BLUE FIRE:
A Season Inside the St. Louis Blues

Dave Simons

Foreword by Bernie Federko

SAGAMORE PUBLISHING CO., INC.
Champaign, Illinois

©1993 Sagamore Publishing Co., Inc.

Production supervision
   and interior design: Susan M. Williams
Cover and photo insert design: Michelle R. Dressen
Editor: Dan Heaton
Proofreader: Phyllis L. Bannon

Printed in the United States of America.

Library of Congress Catalog Card Number:92-82551
ISBN:0-915611-55-4

This book is dedicated to my wife, Susan. I never understood before why authors dedicated their work to their wives instead of a sports idol like Lou Brock, or a favorite rock 'n' roller like REO's Kevin Cronin. (Yep, I had to get those names in the book somewhere). But I certainly understand now why authors honor their wives after undertaking such a laborious task. Despite being ignored for nearly a year, Susan supported my efforts 100%. I guess it's time to re-introduce myself.

Susan, I love you. I am truly blessed.

CONTENTS

Acknowledgments vi
Foreword vii
Introduction xii

1	Camp of Controversy 1
2	A Devil of a Start 29
3	Home Cooking 41
4	Trade Winds 55
5	Paul Bearer 67
6	Curtis the Cat 83
7	Defenseless 103
8	Sutter Home 129
9	The Green Berets 157
10	Sowing Wild Oates 177
11	Slip, Sliding Away 201
12	The Cloud Lifts 219
13	Brett Behavior 241
14	On the Road Again 259
15	Banff Blues 277
16	Purple Heart Blues 305
17	Strike Out 329
18	Playoff Bound 363
19	Over and Out 385
20	End of an Era 403

Appendix A
Team Statistics 418

Appendix B
Final Standings 421

Appendix C
Blues' Game-by-Game Results, 1991-1992 422

ACKNOWLEDGMENTS

My list of people to thank has to start with the Blues' public relations staff, specifically Jeff Trammel and Mike Caruso. Their tireless efforts to get me the facts and figures I needed is very much appreciated. And the best part is, they didn't charge me. (At least I haven't received a bill yet. Uh-oh).

A hearty dose of gratitude is also extended to free-lance photographers Tim Parker and Bill Gutweiler. Tim snapped the black and white pictures you see in the middle of the book, while Bill shot the color photos on the front cover. Thanks to both gentlemen for lending their help and support.

Thanks to Dave Luecking, the hockey writer for the *Post-Dispatch*, and John Kelly, the Blues' play-by-play man, for their insight. You guys were terrific tour guides. Just one question, though. Did anyone ever rescue Pik from the trunk?

Adios to trainer Mike Folga, Coach Brian Sutter, and John Kelly. You guys always found time out of your busy schedules to talk hockey with a pain-in-the-ass reporter. You'll most certainly be missed. Best of luck in your new endeavors.

Thanks to Doug "Oooh, he's hot!" Vaughn for the lead, and everyone else at KMOV for being nice enough to act like you cared when I talked about the book.

And finally, a huge thanks to Bernie Federko. I admired you as a player, but I respect you even more now that I've gotten to know you as a person. You're a prince of a guy, and I consider it an honor to be called your friend. Your assistance with this book will never be forgotten.

FOREWORD

I find it absolutely amazing when I look around St. Louis, my home for the last 16 years, that hockey is as popular as it is today. Wherever you look, you see kids cruising the sidewalks on rollerblades. You see hockey leagues growing by leaps and bounds. You hear more people talking about the sport than ever before. There's no doubt about it. Hockey and the St. Louis Blues are here to stay.

It certainly wasn't that way when I was drafted by the Blues in the spring of 1976. Heck, I didn't even know where St. Louis was. And as I came to find out, a lot of St. Louisians didn't know much about their own hockey team. The glory of the expansion years had worn off, and the Blues' popularity was starting to decline by the time Brian Sutter and I came on the scene.

That changed for one brief moment in the early '80s. Thanks to an infusion of young, talented players, the Blues became a Stanley Cup contender in 1980-81, the organization's most successful season in its 25-year history. Unfortunately, we cooled at the end and were eliminated in the second round of the playoffs. We had just started to bring huge crowds back to the Arena, but they soon disappeared as the Blues became just an average team again after our one shot at winning it all.

The lowest point came a couple of years later, when Ralston Purina was close to selling the team to some investors in Saskatoon, Saskatchewan. As many of you know, that's my hometown. While it would have been exciting to play in front of all my friends and relatives, I had grown to love the city of St. Louis and its people and did not want to leave. As it turned out, I didn't have to. Harry Ornest bought the Blues and kept them right where they belonged.

We suffered through several years of mediocrity under Ornest, and we continued to struggle to fill the Arena on a regular basis. However, when Ornest sold the team to local businessman Michael Shanahan in December 1986, the Blues suddenly became a competitive and exciting team to watch. Slowly but surely, the Blues started to climb into the NHL's elite. With that came an increase in popularity that continues to grow today. And if there's any one person who should be credited for the growth of hockey in this town, it's Brett Hull.

Brett has become the most recognizable figure in St. Louis today. He is the idol of countless young kids who hope to grow up to be just like him. It seems every youngster owns a hockey jersey with No. 16 on it, including my son, Jordy, who probably has more items with 16 on them than my old number, 24. Brett has done more for the sport of hockey in St. Louis than anyone else in the last 25 years. In my opinion, he has single-handedly put St. Louis on the map of great hockey towns in North America. Years from now, after Brett has broken all my scoring records, I will look back and consider it an honor that I got to play with him for one full season.

I have so many fond memories of my 13 seasons in St. Louis, it's difficult to point to just one or two. Certainly, the most memorable event came during a playoff game against Calgary on May 12, 1986, now known as the "Monday Night Miracle." Doug Wickenheiser's overtime goal, which I assisted on, gave us a 6-5 win and evened that third-round series at three games apiece. What made it even sweeter was the fact that it came on my 30th birthday. Some celebration, eh? Unfortunately, we lost the seventh and deciding game in Calgary, which prevented us from going to the Stanley Cup finals. That was a close as I ever got to winning it all, and it's something I'll treasure for the rest of my life.

Of course, that was a team accomplishment. As far as personal milestones, how could I ever forget my first game as a member of the Blues at the Arena? It came on February 5, 1977, against the Buffalo Sabres. At the time, the Sabres were one of the premier teams in the NHL, accumulating more than 100 points four years in a row. But I guess I was too naive to be scared or intimidated. I scored three goals, including the game winner with just a couple of minutes to play in a 6-5 victory. Not too many people can say they scored a hat trick in their very first game in front of the home crowd. I feel very blessed that I was able to do so.

Nearly seven years later, on December 14, 1983, I became the all-time leading scorer in Blues history when I scored my 526th point, breaking Gary Unger's record. Just hours before, my wife, Bernadette, gave birth to our second child, Dustin. Guess I had a little extra incentive to break the record that night.

I'll also never forget Bernie Federko Night at the Arena in 1987, when the Blues honored me for my record-breaking accomplishments, and the night they retired my No. 24 in 1991, after I finally hung up my skates for good. By then, I had played in exactly 1,000 games and recorded more than 1,100 points. (1,073 with the Blues). Every time I visit the Arena, I can't help but look at my jersey hanging from the rafters and remember the wonderful career I spent there.

Unfortunately, there are some very painful memories for me as well during my 13 years with the Blues. By far, the most depressing time of my career came the day Barclay Plager died from cancer, February 7, 1988. Ask any person who's been touched by Barc in some way or another, and they'll tell you they shed some tears on that fateful day. If there's any one man responsible for my success, it was Barc. He put his arm around me from the moment I first arrived in St. Louis in 1976 and never took it off until the day he passed away. He not only made me a better hockey player, he made me a better person.

I wasn't seeing much ice time during my first year and a half with the Blues. All the fans must have been wondering why the team had wasted its first-round pick on me. But when Barc took over as head coach in February 1978, he decided to go with the kids, and the careers of Bernie Federko and Brian Sutter took off. He put us on a line together, where we stayed for the majority of the next decade, breaking just about every team record along the way. I am forever indebted to Barclay Plager. I know that somewhere he is watching me, and I hope that I turned out to be the kind of person he expected me to be.

Another painful moment came a little more than a year after Barc passed away. I never thought it was possible, but the Blues traded me to the Red Wings on June 15, 1989. I assumed I would play another year or two in St. Louis and then retire. Not many guys get to play their whole careers in one city, but I was convinced that I would be one of the lucky ones. I quickly learned that hockey is a business just like anything else. There aren't very many loyalties.

I was never bitter about the trade. How could I be? I spent 13 glorious seasons with the Blues and left my heart with them when I traveled to Detroit. And, as it turned out, the Blues acquired Adam Oates, who established himself as one of the premier centers in the league. I'd say it was quite a steal on the Blues' part.

No, I wasn't bitter, but I was certainly hurt. I just couldn't believe I was being forced to shed the Bluenote. It was an honor to put that jersey on every night and represent the pride of the St. Louis Blues. Barclay Plager taught me to have the utmost respect for the Bluenote, and I did. But suddenly I had to show my loyalty to another organization, and it was extremely difficult to do.

After one unproductive season with the Red Wings, I retired and moved my family back to St. Louis. There was never any doubt where we'd go after my playing days were over. I had too many friends, too many memories, and too many business opportunities to go anywhere but the Gateway City. In fact, within 24 hours of my announced retirement, the news director at KMOV-TV in St. Louis called and offered me a job as a hockey analyst. I've been doing it ever since, and plan to continue doing it as long as I'm asked.

I've been out of hockey a couple of years now, but I'm as busy as ever. I'm involved in a variety of local business ventures, including my own restaurant, Bernie Federko's Bar and Grill. My career as a hockey player has certainly afforded me many opportunities to find success in the business world. But it still wouldn't have been possible without the support of the people of St. Louis. You won't find a friendlier city anywhere in the country. I'm flattered that people still take the time to talk to me about hockey and reminisce about my playing days. I feel bad I was never able to bring them home a Stanley Cup. But now that I'm one of them, a fan cheering on the Blues, I hope and pray this organization will finally win it all. This city certainly deserves it.

And hockey fans certainly deserve this book, *Blue Fire*. It's about time someone took the time and effort to write a book about the St. Louis Blues. Dave Simons has done an excellent job giving the reader a feel of what it was like to be a part of the Blues' controversial 25th anniversary season. Dave is not only a talented sports reporter, but a very gifted writer. He offers you a free ride with the Blues from the moment training camp opens to the day Brian Sutter leaves St. Louis for Boston. And Dave also takes you back in history, describing the backgrounds of your favorite Blues players. I'm sure you'll agree that *Blue Fire* is very difficult to put down once you open the very first page. Happy reading!

—Bernie Federko

INTRODUCTION

I sat in the lobby, tapping my feet, adjusting my tie, crossing one leg, then the other, and occasionally feeling the back of my head to make sure my bald spot was covered up. In other words, I was just a tad nervous. The man I was about to meet was someone I highly respected and admired. I knew him pretty well, but this get-together was a little different. It had nothing to do with my television duties. It had everything to do with a bold, and perhaps foolish, venture I was undertaking.

"Mr. Simons, you can follow me," said a pleasant-looking woman.

I jumped to my feet, gathered my folder of material, and followed her.

We walked down the hallway, passed through one door, and then continued walking down another corridor. I was finally led into the office of the person I was supposed to meet. Problem was, he wasn't there.

"He'll be right with you, Mr. Simons," the woman said. "Just make yourself comfortable."

"Thank you very much," I said as I sat down in the only chair available. It wasn't anywhere near HIS desk, so I moved it a little bit closer. Here I was, a mere peon of a sportscaster, moving office furniture around that belonged to the owner of a multi-million dollar company. Nobody ever accused me of being very intelligent.

"Hello, Dave. How are you?" he said as he entered his domain.

"Fine, Mike. How are you?" I responded.

"Oh, pretty good. Pretty good."

Actually the guy looked great. He was in his early 50s, but you would never have guessed it. With a head full of thick, jet-black hair and a strong Marine-like jawline, Michael F. Shanahan could have easily passed for a man in his early 40s.

Shanahan was the general partner and chairman of the St. Louis Blues Hockey Club. As a sports reporter for KMOV-TV in St. Louis, I had interviewed Shanahan on many occasions concerning the city's hockey team. But this meeting was out of the ordinary. There were no television cameras, no lights, no microphones. There was just me holding a folder of goodies I wanted to share with this man.

I took out a couple pieces of paper and handed them to Shanahan across his desk. One sheet contained an outline of prospective chapter titles, another showed a detailed introduction of the what, where when, and how of my idea. Shanahan looked them over quickly and nodded.

"My first reaction to this is very positive," Shanahan remarked.

Whew. I had passed one of many hurdles to get this project accomplished. We talked for another thirty minutes before we shook hands and parted.

"Let's get together with Jack on this," Shanahan said as I was leaving, referring to the team president, Jack Quinn.

"That'd be great," I said. " I certainly want him to know about this."

And so a book on the St. Louis Blues' 25th anniversary season was born. The 1990-91 season, the second-most-successful year in franchise history, had just ended. Next season was the team's silver anniversary, and I thought it would be a tremendous idea to write a book on the Blues as they skated toward a possible Stanley Cup in their 25th year of existence.

I didn't meet with Shanahan to get his approval. The last think I wanted was to be a public relations shill and write only positive stories while ignoring anything that might show the team in a bad light. But I certainly thought it was fair to let Shanahan know what I intended to do. In fact, I probably would have dropped the idea if Shanahan and his management staff were adamantly against it. As a man who had never undertaken a project like this, I didn't need the hassle. I would have politely bowed out and waited for another subject to come along to tackle as my first book.

But there was no doubt this was the one I wanted. And as I walked back to my car after meeting with Shanahan, I felt a sudden urge to jump up and kick my heels together. As a St. Louis native and huge supporter of the city's hockey team, I had always been disappointed with the lack of hockey coverage in this town outside of the *St. Louis Post-Dispatch*. Every year it seemed there was a book out on the baseball Cardinals. And that was fine. I grew up idolizing Lou Brock while playing Khoury League baseball on Wiethaupt Field, next to Cold Water elementary school in north St. Louis County. My dad took me to the left field bleachers at Busch Stadium in the late 1960s and early 70s so I could watch my hero in action. And, of course straining our butts on those backless pieces of lumber saved my dad a few bucks.

But one of my favorite childhood sports memories occurred on the night of February 19, 1974. I was 11 years old when my dad, after constant pleading on my part, finally took me to my first professional hockey game. I'll never forget the sight of a man who looked like he was about ten feet tall and weighed 400 pounds. In actuality, he was very average in size. But Barclay Plager caught my attention the way he ruled the rink that night. No. 8 skated ferociously from one end to the other while bashing bodies along the way. He helped lead the Blues to a 7-1 thrashing of the Atlanta Flames, and I was suddenly and passionately hooked on the sport of hockey and the St. Louis Blues.

Unfortunately, growing up in the north county suburb of Florissant, I was never in a position to play the sport. A couple of kids in the neighborhood convinced their parents to drive them to the nearest ice rink. But for the most part, we played baseball in the summer, football and soccer during the school year. My only attachment to a frozen sheet of ice was watching Peter Puck on NBC and keeping abreast of the standings in the newspaper.

That didn't change in college. When I was a freshman at Mizzou in 1980-81, my dormmates and I watched the standings in amazement as the Blues raced to the top of the NHL race, even ahead of the defending champions, the New York Islanders. We read how Bernie Federko became the first player in Blues history to score over 100 points (104), while Wayne Babych netted a team-record 54 goals. We noticed how Mike Liut became one of the premier goaltenders in the league, winning an incredible 33 games. We also couldn't help but read about a second-year player named Wayne Gretzky of the Oilers who accumulated a Ruthian figure of 164 points.

That season made hockey fans of just about everyone on the first floor of Hudson Hall. For me, it was just an affirmation of my devotion to the sport. I was heartbroken I couldn't be a part of that record-setting year. The Blues sputtered toward the end, finishing second to the Islanders in the overall standings and being eliminated by the Rangers in the second round of the playoffs. But it was a hell of a run, one I'll never forget.

Now, many years and hairs later, I have decided to write about the sport so little documented in St. Louis. Attendance continues to rise, management continues to shell out big bucks to make the team a winner, and the sport has never been any more popular since the Blues burst onto the scene in the late 1960s. It's time a book was written to reflect the growing popularity of hockey in St. Louis.

Unfortunately, as we all know now, the silver anniversary season was tarnished before it even started. The team captain, its very heart and soul, was sent to New Jersey in a controversial compensation ruling. Without Scott Sevens, the Blues were forced to make a myriad of changes to fill the gap. Nothing worked. The team went from Stanley Cup contenders to also-rans. Everything that could go wrong did. Trades, contract disputes, injuries, a league strike, you name it. The Blues never got on track, and plummeted from elitism to mediocrity. The drop was so dramatic it eventually cost the team its head coach, a man who had been with the organization for 16 years.

This book is written not just for the hockey fan but for all sports buffs who'd like to know what it's like to be a professional athlete. You'll get a free pass into the Blues' locker room and learn about the personalities and backgrounds of your favorite stars. Did you know Curtis Joseph went by the name of Curtis Munro until he signed with the Blues, and recently contacted his biological parents for the first time? Did you know Bob Bassen once played on the Islanders' top line with superstars Mike Bossy and Bryan Trottier? And that Paul Cavallini was so chubby in high school he was almost passed over in the draft?

You'll read about Rich Sutter's arrival in St. Louis, and how his older brother was so hard on him that Harold Snepsts had to intervene. And how Dave Lowry felt like quitting hockey after an incident with a group of Japanese hockey players. You'll also learn about Craig Janney's distaste for the media, and what Brian Sutter, Garth Butcher, Rick Zombo, Lee Norwood, and others were doing the second each was told to pack his bags for St. Louis.

You'll also read about Brett Hull's threat to never talk to a St. Louis television station again, along with surprising comments from Judge Edward Houston, the man who unwittingly changed the course of the Blues' 1991-92 season. And you'll also be shocked to learn what Brian Sutter REALLY thinks about his ex-bosses.

So, for an in-depth look at the Blues' 25th anniversary season, while learning about the players and coaches who filled the roster, dig in. I hope you find the book entertaining, informative, and enjoyable.

Chapter One

CAMP OF CONTROVERSY

"Did you see that?" asked one of the golfers nervously.

"Damn right. That's enough for me," said his partner.

Lightning in the distance sent dozens of golfers scurrying toward the food stand at the end of the 13th hole. The St. Louis Blues/March of Dimes Celebrity Golf Tournament at Norwood Hills Country Club was temporarily halted. No one argued the decision. Playing for charity was admirable, but not at the expense of your life.

While most of the celebrity golfers were exiting the course, members of the St. Louis media were en route to Norwood Hills. The annual tournament usually attracted reporters, but this year's event was especially noteworthy. Two of the men playing in the tourney were probably spending their last day in St. Louis. Blues forward Rod Brind'Amour and goalie Curtis Joseph were on their way to the New Jersey Devils. Or so everyone assumed.

Six weeks before, on July 24, 1991, the Blues signed Devils free agent Brendan Shanahan. Because free agency in the National Hockey League is anything but free, the Blues had to compensate the Devils for "stealing" their fifth-year forward. Blues general manager Ron Caron offered Brind'Amour, Joseph, and a couple of draft choices. Devils general manager Lou Lamoriello scoffed, labeling the Blues' package "unconscionable." He countered with an offer that many hockey observers found even more unthinkable, even laughable. Lamoriello asked for Blues captain Scott Stevens.

Scott Stevens? A three-time all-star defenseman? For a 22-year-old player whose resume listed "potential" but little else?

The Blues had to give the Washington Capitals five first-round picks the year before to snatch Stevens, then a free agent. Would any team in its right mind give up its future for Brendan Shanahan?

The chuckles could be heard in rinks throughout North America. Lamoriello might as well ask for Brett Hull, people thought. An arbitrator, hired by the NHL Board of Governors, would decide whose offer was the fairest of them all, and it seemed no contest. Stevens would keep the captain's "C" on his Blues jersey, and Brind'Amour and Joseph would pack their bags for Jersey.

As a light rain began to fall at Norwood Hills, Brind'Amour, Joseph, and a number of other current and former Blues huddled under cover to wait for the sky to clear. A few reporters were already in attendance, asking the two players about the impending decision that would send them east.

Suddenly, a bolt of lightning crashed through the sky, striking a tree on the 13th fairway, the highest point on the course.

"Man, that was close," said one of the men at the food stand, just a few hundred feet from the lightning strike.

"It sounded like a mortar shell," remarked Blues chairman Mike Shanahan, no relation to Brendan.

As everyone cautiously looked to the sky to see if another bolt was forthcoming, a man ran frantically up the fairway.

"Does anyone know CPR?" he yelled. "Does anyone know CPR? A couple of guys have been hit!"

Don Morrison, a former TWA spokesman who was well known by the local media, and William Eultgen, the senior station manager for the Federal Express office at West Port Plaza, had been standing next to the tree when it was struck. The electrical force jumped from the tree to the two men, knocking them to the ground.

The shock was so powerful it not only shredded the top of the tree into toothpicks, it ripped apart Morrison's coat collar and tore a six inch gash down its back. Two separate lines of electricity raced down Morrison's body. Black lines on the inside of the coat showed the lightning's path.

Within minutes, an ambulance sped across the golf course in a frantic race to reach the stricken men. By the time paramedics arrived, Morrison and Eultgen were thankfully conscious, alert, and responding to questions. What might have been a tragedy was just a close call.

"I'm very fortunate, and I thank the Lord I'm still here," Morrison said from the hospital.

Minutes later, in another city more than 1,000 miles away, a second thunderous bolt rang so powerfully, it too shook St. Louis. However, this flash of lightning was delivered by Edward J. Houston, a retired judge who once sat high atop the Ottawa, Ontario, Court of Justice. Judge Houston had done the unthinkable. As the NHL arbitrator, he had scandalously ruled Scott Stevens was indeed equitable compensation for Brendan Shanahan. Lightning had struck twice.

Brind'Amour and Joseph, now resting in the clubhouse, breathed a heavy sigh of relief upon hearing the news. They were staying. However, many of the other 550-plus players around the league shook their fists in anger. The fix was in, they yelled. Some players publicly accused the NHL and Judge Houston of deliberately penalizing the Blues for aggressively pursuing free agents, paying them big bucks, and forcing other teams to dish out large sums of money to keep up. The salaries were rising, and many team owners pointed an accusatory finger at the Blues.

Few organizations had dared to experiment with free agency because the rules of compensation were just too risky. And no one on the management level complained. After all, signing free agents to multi-year, multi-million dollar contracts would cause the salary structure to skyrocket and eventually kill the game. Or at least that was the general consensus among team owners. That's why few of them bellyached about the free-agent system in place. It was designed to discourage teams from using it.

But Caron, Blues president Jack Quinn, and head coach Brian Sutter were the bad boys. And many players were convinced the NHL, with orders to Judge Houston, its hand-picked "impartial arbitrator," was doing everything within its power to punish the free-wheeling Blues, to bring them back in line with the rest of the league before they destroyed it.

Nonsense, remarked Judge Houston. In a telephone interview this author had with the judge several months after the decision, Houston scoffed at such conspiracies. He adamantly denied any contact with NHL officials regarding the Scott Stevens ruling.

"[NHL president] John Ziegler has never called me in one of these cases," he said. "He'd never even think of contacting me. I take full responsibility for the decision. I didn't have any help."

The players had every right to be skeptical. On July 30, 1991, just six days after signing Shanahan, and five weeks before Judge Houston's decision, the Blues signed Dave Christian, a free-agent forward from the Boston Bruins, to a three-year contract worth $1.78 million. The Blues were trying desperately to improve their second scoring line, hoping to take the pressure off Brett Hull and Adam Oates, the NHL's most prolific scoring duo.

However, Bruins general manager Harry Sinden cried foul, saying Christian was not a free agent at all. He accused the Blues of tampering and turned the matter over to the league office.

This was not the first time Sinden had accused fellow owners of tampering. Back in June of 1976, Sinden was convinced other teams were playing dirty pool in trying to sign his prized possession, Bobby Orr, then a free agent. The Bruins defenseman eventually signed with Chicago for a then-record $3 million over five years. Sinden chided team owners for their "deplorable and discouraging" behavior, but Orr ended his career after a few games with the Blackhawks, and the matter was quickly forgotten.

While the Christian issue was being discussed behind closed doors, the Bruins decided to enter the free-agent market themselves. What team did they raid? The Blues, of course. Sinden signed Glen Featherstone, a tough, stay-at-home defenseman who had racked up 204 penalty minutes for the Blues the previous year, and left winger Dave Thomlinson, who had just 22 games of experience but showed plenty of promise. Suddenly, Sinden withdrew his tampering charge, letting Christian go as compensation for his acquisition of the two Blues. Sinden also threw in a couple of draft choices and the matter was brushed aside. How convenient.

Dave Christian was indeed a free agent. Everyone knew that. But the Bruins waved a red flag anyway, and the league office took notice. The message was clear to the Blues: Big Brother is watching you.

In one year's time, they had signed three quality free agents in Stevens, Christian, and Shanahan. They tried to sign a fourth, Blackhawks forward Michel Goulet, but Chicago grudgingly matched the Blues' four-year, $2.9 million offer, forcing Goulet to stay put in the Windy City. The maverick Blues had to be stopped. Some way. Somehow.

Caron and Quinn knew something was up as they pursued Shanahan. If signing Christian was a headache, inking Shanahan to a free-agent contract turned into a full-blown migraine.

As required, they sent Shanahan's contract to the league office for approval, a process that usually takes a couple of days. However, Shanahan's contract apparently smelled funny. NHL president John Ziegler pulled it off the assembly line for further review. Days dragged into weeks. The welcoming ceremony in St. Louis was put on hold indefinitely. The party hats were put back in the closet. Suspicions arose that Shanahan was not coming after all.

The problem was a case of mistrust, deception, and deceit. Devils general manager Lou Lamoriello was convinced the Blues had signed Shanahan to an outrageous multi-year deal worth millions. But much to his shock and surprise, the contract that turned up in Ziegler's office listed only a one-year deal close to $650,000. Lamoriello thought he had been duped. He could have paid that to keep Shanahan in Jersey, he argued. The Blues had pulled a fast one. They had signed the free agent to a multi-million dollar contract in secret while submitting a bogus one-year deal to the league office.

However, after 29 days of explaining themselves, Caron and Quinn had their man. Without fanfare, Ziegler quietly approved the contract, and Shanahan caught the first plane to St. Louis. No explanation was ever given why the approval process took so long. What did Ziegler find? Was there even a hint of wrongdoing by Blues management? Or was this another attempt to make the Blues sweat it out for diving into the forbidden free-agent market?

Meanwhile, Lamoriello was still grumbling, and officials inside the league office agreed to continue investigating the matter. The Blues could be heavily fined if any inconsistencies were uncovered. The contract was approved, Shanahan was an official member of the Blues, but the heat was still on. For trying to improve its club, St. Louis was being ostracized by the powers that be. And the controversy was only beginning.

The Devils and Blues now had three days to work out a compensation deal for signing Shanahan. Caron claimed he submitted a number of proposed deals, some of them outlandishly lopsided, but Lamoriello didn't want to hear any of it. He was determined to go to arbitration to make the Blues pay.

"I phoned Mr. Lamoriello nine times to offer eight or more players on a package,"Caron said. "It took him about five seconds to say you're not even close. So we were doomed at that time to go through arbitration. We had no idea how the arbitrator would treat us. We found out very quickly."

Two days after scanning written arguments that had been submitted to his office by both teams, Judge Houston first listened to Ron Caron give an impassioned plea as to why Rod Brind'Amour, Curtis Joseph, and two draft picks were more than enough to offset the loss of Brendan Shanahan.

Caron pointed out that Brind'Amour was almost identical to Shanahan. Each was a highly regarded young forward dubbed "the future" by his organization. Each had been a first-round draft pick. Shanahan had four full seasons under his belt, Brind'Amour just two. But the Blues' forward had tallied more points than Shanahan had scored in his first two years.

However, Caron wasn't about to gamble. He added goalie Curtis Joseph to the compensation package. Joseph had a 25-15-3 career record, with an impressive 4-1 mark in playoff competition. Called "The Cat" for his quick reflexes, Joseph was considered one of the top number two netminders in the league, with the talent to be a number one. Even though he found it inappropriate to mention it to Judge Houston, Caron knew the Devils were probably going to lose free agent goalie Sean Burke, who had made it very clear he was not returning to the Meadowlands. Surely, Lamoriello would agree he needed a capable goaltender to back up starter Chris Terreri.

But feeling justifiably paranoid about the league's disdain for his team, Caron threw in two draft choices for good measure. The general manager's oral presentation to Judge Houston was convincing, at least according to those in the room.

"Ron did a very, very, very good job in analyzing his players and his picks versus what they were losing in New Jersey," boasted Blues president Jack Quinn. "He did a very, very fine job."

Judge Houston couldn't have disagreed more.

"Beauty is in the eye of the beholder. That certainly wasn't one of the best presentations I've heard," Houston said bluntly. "Caron spent the first 15 to 20 minutes telling me what my responsibilities were. I had to tell him, 'Mr. Caron, I've done this a few times. Get to your point.' I was rather surprised he didn't give me more material. His argument was not in the least bit brilliant."

Then it was Lou Lamoriello's turn. Instead of arguing why the Devils deserved Scott Stevens, Lamoriello went on the attack, lambasting the Blues' proposal. He conceded Brind'Amour was a quality player, but pointed out that his stock with the Blues had plummeted to the point where Coach Sutter removed him from the power play during his second year. His goals dropped from 26 to 19 while his overall point total fell from 61 to 49.

Lamoriello argued that Joseph would mean nothing to his team. The general manager pointed out the Devils already had two outstanding goaltenders, in Burke and Terreri (even though he was about to lose Burke to Team Canada), as well as three talented young netminders in the minors, including a kid named Craig Billington who had recently made the Canadian National Team. Lamoriello said he wasn't about to pay Joseph's salary of $200,000 when he would be sitting on the bench, or perhaps even sent down to the minors. Besides, he said, Joseph was only 22 years old and had already been injured a couple of times. He had blown out his right knee in February of the previous season and never put on the pads the rest of the year. Lamoriello adamantly argued he had no need for an injury-prone goalie.

As far as the draft picks went, Lamoriello was incredulous. Draft picks are an unproven commodity, he said. Since Shanahan was a proven player, draft selections added nothing to the attractiveness of the Blues offer.

"I would have to say there was only one sentence the Devils used in the entire presentation which related to offense and defense with the two players involved," said Quinn. "They spent the rest of the time basically whining."

Again, Judge Houston begged to differ.

"New Jersey argued they had five goaltenders better than Joseph," Houston said, "while pointing out that Brind'Amour had been taken off the power play. They also made Shanahan out to be a superstar. They prepared very well."

Less than a week after the compensation hearings, on the same day lightning struck a Blues charity golf tournament, Judge Houston rendered a decision in a 14-page report.

"It is my opinion," Houston wrote, "that the New Jersey proposal for compensation is the one which I must accept.

Accordingly, Scott Stevens will be awarded to New Jersey as compensation for the signing of Brendan Shanahan to St. Louis." Apparently, Lamoriello's whining had touched Judge Houston's heart.

Realizing that he was president of the league's renegade team, Jack Quinn was frustrated but not entirely surprised by the ruling.

"It's odd that the same decision affects the first two free agents to move in seventy-some odd years," remarked Quinn, referring to Stevens and Shanahan. "On the surface, at first glance, it appears to be somewhat punitive."

Blues superstar Brett Hull was even more outspoken. Playing in the Canada Cup when he heard the news, Hull reached the boiling point. The Golden Brett fired a few slapshots at the league when Steve Simmons of the *Toronto Sun* asked for a comment.

"The decision was totally fixed," Hull angrily responded. "I'll probably get sued for saying this, but I believe it. Anyone who can look at it any other way has no clue . . . We just got the shaft. The message was clear: Don't sign free agents."

The one player who could claim even more popularity than Hull also landed a few haymakers.

"The decision is just not fair, and they can't possibly say it's fair," complained Wayne Gretzky to the *Toronto Sun*. "Ron Caron has gone out and tried to build a winner, and now he is being penalized."

League officials were on the firing line. The NHL's top ambassadors were publicly denouncing those running the sport.

"You know something is up when guys like Hull and Gretzky are talking like this," said Blues forward Darin Kimble.

The league's players could feel the money drain from their pockets. If a team was punished for signing a free agent, why would any organization risk it again? Free agents would be locked into their current teams, accepting whatever offer their employers deemed fair.

The Blues had been the only team to make a serious offer for either Shanahan or Christian.

"We just let things play themselves out over the course of the summer," said Christian. "St. Louis was the only team that was really serious."

"I was sitting at home waiting for the phone to ring," said Shanahan, who had a similar story to tell. "About a month into my free agent availability, my agent called me to say St. Louis was interested."

In his report, Judge Houston called Shanahan "a power forward who is a star hockey player." If so, why was Ron Caron the only executive to contact the young man? The lack of interest in such a "star hockey player" lent credence to suspicions that the league office had strongly suggested that high-priced free agents be left alone.

At first, Houston couldn't understand what all the fuss was about. The rest of the league certainly knew how dangerous it was to go after Type I free agents like Shanahan. Why didn't the Blues? Why were they so reckless in their pursuit of young talent?

"The Rangers told me they wanted to sign Shanahan," explained Houston, "but they were afraid they'd lose Brian Leetch. (General manager) Neil Smith told me that."

In fact, Judge Houston had a little advice for Blues' management: Do your homework next time. Houston said if the Blues' proposal had included one minor change, he would have had no choice but to rule in favor of the St. Louis contingent.

"If they would have put a defenseman in their package instead of (goalie Curtis) Joseph, my ruling might have been different," Houston said.

You mean someone like Paul Cavallini?

"Then the Blues would've won," he said matter-of-factly.

Wow. Here's the good judge himself explaining what the Blues did wrong. The message was unmistakable. If Caron and company would have substituted Cavallini for Joseph, as some suggested they were close to doing anyway, then the Blues would have Joseph AND Stevens.

Nonetheless, the criticism was aimed at Judge Houston and not the Blues. But the criticism continued to mount until Judge Houston could stand it no longer. Tired of hearing how the "fix was in," Houston responded by calling Brett Hull a "whiner" and a "little jerk" for his earlier remarks. The controversy had now escalated into name-calling.

Hull was not about to let it die there. After hearing the judge's comments, the star right winger remarked, "I think that just goes to prove I was right all along. When a guy of his caliber has to come out and say stuff in the media, it just goes to show how defensive he is about his mistake. I hope it's a cold day in hell when Scottie ends up in New Jersey."

Hull had finally gone too far. Growing weary of having its integrity called into question, the league office took action. It gave a stern directive to Blues management: Make Brett Hull apologize for his remarks, or face the consequences. Not wanting any more trouble, the Blues front office faxed a letter of apology, supposedly written by Hull, to the St. Louis media.

"I realize that my comments were harsh and using the terminology 'the fix was in' was incorrect," Hull supposedly wrote. "I did not intend my comments to reflect negatively on Judge Houston. I was dismayed at the compensation award of Scott Stevens to New Jersey, as Scott was not only an integral part of the St. Louis Blues' 105-point season in 1990-91, but our captain and off-ice leader. Beyond the quality of the player was the additional factor of my heightened emotions due to other events surrounding the decision."

Everyone knew the words were fashioned by team officials and not Hull. In fact, the *St. Louis Post-Dispatch* refused to print the apology for fear of insulting the intelligence of its readers. But league president John Ziegler got what he wanted. Whether they were his words or not, Brett Hull had publicly apologized to Judge Houston, and the insults were forgiven.

Meanwhile, the Scott Stevens controversy was far from over. Like Hull, Stevens was playing in the Canada Cup when Judge Houston rendered his decision. But instead of putting his St. Louis home up for sale, Stevens hinted he would fight the ruling. After all, history was on his side.

In 1978, Judge Houston awarded Red Wings forward Dale McCourt to the Los Angeles Kings as compensation for Detroit's signing free-agent goalie Rogie Vachon. However, McCourt went to court. While his case was being heard, McCourt was allowed to stay with the Red Wings where he played another full year. He later lost the case on appeal, but his lawyers were set to take it to the Supreme Court. That's when the NHL finally backed off, allowing the Kings to trade McCourt's rights back to Detroit for Andre St. Laurent and two number-one draft picks. The mess had been swept under the rug. McCourt got to stay with the Red Wings, and the free agent system was still in place.

Critics have argued that the NHL has always been a business that inhibited the free movement of its employees, violating antitrust laws. But the NHL Players' Association has never had the guts to fight back, allowing the league to take advantage of its union members. The players have always allowed the league to formulate collective bargaining agreements that restrict the ability of players to move to different cities. Bob Verdi, a columnist for the *Chicago Tribune* and *The Sporting News*, said it best when he wrote, "What's remarkable is how hockey players can be lions on the rink and lambs at the bargaining table."

But while Stevens was trying to decide what address he wanted on his business card, the players' association was negotiating a new contract with the league. The timing was impeccable. Because of the Stevens ruling, the players finally had reason to be angry enough to fight the free-agent system. What's more, their old union boss, Alan Eagleson, was gone. Eagleson was the owners' best friend, rarely blinking an eye during union negotiations. He had recently been replaced by Bob Goodenow, a no-nonsense lawyer who had worked for the law firm that represented Dale McCourt 13 years earlier.

Suddenly, there was talk of a full-scale players' strike, unprecedented in NHL history. The old bargaining agreement would expire in a few weeks, and if the owners wouldn't take the locks and bolts off free agency, the players might walk.

"Obviously, it's in the air," said Brind'Amour, referring to talk of a strike. Here was a guy who was happy with Judge Houston's decision because it allowed him to stay in St. Louis. But that didn't mean Brind'Amour thought it was the right decision.

"Things aren't fair. From the players' standpoint, something has to be done," Brind'Amour argued. "If it means going on strike, so be it."

"It'll be very interesting to see what happens," said Blues center Dan Quinn. "St. Louis was very aggressive in signing the two guys. It seems somewhat punitive for the league to do what they did. Players who don't get what they feel they're worth really don't have any way to do it other than to walk out."

The players didn't strike in training camp, starting the year without a new collective bargaining agreement, but the threat of a walkout was still very real. Some Blues players privately mentioned the best time to strike would be right before the playoffs in April, when the owners would stand to lose the most money. The 1991-92 season could end at the conclusion of the regular season.

But for now, the hockey world had turned its attention to Scott Stevens, wondering what he was going to do. He had just helped lead Team Canada to a two-game sweep over the United States in the Canada Cup. As the players packed their bags for home, Stevens had to decide where home was. Would he travel to New Jersey, or back to St. Louis? His lawyer, Richard Bennett, had been hinting Stevens might follow in McCourt's footsteps and fight the decision.

"It is Scott's intention to play out the rest of his career in St. Louis," Bennett said matter-of-factly. "He has no intention to report to New Jersey." The around-the-clock Scott Stevens watch had officially begun.

Two days after the Canada Cup ended, I was sitting at my sports desk when the phone rang.

"Hello?"

"Dave, I got a tip for you. Scott Stevens is here in St. Louis."

The caller was a reliable source who knew almost everything about the Blues. I never questioned him. He was always right.

"That's great, but how do I get hold of him?" I asked. "I don't have his phone number."

"Neither do I. But I think I know where he lives."

The address was a place in Ladue, perhaps the wealthiest suburb of St. Louis. The fact that Stevens lived in a well-to-do community didn't surprise me. That he would pick Ladue did. These days, most of the city's *nouveau riche* were moving to Chesterfield, about 10 miles west of Ladue. Chesterfield is the yuppie's choice of fine living. It's a fast growing city, quickly filling up with luxurious homes. In fact, it was a waste of breath to ask any sports personality in St. Louis where he resided.

Chesterfield is "new" money. Ladue is "old." Stevens' choice of neighborhoods was the first hint of many personality traits I'd learn about him over the next few days.

As we pulled up to Stevens' house, I told my cameraman/driver not to pull into the driveway. For some reason, I thought keeping our station vehicle in the street would appear less intrusive, less obvious. Never mind the fact it had company logos stamped all over it.

Stevens' home was an old English-style, two-story brick house that looked like it belonged somewhere on the New England countryside, not in suburban St. Louis. I knocked loudly on the front door and waited. And waited. I knocked again. Still, no one answered. I looked to the driveway and noticed Scott's truck. Not a BMW, Porsche, or Mercedes. A good old-fashioned American pickup truck. It was Scott's pride and joy and still sparkled like the day he bought it. Another car was parked right next to it. It must be his wife's, I figured. Either they were in a third car driving around somewhere, or they were hiding in a back room, silently demanding I leave.

I looked back at my cameraman, shrugged my shoulders, and started to walk back up the driveway. Then I heard the unlocking of a side door near the garage. A very attractive blonde woman with an equally pleasant smile emerged. It was Scott's wife, Donna.

"Can I help you?" she asked.

"Hi, Donna," I replied in an almost apologetic tone. "I'm Dave Simons with Channel 4. Is Scott here? Can I talk to him?"

"I'm sorry, but he's not talking to anyone right now."

"Oh, he must be sleeping after driving all night from Toronto."

Donna smiled. "Yeah, that's it. He's sleeping."

I smiled too. We both knew Scott was wide-awake. At least he was now after my incessant pounding on the front door. I decided not to press the issue. I politely excused myself, jumped back into the truck, and traveled back to the station.

The next day, Stevens talked. Not to me or any other television sports reporter. He visited with Dave Luecking, the hockey writer for the *Post-Dispatch*. There it was in fine print, Stevens talking about his frustrations, opening up about the pain this was causing his family, and reiterating his desire to stay in St. Louis.

I was frustrated, but not surprised. It's for this reason I've always envied sportswriters, especially the "beat" writers whose sole responsibility is to cover one particular team. During the course of a season, they practically live with the athletes they write about, even traveling with them on the road. The writer becomes a familiar face in the locker room whom most players learn to trust. That's not to say the writer won't occasionally rip a player on the morning sports page. A few choice words might be exchanged after the article appears, but the matter is usually forgotten or resolved. The two sides generally develop a relationship of respect and tolerance.

The television sports reporter also tries to establish a good rapport with the players, but his appearance in the dressing room is too infrequent to develop any real trust. The TV reporter typically rushes in with his cameraman at his side, throws a light on the athlete's face, sticks a microphone under his chin, asks a few quick questions, then rushes out to the next story.

However, no TV journalist should apologize for this. The sports department at a major newspaper will generally employ at least a dozen reporters. A television station in the same city may have just one or two reporters, not counting the sports anchors who are usually unable to leave the building. While a scribe is working on one or two stories that won't appear until at least the next morning, his counterpart on TV is trying to gather material for several stories that have to be ready for broadcast in a matter of hours.

The two media actually complement one another very well. The paper gives its readers an in-depth analysis of an issue that television has little time for. On the other hand, the electronic media are able to give a story emotion so powerful it hypnotizes its viewers. Even the most talented writer cannot accurately describe Brett Hull's wicked slapshot from the circle. Only television can do him justice.

The players are always on their guard when the cameras show up, and I don't blame them. They know anything they say will forever be recorded. There's no taking it back. The players also have to be cognizant of their appearance while the camera is tightly focused on them. You don't see bloopers in the newspaper, only on television.

The day the newspaper article on Scott Stevens appeared, I sat next to its author at the Arena, watching the Blues tirelessly skate through drills.

"That was a good article on Stevens," I said.

"Oh, yeah, I guess," replied Luecking, one of the most humble and unassuming sports reporters in St. Louis. "He didn't tell me anything he hasn't already said, though."

Luecking was right. Stevens had routinely talked to reporters while playing in the Canada Cup. For some reason, his return to St. Louis suddenly made him speechless.

"How did you get him to finally talk?" I asked.

"He called me."

"Oh, yeah? He just called you?"

"Yep, I left a message for him to get in touch with me and he did."

I called Bernie Federko, the former Blues center who holds just about every team career scoring record. Federko is the hockey analyst for Channel 4, so I figured I could put him to work.

"Bernie, is there any way you could get Scott Stevens to talk to us?" I asked, almost pleading.

"Yeah, I've been thinking about that," he said. "I'll get a message to him through the Blues' office to have him call me."

"Well, that could be awhile. I was hoping to get him today. I'll tell you what. I'll pick you up, and we'll go to his house. I'm sure he'll at least talk to you."

"No way," Federko was quick to answer. "When I was a player, I never cared for reporters ringing my doorbell. I'm not going to do it."

I had no choice but to go out there again on my own. This time, no one came to the door after several minutes of knocking. Both vehicles were in the driveway, and I kept expecting Donna to repeat her appearance from the side door. But no one emerged. I thought I'd use the ol' "Why don't you call me?" trick that worked so well for Dave Luecking. Before I left, I wrote my name and number on a piece of paper, along with a short message to please call me, and put it in the Stevens' mailbox. Surely, he'd call me now.

I was wrong. The phone call never came. Stevens had effectively locked himself in, and was keeping his mouth shut. If he had made up his mind to walk the hallowed halls of justice, he wasn't telling anyone. But everyone knew it was just a matter of time. The deadline for all Canada Cup participants to report to their respective NHL teams was Tuesday, September 24, just a few days away. He still might avoid the TV cameras, but at least we'd know what he was up to.

The first thing I did when I reported to work on the 24th was call the New Jersey Devils' front office. I had talked to various officials with that team the last several weeks and always got the same answer: "We still believe Scott Stevens will report to the Devils," and that was the extent of the conversation.

But today was different. The first sentence I heard this time was, "A news conference concerning the Scott Stevens situation will be held today at 4 p.m. Eastern Time, that's 3 o'clock your time." No, they couldn't go into further detail.

I quickly phoned Susie Mathieu, the Blues' vice-president of public relations. If Stevens had made a decision, he certainly told the Blues' office, and Mathieu certainly knew about it.

"No, I haven't heard a thing," she replied.

"Seriously, you have no idea what Scottie's up to?" I asked, not really believing her.

"If he's made a decision, I'm certainly unaware of it," Mathieu said. "But after the news conference, please give me a call back, and tell me what they said."

Fair enough. All I could do now was wait until the meeting in New Jersey was over, call to get the details, phone Susie back with the information, and then try my damnedest to get a reaction from Stevens.

The sports world is full of speculation, and we were doing plenty of that while patiently watching the clock tick down to 3 o'clock. Everyone in the sports department seemed to be in agreement, a rarity in itself. Scott Stevens was going to report to camp all right, but it would be down the street at the Arena, not the Brendan Byrne Arena in the Meadowlands. The news conference, we said, was to announce fines levied against Stevens for his refusal to report to the team that currently held his rights. We had it all figured out.

I waited until 3:30 to call the Devils. The receptionist patched me through to Dave Freed, the Devils' director of public relations.

"Scott Stevens has decided to report to New Jersey," Freed said in a very businesslike tone. "He'll be here in two days."

"Excuse me?"

"Stevens will be here this Thursday. That's about all there is to it."

"Did you guys threaten him with fines or something?" I asked, still questioning what I was hearing.

"No, this decision was made by Scott, and Scott alone. Anything else you'll have to get from him."

I took the cue. Forgetting to call Susie Mathieu back, I quickly grabbed a cameraman and headed to Stevens' house. Hopefully, the third visit would be a charm.

Scott and Donna were home this time. Their front door was wide-open, leaving the inside of their house exposed. I felt a little uneasy standing on the porch being able to look inside like that. I didn't know whether to knock or yell from the driveway. I chose the former. Scott was there right away, followed closely behind by Donna.

"Hey, Scottie. Remember me? I'm Dave Simons from Channel 4." Being a reporter and not an anchor, I always assume people remember the face but not the name.

"Sure, how are you?"

"Fine, thanks." Actually, I was ecstatic. The muscular defenseman in front of me seemed to be in a pretty good mood. I shouldn't have been surprised, though. He always appeared in good spirits to me. Even after a tough loss, Stevens was cooperative and gracious, politely answering all questions. The chance that he would suddenly check me into the side of his house was pretty minimal.

"I understand you're going to Jersey," I said, stating the obvious. "Can I talk to you about it?"

"Um, I don't know. I really shouldn't talk to just one reporter," Stevens said. "I've tried to be fair about this. I should probably get all you guys together at the same time."

"I understand, Scottie. But I'm the one that's made the trip out here for right now. I'm sure the other stations are on their way. Can't I just grab a quick word from you and get out of your way?"

Stevens paused, moving his fingers through his short, curly blond hair. His wife came to his rescue.

"You have to pick up the babysitter right away," Donna said. "It's getting late. You don't have a lot of time."

Scott turned back around and looked at me. He was still having trouble telling me to get lost. And that's when it hit me. Standing face-to-face, watching this man struggle with his decision whether to talk to me, I suddenly realized why he had decided to report to New Jersey.

Scott Stevens was tired of the headlines. He played hockey because it was his passion. He didn't care for the spotlight. He didn't care for the media attention granted star athletes. Although he appreciated it, he didn't care for the richly deserved adulation he received from fans. Scott Stevens wanted to play hockey, period. Away from the rink, he was content with staying at home with his wife, two kids, and black Labrador Retriever. Stevens was as old-fashioned as the house he was about to move from. All Stevens wanted to do was get back to the game he loved. If going to the Devils allowed him to do that, then it was hello, New Jersey. It was a tough decision, sure. But it was the right one for Scott Stevens.

We stood on his porch and talked for a couple more minutes. The camera could stay in the truck for now. I was enjoying my chat without the presence of a lens in Scott's face.

Just then, another television reporter arrived. I felt relieved in a way. I knew Scott would allow the cameras now that two stations in the city were there. He preferred a news conference to take care of everybody at once, but this would have to do.

The two cameramen set up their equipment on Scott's loose-gravel driveway. Once they were rolling, Stevens couldn't hold back the sadness he felt about leaving St. Louis. He was going to the Devils, but his heart would always have a Bluenote emblazoned on it.

"It's been very tough," he said. "We've become very attached to St. Louis. We love the city and the people here. We're really going to miss it."

So why did you make this decision?

"It's time I played hockey again. I can't sit out any longer. I just want to get going."

Are you bitter toward anyone?

"No, not really. It's something no one really had a lot of control over. It's something no one ever expected would happen. It's unpredictable, but it's business."

And that was that. His fellow players could holler all they wanted about the unfairness of free agency, but he wanted no part of it. The league had sold Scott Stevens' soul to the Devils, and he accepted it.

*   *   *

Rod Brind'Amour couldn't help but smile. As he took his first few strides on the ice, the fans gave him a warm reception. All of them clapped. A few chanted his name, "Roddy, Roddy!" Not bad for a guy who wasn't supposed to be here.

It was September 8, 1991, the Blues first practice of the season. A few hundred fans crammed the tiny Brentwood ice rink, the team's practice facility, to catch their first glimpse of the new-look Blues. The first player on the ice was Ron Hoover, a recently signed free agent from Boston. His acquisition didn't create the kind of stir the other free agent signings caused. After all, the 24-year-old Hoover had only 17 NHL games under his belt, scoring just four goals and no assists. This was one free agent deal the league apparently could survive.

Hoover was unknown to just about everyone in attendance, but he still received applause loud enough to drown out the whispers of, "Who's that guy?" The fans were so excited for the new season that they were clapping for anyone wearing a pair of skates and a Blues jersey.

The fans recognized the second guy. It was Brind'Amour. As he hit the ice, the cheers grew louder. He grinned sheepishly, as if the recognition was completely unexpected. It probably was.

Many Blues fans had grown weary of Rod Brind'Amour. As a highly-touted center from Michigan State University, Brind'Amour first put on the Bluenote in April, 1989, at the age of 19. He arrived just in time for the second round of the playoffs, as the Blues took on the Blackhawks for the Norris Division title. Brind'Amour was remarkably poised for being tossed into the fire like that, scoring two goals in five games and throwing his weight around effectively in the corners. The Blues lost the series, but gained a potential superstar.

The following season, 1989-90, Brind'Amour was the early front-runner for rookie of the year. His quick start put him on a pace for more than 35 goals and 75 points.

Brind'Amour slowed the last half of the season, allowing Mike Modano of the North Stars, Jeremy Roenick of the Blackhawks, and Sergei Makarov of the Flames to steal the rookie spotlight. But the Ottawa native still finished with a respectable 26 goals and 61 points. The numbers weren't earth-shattering, but they showed promise.

Despite a flurry of protest, the 31-year-old Makarov won rookie-of-the-year honors that season. Calling Makarov a rookie was stretching it. Sure, it was his first season in the NHL, but only after serving 11 years with the powerful Central Red Army team of the Soviet Union. The NHL grudgingly gave Makarov his Calder Trophy, but changed the rules during the off-season, specifying that all future rookie-of-the-year candidates must be 26 or younger.

As it turned out, the first few months of his rookie season were as good as it would get for Brind'Amour as a member of the Blues. He suffered from the proverbial sophomore slump in 1990-91. His totals plummeted to 17 goals and 32 points. Coach Brian Sutter moved him from line to line, trying to find the right spot for Brind'Amour, hoping to shake him out of his daze.

Nothing seemed to work. Brind'Amour's confidence faded and many fans gave up on him. Every time a trade rumor made the rounds, the name of Rod Brind'Amour was attached to it. And few complained.

"I do have to prove something, not only to everybody but to myself," Brind'Amour admitted at the first day of camp, the start of his third year in the NHL. "I'm just hoping when the puck is dropped at the beginning of the season, I'm ready to go."

The Scott Stevens controversy didn't help Brind'Amour's standing in the community. Blues fans were very angry about losing the team captain, blaming Edward J. Houston for the loss. If he had made the right decision, they yelled, Rod Brind'Amour would be wearing a Devils jersey, not Stevens. Brind'Amour didn't take the fans' outrage personally, but it still made him feel awkward.

"It's a very weird situation," he said. "Unfortunately, I had to be a part of it.

"I haven't looked at it as a personal thing," he added, echoing Stevens: "It's just business."

Brind'Amour's state of mind was certainly in good working order, but his physique was even more impressive. He had been criticized as being too muscle-bound to have the quick reflexes of a high scoring forward. His "hands of stone," as one player derisively called them, had pushed him to the lower rungs of the depth chart.

However, Brind'Amour sported a new look in training camp. He was still well-defined, but that bodybuilder image was gone. So was the excessively high intensity level that almost destroyed him the previous year when his production level dropped off. No matter how he played, Brind'Amour ripped himself apart for not doing better. His self-criticism destroyed any remaining confidence he had. He didn't need to listen to the radio call-in shows. Rod Brind'Amour was his own worst critic.

But the new-look youngster now had a new outlook. A summer of soul-searching gave him the bubbly enthusiasm that had been missing since his rookie year.

"I've learned to relax a little bit when I'm away from the rink and not carry all the garbage of the game with me," he said. "It just builds and builds and wrecks everything for you. I feel different in camp now. I'm not as intense. I think that comes with experience as you get older. After all, I'm 21 now."

After just the first week of training camp, Brind'Amour had established himself as one of the top players. His skating was fluid. His shot was quicker. He banged into his teammates as if the Stanley Cup were on the line. Rod Brind'Amour didn't come just to the make the team. He was going to be an important cog in the Blues' offensive machine. He was going to dare Coach Sutter to move him off the first two lines. This was going to be Brind'Amour's season of redemption.

On just the third day of camp at Brentwood, Brind'Amour knocked into Dave Mackey, a young left winger trying to earn a job. The two exchanged glances, grabbed each other's jerseys, and started throwing punches. Goalie Curtis Joseph, on the opposite end of the ice, yelled to some of his teammates, "Mackey must have told him he was being traded to Jersey anyway."

The players and reporters standing nearby had a good laugh. But we all knew Joseph was right. If you wanted to wipe the smile right off Brind'Amour's face, mention him in a trade rumor. He had grown justifiably tired of hearing his name thrown around North America as trade bait.

The wildest trade rumor was circulated the same night of the Brind'Amour/Mackey fight. On KMOX radio, the self-proclaimed "sports voice of St. Louis," Randy Karraker told his listeners that a high-ranking source said the Blues and Nordiques were very close to making a deal for Eric Lindros, the number-one pick in the 1991 draft. Lindros was touted as the most talented player to come along since Mario Lemieux was drafted number one in 1984. If anyone was a franchise player, Lindros was it.

The 18-year-old Lindros had a business sense beyond his years. The Nordiques had finished with the worst record in the NHL three years straight, and Lindros was very blunt in saying Quebec couldn't afford to pay the world's best young hockey player to work his magic for the world's worst team. Besides, Lindros pointed out, Quebec was a French-speaking city, and he didn't know enough of the language to ask directions to the nearest ice rink. That would diminish his endorsement opportunities, which, in an English-speaking city, might make him millions. Don't waste your time writing a contract, Lindros said. He wasn't coming.

Assuming the Nordiques were interested in unloading their prized possession, virtually every NHL team contacted Quebec general manager Pierre Page, asking him what he wanted in return for Lindros. St. Louis was no exception, according to Karraker. Quoting an unnamed source, the talk-show host said the Blues had offered center Adam Oates, defenseman Paul Cavallini, Brind'Amour, and draft choices in exchange for Lindros. Apparently, the only hang-up was money. Lindros was asking for everything but the Arch, and the Blues reportedly could not meet Lindros' financial demands.

The rumor spread quicker than a forest fire. Fans lit up the Blues switchboard asking when Lindros was coming. Some were already saving money for Stanley Cup tickets. Many others called the Blues foolhardy for giving up so much for a teen-ager who had yet to play one game in the NHL. Team officials were outraged by the reports, calling the media "irresponsible" for reporting such gossip.

"I'm going to declare St. Louis the capital of rumors," an irritated Caron said. "That's the easiest way to do your work. Get it from someone else and bring it back home. My forecast for Lindros is that he will sign with Quebec in a matter of time."

The trade proposal was also a hot topic among the players themselves, especially the three Blues mentioned. Oates tossed it aside like yesterday's garbage.

"I'll deal with it when it happens," Oates said. "I don't pay too much attention to it."

Cavallini was more defensive. He, like Brind'Amour, was frequent trade bait, and it was starting to take its toll on his home life.

"It's hard on our families because your wife reads the paper in the morning how you're going to get traded," said the all-star defenseman. "She doesn't know whether to pack up or relax and be cool about it."

"It's an impersonal business at times," said Brind'Amour, by now an expert on hot gossip. He would learn just how impersonal less than two weeks after the Lindros rumor first surfaced. Brind'Amour was indeed traded, but not to Quebec.

On September 22, Brind'Amour, along with center Dan Quinn, was shipped to Philadelphia for defenseman Murray Baron and center Ron Sutter. Brind'Amour was disappointed, but not completely surprised. With his name being tossed around so frequently, he knew it was only a matter of time before he changed jerseys.

Meanwhile, angry fans flooded the Arena phone lines. Most weren't upset with the loss of Dan Quinn. He was not a favorite of Brian Sutter's, nor with many paying customers. Quinn was a figure skater who got lost trying to find his own zone. He was unwilling to hit or be hit, unacceptable behavior for one of Sutter's employees.

It was the loss of Brind'Amour that irked so many fans. Even though they were on Brind'Amour's back like a tight-checking defenseman, they criticized Sutter for giving up on the kid so quickly. Give him time, they demanded. One sophomore slump, and he's out the door? Blues backers demanded an explanation, forcing Coach Sutter to defend himself.

"Everyone says Brian Sutter lost patience with Rod Brind'Amour. Brian Sutter was Rod Brind'Amour's chief booster last year," the Blues' coach said. "Everyone else criticized him and ridiculed him. This is the first time in my 16 years here (twelve as a player, four as coach) that we dealt from strength at a position. We had Dave Christian, Dave Lowry, and Brendan Shanahan, so we could deal someone. It was a bonus to get Ronnie, believe me."

It was that last sentence especially that made fans, and some members of the media, cringe. Three of the six Sutter brothers affiliated with the NHL were now in St. Louis. Brian's younger sibling, Rich, was acquired from Vancouver in March of 1990. And now Richie's twin brother, Ronnie, was joining the family at the Arena. Cries of nepotism rattled the rafters. Instead of the Bluenote, the team should wear a picture of the Sutter family on the front of its jerseys, fans yelled. The public relations department should print two media guides, one for the Sutters and one for the rest of the team. If you couldn't tell the difference, the Sutter guide was the thicker one.

In a well-written and highly critical article, *Post-Dispatch* columnist Tom Wheatley slammed the Blues for turning the team into a Sutter family reunion.

"The Blues should deal Adam Oates for Brent Sutter, the only active Sutter not here," Wheatley sarcastically wrote. "Then the Blues could try to have Bruce Sutter come in from the bullpen, and David Souter come off the bench at the Supreme Court."

Wheatley also suggested the growing Sutter presence in the locker room was resented by some players. Even Brett Hull admitted that several of his teammates were grumbling, but was quick to say he wasn't one of them.

"Except for a few people in here, the general consensus is you can't give up enough to get a Sutter," said Hull. "Those guys are heart and soul every time they come and play the game."

"I haven't heard any grumbling," said Oates when asked about the Wheatley article. "In fact, Richie Sutter called me at home last night and talked about it. I know Hullie and myself feel very strongly about the trade."

Even so, the head coach was forced to respond to the mounting criticism.

"If we're going to upgrade our hockey club, I don't care if it's [with] five guys named Jones, or Caron, or Federko," said Sutter. "We want to win, and we will put the best team possible on the ice."

The Blackhawks certainly followed that approach. Reports out of Chicago had Ron Sutter going to the Hawks in a preseason deal. Coach Mike Keenan admitted he had been trying to land the Flyers' captain for two years. And yes, the Blackhawks already had two Sutters in their organization, Darryl, an assistant coach, and Duane, a scout.

Failing to acquire Ron, the Hawks went after the only remaining Sutter still playing. Keenan traded forwards Steve Thomas and Adam Creighton to the New York Islanders for center Brent Sutter. It was now even. The Blues and Blackhawks, those hated rivals, each had three Sutters.

Nonetheless, conspiracy-minded Blues fans were convinced that Brian Sutter was engineering all the trades. Surely, Ron Caron wouldn't stockpile so many members of one family. It was so obvious, they said. Team President Jack Quinn had stripped Caron of some of his power, giving Coach Sutter the freedom to make any trade he wanted.

Nonsense, team officials shot back.

"Brian and I have a great relationship," said Caron. "I enjoy working with him very much. People have to remember one thing when it comes to trades. If you're going to make a team nowadays strictly with draft picks, you're in for a surprise. I don't think ownership or fans are patient enough to build strictly with draft picks. You must produce at present."

Sutter agreed.

"We're easy to get along with that way," he said. "It's not my hockey club. It's our hockey club."

Perhaps, but it was a hockey club that was quickly acquiring Brian Sutter-like players. As the captain of the Blues for nine years, "Sudsy" was an aggressive left winger, who still holds the team's career penalty minutes record with 1,786. If there was ever a player who used every ounce of his God-given talent, it was Sutter. Never known as a pure goal scorer, he managed to find the back of the net 303 times in his career, second only to Bernie Federko's 352 on the team scoring list.

But he was also a terrific defensive player who took as much pride in banging an opposing player as banging in a goal. He was the ultimate two-way hockey player, skating into his own end to smother the opposition, then rushing up ice the other way to lead a break.

To play for Brian Sutter, you had to play like Brian Sutter. That's why the twins, Rich and Ron, were on the team. That's why Dan Quinn was not. That's why Bob Bassen and Dave Lowry were on the team. That's why Steve Tuttle was not. Tuttle was a very talented offensive player whose defensive work did not impress Sutter. For that reason, the 26-year-old Tuttle has spent much of his young career in Peoria, the Blues' top minor league affiliate.

Many hockey fans disagreed with that philosophy, saying Sutter was acquiring too many "muckers and grinders" and not enough goal scorers. The players came to their coach's defense.

"Every fan has a right to their opinion, but I just don't think a lot of them understand the game," said Hull. "We need guys who intimidate the other team with hard work and tenacity. That's what wins games. I don't win games. I may get a goal to win, but in the overall picture, it's guys like Ron Sutter who win games."

Hull's playmaking centerman agreed.

"We've got guys like Hullie, myself, Brendan, Dave Christian, a lot of offensive talent," said Oates. "Now we're getting some great checkers and physical players. We just need to fill the void of Scott Stevens, and I think we've got a very solid hockey team."

Interestingly, it was the acquisition of Ron Sutter that eventually forced Stevens to decide to play in New Jersey. Even though he had privately made up his mind not to fight the compensation ruling, he still held out hope that the Blues would swing a deal with Jersey to reacquire his services. But Dan Quinn and Brind'Amour were necessary pawns in any trade talk with New Jersey. When Ron Caron sent that pair to the City of Brotherly Love, Stevens knew the Blues were going on without him.

With the arrival of Murray Baron, the Blues were admitting they had a huge defensive hole to fill, even though Stevens had yet to announce his intentions. Just two days after the trade, Scottie moved to New Jersey.

"It just didn't seem like much was going to happen in St. Louis with some of the other stuff going on," Stevens said, referring to the Philly trade.

Also, Stevens undoubtedly heard some of his teammates say it was time to move on and prepare for life without their captain even before he made up his mind what he was going to do.

"Scott means an awful lot to this hockey club," said defenseman Garth Butcher. "But as it sits right now, he's not going to be with us, so we all have to pick it up a notch."

"Let bygones be bygones," said Harold Snepsts, a team-mate of Stevens' the year before who had become the Peoria head coach. "We can't think about what we lost. We've got to think about what we've gained."

Murray Baron for one. He was the "other" guy in the Blues/Flyers swap. While everyone debated the merits of Ron Sutter, Murray Baron was largely forgotten. However, his output could determine how far the Blues would go in the playoffs. Few questioned the Blues' offensive prowess. It was the defense, or lack thereof, that concerned fans and players alike. Stevens was gone, as was tough-guy Snepsts, who had retired to take the Peoria job. You could just see high-scoring forwards licking their chops at the Blues' Swiss cheese defense. Murray Baron had to stop the opposition's hunger pangs.

Few St. Louis fans knew anything about Baron. The 24-year-old had played in 87 NHL games, racking up 10 goals, 20 assists, and 86 penalty minutes. No one expected him to replace Scott Stevens. But at the very least, the Blues were hoping his 6' 3," 215-pound frame could help solidify the blue line corps.

"The coaches here want me to use my size and be physical," said Baron. "I work hard and come to play every night."

In other words, a Brian Sutter-type player.

*   *   *

An early October thunderstorm was fast approaching from the west. St. Louis was not immune to severe weather, but it was usually reserved for the spring and summer months. However, on October 4, 1991, a monster of a storm was sweeping across Missouri. It had been dumping hail and heavy rain, and producing lightning and damaging winds. A severe thunderstorm watch was in effect for the entire St. Louis area.

The storm was about twenty miles west of the city as the Blues gathered at Lambert International Airport. Several of the players gazed out of the window at Gate 55, watching the sky grow darker.

"Ole Doggy's gonna be hiding behind the seats," joked Gino Cavallini. He was referring to Ron "Dog" Wilson, the Blues' center known for his disdain of air travel even on the most gorgeous of days. As Cavallini chuckled, Wilson looked straight ahead, unamused by his teammate's attempt at humor.

The other players didn't seem to notice the impending storm. Coach Brian Sutter was making a last-minute call on one of the public phones near the gate. Standing right next to him was his brother, Ron, also yapping away on a phone. When people said these guys were alike, they weren't kidding.

Jeff Brown was munching on a burrito he had just purchased at the Taco Bell Express. Brendan Shanahan was finishing a cup of frozen yogurt. The others were mingling among family and friends who were wishing the players good luck.

The Blues were about to fly to Newark, New Jersey, for the season opener in nearby East Rutherford. The schedule makers couldn't have designed a better script. After weeks of battling one another at the bargaining table, the two teams were starting the season by battling one another on the ice. Scott Stevens would be there, but wearing a Devil instead of a Bluenote. Brendan

Shanahan would also play, but as a visitor, not a member of the home team.

"I have lots of butterflies," admitted Shanahan. "But that first shift I'll try to get a big hit or take a big hit. After that, I'm sure I'll be a bit looser."

And what about going up against Scott Stevens, the player who was forced to go to New Jersey because of your arrival in St. Louis?

"I hear that name at least a dozen times a day now," said Shanahan, growing irritated with all the Stevens-related questions. "He plays for New Jersey, and I play for St. Louis, and we want to beat them. He's the opposition now."

"I really feel for Brendan," said Kelly Chase. "Every time he opens a newspaper or watches a newscast he hears everyone saying how we lost Scott Stevens and all we got was Brendan Shanahan. But let's face it. Brendan Shanahan is a quality player."

As the players boarded the plane, the storm suddenly took a turn toward the north. The sun began to shine and the temperatures started to fall, an offshoot of the passing front. As the last few players walked down the ramp, a puzzled woman asked what all the commotion was about. When told it was the Blues traveling to play their season opener in New Jersey, she shrugged her shoulders.

"Oh, I thought it was somebody important or something," she said, obviously unimpressed.

No, ma'am, it's just your local hockey team traveling to the east coast. There were more pressing issues in the world, to be sure. But the people boarding the 1:35 p.m. flight to Newark were thinking only of hockey. Less than 27 hours later, they would play their first game of the year, the first step on the road to a possible Stanley Cup. Hopefully, the storms of training camp had passed, giving way to a brighter season ahead.

As the clouds cleared, the TWA flight took off toward the sky, carrying the St. Louis Blues to the start of the 1991-92 season.

Chapter Two

A DEVIL OF A START

There was confusion in the Blues' locker room. The players appeared a bit puzzled as they looked around the room. Who are some of these guys?, the players wondered. Who let them in here? Isn't there a guard checking passes? They looked like hockey players. They even talked like them. The evidence seemed clear. These guys must be members of the St. Louis Blues.

That's overstating it, of course, but the team about to take the ice consisted of players who had never skated together before the opening game against the New Jersey Devils. Garth Butcher had been out of action nursing a sore back. Ron Sutter and Murray Baron had been acquired less than two weeks before the season opener. Vincent Riendeau, Paul Cavallini, Jeff Brown, and Adam Oates missed the start of training camp after trying out for the Canada Cup. The players who actually played in the Cup—Brett Hull, Brendan Shanahan, Dave Christian, and Pat Jablonski—didn't report to St. Louis until 13 days before the season officially started. Even head coach Brian Sutter had missed the first two weeks of camp after assisting Team Canada in its triumph over the Americans.

Here it was, just minutes before the opening faceoff of the 1991-92 season, and the St. Louis Blues were playing together for the first time. To make matters worse, the team was road-weary. Players who had been at camp since day one had just completed a grueling ten-game exhibition schedule, nine of them away from home. They won eight, more than any other team, but at what price? Even Ron Caron was worried about the hectic pace, calling his team "the Globetrotters of hockey."

"I've been back almost three weeks since the Canada Cup," said Coach Sutter, "and have spent about three nights in my own bed."

But the Blues looked anything but tired when they left the locker room and headed toward the ice. More than 15,000 fans crammed the Byrne Meadowlands Arena, jeering the visiting team when it stepped into the rink. That only pumped up the boys in blue, who were ready to start the campaign on a winning note. Hockey was back, and all was right with the world.

"The excitement is here," said Ron Sutter. "Everyone's ready."

Including Vincent Riendeau. The Blues goalie who led the NHL in winning percentage the year before was a surprise starter against the Devils. Many assumed Curtis Joseph would get the nod. Weeks before, Devils general manager Lou Lamoriello had criticized Joseph's abilities as a goalie in the Scott Stevens arbitration hearings. What better way for Joseph to show up Lamoriello than by shutting down his team? But Coach Sutter wasn't going to base his decision on off-ice considerations, especially ones involving management. Sutter likes to show loyalty to players who have gone to battle for him on the ice. With a 29-9-6 record and a 3.06 goals-against average the year before, Riendeau deserved the starting job. Politics weren't going to enter into the decision.

"If Jersey and the Blues have a problem, it's not between the players," said Brett Hull. "It's between the management."

The Blues showed off their new look as soon as the puck was dropped. On the ice was the familiar duo of Hull and Oates, but taking care of business on the left side was none other than Brendan Shanahan. The new first line for the Blues was expected to develop into one of the most explosive top lines in the league.

Everyone knew the exploits of Hull and Oates. But now they had a physical forward in Shanahan to bang into the boards and throw his weight around in front of the net. His physical style of play was supposed to open up the ice for Brett and Adam to work their magic. And if the opposition started pushing the Golden Brett around like the North Stars did in the playoffs the year before, then Shanahan would skate to the rescue.

"The opposition isn't going to be able to do what they did last year and get away with it," said Hull.

The impartial partisan was not impressed. The fans booed Shanahan unmercifully from the moment he touched the puck. He later said he was a bit hurt by the hostile reception. As a Devil for four years, Shanahan had played every game as if it were his last, skating as hard and fast as his big frame would carry him. His blue-collar work ethic on the ice, and his "media darling" presence off it had made Brendan Shanahan an idol of many in New Jersey. He was a role model for young men, a pin-up for young women. But when he bolted for greener pastures in St. Louis, his posters were ripped down. His fans felt betrayed. Few would ever forgive him. So on opening night, they made their feelings known every time No. 19 touched the puck.

The negative reception made Shanahan a bit surly. As a Devil, Shanahan had won an award from the New Jersey media for his cooperation with the press. But tonight Shanahan shed his "nice-guy" image and told reporters that if they wanted to discuss his move to the Blues and the subsequent Scott Stevens controversy, they could get lost.

"Hey guys, I was more than willing to talk about it during the Canada Cup," Shanahan said. "But we're into the season now. It's time to drop it and move on."

Shanahan's teammates were equally frustrated once the game started. Just 49 seconds into the season, the Blues found themselves behind. Stephane Richer, the newly acquired center from the Canadiens, flew into the Blues' zone down the left side. He quickly stopped at the bottom of the circle, letting Garth Butcher slide past him. Richer patiently waited for a teammate to crash the net. But with Adam Oates skating back to interrupt the play, Richer had no choice but to let one fly at a seemingly impossible angle.

Riendeau never saw it. He was screened by Paul Cavallini and Tom Chorske fighting for position. Before Riendeau knew it, the red light was flashing and the packed house erupted into a frenzy. The Devils were up 1-0.

The first period was dominated by the home team. New Jersey outchecked, outskated, and outplayed St. Louis. The only thing the Blues had done right so far was stand at attention for the national anthem. The team was out of sync. It was painfully obvious that the players were unfamiliar with one another. Guys were out of position all night.

Not only did the first line have a new left winger, the second line had a new everything. Left winger Dave Christian was a free-agent acquisition, center Ron Sutter had come from the Flyers just a week before, and right winger Nelson Emerson was a rookie. The defensive pairings were also new, with Murray Baron and Rob Robinson added to the squad. The players barely knew each other's names, and here they were trying to win a hockey game together.

It didn't take long to see the Blues' power play was also out of whack. With so many new faces, Coach Sutter had to experiment with different power-play formations. He put Baron and Brown on the points, with Shanahan, Hull, and Oates down in front. The early reviews were unfavorable. The Blues managed only one shot on goal during their first power play.

Just a few minutes later, they were given a second chance when Devils defenseman Bruce Driver was called for interference. Still no luck. The second try, in fact, was disastrous.

As the puck lay along the right boards in the Devils' zone, four Blues and two Devils raced to get it. The laws of math holding true, that left just one Blue to guard two Devils. Sure enough, when the puck was kicked loose, Richer had a two-on-one break with Viacheslav Fetisov. Mario Marois hurried back to help his defenseless goalie. Fetisov glided down the left side and slid the puck under Marois' stick to Richer, who easily beat Riendeau on the glove side. The Devils' short-handed goal made it 2-0.

To make matters worse in the first period, the Blues' newly named captain, Garth Butcher, was kicked out of the game.

During the off-season, the NHL had instituted a new rule slapping a five-minute major penalty and a game misconduct on any player guilty of misusing his hockey stick or throwing a blindside check. If blood is drawn, the perpetrator is automatically tossed. Otherwise, it's a discretionary call made by the referee. Too many players had been seriously hurt because of high-flying sticks and checks from behind, and the league was trying to stop it. Butcher was the rule's first casualty.

While Rich Sutter and Richer were fighting for the puck along the boards, the Devils' Peter Stastny slowly moved toward the play. Butcher followed Stastny like a cop stalking a criminal. As soon as Stastny got near the action, Butcher cross-checked him from behind, sending Stastny into the boards headfirst. Referee

Ron Hoggarth quickly called the penalty. Butcher knew he was guilty and slowly skated toward the penalty box. However, before he could even sit down, Hoggarth informed Butcher he had gone to the wrong place. The locker room is where you're going, Hoggarth said. You're done for the night.

At the end of one period, the Blues were down by two goals, had managed only one shot while giving up 14, and were without their captain for the final forty minutes. If the Blues came back and won this one, the league might as well stop playing the season and ship the Stanley Cup to St. Louis right now.

The Blues were much more inspired at the start of the second period. The teams traded quality scoring opportunities, until the Blues finally got on the board at 8:37. Adam Oates, the stick-handling wizard, was to the left of the Devils' net when he passed across to defenseman Jeff Brown, who was pinching in to try to shake up the team offensively. The puck bounced over his stick, and Brown had to retrieve it. As soon as he got to it, near the circle, Brown quickly spun around and passed it to Shanahan ten feet in front of the goal. Shanahan swiped at the puck, didn't get very good wood on it, but still managed to beat Chris Terreri, who was out of position awaiting a potential shot from Brown.

Fittingly, Shanahan scored the Blues' first goal of the year in his old workhouse. The fans booed, hissed, and jeered. But it didn't matter. The Blues suddenly were down by just a goal, and that nightmarish first period was all but forgotten.

Playing with a new-found passion, the Blues had a couple of golden opportunities to tie it up. On the power play, the Golden Brett tried to poke the puck past Terreri, who had to make a sweeping glove save to bat it away. A few seconds later, Christian fired a slapper from 15 feet out that appeared destined for the left side of the net. But Terreri came up big again, making a sprawling save to thwart the Blues' chances.

New Jersey killed that penalty but gave the Blues plenty more. The Devils committed their seventh infraction late in the second period, handing the Blues yet another opportunity to establish their power play. However, the Blues continued to have problems moving the puck, even with the extra man. With less than five minutes to play in the period, Chorske picked up a loose puck at the red line, skated unmolested into the Blues zone and fired a long shot on goal. The puck hit Jeff Brown's left foot, creating a knuckleball effect that handcuffed Riendeau. The puck bounced once in front of the goalie before slipping between his pads. The Blues were not only behind 3-1, they had been outscored 2-1 on their own power play.

"It's not so much that five guys aren't working hard," said Coach Sutter, referring to his powerless power play. "It's that five guys aren't working hard together. There's a difference. We just have to have patience while expecting a little more of ourselves."

The ultimate embarrassment came just a minute later, with the teams at even strength. Once again, the Devils had a two-on-one break, with Jason Miller and Fetisov racing toward the net and Jeff Brown trying desperately to break up the play. Just when it looked like Fetisov would pass off to Miller, Brown went down in an effort to block it. However, Fetisov kept the puck, let Brown slide into the boards, and was now all alone in front of the net. There was not a single Blues jersey in the vicinity except for the one that had "Riendeau" stitched across the back. Fetisov just stood there. Riendeau crouched into position, looked at Fetisov, and begged for mercy. Finally, after what seemed an eternity, Fetisov moved the puck from his forehand to his backhand and flipped it past Riendeau's left foot. An empty-net goal would have been more challenging.

That one play was indicative of the Blues' performance on opening night. The Devils abused, humiliated, flustered, and agitated St. Louis into submission. Riendeau was yanked in favor of Curtis Joseph, but the damage had been done. The Blues couldn't have beaten a minor league team that night.

With the score 6-1 in the third period, Blues' tough guy Kelly Chase decided to see whether his fists were in midseason form. Chase knocked Devils defenseman Eric Weinrich heavily into the boards to try to get something started. Weinrich is not a fighter, racking up only 59 penalty minutes his first two years. So his teammates came to the rescue, trying to get at Chase. One of the Devils especially interested in landing a few blows on Chase's noggin was none other than Scott Stevens. Just a few months earlier, Chase and Stevens had fought for the same cause. Now they were on opposite sides of the battle line.

"Just because you went to the wall for each other as team-mates doesn't mean you won't play hard against him when he's on the other side," said Chase.

Gino Cavallini agreed.

"There are no friends when the puck is dropped," Giant Gino said. "You talk to your friends after the game."

Stevens was in no mood to exchange pleasantries with his old working buddies. Adam Oates tried to get between Stevens and Chase to prevent a full-scale war but was rudely pushed away by the former Blues captain. Mario Marois also attempted to play peacemaker by holding onto Stevens' arm, but Stevens shook him off. Finally, the linesman interceded, taking the two to the penalty box without any punches being thrown. As they were being led away, Chase and Stevens continued to jaw at one another. What were they talking about?

"I wasn't quite sure when we would play them again," said Chase. "So we were exchanging Christmas greetings just in case it would be awhile."

However, the Blues' performance on opening night was no laughing matter. If it had been a Broadway play, the Blues would have lasted only one night. The critics would have been so harsh, the "players" would have never performed again in any venue. Final score: Devils 7, Blues 2. The early review was a big thumbs down.

"We just have to keep working hard," said Jeff Brown after the game. "Things will happen for us."

The Blues had been bludgeoned, but their optimism was still alive.

*   *   *

As the crowd rolled in, and the clock ticked down to the start of the game, Toronto goalie Grant Fuhr was limbering up in front of his bench. If tonight's game was like the first two, Fuhr knew he would be busy. He had been pelted with 70 shots by Montreal and Detroit. And now Brett Hull and Company were in town, promising to be another shootout.

Hull spotted Fuhr along the boards. Flashing his million-dollar smile, the Golden Brett skated over to make small talk.

"What are you going to give me tonight?" asked Hull. "Top shelf or bottom shelf?"

"How about the top?" Fuhr was quick to respond.

"You got it," said Hull as he skated back to his own end.

Brett knew he would have to work for his goals tonight. Fuhr is considered one of the best netminders in the league. He has five Stanley Cup rings to prove it, all with the Edmonton Oilers. And no goalie was more durable. Fuhr appeared in 75 games in the 1987-88 season, an NHL record. He won the Vezina Trophy that year as the league's top goaltender.

When the Oilers traded Fuhr to the Maple Leafs just weeks before the start of the 1991-92 season, he gave Toronto instant credibility. The Leafs were considered the weakest team in what many experts predicted would be the strongest division in 1991-92. They were supposed to be the doormat for the other four Norris Division squads making a run at the playoffs. But with Fuhr on board, Toronto suddenly was no cakewalk.

Frustrated by his team's performance two nights before, Blues coach Brian Sutter made several personnel changes. He switched left wingers on the first two lines, dropping Shanahan to the second line and moving Christian to the first. He also flip-flopped Nelson Emerson and Ron Sutter on the second line, moving Emerson back to his natural position at center. Gino Cavallini, scratched from the New Jersey game, was in the lineup in place of Ron Hoover. Cavallini was the second-biggest forward on the team, after Shanahan, and in an important divisional game, Coach Sutter wanted some extra beef on the ice. And Curtis Joseph was given the starting job in net, continuing where he left off after taking over for Riendeau in the second period of the Devils game.

However, all the strategic planning in the world could not have prevented the mishap that occurred just six-and-a-half minutes into the game. The Blues were on their second power play and already reprising their frightful performance of two nights earlier. Once again, they were having trouble moving the puck into the Leafs' zone, so they just dumped it in behind the net. Leafs defenseman Dave Ellett skated back to retrieve it. The puck bounced off the boards right to Ellett, who, without looking, quickly turned and fired a clearing pass. Nelson Emerson was merely a bystander on the play, slowly trailing Ellett to see what he was going to do. Unfortunately, he saw it a little too closely.

The puck smacked Emerson in the face, catching him on the left side of the nose. The 5' 10" center crumbled to the ice as if he had been shot. He quickly got to his hands and knees and watched the blood flow from his face, creating a red puddle on the ice beneath him. He shook off his gloves and put his hands to his face to make sure everything was still intact. Blues trainer Mike Folga carefully jogged across the ice to the fallen player. Folga placed a towel across Emerson's nose and hurriedly escorted him to the locker room. Once there, Leith Douglas, Toronto's "cut" doctor for 25 years, forcefully moved Emerson's nose back into its proper socket. It was broken in two places and required a dozen stitches to sew up the gash.

"I was in a bit of a shock and I was kind of scared," Emerson said. "The first thing I thought of was my eyesight. If the puck had hit me in the eye the same way it hit me in the nose it could have been a lot worse. Fortunately, I didn't lose any vision over it."

After hearing the rookie center was going to be okay, general manager Ron Caron relayed his frustration over the incident from the press box.

"I was hoping Emerson would stay on his feet for one more second," said Caron. "Our man at the right point was about to fire a slapper, but the linesman stopped play when Emerson went down."

When your team is having trouble scoring goals like the Blues were in the season's first four periods, a broken nose takes a back seat to putting points on the board. The Blues now needed to catch a few lucky breaks.

The first period ended in a scoreless tie, Fuhr and Joseph making spectacular saves. Once again, the Blues had failed to take advantage of their extra man. They managed only two shots on three power-play opportunities. For the Blues to have any chance tonight, Joseph would have to match Fuhr save for save.

However, the Blues' defense didn't give its goalie much support. Just 1:46 into the second period, Toronto had a two-on-one break. Wendell Clark skated down the right side and ripped a slapshot from the top of the circle. Joseph made a nice pad save, but the puck bounced right back to Clark, now just a few feet away. Instead of shooting again, Clark slid a pass across the crease to Peter Zezel, standing near the left goal post. Zezel tapped the puck in for the easy goal, and the Maple Leafs had the 1-0 lead.

A little more than 5:30 later, Toronto lit the lamp again. Defenseman Bob Rouse skated unchecked into the Blues zone along the left boards. Sensing teammate Dave Ellett trailing him, Rouse left the puck at the top of the circle. Ellett scooped it up, skated a few strides toward the net, and rifled a shot that beat Joseph on the left side. Suddenly, the Maple Leafs were up by two. And with Grant Fuhr in goal, the lead seemed insurmountable.

Shortly after Ellett's goal, the Blues went on the power play when Gary Leeman was slapped with a five-minute major and a game misconduct for slashing Paul Cavallini. Unfortunately, the Blues' defenseman had to serve two minutes in the penalty box himself for slashing Leeman in retaliation. After Cavallini served his time, the Blues had the man advantage for three minutes, plenty of time to practice their woeful power play.

This time, they worked it to near-perfection, meaning the Blues continuously fed Brett Hull and his cannon disguised as a stick. Hull launched a slapper from his favorite spot, just inside the left circle, but Fuhr made a nice pad save and kicked it out. The Blues regained control of the puck and passed it to No. 16 once again. Hull wasted no time, sending another ferocious slapper toward Fuhr. The puck missed its intended target and smashed into the glass behind the net. The glass instantly cracked, but the officials didn't notice it at first and allowed play to continue. For the third time in a matter of seconds, the puck found its way to Hull's stick. Standing near the left circle, he let a rocket fly that hit Fuhr on the mask so hard the puck ricocheted about twenty feet in front. The Toronto goalie skated after it, coming way out of his net to smother it. Fuhr had seen enough of Hull and needed a breather.

While workers attended to the broken glass, referee Denis Morel skated to the official scorer to call a delay-of-game penalty on Fuhr. The Leafs argued vehemently that Fuhr had every right to pounce on the loose puck. But Morel pointed to the spot where Fuhr had fallen to the ice. A goaltender can't come out that far to fall on a puck, he said. The call stood.

It was too bad for the Blues that a goalie doesn't have to serve his own penalties. Mike Foligno was sent to the box as the sacrificial Leaf, and Fuhr was allowed to continue teasing the

Blues and Brett Hull. Shortly after the new power play started, Hull was all alone in front of the net, but he pushed the puck right into Fuhr's midsection. A few seconds later, Hull returned to his spot between the circles and rifled a low, hard slapper that Fuhr managed to kick out. The Golden Brett skated in, picked up the rebound, and tried to flip it past the Leafs' goalie. You guessed it. Fuhr also stopped that shot. The puck lay loose in the goal crease, but Fuhr fell on it to stop play. Six consecutive shots. Six consecutive saves.

The 15,375 fans in attendance had just witnessed a spectacular one-on-one battle between Brett Hull and Grant Fuhr, two of the world's best hockey players. The others on the ice were merely spectators. The game between the Blues and Leafs had become a head-to-head challenge between an out-of-town sniper and a local sheriff aiming to stop him. Hull pulled out his most explosive arsenal, firing shot after shot in rapid succession, but Fuhr heroically protected his territory. It was a shootout on ice, with the expert marksman going home with nothing to show for it but an empty six-shooter.

As the crowd stood on its feet and roared its approval, Hull slowly skated to his bench. He looked to the rafters of the Maple Leaf Gardens as if to ask for divine guidance. He then lowered his head toward the ice as if he had been told, "not tonight."

With Hull shut down, the Blues were shut out. Grant Fuhr recorded his tenth career white washing, stopping 33 shots. Toronto center Claude Loiselle added an empty-net goal with 44 seconds to play, to finish the scoring at 3-0. The Blues performed much better than on opening night in New Jersey, but had zero to show for it.

"We ran into a hot goalie and couldn't put the puck in the net," said Coach Sutter. "They won the hockey game, but we can't let that get us down. We need to keep our perspective."

His players agreed. The team played well, even getting quality shots on the power play, but the opposing goalie was Fuhr-ocious. An NHL all-star team wasn't going to score tonight.

"He can still stop the puck," said Jeff Brown. "He proved it tonight, and I'm sure he's going to continue to prove it the whole year."

Hull was frustrated but not entirely disappointed. His slapshot was still intact. Against a mere mortal, Hull would have racked up at least a couple of goals. But on this night, he ran into an impregnable wall named Grant Fuhr.

"As long as the chances to shoot keep coming, I'm not worried," said Hull. "When the chances stop, then I'll worry about it."

The team as a whole, however, had plenty to worry about. Even though the Blues played better in Toronto, statistics couldn't lie. In two games, the Blues were 1 for 17 on the power play. That's a minuscule .059 success rate.

Overall, the Blues had been outscored 10-2 by teams not expected to contend for the Stanley Cup. For the first time in Brian Sutter's coaching reign, and only the third time in 15 years, the St. Louis Blues had started a season with two losses. That meant that for the Blues to win it all, they would have to break an 11-year-old tradition. They would have to become the first team since the 1979-80 New York Islanders to win the Cup after losing its first two regular-season games.

Chapter Three

HOME COOKING

"Brian Sutter is ruining this team!" screamed the caller. "He lets scorers like Geoff Courtnall and Dan Quinn go and picks up slugs like his brother!"

"There's too much change," points out another fan on the phone. "How can a team that finished second overall the year before make wholesale changes like this? It's crazy."

The local talk shows were filled with the tirades of angry Blues fans. The season was still in its infancy, but people had seen enough. They were already throwing in the towel. Fans across St. Louis were jumping off the Blues' bandwagon. Forget about the Stanley Cup, some yelled. We'll be lucky to make the playoffs.

Except for the expansion years of the late 1960s and an aberrant 1980-81 season when the team tallied 107 points, the St. Louis Blues had puttered along in mediocrity through their 25-year existence. That's strange, considering the all-stars who have worn the Bluenote. The roster reads like a Who's Who: Red Berenson, Garry Unger, Barclay Plager, Glenn Hall, Doug Harvey, Jacques Plante, Bernie Federko, Brian Sutter, and a host of steady, if not spectacular, performers. Coaches Al Arbour and Hall of Famer Scotty Bowman shouted instructions from behind the Blues' bench. Contributing to the organization's heritage, if not to its won-lost record, the Blues also possessed arguably the greatest hockey announcer in the history of the game, Dan Kelly. His death in 1989 was mourned by hockey lovers across North America.

And yet, despite that rich heritage, the Blues had never sipped champagne from Lord Stanley's Cup. In fact, they had never even gotten near enough to smell the bubbly. Sure, they played for the Cup in the team's first three years, 1968-70. But the Blues got there only by winning the inferior six-team expansion division. When they arrived at the finals, they became the whipping boys for established powerhouses like Montreal and Boston. Even though the Blues played tough and many games were decided by a single goal, St. Louis was still swept in four straight by the Canadiens in 1968 and '69 and shut out by the Bruins in 1970. Their all-time record in the Stanley Cup finals is an embarrassing 0-12.

However, most long-time Blues fans ignore those early years, tossing them aside as an unfair blot on team history. It was like expecting a sixth-grade math student to match wits with Albert Einstein. It was certainly exciting to play for the Cup as an expansion team. But no one mistook the early St. Louis Blues for a dynasty. They were merely the best of six new teams added to the league, no more.

But two decades later, led by the dynamic and debonair Michael Shanahan, who purchased a small portion of the team in 1986 and was made its general partner and chairman, the Blues entered the uncharted waters of success. Not just the one-year wonder of success that teases so many fans. No, this was turning into the real thing. A solid foundation was being laid on which to build a high-rise of achievement. Led by general manager Ron Caron, whose hockey insight seems almost mystical, the Blues started gathering talent at a dizzying rate in the late 1980s. Brett Hull, Adam Oates, and Paul Cavallini were acquired in trades. All three were decent players at best with their former organizations, but Caron saw the glimmer of stardom in all of them, and each became an all-star with the Blues.

Curtis Joseph, Scott Stevens, Brendan Shanahan, and Dave Christian were signed as free agents. The Blues' aggressive approach would later cost them Stevens, but team president Jack Quinn had sent word to the rest of the league that the Blues meant business.

Rising stars like center Nelson Emerson and goalie Pat Jablonski were draft picks, proving that team management, while shuffling players as fast as a Las Vegas card dealer, was willing to breed and nurture its own talent. Some kids were used as trade bait to acquire more experienced players; others, like Emerson and Jablonski, were groomed for permanent spots on the Blues' roster.

The Blues had used every avenue possible to drive to the top. They hadn't made it yet, but the improvement in the standings in each of Brian Sutter's three years showed they were on the right track.

That's why Blues fans were so irritable after the first two games. An 0-2 start was tolerable a few years ago, but not now. Not with this team. Blues backers were justifiably concerned about a repeat of a decade ago. In 1980-81, the Blues finished second overall in the NHL with 107 points, the most in team history. However, the Blues suffered a disappointing loss in the second round of the playoffs. Later that summer, Coach Red Berenson went on to coach in the Canada Cup, while management made a number of personnel changes to avoid a similar collapse in the playoffs in 1982.

The comparisons between then and ten years later were eerily similar. In 1990-91, the Blues finished second overall in the league with 105 points, but lost in the second round of the playoffs. Coach Brian Sutter went on to the Canada Cup, while management busily changed the structure of the team. St. Louisans were praying the comparisons stopped there.

In 1981-82, the team plummeted 35 points to a third-place finish in the Norris Division. They fell even farther the next season, managing just 25 wins and a fourth-place finish, barely making the playoffs. That flash across the St. Louis skyline in the early '80s was the meteoric plunge of the city's hockey team. Would history repeat itself ten years later? If early indications were accurate, well, no one wanted to think about it.

"You're next."

"Am I on?"

"Yes, please go ahead."

"I think the hockey fans in St. Louis are in for a big letdown."

"Can you explain?"

"Well, the first two games proved we have too many grinders and, you know, not enough scorers. I think we're in big trouble."

"Thanks for the call. Next."
"Rich and Ron Sutter have no business being here, and furthermore . . . "

*   *   *

If Curtis Joseph had not become a professional hockey player, he might have made a successful living as an architect. He was certainly showing off his talents the day the Blues returned home for practice after their dreadful two-game road trip to start the season. While most of his teammates huddled around Coach Sutter at the other end of the Brentwood ice rink, Joseph used the idle time meticulously constructing a one-inch-high wall of ice shavings along his goal crease. Joseph kept scooping up handfuls of ice around the net and adding them to the ends of the growing structure. By the time Sutter broke the huddle, Joseph had built himself a nice little five-foot-long wall of packed ice.

What was he doing? Didn't he know Sutter would chew his head off for goofing around? The Blues' no-nonsense coach was in no mood for levity. After all, the players proved in their first two games they needed to practice hockey, not ice sculpture.

However, as Sutter and his players skated toward Joseph, the only recognition of "the wall" was a few smiles and a couple of chuckles. One player gently shot a puck right through it, destroying it on impact. Coach Sutter paid no attention, if he even saw it in the first place.

The players were loose as they smiled, joked, and laughed during practice. Even Brett Hull, stifled the night before in Toronto, was in a light-hearted mood. He fastened a piece of masking tape over the No. 16 on the back of his helmet. Written on the tape was "-7," a reference to his plus/minus rating. Instead of hiding from his embarrassment, he wanted the whole world to know how disappointed he was in his play.

Make no mistake, despite their jocularity, the players also worked extremely hard in practice. Coach Sutter ran them through a grueling, two-hour practice that left them drenched with perspiration. But there was no cloud of despair hanging over the practice rink. There were no frowns or expressions of concern. The fans could predict the team's demise if they wanted. That was their right. But the players wanted no part of it. Two games does not a season make.

"The boys are really upbeat, as you can see," said Jeff Brown as a couple of teammates walked by and knocked his helmet off. "We just have to keep working hard, and things will happen for us. We're going to be there at the end of the year."

"It's not something you can just snap your fingers at and make happen," said Sutter. "We obviously tried to get two points in Toronto, but we didn't get them, and that just makes us more ornery for our game tomorrow against Edmonton."

If the players were even half as ornery as their fans, the Blues were going to come out like gang-busters in their home opener.

*   *   *

At 7:30 p.m. on the night of October 10, 1991, the lights inside the St. Louis Arena were suddenly turned off. The more than 17,000 spectators roared their approval. They knew the darkness meant the opening ceremonies were about to begin.

A narrow strip of carpet was rolled out from the penalty box area to near the faceoff circle at center ice. With a spotlight shining brightly on him at the end of the carpet, Blues Chairman Michael Shanahan thanked the fans for coming, made a few brief remarks about the silver anniversary of the Blues, and then gave the microphone to play-by-play announcer John Kelly, son of the late Dan Kelly.

"Welcome to the 25th year of Blues hockey!" Kelly yelled. The fans responded as if at a rock concert, listening to Mick Jagger introduce the members of his band.

"Goaltender Vincent Riendeau!" Kelly barked with authority. The spotlight followed Riendeau who skated from one end of the rink past Kelly at center ice, to the far blue line. The spotlight returned to the other end of the rink to pick up the next player, who repeated the process.

When Kelly read the name of Bob Bassen, the spotlight was unable to find him right away. Bassen skated in darkness toward center ice when BOOM!—he hit the carpet in full stride. Bassen flew through the air as the fans ooohed and aaahed. The scrappy forward somehow managed to land on his skates and avoid serious injury. It was one thing to be cross-checked into the boards by an opposing player. It was quite another to be blindsided by a piece of immovable carpet in complete darkness.

"Oh, man," Bassen exclaimed after the game, still in disbelief. "I was just skating along when I felt my skate leave the ice. Before I knew it, I was flying over the carpet!"

That wasn't the only near-mishap. As the players were standing along the blue line for one last round of applause, fireworks were set off overhead. Right overhead. Right above the players. It was an impressive sight, and the spectators clapped and yelled wildly. But a few sparks found their way to the ice below, forcing some of the players to skate out of harm's way.

"Did you see that?" asked Paul Cavallini. "Those fireworks were awful close."

Fortunately, the opening ceremonies ended without any injuries. But even the non-superstitious had to wonder whether this foreshadowed tragic consequences for not only this particular game, but for the entire season.

Any negative thoughts, however, quickly disappeared once the game started. The Blues put the pressure on the Oilers early and often. Just fifty seconds into the contest, Garth Butcher let go a slapper from the blue line and hit the post. Thirty seconds later, Hull tried to poke the puck past Oilers goalie Peter Ing, but Ing made a wonderful pad save.

Halfway through the first period, the Oilers went on the power play when Kelly Chase was caught cross-checking. However, it looked more like the Blues had the man advantage. They surrounded the Oilers' goal, forcing Ing to come up big on several occasions. Edmonton was given two power plays in the period but had to struggle to keep the puck out of its own net.

The Blues played inspired hockey in that first period, much to the delight of the near-sellout crowd. The home team outshot the visitors 12-6, but those numbers weren't indicative of how one-sided the hockey game was. If not for Ing, the Blues would have been up by a handful.

"That was our best period of the year, and we have much more to come," said Ron Caron during intermission. "I thought our guys were good in the transition game. They were jumping at the loose puck."

However, nearly eight minutes into the second period, the Oilers struck first. All five Blues were in the Oilers' zone trying to create some offense. As Hull and Geoff Smith were fighting for the puck along the boards, Smith managed to kick it ahead to Craig Muni. The Oilers' defenseman quickly backhanded a pass to Joe Murphy who was skating up-ice. Blues defensemen Murray Baron and Garth Butcher, caught up-ice, were out of the play.

Murphy raced down the left wing and fired a slapper from the top of the circle. The puck whizzed past Joseph low on the left side. The red lamp flickered, the crowd groaned, and Edmonton had a 1-0 lead.

Meanwhile, the Blues' offense continued clicking, but still couldn't score. Hull ripped his first big shot of the game with six minutes remaining in the period. Ing made the glove save to stop play, but that didn't stop Hull. Thirty seconds later, Hull fired another slapper from the left circle. Once again Ing made an Ozzie Smith-like glove save to force a faceoff.

Less than two minutes later it was Oates' turn. The Blues' playmaker was all alone to Ing's right. Instead of shooting, Oates waited for an open teammate to appear. He took a step back in an effort to draw attention toward him, but it didn't work. Oates, who is gracious to a fault, had no choice but to shoot on net. However, he had waited too long. Ing gave Oates virtually no opening at which to shoot, and easily stopped the shot between his pads.

Seconds later, with the puck still in the Oilers' zone, Hull decided to give it a couple more chances. He first tried to poke the puck into the net, but Ing kicked it out. On the ensuing scramble for the puck, Hull managed to pick it up and rifle a slapshot from his home near the left circle. However, the Oilers' netminder turned in another amaz-Ing save.

"You just feel like giving up," said Hull. "What can you do? You give him your best stuff and nothing goes in."

Incredibly, the Blues had outshot Edmonton in the second period 14-6 and held a 26-12 advantage for the game. But the game's only goal belonged to the Oilers. It was deja vu all over again. As in Toronto two nights earlier, the Blues were getting

quality shots but were being stymied by a spectacular performance from the opposing goalie.

Interestingly, Grant Fuhr and Peter Ing had been traded for
one another just weeks earlier. Was this evidence of another
league directive aimed at getting back at St. Louis? Had the trade,
which had to be approved like all trades by the league office,
contained a clause demanding the two goalies shut out the Blues?

A little more than two minutes into the third period, Oilers
left winger Craig Simpson struck what appeared to be the fatal
blow. Teammate Joe Murphy ripped a shot from the top of the
left circle. Curtis Joseph made a nice blocker save but was unable
to gain control of the puck, letting it bounce out in front of the net.
Simpson, patrolling the crease area, went for the loose puck.
With Garth Butcher and Rob Robinson draped all over him,
Simpson managed to put his stick on the puck as he was being
knocked to the ice by the two defensemen. He expertly flipped
a shot over Joseph's stick for his first goal of the year. The Oilers
had a 2-0 lead with less than a period to play.

The way the Blues had been scoring, it might as well have
been 12-0. A come-from-behind victory seemed not only improbable but impossible. St. Louis had netted only two goals in
the season's first 162 minutes. Now the team had to equal that
output in just 18 minutes to gain a tie. The expansion San Jose
Sharks had better odds to win the Stanley Cup.

"C'mon boys, c'mon boys!" Coach Sutter ordered from his
bench. There was still a lot of hockey left to be played, and Sutter
wasn't about to let his players hang their heads. If they wanted
to feel sorry for themselves, then fine, do it privately in the locker
room, not on the ice in front of 17,000 paying customers.

But Sutter didn't worry about this team giving up. During
his three years as a head coach, he had built a team of what he
called "character players," guys who didn't know when to quit.
He had been widely criticized in recent days for letting so many
offensive weapons go. But he had replaced goals with gristle.

Most fans who chided the Blues head coach knew only what
they read in the game summaries or saw in the few highlights
shown on the evening news. But the muckers and grinders of the
world rarely make the headlines. There weren't any statistics for
banging into the boards, forechecking, or forcing turnovers.
There were no records kept for intimidation, irritation, or just
plain being a pain in the ass to the opposition. If you could poke,

jab, and jaw your opponent into submission, you had a place on Brian Sutter's team. Those were the types of players, in Sutter's opinion, that made a team successful. You could have all the goal scorers you wanted, but if they lacked heart,they were as worthless as Confederate money.

With a little more than 13 minutes remaining in the game, Oilers defenseman Jeff Beukeboom was sent to the penalty box for tripping Nelson Emerson. Edmonton sent out its penalty-killing unit, but why worry? After all, the Blues were one for 22 on the power play after nearly three games, including 0 for 5 on the night against the Oilers.

As the clock counted down the penalty, it looked as though the Blues would fail once again. With seconds remaining in the penalty, Beukeboom prepared to dash back onto the ice. Sensing the penalty was about to expire, Paul Cavallini desperately wound up for a slapshot from the left point as Beukeboom rose from his seat to get ready for his return. Cavallini's shot hit Ing on the left shoulder and ricocheted out to the slot. At least a half-dozen players scrambled for the puck, including Hull, who backhanded a shot toward the net. The Oilers' Kelly Buchberger, perfectly positioned in front of Ing, stopped Hull's shot.

For a split second, no one knew where the puck went. No one except Cavallini. The man who started the action with a shot from the point found the loose puck in the left circle. Cavallini wasted no time. He one-timed a shot that managed to find its way through a crowd of players and beat Ing high on the stick side. The Blues had gone nearly 120 minutes, two full games, without a goal. But Cavallini's power-play goal not only stopped the offensive dry spell, it cut the Oilers' lead in half. St. Louis still had more than half a period to tie it up.

The Oilers gave the Blues plenty of chances, too. Dave Manson was escorted off the ice for high-sticking Rich Sutter. The Blues failed to capitalize on the two-minute power play, but not to worry. Almost as soon as Manson left the penalty box, Craig Simpson took his place for tripping Garth Butcher.

Less than a minute into this power play, Dave Christian was fighting for the puck in the corner of the Oilers' zone. Despite being hounded by Esa Tikkanen and Geoff Smith, Christian did a marvelous job of directing the puck toward the net. Cavallini, about ten feet to the left of Ing, retrieved the puck and quickly passed to Oates in the slot. Oates unleashed a shot that hit Ing on the left shoulder, the exact spot Cavallini had hit just five minutes earlier that led to the first goal. The puck rolled over Ing's shoulder and down his back, landing just inches from the goal line. Cavallini, who had moved toward the net after his pass to Oates, was in perfect position. As he was being knocked down from behind, Cavallini tipped the puck into the net. The Blues were suddenly even with the Oilers after scoring two power-play goals in less than six minutes. The team had overcome enormous odds.

"We never gave up," said Nelson Emerson. "We stuck to our game plan and knew what we had to do. We were playing well, even though we were down two goals."

Neither team scored the remainder of the period, sending the game into overtime. If shots-on-goal counted for anything, the contest would have ended after three periods. The Blues dominated the Oilers in that category, 42-15. They did everything but outscore the Oilers. But the Blues had five extra minutes to complete their remarkable comeback and earn their first win of the year.

There's an unwritten rule in hockey, a belief shared by players and fans alike, that a player practically has to be guilty of murder before he's called for a penalty in overtime. Referees don't want to be blamed for the outcome of a game that's decided on the last shot. However, Paul Stewart doesn't subscribe to that theory. At least on this particular night he didn't. The referee sent Blues winger Dave Lowry to the penalty box for hooking. It was actually a smart penalty for Lowry to take because it might have saved the game. The Oilers had a three-on-two break led by center Scott Thornton. Just as a wide-open Craig Simpson was about to take a pass from Thornton, Lowry caught up to Simpson and hooked him down from behind. If he had been allowed to take the pass, Simpson would have skated in alone down the right side.

Even though he had clearly committed a foul, Lowry was outraged that Stewart made the call. As he took his seat in the box, Lowry threw down his stick in frustration and shook his head back and forth as if he couldn't believe he'd been called for a penalty in overtime. So much for the unwritten rule.

After living in the Oilers' zone most of the game, the Blues suddenly had to retreat to their own end to kill off the two-minute penalty. And what a job they did. The Blues' penalty killers smothered the Oilers' power play, never giving it a chance to set up. Edmonton failed for the fourth time to score with the man advantage.

After serving his time, Lowry raced across to the Blues bench, where he watched the final minute of the game unfold. Coach Sutter had his number-one line on the ice. There would be no more substitutions. It would be up to Dave Christian, Adam Oates, and Brett Hull to win it now.

As hundreds of fans made their way to the exits, more intent on beating traffic than watching the final thirty seconds of play, Beukeboom controlled the puck behind his own net. He tried to clear it around the boards, but Paul Cavallini, the man of the night so far, was perfectly positioned at the blue line along the left side. He stopped the puck right on the line. Another inch more and the play would have been called offside.

Cavallini dumped the puck toward the net. It hit Beukeboom's skate and bounced toward the open area between the circles. As if following a pregame script, the Golden Brett was the closest person in the building to the puck. Inexcusably, the Oilers had lost track of Hull. He grabbed the puck and moved to his right, showing remarkable patience. He waited for Luke Richardson to throw himself to the ice to block a potential shot. Instead of slapping it into Richardson's gut, however, Hull took another step to his right, his built-in radar now firmly affixed to the back of the net.

Ing never had a chance. It was more of a snapshot that a slapshot. Possessing a pair of lightning-quick wrists, Hull lifted a shot just inside the crossbar over Ing's right shoulder. With just 29 seconds left in overtime, Brett Hull gave the Blues their first two points of the season and sent the fans into uncontrollable delirium.

As Hull stood there with his arms raised, his teammates rushed from the bench and smothered the superstar. Coach Sutter waited at the gate where the Blues enter and exit the ice. With the spectators still wildly whooping and hollering, the players exited the rink, shaking hands with their coach as they passed him. Fittingly, the last player to step off the ice was Hull. He and Sutter embraced in a joyous hug, much to the delight of the crowd.

As one would expect, the locker room was one festive place. There were more hugs, handshakes, and high-fives. It was just one game, to be sure. But the Blues had silenced their critics, if only for a few hours.

"One week you're in the penthouse, and the next week you're in the outhouse," said Coach Sutter, grinning widely behind his desk after the game. "When you lose, it's absolutely devastating to the players and coaches. That's what makes it so tough when people criticize you."

After talking to reporters, Sutter walked through the locker room, patting his players on the back for a job well done. Sutter understood the importance of this kind of game so early in the season. It gives players something to draw upon during the low points of the season. It reminds the guys that despite the odds, anything is possible. And for a team with so many new faces, an in-house celebration like this one at the start of the year helps to establish a healthy and positive environment in the locker room. The friendships that develop over the course of a season begin with games like this one.

"We have a lot of character in here," said newcomer Dave Christian. "We have a lot of guys who are going to work hard game-in and game-out. The last couple of years playing against the Blues, you knew you had to play well and work hard in order to beat them. That will continue."

"It's knowing how to win that matters," said Brendan Shanahan, another new face impressed with the character of the Blues. "You have to know how to make sacrifices during crunch time. This team does that, and it filters down from Brian."

As in Brian Sutter, the man charged with impersonating a head coach. The man many accused of incompetence. However, the jury asked for more evidence, and it got it in the form of a scintillating, come-from-behind victory by Sutter's Blues. Case dismissed, at least for now.

*   *   *

The thrilling win over Edmonton was just the start of a very successful three-game home stand. Two nights after beating the Oilers, the Blues got past the San Jose Sharks 6-3. The game was actually a lot closer than the final score indicated. After rookie Pat

Falloon scored early in the third period, the Sharks trailed by only a goal, 4-3, with 17 minutes to play. San Jose threw everything it had at Curtis Joseph, but the Blues' goalie made several spectacular saves to keep his team up by a goal. Then with 3:30 left in regulation, Garth Butcher was called for high-sticking. The Sharks were already 1 for 2 on the power play, showing remarkable ability for a group of players no other team wanted. The Blues were suddenly in danger of giving this game away.

However, thanks to pesky penalty killers Ron Wilson and Bob Bassen, the Sharks had to retreat to their own end during much of the power play. Both Bassen and Wilson had quality scoring chances short-handed, taking the wind out of the Sharks' sails.

After failing with the extra man, San Jose pulled its goalie, Jarmo Myllys. Murray Baron and Bassen took advantage by scoring empty-net goals to give the Blues the 6-3 win. It wasn't the prettiest victory, but it was two points nonetheless, and moved the Blues to the .500 mark, with two wins and two losses.

Three nights later, on October 15, the Blues got their revenge against the Maple Leafs and Grant Fuhr. Nine minutes into the game, Butcher emerged from the penalty box after serving time for high-sticking. With the puck in his own end, Rich Sutter flipped it ahead to Butcher, who was behind the defense. "The Strangler" suddenly had a breakaway. Fuhr raced out of his goal to cut off the Blues' defenseman. But just as Fuhr went down to try to smother the puck, Butcher moved the rubber disk from his backhand to his forehand and nudged it past Fuhr. As the puck slid unmolested into the net, Fuhr crashed into Butcher, sending him somersaulting through the air before crash-landing on his back. Ouch!

"It hurt for about a half-second," said Butcher. "But then I saw the puck was in the net, and I felt good. I'm sure I'll be a little sore tomorrow, but what the heck."

That first goal was the start of a 5-1 victory for the Blues. As a special treat, they chased Fuhr in the third period after Ron Sutter scored the team's fifth goal. After shutting out the Blues one week earlier, Fuhr found himself on the bench watching his replacement, Jeff Reese, shut down the Blues the final 13 minutes.

For the first time in the 1991-92 season, the St. Louis Blues were above .500, 3-2. As if rediscovering life, everything suddenly looked, smelled, and tasted better.

"It's been nice to get the home cooking again," said Butcher, referring to the Blues' 3-0 record at home after losing their first two games on the road. "As the year progresses, I think we'll get better and better."

Especially thrilled with the win over Toronto was Brendan Shanahan who scored his second goal of the year, his first at the Arena.

"Everyone's been watching me work hard and bang my head against the glass," said Shanahan. "So it's nice to get a goal at home."

What made it so special for Shanahan was the reaction of the crowd. Still haunted by the Scott Stevens controversy, Shanahan was unsure how the fans in St. Louis would react to him. Would they blame him for the loss of Stevens? Would they boo his every move? Shanahan was worried about the reception ever since having a nightmare about it earlier in the summer.

"Before I even heard that St. Louis was interested in me, I had a dream that I was traded to the Blues, and I was booed during the introductions," Shanahan said, his eyes growing wider as he retold the story. "The very next day after having that dream, my agent called to tell me the Blues were interested and I said, 'Oh, no!' I really didn't know how the fans would react. But now I can say I've been really pleased with how I've been received."

Also pleased was Vincent Riendeau. He was given the start in goal against the Leafs, his first assignment since being unceremoniously yanked in the season's first game against New Jersey. Riendeau was brilliant this time, stopping 37 of 38 shots to earn his first win of the year.

"Toronto is not really my team, but I was happy to play," said Riendeau. "If I couldn't play, I wouldn't be here."

At the time, no one knew how prophetic his words were. Vincent Riendeau had just played his last game at the Arena as a member of the Blues.

Chapter Four

TRADE WINDS

Brian Sutter was in a foul mood. His frown was so pronounced it looked as if ten-pound weights were attached to the
ends of his lips. The night before in Detroit, October 17, the Blues
looked silly in a 6-3 loss to the Red Wings. The score should have
been 16-3. The Blues were outmuscled and outhustled in every
facet of the game. Their defense looked as if it was having a party,
inviting in as many guests as possible.

And though they were the visitors on the scoreboard, the
Blues were gracious party hosts, letting their winged friends
surround Vincent Riendeau and not kicking them out until the
lights were out. Detroit took advantage, pummeling Riendeau
with 29 shots in just the first two periods. No doubt, the Blues'
netminder gave up a couple of soft goals. But for the most part,
his teammates in front left him unprotected. The Wings obliged
and skated in untouched.

The pathetic performance was another disturbing indication that the Blues could not play well on the road. They had been
outscored 16-5 in three games away from the Arena. For a team
that had led the league in road wins the year before, the sudden
ineptness was intolerable.

As the players slowly made their way onto the Arena ice for
their morning practice, a scowling Brian Sutter followed closely
behind. Last night's game was only about 12 hours old, and the
nightmarish memories kept swirling in Sutter's head. And he
wasn't going to let his team forget it either. This was going to be
one grueling practice.

Just as Sutter was about to step into the rink, I waved a hand and asked him if he had just a minute to spare. The technique was not uncommon. When a television reporter is unable to keep his cameraman through the entire practice, which unfortunately is quite often, the reporter has to grab his interviews before practice instead of after. It's not the best way to do business, but many times it's the only way. Fortunately, the players and coaches are always gracious enough to stop for a minute or two before starting their morning drills.

However, this time I thought I was about to get turned down for the first time. After I asked Sutter if he had just a minute, he stopped, looked out at his players on the ice, looked at me, then turned again toward his team. I was delaying him from making life a living hell for his employees.

"All right, but quickly," Sutter said.

I asked the head coach if the team needed more time to gel. After all, there were so many new faces. Maybe they just needed another month or two before they were comfortable with one another.

Sutter didn't want any part of that theory.

"That can be an excuse," he said. "I wasn't pleased at all with what went on last night. Some of the guys need to shake their heads and get themselves going. When you lose it's got to hurt you a little bit. You have to demand a little bit more of yourself and expect a little bit more of yourself."

Are the players starting to point fingers at one another?

"No, no, no, no," Sutter said, violently shaking his head back and forth. "You don't point fingers. You look in the mirror."

And with that the interview was over. Sutter raced onto the ice to start working over his players.

I said goodbye to my cameraman and took a seat in the stands next to Garth Butcher, who was in street clothes, watching his teammates from a safe distance.

"I'm just nursing a few bumps and bruises," said the Blues' captain.

Practice was but a few minutes old when Coach Sutter was summoned from the ice. After disappearing for a brief period, he re-emerged long enough to motion Butcher to join him in the locker room.

What's this all about? A little secret planning behind closed doors? They only did that after practice. Why suddenly do it right after the team's just getting warmed up?

As I sat there contemplating the possibilities, Riendeau slowly made his way off the ice. What the...?

It immediately hit me like a Brett Hull slapshot. For the first time, I was actually witnessing a trade. A deal had just been made seconds ago, and it was unfolding on the ice. Vincent Riendeau was about to be informed he was no longer a member of the St. Louis Blues. He was going to take off the Bluenote for the last time.

It didn't take a genius to figure it out. Riendeau had been the subject of trade rumors the past week, specifically with the Red Wings. The Wings were looking to unload a defenseman, something the Blues desperately needed. And the Wings were shopping around for a goaltender, something the Blues had in abundance. The question wasn't whether the two teams were going to make a deal, but when.

I sat there trying to picture what Riendeau must be going through. The man loved St. Louis. He had known absolutely nothing about the city when he first arrived here in a trade with Montreal in August of 1988. But it didn't take long for him and his wife, Marie-Josee, to make St. Louis home. He was very open about his affection for the people of the city, and for the hockey fans who jammed the Arena for every home game.

"I love this place," Riendeau would say. "I've met a lot of people and made a lot of good friends."

That's why the trade rumors turned his stomach inside out. He understood that being swapped around the league was part of the business. But that realization didn't make it any easier. He hated the thought of leaving his teammates, his friends, and the weather that allowed him to play golf almost year-round. Vinnie was an outstanding golfer, consistently shooting in the mid-to-upper 70s. Being forced to move north would severely cramp his tee times.

Ten minutes after Riendeau left the ice, Butcher reappeared. But instead of taking his seat in the stands, he walked to the rink's entrance gate. Alternate captain Ron Sutter cruised over, let Butcher whisper something into his ear, then skated back to practice. That was the last piece of evidence I needed.

My first thought was to get my cameraman back. If my suspicions were correct, Riendeau was going to quickly grab his belongings and head home to tell his wife. If I didn't have someone here within a few minutes, I was going to lose the only chance I had for an interview.

I jumped out of my seat and headed toward the nearest pay phone. As I walked down the exit ramp and turned the corner to the Blues' offices, I stumbled into a private meeting between two people. Brian Sutter and Vincent Riendeau. Brian was in a Blues warm-up suit, Vinnie in street clothes.

I quickly turned my eyes to the ground and walked in the opposite direction. The phone call would have to wait a few minutes. I didn't want to be accused of eavesdropping, especially during such a delicate moment. But at least I didn't need confirmation anymore. Riendeau had indeed been traded.

Minutes later, the Blues public relations staff made it official. Riendeau was being sent to Detroit for defenseman Rick Zombo. Detroit was getting a more than capable backup to starter Tim Cheveldae. St. Louis, on the other hand, was still trying to plug the gaping hole left by Scott Stevens. No one pretended Rick Zombo was the answer. But at least he brought seven years of experience and a reputation as a fierce defender of his own net. Zombo would certainly strengthen a blue line corps that performed decently at home but meekly on the road.

As it turned out, there was no rush to get a photographer. Riendeau had agreed to hold an informal news conference once the St. Louis media were informed of the trade and able to send representatives to the Arena.

After a number of media types had gathered in one of the conference rooms, a red-eyed Vincent Riendeau strolled in to take questions. A reporter is supposed to remain objective and not get emotionally involved in a story. But damn, it was hard not to feel for this guy. He had worked so hard to establish himself as the Blues' number-one goaltender. The team even traded its former number-one man, Greg Millen, in December of 1989 to make room for Riendeau.

But the Blues faltered in the 1990 and '91 playoffs, and much of the blame was leveled at Riendeau. His ability to lead his team through postseason play was questioned. It was proved year-in and year-out that a hot goaltender was essential for a club to win the Stanley Cup. The North Stars, of all teams, came within a couple of games of winning it all in 1991 thanks to Jon Casey. The Oilers rode Bill Ranford to the championship in 1990. The year before that, Mike Vernon suddenly became impenetrable, and the Calgary Flames won their first Stanley Cup. And during Edmonton's four titles in the mid-80s, Grant Fuhr established himself as one of the greatest clutch goaltenders of all time, always picking his game up a notch once the second season started.

During the Oilers' first Stanley Cup year in 1983-84, Fuhr posted a 3.91 goals-against average during the regular season. However, when the playoffs rolled around, Fuhr kept the goals-against under three. Same story the next year. And again in 1986-87, when Fuhr allowed 3.44 goals per game during the regular season, but only 2.46 during 19 playoff games. If Reggie Jackson is Mr. October, Grant Fuhr is certainly Mr. April and May.

Riendeau proved unworthy of such praise. It didn't matter that his teammates were nearly as much to blame for the early playoff exits. When you give up eight goals in a postseason game, which the Blues did to the Stars in '91 and the Hawks in '90, the goaltender becomes the scapegoat. If he had been sharp, the critics would say, he could've made up for the mistakes made in front of him.

But now, just as the Blues had made room for Riendeau nearly two years before, they were now making room for Curtis Joseph. It was time to see if "The Cat" was the man who could carry the team through the playoffs.

Riendeau took a seat facing reporters. He managed a weak smile as he said hello to everyone. The new Detroit goalie was full of mixed emotions, staring at the table in front of him as he answered questions. There was no doubt he hated saying good-bye. But at the same time, he was thankful the rumors had finally stopped.

"I just wanted to get the trade over with," Riendeau said. "It's no fun to always be in the middle like that. It's not what I wanted, but something happened. The rumors have been going on forever. I knew I was gone right after Brian pulled me off the ice."

After talking to the media for nearly 30 minutes, Riendeau had to do the hardest thing yet: say good-bye to his teammates. Ask any athlete who's been traded, and he's likely to say the most difficult part of being dealt, at least for those who don't want to be, is walking into the locker room one last time for a final farewell. Those are not just fellow players the athlete is saying good-bye to. Those are members of his family. And for Riendeau, who was liked by every last one of his teammates, it was like bidding adieu to a roomful of brothers.

Vinnie made his way around the locker room, shaking hands and telling everyone good-bye. He grabbed a few belongings and headed out of the Arena alone. As he was about to jump into his car, he was asked one last time what he was going to miss most.

"Everything," he said. "I love St. Louis. My wife and I will come back here because we've got good friends. We won't forget this place."

*   *   *

Terri Zombo couldn't believe what she had just heard. As her husband would later say, she "freaked." Their good friend, Adam Oates, had called from St. Louis with some information that was sure to blow his former teammate, Rick, away. It certainly stunned Terri. She was from the Detroit area, and the thought of moving to . . . Well, she'd have to talk this over with Rick.

It was September, the middle of another training camp for Rick Zombo. The Red Wings' defenseman had enjoyed five solid seasons in Detroit, the last three appearing in at least 75 games and scoring more than 20 points in each. His resume did not boast offensive prowess, but Zombo was not paid to score goals. He was a "stay-at-home" defenseman, the kind of player who likes to take care of business in his own end before venturing into the offensive zone.

When Zombo was on the ice, he protected the goal crease as if it were the driveway leading to his own house. The 6' 1", 190-pounder used every ounce of muscle to bash opponents out of the way. His philosophy: only two people belong near our own net. Me and my goalie.

Brett Hull learned that in the 1991 playoffs. Hull tried to station himself near the Wings' net one game but was crunched so hard from behind his helmet flew off. The perpetrator was none other than Rick Zombo. The season before, Zombo was suspended for three games after high-sticking Al Iafrate.

Zombo was not considered one of the premier defenseman in the league. Far from it. But he was a coach's dream. He was extremely dedicated to his profession, busting his butt every time his skates hit the ice. There aren't too many eighth-round draft picks who become everyday players, but Zombo was one of them. His work ethic and leadership abilities were the reasons for his success, traits that weren't lost on Wings coach Bryan Murray. He named Zombo an alternate captain before the start of the 1990-91 season.

"What an honor that was," Zombo said. "To think of the great Red Wings tradition and the players who've worn a letter on their jersey. And I was one of them."

But a few things happened on the way to training camp the following season. They were called Niklas Lidstrom and Vladimir Konstantinov, two young foreigners competing for Zombo's job. For Zombo, it wasn't a matter of "What have you done for me lately?" but "When can you step aside and let the younger guys have a shot?" Detroit's defense was showing some age, and Bryan Murray decided it was time for a youth movement on the blue line. Zombo, a mainstay on the Red Wings' defense through the late 1980s, was suddenly expendable.

After the call from Oates, Terri Zombo realized just how expendable. She immediately called Rick, who was out of town for a Red Wings exhibition game.

"Adam called today," Terri told her spouse. "Brace yourself. Apparently, you're going to the Blues."

There was silence on the other end of the line.

"Adam said the Blues are all set to trade Vincent Riendeau for you," Terri continued. "He said the deal's done."

Rick didn't want to hear any of it. He told his wife to drop the subject. He couldn't bear the thought of leaving the only NHL team he had ever played for. He was also angry, wondering why Detroit management had suddenly soured on him to the point it was willing to trade him to another team in the division.

Zombo was so flustered by the sudden revelation, he refused to even call Oates back. He attempted to bury the trade news in his memory banks, where he hoped it would disappear forever. He was having a bad enough camp as it was, trying to prove that he still belonged on the team. Now he had this to deal with.

Zombo simply decided to work his tail off as he always did and not let any rumors bother him. But that would eventually prove impossible.

"Bother me it did," admitted Zombo. "I knew Adam was close to management, so I knew there was a lot to it. I knew it wasn't something that just crossed the wire that some reporter picked up."

Rick couldn't handle waiting for something to happen. If they were going to make the deal, then do it. Otherwise, just come out and say it's not going to happen. He asked captain Steve Yzerman if he had heard any murmurings about a trade. Yzerman assured him that he hadn't, but he'd keep his ears open.

Zombo did such a poor job of hiding his frustration that even the coaches noticed it. A couple of days after talking to Yzerman, Zombo was called in to Bryan Murray's office.

"I've been watching you walk around, and I know you're upset about things you're hearing," said Murray. "I know how close you are to Adam. But I can tell you the deal is not going to be made. It's been mentioned. Ron Caron asked if you were available, and we talked about it. But it's not going to happen."

Was Adam wrong? Or did something happen to make one of the teams back out at the last second? Either way, Murray had confirmed that Zombo was indeed a part of trade talks. And now that the Blues were out of the picture, who was next?

Rick Zombo did a lot of soul-searching the next couple of weeks. He was never one to question moves made by management, because it just drove him crazy. But he still had a difficult time accepting that he was unwanted in Detroit. He was more than just a well-respected veteran. He was the "go-to" guy. Every team has one, the player to whom all new players and rookies are sent. The "go-to" guy gives advice on where to look for homes, where the best shopping places are, and what businesses cater to athletes.

Zombo took great pride in his "go-to" role, always remembering an incident during his rookie season. On his first trip to Chicago, the entire team was supposed to meet in the hotel lobby for a day on the town. It was an off-day, so the players were free to roam the streets until curfew later that night. Zombo was the new kid on the block and wanted to make a good impression on his older teammates. He put on his best suit and tie and hurried downstairs.

Zombo almost fell over when he got to the lobby. He was completely overdressed. Every one of his teammates had on a golf shirt. Most were wearing shorts. No one had told the red-faced rookie there was no dress code the day before a game, only game day. Zombo suddenly felt about two inches tall.

Amid much teasing and verbal abuse, one of the most respected players in the game approached the youngster and told him not to worry about it. They were going shopping. His name was Harold Snepsts.

Snepsts played on four teams in his 17-year career, and he commanded the same respect wherever he went. After all, a player who threw his body around on the ice as though it were a worthless hunk of scrap iron stood out in the locker room. Some thought him crazy, but all thought him courageous.

Snepsts not only took great pride in his work habits, but he took great care of his teammates. And on that day in Chicago, he was watching out for young Rick Zombo.

Snepsts took Zombo down to Michigan Avenue, walked into the finest polo shop, and dressed the rookie from head to toe.

"Thanks, Snepstsy," said Zombo sheepishly.

"Don't worry about it, kid," said Snepsts. "Next time, wake up."

Zombo was awestruck. From that moment on, he promised to take on the responsibility of helping lost little rookies if he ever got the opportunity.

"I'll never forget that," Zombo said. "Here's Harold Snepsts going into his top pocket to shell out a couple of hundred bucks for me. That's when I decided that when I got my career going and got the stability Snepstsy had, I was going to do the same for someone else.

"When you're one of the young guys, you're so in awe of everything. Just to have a veteran ask you to lunch means so much. As a veteran, you don't really care who comes along. You're going to lunch anyway. But it means a lot to the rookie."

Now the Red Wings would have to find a new "go-to" guy. Two weeks into the season, and a full month after Adam Oates' call, Zombo was indeed traded to the Blues. He sat and listened to Bryan Murray explain the philosophy of the deal. But his explanation only made it worse.

"I was ready to get up and walk out," Zombo said. "I was really burned up inside."

After Murray finished his speech, Zombo walked through the Red Wings' locker room one last time, just as Vincent Riendeau was doing in St. Louis. The Wings were about to hit the road, so Zombo had to retrieve his sticks from the stick bag and his other belongings from the bus. He preferred to sneak out without anyone noticing. Zombo is a rather quiet, soft-spoken individual who enjoys nothing better than spending a day in the great outdoors.

"I wanted to put up a sign that said, 'Gone fishing, see you next year,'" said Zombo. "It was just very difficult."

The next day, just hours before his flight to St. Louis, Zombo could not get out of bed. His legs were as stiff as an old tree. The last 24 hours had been so emotionally draining, his body had shut down. When he wasn't talking to out-of-town reporters on the phone, he'd been standing in his front yard yapping with the local media. Somehow in between he'd managed to talk to friends and relatives. He even took time out to answer a call from Blues captain Garth Butcher, who welcomed him to St. Louis.

Then there were moving plans to be made and living arrangements to be ironed out. When would Terri and their six-month-old baby move down? And nearly as important, where are the best hunting and fishing spots in Missouri? Priorities, priorities. (In a move heaped with irony, Zombo and his family eventually settled into Scott Stevens' old house.)

Zombo did gather up enough strength to get himself to the airport that morning for a trip to his new home. As expected, Adam Oates met him at Lambert Airport, where they grabbed a cup of coffee and headed to the rink.

"Just like old times," said Zombo.

Indeed. There wasn't a friendship between two players any stronger in the National Hockey League. Zombo and Oates had been inseparable during their playing days together in Detroit during the late 1980s. They shared a condominium and, when Zombo moved out to buy his own condo in the same complex, it wasn't long before Oates sold his unit and moved in.

"We did everything together," explained Zombo. "We ate at the same places, went to the same bars, drank the same coffee. We never got bored of it. It almost gave you a cavity it was such a sweet relationship."

They hit it off so well because they're a reflection of one another. Both are extremely intelligent men who display a quick, dry wit and unabashed candor. Each is wary of outsiders and rarely starts a conversation with someone he doesn't know. Their aloof behavior, especially Oates', is interpreted by some as being arrogant, if not downright snotty.

But get either one of them talking, and their true characters emerge. Both are intensely competitive. It's essential for both men to be taken seriously outside of hockey. The "dumb jock" image grates on them. After finishing only three years of college before he turned pro, Oates went back to school to earn his business degree in the summer of 1991. Zombo, meanwhile, is not only an avid outdoorsman, he's an expert artist. His drawings have been auctioned at art sales and featured on Detroit television.

Zombo was a picture of nervousness when he walked into the Blues' locker room that first morning. He had never been traded before and didn't know how to act. Do I just sit here and act like I belong? Or do I make my way around and introduce myself? What will everyone's reaction be?

As it turned out, there was no reason to sweat. As soon as Zombo stepped in the door, his new teammates were almost falling over one another to meet him. The Sutter twins were the first to offer a hearty welcome, followed by the rest of the pack. Brett Hull even served up a few Don Rickles-type jabs to break up the tension.

"I quickly learned what a class organization this was," Zombo said.

He also quickly learned what kind of backbone his new team had. In a classic Blues-Blackhawks thriller, Brendan Shanahan scored with five seconds remaining in regulation to salvage a 4-4 tie in Zombo's first game with St. Louis. His new team trailed 2-0 early in the second period and had to play catch-up hockey all night.

Trailing 4-3 with under a minute left in the game, Curtis Joseph skated to the bench for the extra attacker. The Blues swarmed the Hawks net until Shanahan poked in a loose puck with just a few short ticks left on the clock.

"We were relentless," Zombo said after the game. "That's the kind of Blues team I played against. These are a great bunch of guys to play with. Everyone has the same work ethic."

Zombo played a strong defensive game in his debut, impressing his teammates and coaches. But after the game, the only thing people wanted to talk about was a mistake he made that almost gave the game away in overtime.

Zombo had scooped up a loose puck behind his own net. As he started up-ice, he fired a pass across to his defensive partner, Murray Baron. Unfortunately, the pass never arrived at its destination. Steve Larmer, one of the Hawks' deadly marksmen, was minding his own business in front of the Blues goal when he suddenly found the puck on his stick. Zombo had given him a perfect pass. Larmer immediately tried to slap the puck in, but Curtis Joseph came up with a pad save, his biggest and most important of the game. Not only did Joseph preserve the tie in his first start as the Blues' number-one goalie, he saved his new teammate from jumping off the Arch.

"That's not one of my better plays," Zombo said, laughing. "I knew my partner was over there. I just didn't see their guy. I about swallowed my heart."

It was a memorable start to Rick Zombo's new career with the Blues, a career that would grow in importance the very next night.

Chapter Five

PAUL BEARER

One complaint against the sport of hockey is unruly fan behavior. Many fine, upstanding citizens of the community would rather see a pro wrestling event with thousands of screaming adolescents than endure three hours of drunken lunatics yelling profanities and spilling beer on the people in front of them.

A message to you Blues fans who feel that way: You don't know how good you have it. Try watching a game in Chicago. Every Blackhawks game is an excuse for fans to completely lose all sense of responsibility and decency.

What's worse, many Blackhawks fans like to take their act on the road. An hour after the Blues tied the Hawks 4-4 in Rick Zombo's debut, two Chicago fans were escorted through the back halls of the Arena. They had blood on their knuckles, handcuffs on their wrists, and smiles on their faces.

For a player, however, Chicago Stadium is usually a more enjoyable experience. Players don't have to sit next to the fans, only hear them. And boy, do they hear them. The fans are loud and obnoxious, creating an atmosphere many players love. It pumps them up. It excites them. It gets their juices flowing. If a hockey player can't get motivated in Chicago Stadium, it's not because he's a laid-back guy, it's because he's dead. He turned pale and cold before the game, but no one noticed.

One night after Brendan Shanahan's dramatic game-tying goal against the Hawks, the Blues travelled to Chicago for a

Sunday night rematch. The fans started partying early, like Thursday. They were primed and ready to go.

"They'll all have a little juice in them," Shanahan joked before traveling to Chicago. "It'll be loud, but those are the kinds of games I really enjoy playing in."

"That's an exciting place to play and the fans really get behind them," said Kelly Chase, thrown out of Saturday night's game for high-sticking Steve Konroyd, who'd had to have his mug stitched up. "We can use their fans to our advantage. We need to go in there with the intention of trying to make the fans leave early and get something out of the building."

Which was no easy task. The Blues had not won in Chicago in their last seven trips, being outscored 37-21. They failed to win a game in the Windy City in 1990-91, the 11th time in 24 years the Blues had been swept there in a season series.

The Hawks were tailor-made for their small rink. Just as Whitey Herzog assembled the Cardinals to fit the dimensions of Busch Stadium, Blackhawks general manager/coach Mike Keenan built a roster and implemented a game plan that worked perfectly in his own rink. He sent his forwards flying in to forecheck their opponents into oblivion, pinning them against the boards and forcing turnovers. Because Chicago Stadium is so tiny, opposing teams have a devil of a time trying to move the puck out of their own end with red and black jerseys swarming everywhere. When the Hawks are on top of their game, they are virtually unbeatable at home.

For the Blues to have any chance, their forwards had to come back and help out their defensemen. They had to take the Hawks' forwards out of the play, allowing the Blues to gain control of the puck in their own end and work it up-ice. St. Louis was in for a long night if its forwards didn't feel like playing in both ends of the rink.

The Blues employed a new weapon on this night, Pat Jablonski. The backup goaltender was getting his first start of the season between the pipes. The trade of Vincent Riendeau not only opened the door for Curtis Joseph, it also gave Jablonski a chance to show his mettle. What better place to throw a kid into the fire than Chicago Stadium? If Jablonski was weak-kneed, he was going to crumble in this place.

This was not the first time "Jabber" had seen the Hawks. In one of the most dramatic and inspirational Blues victories in recent years, Jablonski stonewalled Chicago in a remarkable 3-1 win February 26, 1991, in St. Louis. Riendeau wasn't dressed for that game due to an injury, and when Joseph injured his knee early in the contest, there was no one else to go to but Jablonski. A nervous crowd looked on as the youngster grabbed his all-white helmet and headed to the Blues net.

But for the next two hours, the fans witnessed a masterpiece. Jablonski was absolutely brilliant, stopping 31 of 32 shots, including two breakaways and a penalty shot by Michel Goulet. It was Jabber's first win in the National Hockey League, and it immediately established him as a legitimate NHL goaltender.

The Blackhawks must have remembered that game from eight months before. Here on Sunday, October 20, they pelted Jablonski with an incredible 17 shots in the first period. As expected, the Hawks darted into the Blues' zone, pinned them in deep, and set up target practice. A little more than 7:30 into the period, Chicago solved Jablonski, thanks in part to a lackadaisical effort by his teammates.

Hawks left winger Steve Thomas beat the Cavallini brothers to a loose puck behind the net and backhanded it out front to a wide-open Mike Stapleton. The Chicago center quickly flipped the puck past Jablonski to give the home team a 1-0 lead.

The period continued to be a Chicago shootout. If not for the stellar performance turned in by Jablonski during the first 20 minutes, the Blues could have been hopelessly buried after just one period. The 24-year old netminder stopped a couple of two-on-one breaks and several drives from close range.

But as the Blues sat in the dressing room during intermission, they exuded only confidence. Not only was their goaltender "standing on his head," a popular hockey term to describe an outstanding performance by a goalie, their checking line and penalty-killing unit were just as impressive.

The Hawks, stymied on four power plays the night before, couldn't score on three power plays during the first period of this game. Dave Lowry (with Dave Christian occasionally filling in for him on left wing), center Bob Bassen, and right wing Rich Sutter, all members of the penalty-killing unit, also formed the checking line employed to smother Chicago's top-scoring trio of Michel Goulet, Jeremy Roenick, and Steve Larmer. And what a job they were doing.

Twenty-four hours earlier in St. Louis, the Hawks' number-one line managed only five shots while failing to tally a single point. The Blues checked them so persistently, they must have felt like they were skating through a rink full of syrup.

The change in venues made no difference. The Chicago Three was again a non-factor after the first 20 minutes. It was as if Lowry, Christian, Bassen, and Sutter had handcuffed themselves to the Hawks' three snipers and said, "Boys, you ain't going nowhere!"

Those are the kinds of performances Brian Sutter demands of his players. He's a man who rarely, if ever, stresses the negative. Sure, the Blues had been dreadfully outshot 17-8 in the first period. But that fact wasn't mentioned. He instead pointed to the stellar work turned in by Jablonski, the aggressiveness of the checking line, and the hustle of the penalty killers. The shots on goal might have been lopsided, but the Blues were still in this game. That was the message everyone took to the ice to start the second period.

Just 20 seconds into it, St. Louis got the break it was looking for. Michel Goulet, starting to exhibit some frustration, high-sticked Garth Butcher, giving the Blues their third power play of the night. The Blues wasted no time in taking advantage of the extra man.

Paul Cavallini, perched near the blue line, expertly passed the puck down low to Brendan Shanahan, who had taken up residence in Hull Territory, otherwise known as the left slot. Just like Hull, Shanahan ripped a shot right on goal. Ron Sutter, standing near the goal crease, tipped it past Jimmy Waite to tie the score at one. It was Brendan's first assist of the year to go with his six goals.

However, the score failed to ignite the Blues' offensive firepower. They retreated to their own zone once again, more intent on limiting Chicago's scoring chances than creating any of their own. The Hawks continued pelting Jablonski unmercifully. It's a wonder the Blues' goalie didn't start carrying the puck up ice on his own, since his teammates seemed uninterested in doing so. The guy deserved a purple heart for sacrificing his body to stave off the enemy.

With 2:30 left to play in the second period, the Blackhawks were given a power play and a chance to take the lead. They should've had the lead by now. A big lead. A huge lead. The only reason for the 1-1 tie was Pat Jablonski and the goaltending clinic he was putting on.

As usual, the Blues' penalty killers were ruthless, stalking their prey with little compassion. They smothered the Hawks, giving them no room to breathe. Every time the Blackhawks tried to set up camp, the Blues rudely pulled up their stakes and sent them packing into their own end. Chicago had completely dominated when the teams were at even strength. But inexplicably, the Blues were playing some of their best hockey a man short.

A minute into the latest penalty, Ron Sutter and Dave Christian nearly scored on a two-on-one break. Sutter picked up a loose puck deep in the Blackhawks' zone and passed it to Christian all alone near the goal crease. However, Christian couldn't connect, the puck sliding past him.

No matter. A few seconds later, the two players found themselves on another two-on-one. This time they connected. Sutter slapped a shot toward the net that Christian deflected past Waite to give the Blues a 2-1 lead on a short-handed goal.

Unbelievable and perhaps undeserved. But fairness and equity never won a hockey game. The Blues had a one-goal lead because, unlike the Blackhawks, they had taken advantage of the few opportunities presented them. Chicago had racked up a lopsided 32-14 advantage in shots-on-goal after two periods but was able to poke the puck past Jablonski only once.

The third period was a repeat of the first two. The Hawks forechecked with reckless abandon, outshot their opponents by a 2-1 margin, and yet fell behind by another goal when Gino Cavallini netted his third of the year. The Blues must have gone to church right before the game. Divine intervention it seemed was the only explanation for the Blues' 3-1 lead.

Unfortunately, the hockey gods left prematurely. Halfway through the third period, St. Louis was struck with a dagger in its heart. Paul Cavallini, the team's only all-star defenseman, collided with Hawks defenseman Steve Smith. Their legs entangled, stretching a ligament in Cavallini's left knee. He hobbled to the bench and was immediately escorted off the ice.

As he started to limp down the runway, a group of boisterous Blackhawks fans began cursing Cavallini. Cavallini should have been thankful a few of them didn't jump to the ice to try to take out his other knee. The Blues defenseman shouted a few choice words at his antagonists before continuing down the stairs to the locker room.

Meanwhile, the Blues—or should we say Pat Jablonski?— shut down the Blackhawks the remaining ten minutes of the game. Ron Wilson added an empty-net goal to end the scoring at 4-1. It was the Blues' first road win of the year, their first win in Chicago Stadium in eight tries. Incredibly, the Blues managed four goals on only 20 shots, while the Hawks could only muster one score on a barrage of 44 shots. Jablonski was named the game's number-one star, which was an injustice. He should have been named the game's number two and number three stars as well.

"All I had to make was the first save," Jablonski said modestly. "Our guys played very well in their own zone. It was an all-round team effort."

His teammates agreed.

"Bobby Bassen, Richie Sutter, Dave Lowry, and Ron Wilson played great," said Darin Kimble. "When you shut down guys like Roenick and Larmer, it's a bonus. Winning in Chicago is one of the best feelings ever."

"It just comes down to hard work," said Bassen. "When you work hard as a team, you win games. We're going to have to pull together now with Paulie out."

That last sentence was repeated throughout the locker room. The Blues watched in stunned silence as "Paulie" hobbled out of Chicago Stadium on crutches after the game. He waved off questions, declining to utter a word about what had happened. An emotional and highly sensitive man, Cavallini couldn't bear to consider the consequences of his injury. Offensively, he was off to his best start in his five-year career. After eight games, he was the team's third-leading scorer, with seven points. His 70-point pace would shatter his career high of 47 points he accumulated during the 1989-90 season.

Cavallini had been looking forward to this year ever since the Blues were ousted from the playoffs the spring before. In a freak accident against the Hawks on December 22, 1990, Cavallini had the tip of his left index finger sheared off after it was hit by a Doug Wilson slapshot.

"The doctors thought it might be a career-ending injury," he said. "That certainly gives you an outlook on your future. You start thinking about life after hockey."

However, Cavallini missed only 13 games. He stayed in shape while limiting the use of his damaged finger so it could heal properly. But when he returned to the ice, he seemed to lack the same intensity. Virtually every day people were asking him if the finger injury was to blame for his drop in performance. Some even suggested Cavallini was scared to play the game with the same ferocity. The sight of his mangled finger had certainly turned his gut. It would've had the same effect on anybody.

But Cavallini became hypersensitive to all the attention. In one unforgettable incident, an employee of the hospital that operated on Cavallini's finger called a morning radio show and claimed she had the severed finger and was willing to auction it off. As it turned out, the woman was not lying. She had indeed taken the finger from the hospital and decided it would be hilarious to talk about it on the radio. The disc jockey agreed, and the "auction of Paul's finger" became the theme that morning.

As you might imagine, Cavallini found no humor in it. In fact, the so-called joke made him sick to his stomach.

"I was totally appalled and very upset," he said. "I know they do a lot of sick things, but I thought that went over the line."

Cavallini didn't hesitate to call the station and berate the managers and the disc jockey. Paul and the DJ are acquaintances but have not spoken to one another since. Meanwhile, in an effort to repair the damage to its image, the hospital fired the employee responsible.

No question, the joke was tasteless and rude. But in the annals of "shock" radio it was hardly criminal. Even some of his teammates thought he was overreacting to the whole incident.

"He should relax and just let it go," said one teammate.

But he couldn't. Cavallini had grown weary of people pointing, uh, fingers at him.

"Everyone has their own analysis on what happened," said Cavallini during training camp. "It's hard for me to look at my season and say it was my finger that led to my downfall, if that's what you want to call it. I have to look forward to this season with more expectations of myself."

He was excited about the upcoming year and eager to put the past one behind him. He even found room to joke about his shortened index finger.

"It's a weather guide right now," he said. "The skin hasn't completely healed over it, so when it gets cold, I know it."

That's why the sudden knee injury was so devastating. He had put the past behind him and was enjoying a terrific start in 1991-92. That's also why he couldn't bear to talk to reporters right away. He was absolutely desolate as he limped out of Chicago.

The next day in St. Louis, with the team given the day off, Paul Cavallini received both good and bad news. Blues orthopedic surgeon Dr. Jerome Gilden told him the good news was that the ligament was not torn and he would not need surgery. But before Cavallini could breathe a sigh of relief, he was informed that he had suffered a sprained knee ligament that would sideline him indefinitely, perhaps up to six weeks.

The news hit Cavallini like a puck between the eyes. He was stunned. For the second year in a row, the talented defenseman would have to spend considerable time off his skates.

Coach Sutter tried to downplay the injury. No team goes through a season without losing at least one quality player to an injury. It's part of the game. It's something good teams overcome. And it's something on which Sutter wasn't about to dwell.

"Obviously, we're disappointed he's not going to be in the lineup," he said. "But that's the last time you'll hear me talk about it.

"It takes away from the character of the dressing room when you talk about the people who aren't there," he continued. "That's the last time we'll talk about it.

"We had people hurt last year," Sutter said. "We had Hullie hurt and we had Oatsie hurt for an extended period of time. It doesn't do any good to talk about it."

Fair enough. We'll leave it at that.

The most devastating blow to any professional athlete is a debilitating injury. Their careers are so short, so fleeting. Many make wheelbarrows full of money, but only over a short period of time. And when an injury cuts an athlete's season short, he can feel the money drain from his pockets. The next time he negotiates a contract, his employers remind him how "injury-prone" he is. You'll recall that's one of the main complaints Devils general manager Lou Lamoriello had against Curtis Joseph during the compensation hearings for Brendan Shanahan. Joseph had injured his knee the year before and was considered damaged goods.

Paul Cavallini could only shudder when confronted with the possibility of an injury-filled career. The 26-year-old Toronto native was considered the top offensive defenseman on the Blues. An adept puck handler, he was added to the All-Star team during the 1989-90 season, when he led the league in plus/minus, his plus 38 earning the first Alka-Seltzer Award. He was a workhorse, skating in all 80 regular-season games and 12 playoff contests.

Frankly, his success surprised many NHL observers. He was a 10th round draft pick of the Washington Capitals in 1984, the 205th selection overall that year. At the time, he weighed a hefty 245 pounds. He looked like Spanky of the Little Rascals on skates.

"I didn't think I'd be drafted," said Cavallini matter-of-factly.

But drafted he was after graduating from Henry Carr High School in his native Toronto. The pudgy 18-year-old decided against signing right away and instead attended Providence College in Rhode Island. During his freshman year there, the Friars made it to the NCAA title game only to lose to Rensselaer Polytechnic Institute. One of the stars on that RPI championship team was a third-year player by the name of Adam Oates, who had tallied 91 points in 38 games and was named to the NCAA All-America team.

Oates signed a free-agent contract with the Detroit Red Wings a couple of months later. Meanwhile, Cavallini had to choose between continuing his education or signing with the Caps and beginning his pro hockey career.

"I chose to see the world," he said.

Which is exactly what he did. He made the Canadian Olympic team, with whom he traveled the globe. He played 52 games during that 1985-86 season and racked up one goal and 11 assists. Those were hardly eye-opening numbers, and they did little to shake the common assumption that Cavallini was a marginal pro prospect at best.

He spent the next season mainly at Binghamton, a minor league team the Caps shared with the Hartford Whalers. He showed marked improvement in all facets of the game, but it wasn't enough to impress the parent club. After playing in only 30 games over two seasons with the Capitals, he was shipped to St. Louis on December 11, 1987, for a second-round draft pick.

The rest, as they say, is history. He joined his older brother Gino, who had come to the Blues nearly two years earlier, and slowly established himself as one of the better defensemen on the team. So how does an overweight teen-ager, who didn't think he'd be drafted, turn into an all-star?

"Through hard work, setting goals for myself, and learning from my mistakes," Cavallini says. "Any goal is attainable. I'm still learning every night."

However, since his all-star year in 1989-90, Cavallini has struggled to stay healthy and on top of his game. He discarded the 1990-91 season as an aberration caused by his freak finger injury. He still managed 10 goals, a career high, but the year was a wash. He wasn't the same player the second half of the season, and the Blues collapsed in the playoffs. It was a forgettable year for Cavallini.

He couldn't throw away another season. Not two in a row. He had to heal his injured knee and hit the ice as quickly as possible.

Cavallini immediately began an excruciating regimen of exercises to strengthen his damaged knee, which was locked in an ankle-to-thigh brace. The Blues' fitness coordinator, Mackie Shilstone, along with team trainer Mike Folga, developed a routine of leg exercises that included lifting, bending, stretching, extending, flexing, and everything else a human knee is capable of withstanding before actually ripping to shreds.

The doctors predicted a six-week rehabilitation period before Cavallini could return to the ice.

He didn't want to hear any part of that. The 6' 1", 202-pound defenseman decided it would take four weeks at most to rebuild his left knee. And for the Blues' sake, he had better be right. Cavallini's indefinite departure further weakened an already suspect defense. That sound Blues fans heard was Norris Division opponents licking their chops at a chance to roll into the Arena and pad their offensive statistics. This was about to get ugly.

*   *   *

Brian Sutter is not a man who laughs publicly very often. But if splitting a rib helps ease other pains, Sutter is more than willing to let out a chuckle or two.

"I guess Ronald and I look like geniuses," Sutter laughed. The trade the Blues' head coach and general manager Caron had engineered—Vincent Riendeau for Rick Zombo—suddenly had a clairvoyant appearance to it. Just one day after Zombo's first game, Paul Cavallini was shelved for at least a month. Zombo's perfectly timed acquisition was expected to help lessen the impact of Cavallini's absence.

To make the trade even more acutely intuitive, Riendeau himself suffered a knee injury just days after reporting to Detroit and wasn't expected back until the playoffs.

This was unbelievable. The Blues acquire a defenseman right before one of their own suffers a knee injury, and get rid of a goalie days before he also blows out a knee. What timing.

Meanwhile, the Blues' defensive picture was a bit blurred. Not only was Cavallini out, but rookie Dominic Lavoie remained sidelined after breaking his left heel during training camp, and Murray Baron was still feeling the effects of a mild shoulder separation he had suffered against the Blackhawks in St. Louis.

Throw in the other defensive movements since last March— Robert Dirk's trade to Vancouver, Harold Snepsts' retirement, Glen Featherstone's free-agent signing by Boston, and Scott Stevens' forced move to New Jersey— and you've got one befuddled mess in the Blues' zone. The team's revolving door on defense had to be constantly greased, it was moving so fast. The goaltender had to introduce himself to his defensemen every night just to make sure they knew who he was and what net they were supposed to be defending.

Due to all the player movements and injuries, Jeff Brown and Mario Marois were the only defensemen in the lineup who had started with the Blues the year before.

Brown was an all-star waiting to happen. He was skilled at moving the puck out of his own end and starting a fast break in the other direction. He was used as a quarterback on the power play, controlling the puck at the point before deciding to take a shot or pass it down low. He was also seeing more time on the penalty-killing unit since his defensive play had begun to improve. But Brown was still susceptible to mental lapses, dangerously giving away the puck in his own end and occasionally getting caught too far up-ice. The team was now counting on him to minimize his mistakes and take more of a leadership role with Cavallini gone.

Marois was in his 14th NHL season and second with the Blues. In his prime, Marois was a solid, unfailing defenseman who showed remarkable passing skills for a man relatively slow on skates. He had accumulated more than 400 points in his career and amassed more than 1,700 penalty minutes, some noteworthy numbers for a guy who will be forgotten the day after he retires.

Unfortunately, the 34-year-old defenseman's skills had eroded by the time the Blues acquired him from Quebec in the fall of 1990. At times, he resembled a construction pylon, letting traffic move freely around him. With such youngsters in waiting as Rob Robinson, Randy Skarda, Jason Marshall, Bret Hedican, and Dominic Lavoie, it appeared Marois' days in St. Louis were numbered. For now, though, the Blues needed him as a temporary expedient while mending their wounds.

In the first game of Cavallini's absence, the Blues hosted the struggling Boston Bruins, who were dead last in the NHL in scoring goals. The game could prove to be pivotal in terms of the Blues' fragile psyche. If they shut the Bruins down like every other team had so far in the early going, they'll have shown they can compete defensively just fine, thank you. However, if the Bruins suddenly overpower Pat Jablonski, given his second start in a row, then be prepared for the Blues' self-confidence to self-destruct.

The key to the team's success on this particular night was to score early and often. And that's exactly what the Blues did. Just 47 seconds into the game, Dave Christian, who had fallen to his knees, swiped at the puck from the slot and beat Bruins goalie Andy Moog between his pads.

Twelve seconds later, only a few seconds longer than it takes Ron Caron to formulate a trade, Christian again hit the back of the net when he tipped in a Jeff Brown slapshot from the left point.

The home team was off and running, er, skating. The Blues raced to a 4-0 lead and appeared to have the game in hand. Most important, the team's defense was holding up beautifully, limiting the Bruins to seven shots in the first period. Not only were the defensemen playing strong in their own end, they were expertly controlling the puck in the offensive zone by pinching in along the boards and continuously feeding the puck down low to their forwards.

Surprisingly, Blues defensemen had racked up five assists on the first four goals. Brown and Butcher had two apiece, Robinson the other one. In a serious violation of Murphy's Law, everything that could go right, was.

However, Mr. Murphy was not going to be made a fool of. Bad luck interceded five minutes into the second period, when Marois was thrown out of the game for high-sticking Steve Leach in the face and cutting his nose. Not only were the Blues down yet another defenseman, they had to kill off a five-minute penalty.

Three-and-a-half minutes into the penalty, Leach got revenge for the nice little cut he was now sporting on his schnoz. His drive from the right circle was stopped by Jablonski, but the rebound slowly trickled back through the slot. Leach had smartly skated toward the net after taking the shot and easily flipped the rebound over Jablonski for the Bruins' first goal.

Barely 30 seconds later, Boston still on the power play, Leach again controlled the puck in the right circle. Fearing a repeat of the last goal, Jablonski skated a couple of feet toward him to cut off the angle. But instead of firing another shot on net, Leach passed the puck straight across the slot to a wide-open Andy Brickley, stationed at the far post. He redirected the pass into the open net, and the Bruins had suddenly cut the lead in half.

Proving they didn't need the extra man to score, the Bruins added another goal less than three minutes after Marois' penalty had expired. Glen Wesley skated over the blue line and ripped a slapshot from the left circle. Jablonski once again couldn't control the puck and let it slide dangerously through the slot. Andy Brickley took advantage and banged it into the back of the net.

Jablonski's failure to control shots from the perimeter, combined with slow reaction by the Blues defensemen, had allowed Boston back in the game. Mimicking the Celtics, the Bruins were crashing the "boards," pulling in the offensive rebounds, and shooting it right back in for the score. The Blues defense, which had looked remarkably solid the first 30 minutes, suddenly appeared incapable of shutting down the Bruins' newly-charged offense.

"Why do we hang back?" Hull questioned. "Why don't we keep going forward? It boggles my mind."

"You gamble a bit when you're that far ahead," added Oates. "You make dumb decisions. You relax a little bit."

Relax? More like a deep sleep. Just 32 seconds into the third period, ex-Blue Glen Featherstone tapped in a rebound (what else?) and the Bruins had tied the game after being down 4-0 just 12 minutes before. The Blues were suffering a slow, tortuous death. It was excruciatingly painful to witness. And worst of all, it wasn't over.

Two-and-a-half minutes later, with Murray Baron off for tripping, the Bruins pounded in what appeared to be the final nail in the Blues' coffin. Leach was allowed to stand untouched near the goal mouth and casually scored the go-ahead goal after taking a pass from Vladimir Ruzicka.

As the hometown crowd booed, reporters scurried through the record books to uncover the last time the Blues had blown a four-goal lead. But before they could even start flipping through the pages, Oates backhanded a loose puck into the net while Bobby Carpenter was cross-checking him from behind. Oates' second goal of the year, just 27 seconds after the Bruins had taken the lead, finally stopped the bloodletting and gave the Blues a chance to save face.

Sure enough, with less than eight minutes to play, Hull and Oates worked their magic again. Oates, who had played an incredibly strong game all night, was behind the Bruins' net with the puck at his stick and Stephane Quintal on his back. With one arm pinned behind him, Oates used his only free limb to stick the puck out to Hull in the slot. Just as Featherstone was about to pounce on his former teammate, Hull wristed a shot past Moog's left skate to give the Blues a 6-5 lead. It was a lead they would not relinquish.

"That tying goal really took the wind out of their sails," said Oates. "They fought so hard to come back, and all of a sudden they're looking at a tie game."

With Moog pulled during the last thirty seconds of play, the Bruins buzzed the Blues' net like bees on honey. They swarmed Jablonski, making him look like a rag doll the way he had to flop around on the ice to preserve the one-goal lead. No question, the Bruins deserved at least one point because of their ferocious comeback, especially considering it was on the road. But the Bruins ran out of time and miracles, and the Blues skated off with 6-5 victory.

"Good teams win these hockey games," said a relieved Coach Sutter. "We played a good hockey club tonight, and it took a damn good hockey club to beat them."

Perhaps. But the final statistics revealed a couple of disturbing figures. The Blues' defense had done little to quiet the concerns about their ability to play without Paul Cavallini. They gave up five goals in a little more than 14 minutes, an intolerable breakdown to say the least.

The Blues may have outshot Boston 38-33, but it was nothing to celebrate. It marked the fifth game in a row the Blues' goaltenders had been hit with more than 30 pucks. As it turned out, that number would not improve until the day Cavallini returned.

Over the next month, the Blues would play below .500 hockey and fall from first to third place. That was no surprise, considering what had happened the year before when Cavallini missed 13 games. In 1990-91, the Blues were 5-6-2 without him and 42-16-9 with him. The team was riding a nine-game unbeaten streak when Cavallini suffered his finger injury but failed to win its first three games after he was sidelined. Upon his return, the Blues won five straight and nine of their next ten.

The numbers don't lie. They're more than just coincidence. The hard, cold truth is the St. Louis Blues are a much better team with Cavallini in the lineup. At least that held true the year before.

Unfortunately, his stock with the Blues would gradually decline after his return. Despite the team's troubles during his absence, it was soon learned the team was no worse off without him. Cavallini's play slowly deteriorated through the end of the year. By the time the season came to an end, the former All-Star would find himself riding the bench, a punching bag for both Coach Sutter and the usually tolerant fans.

Chapter Six

CURTIS THE CAT

Grant Eakins was the most excited kid in all of Newmarket, Ontario, perhaps in all of Canada. He was only five years old on that April day in 1967, but he felt as tall as a grown-up. Today he was becoming a big brother.

For some time Grant had pleaded with his parents to give him a playmate. While most kids his age were screaming for a new bike or a pair of ice skates, he wanted nothing more in the world than a baby brother.

Grant was not exactly an only child, but close enough. He had been adopted in 1962 by Jeanne and Harold Joseph, who were old enough to be his grandparents. Their biological daughter, Grant's half-sister, was already well into her 20s. He longed for a sibling nearer his own age. And not a girl. He wanted a kid brother. Someone he could play with. Someone he could help take care of. Someone he could grow to love.

Grant knew he was adopted, but he couldn't have cared less. All that mattered was Harold Joseph was his dad, and Jeanne Joseph was his mom and together they were bringing home a baby brother.

When the newborn arrived home, Grant was wide-eyed. How can anything be so small? Why does he keep crying? What's that smell?

Grant couldn't leave his brother alone, spending every possible second right by his side. It was the start of a special relationship biological brothers would envy.

"What's his name?" Grant asked.

"Curtis. Curtis Munro," he was told.

Curtis was also adopted. His biological parents were 17-year-old high school sweethearts. The problem was, they weren't married. There were some hard feelings between the two families so a quick wedding was out of the question. Wendy Munro and Curtis Nickle were passionately in love but forced apart because of their parents' ideological differences. Wendy had no choice but to give her baby away and say good-bye to her young love, Curtis. So she would never forget him, Wendy named her child after the boy's father.

At the time, Wendy did not think she was losing her son forever. Instead of handing him over to an adoption agency, she gave him to Jeanne Joseph, a co-worker more than 30 years her senior. Wendy knew Jeanne had already adopted one son, so she figured Mrs. Joseph was the perfect choice to look after her baby.

As it turned out, Wendy would not see her son until 23 years later, in the summer of 1990. Just the year before, 22-year-old Curtis Munro had legally changed his name to Curtis Joseph, the last name of his adoptive parents. Curtis felt it necessary to finally set the record straight. After all, he was now an adult, embarking on his new career. He had just signed a free-agent contract to play goaltender for the St. Louis Blues.

Joseph can relate to the character Jimmy Stewart played in "It's a Wonderful Life." Stewart's guardian angel proved that one person greatly affects the lives of so many around him. Go back in time, take that person out of the mix, and history is rewritten in an infinite number of ways. It's only a movie, but for Curtis Joseph the theme is very real.

If his biological parents had been allowed to marry, and he'd been raised in a more traditional family setting, there's no telling what he'd be doing today. But as Curtis Nickle, it's highly unlikely he would be stopping hockey pucks for a living. That's because he would have never met a boy named Grant Eakins.

The boy who had begged his parents for a baby brother was instrumental in Curtis' development as an athlete and eventual NHL goalie.

"He really played the big-brother role," Curtis said of Grant, now an accountant with a fire extinguishing company in Canada. "He really did a lot of things with me. He got me involved in all the different sports. He made me very athletic.

Whether it was basketball, soccer, baseball, or track, he really spent a lot of time with me."

Notice Joseph didn't say hockey. That's because he never touched the sport until he was 11 years old. And in Canada, that's intolerable. Most kids are skating before they can even walk. To say you didn't lace up a pair of skates until age 11 is akin to treason.

Joseph remembers losing his hockey virginity very well. It was an embarrassing experience. But great success stories are often built on humble beginnings.

"I couldn't skate at all," he recalls. "The kids told me to play goalie because no one else wanted to. So I went into the net and fell down a lot. I'll tell you, I stopped a lot of pucks that way. After the game, the kids came up to me and said, 'Oh, you played great. You were really good.' So I just kept on doing it."

Curtis laughs when he tells that story. He knows now the kids didn't mean a word of what they said. They had finally found some poor sucker to play goalie, and they weren't going to blow it by telling him how bad he really was. So 11-year-old Curtis Munro kept falling down, kept stopping pucks, and kept receiving fake praise for his efforts.

Over the next few years, however, Curtis turned into a remarkably versatile athlete. Because of Grant's guidance, Curtis could compete in every sport imaginable.

Grant also worked at a golf course during his late teens. He took advantage of the opportunity by getting his kid brother on the links and teaching him the finer points of the game. Curtis remains passionate about the sport to this day.

"He even took me out to the garden to teach me to triple jump," Curtis chuckles. "None of the kids knew how to triple jump. That's the hardest thing to do, and I know how to do it."

Grant Eakins and Curtis Munro did not share a last name. They did not share biological parents. They had no physical characteristics that were similar, other than they were both boys. But there was no set of brothers anywhere that was closer than these two adopted boys. Grant never backed down on his promise to his adoptive parents that he would be the best big brother in the whole wide world.

"He always wanted to be a big brother," Curtis said. "He was really, really happy when I came along. Because he spent so much time with me, we shared the same interests."

Through his teen years in the early 1980s, Curtis' interest in sports took on a much more serious tone. He started to think about a professional career. He was extremely athletic and quite talented in a variety of sports.

But by now, he had narrowed his focus to baseball and hockey. In fact, baseball was his strongest love. While he had no idols in hockey ("I just enjoyed good performances"), he watched in awe a young shortstop in a faraway place called St. Louis.

"I was a shortstop, and Ozzie Smith was my hero," he remembers fondly.

Meanwhile, Curtis slowly improved as a goaltender through high school. He was no longer an uncoordinated kid who managed to stop a few pucks while falling down. His all-around athleticism spilled over to the ice and helped him become an above-average goaltender. Not a superior one. Not even a really good one. But one whose skills were above average and slowly getting better.

Few, if any, NHL scouts noticed Curtis. There were no fewer than two dozen goalies Curtis' age who were being drafted straight out of high school during the mid-1980s: Sean Burke, Tim Cheveldae, Kirk McLean, Bill Ranford, Mike Richter, Ron Tugnutt, Daniel Berthiaume, Craig Billington, and the list goes on.

In 1985, there were two 18-year-olds drafted in the second round who were just three weeks older than Curtis. Their names were Troy Gamble and Kay Whitmore, now playing between the pipes for the Canucks and Whalers, respectively.

Heck, there was even a kid from Toledo, Ohio, who was drafted that year by the Blues in the seventh round. Some guy named Pat Jablonski. How good can a kid from Toledo be, anyway?

Joseph's name was never called. His teen years passed; his desire to play in the NHL did not. He tirelessly worked to refine his goaltending skills. As a late bloomer, he wasn't surprised that he was still looking for a pro contract. Other goalies his age had been wearing hockey masks since they were big enough to hold goalie sticks. He just had to keep practicing his game, hoping that someone would eventually notice.

During the 1987-88 season, at the age of 20, Curtis played for Notre Dame, a Tier II Junior A team in the Saskatchewan Junior Hockey League. There he teamed with a 17-year-old fledgling superstar named Rod Brind'Amour. The young center would rack up 107 points in just 56 games. The Blues drafted him in the first round after the season was over.

It was also Joseph's first real chance to shine, and he wasn't about to waste the opportunity. He lost only four games out of 36 that season. He logged more than 2,000 minutes in net and posted an impressive 2.59 goals-against average. He would certainly be drafted alongside his teammate, Brind'Amour, right?

Wrong. At 21, Joseph was a senior citizen, too old by NHL rules to be taken in the draft. Anyone older than 20 born in Canada or the United States can enter the NHL only as a free agent. Players born outside of North America can be drafted at any age. (With the rapid influx of foreigners into the NHL, don't be surprised to see the rule changed in the near future.)

Not that Joseph's age mattered. Even after his stellar performance at Notre Dame, there still was little interest in his services. He decided to go to the University of Wisconsin, a school with a proud record of hockey achievement. The Badgers had won four NCAA titles in 16 years. Three of those championships came under the guidance of "Badger" Bob Johnson, who would later take the Pittsburgh Penguins to the 1990-91 Stanley Cup before succumbing to a brain tumor just months later.

Joseph's season at Wisconsin finally opened some eyes around the NHL. He recorded a 21-11-5 mark with a minuscule 2.49 goals-against average. He won the triple crown of Western Collegiate Hockey Association awards at the season's conclusion: Player of the Year, Rookie of the Year, and starting goalie on the All-Star team.

Finally, after several years of begging for attention, Joseph couldn't hide from it. Fourteen of the 21 NHL teams called to talk business. His phone was one of the busiest in Canada.

Missing the draft proved to be a blessing. Lacking the star quality of an Eric Lindros, if he had been selected at any time in the previous few years, he would've had no choice but to report to his team and sign for whatever that organization thought was appropriate.

But now Joseph and his newly-hired agent could do all the talking. They were in the driver's seat. If any team wanted this hot young goalie from Wisconsin, it was going to have to loosen its purse strings and shell out some major cash.

"It was nice I was a free agent," Joseph said. "I had teams coming in and looking at me and bidding on me. They knew all they had to do to get me was to pay me."

And pay him big. Joseph was hoping for a million-dollar package, an unheard-of amount for a goaltender who had yet to prove himself in the big leagues. He narrowed his choices to four teams: the Oilers, Whalers, Islanders, and Blues.

He was especially impressed with St. Louis. The management team there was trying to build a winner and made it clear to Joseph that he could be a major part of an up-and-coming hockey club. The numbers they were throwing at Curtis were staggering, but it was several other factors that finally convinced him to sign with St. Louis.

"They had a young team and stressed team defense, which is important, of course, to a goalie," he said. "They had played well the last half of the season. They seemed like a team that was coming up."

Indeed. The Blues were struggling in late February of that 1988-89 season with a 21-31-10 record. But starting with a 7-5 victory at Toronto on February 27, the Blues raced to a 12-4-2 record the final month of Brian Sutter's first season as head coach. They lost in the second round of the playoffs to the Blackhawks, but Curtis liked what he saw in the team.

And there's no mistaking he liked what he saw in the team's contract offer. After officially changing his last name from Munro to Joseph, he signed a four-year deal worth $1.1 million. Just months before, Brind'Amour, who had decided to end his college career after only one season at Michigan State, inked his name to a similar contract after being drafted the year before.

Together, they were known as the "bonus babies," touted as part of the cornerstone of the rebuilding Blues. In the 15 months from March of 1988 to the day Joseph signed on June 16, 1989, the Blues acquired Brett Hull, Sergio Momesso, Vincent Riendeau, Dave Lowry, Peter Zezel, Adam Oates, Paul MacLean, and a host of lesser-known players.

At the same time, General Manager Ron Caron purged the team of Rob Ramage, Rick Wamsley, Jocelyn Lemieux, Doug Gilmour, Mark Hunter, and Bernie Federko. That's hardly a list of throwaways. Give those guys to an expansion team, and it'll win a lot of games.

But Caron was willing to take the risk of starting from scratch and building a new and improved hockey club under the leadership of his rookie head coach. The plan paid immediate dividends. During the 1989-90 season, the Blues finished over .500 for the first time in four years and took Chicago to game seven in the second round of the playoffs, the farthest the Blues had advanced since 1986. Hull emerged as the league's newest superstar, scoring 72 goals, an NHL record for right wingers.

One performance largely overlooked that year, though, was the impressive work turned in by rookie Curtis Joseph. After the Blues' number-one goalie, Greg Millen, was traded to Quebec in December of 1989, Joseph moved up a notch to number two behind the team's new top man, Riendeau.

Curtis appeared in 15 games for the Blues and posted a 9-5-1 record with a 3.38 goals-against average. Riendeau had a much lower winning percentage, a higher goals-against mark, and a lower save percentage. But fair or not, Joseph had been given the label of "backup goalie," and there wasn't much he could do about it. He knew he'd go into training camp the next season as Riendeau's understudy. So instead of getting mad or angry, Joseph just decided to work as hard as he could and hope that somewhere, somehow, some day he'd catch a break.

"When things are frustrating, I just realize how fortunate I am," he said. "Everybody gets mad at times. When I get frustrated, I have to remind myself that I couldn't have a better job. I couldn't ask for anything better. I've always wanted to play in the NHL."

Joseph went home to Newmarket after his rookie year and experienced the most memorable summer of his entire life. Not only did he marry his high school sweetheart, Nancy, he met his biological mom, Wendy, for the first time.

Like so many adopted kids, he had always been curious about his real parents. What did they look like? Did they ever think of him? Why did they have to give him away? Curtis' adopted mother, Jeanne, had passed away when he was in his late teens. Her daughter, the older sister Curtis and Grant never felt particularly close to, was responsible for the first reunion of biological mother and son. She made the initial contact to arrange a meeting between the two.

Curtis' mom had married another man soon after she was told she couldn't wed Curtis Nickle in 1967. She had one son and one daughter, both just a couple of years younger than Curtis. Both were present during that first meeting.

"It was a nervous time for everybody," Curtis explained. "My mom knew how I felt, and I knew how she felt."

The group spent the entire afternoon together, trying to describe lifetimes in just a few hours. It was the start of a new-found relationship that continues today.

"I talk to them often now," Curtis said. "It's a regular thing."

Meanwhile, his biological father, who never married, began exchanging letters with Curtis. The two have talked on the phone a couple of times and made plans to meet sometime in the near future.

After that eventful off-season of '90, Joseph returned to St. Louis with his new bride to begin his second year with the Blues. Because of Joseph's fine play during the previous season, the Blues' coaches had a difficult decision to make. They couldn't exactly demote Riendeau. He had shown steady improvement to emerge as the team's number-one goalie. But they also didn't want to bury a 23-year-old sophomore who looked like the real thing.

To make it even more complicated, waiting in Peoria was Pat Jablonski, a goalie who later proved talented enough to make Team USA during the Canada Cup in 1991. Other teams may have had better-known superstars between the pipes, but no squad had a more impressive trio of young netminders than the St. Louis Blues.

As it turned out, the team made several brilliant moves to help establish itself as one of the top defensive clubs in the league. Besides signing free-agent defenseman Scott Stevens to intimidate opposing players who got a little too close to the Blues' net, they brought up Peoria Head Coach Wayne Thomas as assistant coach in charge of goaltending. Thomas wore the goalie pads for nearly a decade in the NHL, winning more than 100 games and compiling a 3.34 goals-against average. He would be the perfect tutor for the team's kid goalies. In fact, both Joseph and Jablonski had played for him in Peoria.

And finally, the Blues' top brass decided against naming a number-one goalie while letting the others rot. Instead, they split the chores almost equally between Joseph and Riendeau, sending Jablonski back to Peoria, where he could play almost every night. The moves worked beautifully.

By the middle of February of '91, Joseph had started 24 games, while Riendeau got the nod 36 times. The two were sharp night-in and night-out. Although no one on the team would admit it, Riendeau was still the club's number-one goalie. But Joseph got enough starts to quiet any talk of a goaltending controversy.

"I've always said there's no number one," claimed Riendeau at the time. "The goalie who plays the game is number one. I just go out and do my job, and whoever they want to put in the net, they put in the net."

However, when Vinnie pulled his groin at Calgary on February 17, Curtis suddenly got his chance in the spotlight. There was no mistaking now who was number one. Joseph was the new top dog, and Jablonski was recalled from Peoria to back him up. Curtis did not disappoint.

He won the next three games, limiting the Maple Leafs, Islanders, and Bruins to two goals apiece. He was in his glory, finally catching the break he had hoped for. He obviously felt sorry for Vinnie. The two of them were very good friends. But Riendeau would only be out a couple of weeks, and Joseph knew this was a golden opportunity to showcase his talents to the rest of the league.

However, Joseph's stay in the spotlight was brief. Just nine days after Riendeau was sidelined, Joseph was stricken with a more serious injury. While stopping a Doug Wilson slapshot on February 26, (yes, the same Doug Wilson who had torn off the tip of Paul Cavallini's left index finger two months before), Joseph strained ligaments in his right knee. He was finished for the year. Just like that. He went from standing on top of the world to having the world crashing down upon him. The spotlight had burned out.

Riendeau soon reclaimed his starting job and ended the season with remarkable numbers. He went 29-9-6, the first Blues goalie in history to finish 20 games over .500. He allowed an average of exactly three goals a game, by far the best percentage of his young career.

During his emergency recall, Jablonski turned in a 2-3-3 mark and a 3.33 GAA. Respectable numbers, but they pale in comparison to the figures he established while in Peoria, where Jabber rolled to a 23-3-2 record while leading the Rivermen to the

International Hockey League championship. That is not a misprint. He really did lose only three times in 28 games.

Even though his season ended prematurely, Joseph also racked up some pretty impressive statistics. He finished with a 16-10-2 record and 3.12 GAA. Together, the three goalies combined for the third-best goals-against average in the league. Only the Blackhawks and Canadiens allowed fewer goals.

Watching the team from the press box the last two months of the season could have destroyed Joseph's morale and confidence. But instead of feeling sorry for himself, he remained positive and upbeat while quietly counting the days until training camp the following September.

Sure enough, when the players started arriving in St. Louis to begin the 1991-92 season, one of the widest grins in camp belonged to Joseph.

"You know, I thought I had a pretty good season last year," said Joseph during the first day of camp. "I'm confident. You never go in with a negative attitude."

Perhaps the biggest reason for Joseph's positive demeanor was that he was in St. Louis, not in New Jersey as compensation for Brendan Shanahan.

"I wasn't sure what would happen that day," Curtis said of the fateful afternoon when lightning struck twice. "I prepared myself either way. If I went, it wasn't going to be a big shock to me. The cameras were following us around the whole golf course. It was actually kind of fun."

Indeed. Instead of fretting over his immediate future, Joseph had a good time with the television cameramen as he toured Norwood Hills.

"Whenever I hit the ball, the cameras would turn to the people playing with me to get their reaction," Curtis said. "So I told the guys to really start clapping and yelling out what a nice shot it was. I remember teeing off and the ball going down one side of the fairway. It wasn't that great of a shot. But the guys were clapping and shouting, 'Oh, man, what a great shot! Did you see that?!' Sure enough, when I watched the sports that night, there was my golf swing followed by everyone clapping and everything."

It's that kind of fun-loving humor that makes Curtis Joseph one of the most genial, down-to-earth guys in the locker room. There's not a more pleasant person on the team. And if a teammate needs to be humbled, Joseph is quick to offer a cut-down line that puts the player in his place while cracking up the guys around him.

At the same time, Joseph is perhaps the most fiery competitor on the ice. Behind that hockey mask is an intense young man who becomes absolutely crushed every time the puck gets past him. After a bad game, it is not uncommon to see Joseph fire his stick like a javelin as he walks into the locker room. Those kinds of emotional outbursts may be wonderful therapy to let off steam, but Joseph has had a problem with carrying that anger into the next game. Wayne Thomas has worked closely with his goalie to stay focused on the game at hand without worrying about the last game, or even the last goal for that matter.

As a goalie, it's imperative to maintain some sense of drollery. The physical and psychological demands can be overwhelming. There are few athletes in any team sport more susceptible to criticism than the man in the hockey mask. If the puck is in the back of the net, it's the goalie's fault. Period. It doesn't matter that a forward was too slow in getting back. Few people notice the defenseman failing to clear the puck. That's quickly forgotten. All that matters is the goalie goofed. If he had just been prepared, if he was on top of his game, if he was just a little more talented, he wouldn't be fishing the puck out of his net.

"You make a mistake and everyone sees it," Joseph says. "You make a mistake, and it costs the game. You really do have to be tough mentally. You have to be prepared. You have to be sharp."

Few would argue that Joseph is sharp virtually every night he takes his position between the goal posts. It's hard to imagine that just 14 years ago, he was an awkward kid on skates who was made to play goalie because he couldn't stand up long enough to compete at any other position. But thanks to the perseverance and athletic ability instilled in him at an early age by his older adoptive brother, Grant Eakins, Curtis Joseph has developed into one of the most promising young goalies of the 1990s.

What a long, strange trip it's been.

*   *   *

Rod Brind'Amour skated slowly around the Arena ice, occasionally looking up at the empty seats. He looked as out-of-place as he probably felt. He had performed here as a member of the Blues for more than two years. But now, on the morning of November 5, 1991, he had returned wearing a different jersey and representing a different city.

The Philadelphia Flyers were in town to take on the red-hot St. Louis Blues. The Blues were riding an eight-game unbeaten streak, with three wins and five ties. They had just returned from a four-game road trip during which they played a spectacular game in Vancouver, beating the vastly-improved Canucks 3-2, while tying Toronto, Edmonton, and Winnipeg. It appeared their early-season road woes had been laid to rest.

Rick Zombo had yet to taste the agony of defeat as a member of the Blues. He arrived the day after the team's last loss at Detroit, October 17. Curtis Joseph had yet to lose after officially taking over as the team's number-one goalie.

The team was in sync. They had become smooth operators. And just as important, most of their sniping fans had stopped their finger-pointing and jumped back on the Blues' bandwagon. Why not? The team was 6-1-5 since losing its first two games of the year on the road and had leapfrogged into first place in the Norris Division, one point ahead of Chicago.

It was quite a different story for the Flyers, mired in last place in the Patrick Division with just nine points. Only the pathetic Nordiques and expansion Sharks had fewer points. Only the Sabres had scored fewer goals. Brind'Amour was perhaps the only bright spot on this once-proud franchise that had missed the playoffs the previous two years. Roddie was leading the team with nine points on four goals and five assists.

While Brind'Amour and his teammates were working through their morning drills, Curtis Joseph was sitting in the Blues' locker room, shedding his goalie equipment following practice. With sweat dripping from his face, he smiled while contemplating tonight's game against his old buddy.

Joseph and Brind'Amour had spent much of the previous day together when the Flyers arrived in St. Louis. The two former teammates relived old times and recounted old memories. They had practically grown up together in their short but prosperous hockey careers. After starring in junior hockey together at Notre

Dame, they signed with the Blues just months apart. With all the accolades bestowed upon them by Blues management, Joseph and Brind'Amour figured to be a major part of the team's future success. But here was Joseph sitting in the Blues' locker room while Brind'Amour was skating around the rink wearing an orange and black "P" on his jersey.

"It's going to be a little strange seeing him across the ice," said Joseph as he unsnapped his goalie pads. "I'll talk to him after the game, but when we're on the ice we'll play hard against each other."

After skating through light drills, Brind'Amour walked back into the visitors locker room, the inside of which he thought he'd never see.

"It feels really strange," he admitted. "I'll be nervous once game time comes around."

Brind'Amour agreed that the perfect scenario would be to score the game winning goal against the team that gave up on him. But he was quick to point out he wasn't angry about the Blues' decision to move him east. He was only 21 years old, but he understood the business side of hockey.

"I'm not bitter about anything," Brind'Amour said. "Supposedly the Blues made the trade to better their team, and it's worked out so far. They're first in their division.

"From my standpoint, it's helped me. I got away from the shadows here and got to prove what I could do in Philly. It's been best for both parties."

Brind'Amour did have one advantage on Joseph that most opposing players didn't have. He knew Curtis' weaknesses as a goalie. If he found himself standing alone in the slot with the puck on his stick, he felt fairly confident he could hit the back of the net.

"He knows that I know where to go, and it's just a question of doing that," Brind'Amour said, grinning from ear to ear.

Joseph laughed when told of Roddie's comment. "I hope he doesn't know my secrets," he said. "I guess we'll see."

Close observers, however, did know Joseph's secrets. His first reaction to almost any shot was to drop to his knees, leaving him dangerously vulnerable to a shot in the upper half of the net. Joseph had been burned on more than one occasion by a well-read goal scorer who scanned the scouting report before the game. The scorer skates in, Joseph flops to the ice, and the puck flies over his shoulder. That's why backup goalie Guy Hebert was such a pleasant sight to many fans when he was first called up from Peoria. Hebert was a more traditional stand-up goaltender who, in some circles, was regarded as a more talented goalie than Joseph.

"If only I was still playing today," said one former player, licking his chops. "I'd score on Joseph every time."

Curtis has heard the criticism and knows every opposing team has his "weakness" listed in their reports. But is he bothered by it? Hardly. He's played long enough to know that the majority of shots stay within a few inches of the ice anyway, especially when the puck is lying near the goal crease, and players are trying to nudge it or poke it into the net.

Besides, Joseph points to another goalie known for taking dives. The Blackhawks' Eddie Belfour is well-known for his "butterfly" saves, an art where the goalie drops straight down to the ice while turning his knees inward and extending his skates to either side of him (Please don't try this maneuver at home. I just did the butterfly in an effort to better describe it, and I'm now sitting in extreme pain).

All Belfour did in his rookie year of 1990-91 was win the Vezina Trophy as the NHL's top goaltender, the Calder Trophy as the league's best rookie, and the *Sporting News* Player of the Year award.

Joseph hasn't won any of those prestigious awards, but his numbers take a back seat to few goaltenders'. Going into the Flyers game, he had compiled a 28-16-8 record in his NHL career while logging a 4-1 record in the playoffs. Hall of Famer Jacques Plante is the only other netminder in Blues history to post a winning record in the playoffs.

Fifteen games into the 1991-92 season, Joseph had a 2.44 goals-against average and .915 save percentage, third-best in the league on both counts. Not bad for a guy who supposedly drops to the ice prematurely.

"I'm going to go down early," Joseph says with no remorse. "You have to go down at times. As long as you block the puck, you can block out what the critics say. It's only when you start to struggle that you think, 'Oh, maybe they're right.' You've got to be mentally tough. Even when you're struggling, you've got to stick to your game plan."

And Joseph's game plan on this particular night was to stop Brind'Amour and the Flyers. It didn't appear to be a difficult task. The Blues were in first place and unbeaten at home. The Flyers were in last place and sported the league's worst power play, netting only five goals in 65 chances, a dismal 7.7 percent success rate.

The game also marked the first time in Ron Sutter's career that he was in the same building as the Flyers but sitting on a different bench. After nine seasons in Philadelphia, Sutter was playing against the Flyers, not with them. But just like Brind'Amour, Sutter refused to call this a game of revenge.

"I've just got to come out and play and be myself and try not to do too much," he said. "Once the game begins, the emotions will take over."

However, the Flyers were the only team showing emotion after the puck was dropped. With just under four minutes gone in the first period and the Blues on the power play, Jeff Brown skated out of his own end down the right side. His dangerous cross-ice pass to Brendan Shanahan on the left wing backfired. The Flyers' Steve Duchesne looked like Ronnie Lott as he picked off the pass at the center line and headed in the opposite direction. With teammate Steve Kasper to his left and only Adam Oates between them, Philly had a two-on-one short-handed rush.

Duchesne passed it over to Kasper, who quickly gave it back. Duchesne tried to shoot before gaining control of the return pass, but the puck bounced off his skate—right back to Kasper.

Joseph was dead meat. He was playing Duchesne to shoot and was hopelessly out of position when the puck ricocheted back to Kasper, who easily found the open net. If the Flyers could do anything right, it was scoring while a man short. With their league-leading fifth short-handed goal of the year, Philly was on the scoreboard first.

Using that as motivation, the Flyers overwhelmed the Blues that first period. Joseph was left to fend for himself as his defense decided to take the night off.

Less than two minutes after Kasper's goal, the Flyers scored again after forcing the Blues to turn over the puck in their own end. With the Flyers forechecking relentlessly, Brendan Shanahan tried to clear the puck along the boards but instead handed it right to Gord Murphy, stationed at the blue line. The Philly defenseman immediately whacked the puck toward the net, where Rick Zombo managed to block it with his chest. The puck dropped right to Keith Acton, bouncing off his skate to Rick Tocchet, who shot the puck over Joseph's right shoulder to make it 2-zip.

The Flyers were the beneficiaries of lucky bounces on both goals, but they certainly deserved them. They were completely outclassing the home team, and probably wondered why other teams this year had so much trouble winning here.

Unfortunately, the breakdown was occurring during Dominic Lavoie's first game of the season. After recovering from a broken left heel and finishing a two-week rehabilitation assignment in Peoria, the 23-year-old defenseman was playing in just his 21st NHL game over three years. The Blues had sent down Randy Skarda to make room for Lavoie. This was probably his last chance to prove to Brian Sutter that he belonged with the big boys. If not, Lavoie would probably languish in the minors or be shipped off to another club willing to take a chance.

By no means was the Blues' poor effort Lavoie's fault. Heck, he wasn't even on the ice for the Flyers' two goals. But just being in the building for this game hurt his cause. His timing couldn't have been worse.

With 11 minutes gone in the first period, Lavoie and his teammates breathed a heavy sigh of relief as the Blues cut the lead in half. As Brind'Amour tried to control the puck behind his own net, Hull came crashing in like a runaway train. Perhaps it was shock that the guy who hit him was wearing No. 16 that made Brind'Amour flutter an aimless clearing pass to Oates in the right circle. Oates paused long enough for Hull to skate to the open slot, then fed him with a perfect pass. Every man, woman, and child in the joint knew what would happen next. Hull one-timed a slapshot past Flyers goaltender Ron Hextall's right ear for the Blues' first goal.

But as the Arena announcer was shouting out the names and time of the goal, the place suddenly grew silent as the Flyers lit the red lamp again. Just 14 seconds after Hull's tenth goal of the season, Tocchet sped around a flat-footed Jeff Brown on a breakaway. The Flyers' rugged forward waited until Joseph went down, then flipped the puck under the crossbar for a 3-1 Philadelphia lead.

Brian Sutter went absolutely bonkers on the bench. He threw everything he could get his hands on, including a towel he tossed into the stands.

Sutter pulled out his cane and yanked Joseph from the net, replacing him with Jablonski. The move was intended to fire up the team, to show the players that this was the most pathetic display of hockey he had ever seen. Everyone wearing a Blues jersey knew it wasn't Joseph's fault the team was down two goals. But because he was now sitting on the bench acting as the fall guy, maybe his teammates would start showing a little life.

Instead, the Blues became even more lifeless. Exactly 97 seconds after the goalie switch, Duchesne ripped a slapshot past Jablonski to extend the Flyers' lead to 4-1.

Sutter played musical goaltenders again, a move Blackhawks coach Mike Keenan employs on a regular basis. Out came Jablonski, back in went Joseph. For the fans, it was like watching a tennis match, following the goalies back and forth between the bench and the net.

Hull scored his second of the game just before the horn sounded, but the first-period damage had been done. Incredibly, the Flyers had rifled 19 shots at the tag-team duo of Joseph and Jablonski en route to a 4-2 lead. The Blues could be thankful they were down by only two goals. They had no business still being in this game.

It's a miracle a blood vessel didn't pop in Sutter's head as he stormed into the locker room. A barrage of the most vile words in the English language was tossed around the room, along with a number of other objects within Sutter's reach.

"I heard a lot of crashing sounds in there," said an Arena worker. "The place was pretty torn up."

The message got through. After killing a two-man advantage at the start of the period, the Blues began their first steady assault of the game. Hull fired back-to-back slappers from the deep slot but was stymied each time by Hextall. Oates then missed a wide open net as Hextall was out of position after stopping a Gino Cavallini shot.

Finally, at 13:25 of the second period, Shanahan tipped in a shot by Garth Butcher from the point to cut the lead to 4-3. With almost half of the game still to play, the Blues were back in it. They had come back in dramatic fashion in several games already, and it appeared another heroic performance was in order.

Unfortunately, the Blues never gave themselves a chance. Or referee Terry Gregson never gave them a chance, as some players would privately grumble later. While the Flyers were called for only three penalties during the game, the Blues were called for three penalties in the third period alone and eight overall, severely limiting their chances of going on the offensive.

It seemed the Blues were always killing off a penalty. They had to worry more about stopping shots than creating any of their own. The penalty killers were outstanding, shutting down the Flyers all eight times, dropping Philly's power-play success rate to an anemic 6.8 percent. They had scored only one goal in 38 power-play opportunities on the road, a nearly invisible 2.6 percent ratio.

Nonetheless, the Flyers played the perfect road game. They came out smoking, raced to a big lead, then played smart, defensive hockey the rest of the way as they edged the Blues 4-3 while outshooting them 45-25.

It was St. Louis' worst game since its opening-night debacle in New Jersey. Gone was the Blues' eight-game unbeaten streak. Gone was the undefeated record at home. And gone was their brief stay in first place, a spot they would not see again the rest of the year.

The Blues' locker room was silent after the game, a far cry from the sounds emanating from it after the first period. They had just returned from a successful four-game road trip only to lose to one of the league's worst teams at home. Did coming back home to play an inferior team make it more difficult to get motivated?

"What's so tough about it?" snapped Hull. "You get to sleep in your own bed when you're at home. You don't have the maid waking you up before you're ready to wake up. How can't you be prepared? You either want to come out and play or you don't. Obviously, we weren't ready. It was a horrible game."

"We've got to be more prepared for the start of games," Shanahan added. "It seems we're waiting for the other team to get ahead of us before we light a fire under ourselves. Brian shouldn't have to kick us in the pants every night."

A few feet away from Shanahan, a solemn Rick Zombo slowly got dressed while reflecting on his first loss as a member of the Blues.

"We've got to start putting together some good first periods," Zombo admitted. "It's tough to keep going to the well game-in and game-out. We have no one to blame but ourselves. We just have to go in front of the mirror."

It wasn't exactly fair, but Jablonski was rewarded with the loss for his 97 seconds of play. He just happened to be in the net when the Flyers scored their fourth goal, which proved to be the game-winner. The quirk of fate allowed Joseph to keep his personal unbeaten streak alive at eight, but he was hardly taking any delight in it. He was short and to the point when asked about the loss to the Flyers.

"We thought we were ready, but we obviously weren't," he said. "We've got to be better than that."

Joseph had lost the first battle against his old friend, Brind'Amour. He would get a chance for revenge in Philadelphia in three months. But there were 37 hockey games before then, starting with a road game in Detroit two nights from now. The Blues had a chance to show how much character and pride they possessed. They had a chance to redeem themselves after their troubling loss to Philly. The game coming up against the Red Wings was going to tell a lot about the 1991-92 St. Louis Blues.

Chapter Seven

DEFENSELESS

It's time for the city of Detroit to take a bold, new step. As we near the 21st century, Detroit city officials need to rethink their city's motto to reflect the changing times.

These days, more people seem interested in buying American pizza than American cars. After all, pizza costs a little less and doesn't depreciate as rapidly. I would bet on any given day, more people are inclined to ask, "Can I get mushrooms on only half of that?" than inquire, "What would it cost me to get tinted windows on that thing?"

Therefore, Detroit should officially change its slogan from "The Motor City" to "The Pizza Capital of the World." It's a perfect fit. The Detroit area may be the home of the big three U.S. automakers, but it's also the location of Domino's and Little Caesars Pizza, two companies that thrive even during a recession and aren't subject to unfair trade barriers.

And how many car companies own professional sports teams in Detroit? The answer is a big, fat zero. Meanwhile, Domino's main man, Tom Monaghan, owns the Tigers, while Little Caesars head honcho Mike Ilitch runs the Red Wings (During the summer of '92, Monaghan sold the Tigers to Ilitch, giving the Little Caesars owner control of the city's hockey and baseball teams). That's the great thing about taking trips to Detroit to cover sporting events. Unlike other professional teams that feed the media soybean burgers and undercooked hot dogs, reporters can count on freshly made pizza in Detroit. You fill up the bellies of media folks, and you've made friends for life.

And do Detroit athletes notice any difference being owned by a pizza company? Have you looked at Cecil Fielder's physique lately?

Rick Zombo knows all about the pizza influence in Detroit. He was used to seeing the Little Caesars advertisements around the rink at Joe Louis Arena. He had grown accustomed to hearing little men in Roman togas yelling, "Pizza, pizza!" He had spent his entire hockey career in "The Pizza Capital of the World" until he was traded to the "The Toasted Ravioli Capital of the World," otherwise known as St. Louis.

For the first time, Zombo was entering the arena as a visitor. His memories of the last few weeks he had spent here were very unpleasant. He had been unceremoniously dumped on the bench before being shoved out of the door.

But Zombo also remembered the more positive experiences during his seven years with the Detroit organization. His friendship with Adam Oates; the 1986-87 and 1987-88 seasons, when the Red Wings, led by coach Jacques Demers, played for the Campbell Conference championship; being given the "A" as the team's alternate captain; the honor and pride of being looked to as a team leader. The house was chock full of memories Zombo could never forget. Coming back here as the enemy was one of the most difficult trips Zombo would ever make.

"This is the hardest game that I'll ever play in my career," said Zombo. "But after that first hit, it'll go well. As long as we win, I'll be pumped."

For the Blues, the last trip here, October 17 was a nightmare. The Wings, with Zombo still a member for about 12 more hours, exploded for five goals in the second period and coasted to a 6-3 win.

If the Blues had any chance tonight, they had to smother Detroit's potent offense and clog up the center lane. Give the Wings open ice and allow them to roam freely around the rink, and the scoreboard was going to get a workout.

Right away it was easy to predict this game was going to get out of hand. The Blues played like scared children. They didn't hit anything but the panic button. The Red Wings skated into the Blues' zone on rush after rush, the visitors trying desperately to keep up.

Just 50 seconds into the game, bad boy Bob Probert crashed into Blues goalie Pat Jablonski. That's perhaps the biggest no-no in all of hockey. You run a goaltender and you pay the price. No questions asked. Be prepared to be pummeled like Beetle Bailey.

So what did the Blues do to retaliate? Absolutely nothing. The men in blue stayed away from Probert for fear of making him really, really sore. Only Garth Butcher got within arm's reach. He pushed at Probert, telling him "That's fucking bullshit." Yep, that'll show him.

That one incident, more than anything, proved the Blues desperately missed the physical play of defensemen like Scott Stevens and Harold Snepsts. Without question, the Blues were not the intimidating force they had been the year before. Teams like the Red Wings were quickly learning they could punish the Blues without fear of retaliation.

Just three minutes into the game, with Oates off for interference, Steve Yzerman took the puck right off Rich Sutter's stick along the far boards. The talented Wings center took a few strides back toward the blue line to survey the situation, then slid a backhand pass across to Paul Ysebaert. From the top of the right circle, Ysebaert wristed a shot past Jablonski to give the home team a 1-0 lead.

After that early goal, the Blues seemed to settle down. Halfway through the first period, their confidence grew as they started to venture into uncharted territory known as the offensive zone. Brett Hull, Dave Christian, and Murray Baron all had quality shots on goal that were turned aside by Tim Cheveldae.

That apparently served only to irritate the Wings. Detroit went back on the assault and crushed the Blues like a pesky swarm of gnats. The Red Wings buzzed into the Blues' zone, forcing turnovers and generally wreaking havoc. With seven minutes left in the opening period, Jeff Brown tried to get out of his own end by passing weakly ahead to Hull. However, the puck was picked off by Shawn Burr, who skated in alone and slid a backhand past Jablonski's left skate. 2-0, Detroit.

A minute later, Rob Robinson's clearing pass was intercepted by Vladimir Konstantinov, who quickly fired a slapshot from the blue line. The puck hit a crowd of players in front of the net, bounced to the ice, and was scooped up by Jimmy Carson, who flipped a backhand under Jablonski. Make it 3-zip.

Forty seconds later, Sergei Fedorov won a faceoff in the Blues' end and kicked it back to Niklas Lidstrom at the top of the circle. Lidstrom blasted a shot just inside the left post. Add another one. It's 4-nothing.

Forty-five seconds later (I'm not making this stuff up, really I'm not), Ysebaert skated in alone on a breakaway and slid the puck under a worn-out Jablonski for a 5-0 lead. That's four goals in just two minutes and 25 seconds of play. Welcome home, Rick Zombo.

Brian Sutter was absolutely motionless. Unlike two nights before when he looked like Jimmy Swaggart storming up and down the bench and swinging his arms wildly, Sutter now had his arms tightly nestled across his chest. He just stood there, his face showing no sign of expression. In a strange sort of way, he looked very peaceful.

The Blues finally ended the bombardment with a goal of their own late in the period. With Detroit defenseman Yves Racine in the penalty box for elbowing, Oates picked up a loose puck and cruised along the right boards looking for a guy wearing No. 16. He found him. Oates threw the puck across the ice to the left circle, where Hull ripped one between Cheveldae's legs for his eleventh goal of the year.

The best thing about the second period, besides the fact the first one was over, was the Blues would get to shoot at the net that had been so kind to the Red Wings the first 20 minutes. Perhaps there was an advantageous wind current in that end of the rink. Or maybe a fan's wristwatch created a blinding reflection that interfered with the goalie. Or perhaps the net was larger. Or maybe. . . .

Forget it. All the excuses in the world weren't going to help the Blues on this night. Exactly 59 seconds into the period, Shawn Burr tipped in a Brad McCrimmon shot from the right point to give the Red Wings a 6-1 lead.

Less than 30 seconds later, Burr gained control of the puck behind the Blues' net and passed out front to a wide-open Lidstrom in the slot. The Wings' defenseman beat a defenseless Jablonski for a 7-1 lead.

But this massacre was not exactly Pat Jablonski's fault. He just happened to be the nearest guy to the puck as it hit the back of the net. After giving up his eighth goal of the game a few minutes later, Jablonski was mercifully sent to the bench in favor of Curtis Joseph, who allowed two goals himself.

The final tally showed a 10-3 victory—or should I say flogging?— by the Red Wings. Mike Ilitch must have thrown a little extra protein in the pepperoni. His employees on the ice showed absolutely no mercy as they handed the Blues one of their worst defeats in the organization's 25-year history, and their most lopsided loss in Brian Sutter's four years as head coach.

The Blues hadn't given up 10 goals since a 10-8 loss to the North Stars on January 27, 1984. That was just one goal short of their all-time record of generosity, when they permitted the Canadiens to score 11 times on March 24, 1973.

The team flew back to St. Louis that night, expecting a horrific workout the next day at the Arena. Instead, Sutter canceled practice and held a 90-minute, closed-door meeting with his battered and beaten players. He was especially distressed about the way his team had responded after the dreadful 4-3 loss to Philly two nights earlier. They had a chance to come back and show some character, an opportunity to flaunt their mettle in their very next game. Instead, the Blues meekly retreated into a shell and allowed the Red Wings to humiliate them.

At the meeting, Sutter stressed the fundamentals and preached the basics. Work hard, play your position, don't take unnecessary chances, and concentrate on defense first, offense second. The message was simple and to the point. It was the only way Sutter knew how to coach.

Despite the continued improvement the Blues had shown his first three years, Sutter would never be regarded as a coaching innovator. It didn't take a brain surgeon to understand his technique. He was a man who was convinced that a marginal player who worked hard was much more valuable than a superior player who played soft. That philosophy had never changed since the day he first put on the Bluenote in 1976. If, as a player, you wanted to get along with Brian Sutter, all you had to do was show concern and compassion for the game.

The day after their meeting, the Blues hosted the Hartford Whalers, an offensively impotent team that had scored just 43 goals a month into the season. Only the Sabres and Sharks had netted fewer. The Whalers seemed to be the perfect tonic for the sickly Blues.

Unfortunately, St. Louis remained bedridden at the start of the contest. The Whalers must have seen the tapes of the last two Blues games. They took a page right out of the Flyers' and Red Wings' playbook and blitzed the Blues the moment the first puck was dropped. You would've sworn the Whalers had too many men on the ice, but they were moving around so quickly, it was difficult to count them.

Just like their previous two games, the Blues stood around as if marveling at the skating ability of their opposition. Even the Blues' strongest points, their penalty-killing and goaltending, were no match on this night. The Whalers scored on their first two power plays to take a 2-0 lead after only 10 minutes of play.

Then, just 49 seconds later, Joseph skated behind his own net to stop a Whalers' dump-in pass along the endboards. After missing it, he nonchalantly retreated to the front of the net a bit too late. Mikael Andersson got to the puck and rifled one just inside the left goal post while Joseph was still trying to get set.

"That was just a really bad play," admitted Joseph. "I didn't even see the guy there."

Once again, the Blues were digging themselves a hole from which they could not emerge. Despite the preachings of Coach Sutter the day before, the Blues weren't paying attention to the small details that had made this club a winner the year before. They were getting knocked off the puck, they were losing track of the opposing players, and they were getting caught in the offensive zone, allowing the other team to rush back the other way. In other words, the Blues just didn't seem like they knew what the heck they were supposed to be doing once they took the ice. This was a team without any sense of direction. Seventeen games into the season, the Blues hadn't shown much improvement from their opening-night loss in New Jersey.

But just when it seemed the Blues were about to suffer another first-round knockout, Brett Hull sent the Whalers reeling with a couple of right-handed shots of his own. Just 28 seconds after Andersson's goal made it 3-0, Hull managed to poke in a loose puck in front of the net to give the Blues their first goal.

Barely a minute later, Blues center Michel Mongeau, just called up from Peoria the day before to add some offensive spark, won a faceoff in the Whalers' zone and dumped the puck back to Hull. The Golden Brett unleashed a bullet of a shot that beat

Whalers goalie Kay Whitmore. Suddenly, the Blues were back in the game, cutting the lead to 3-2.

Just as suddenly, though, Hartford recovered its two-goal lead. Fifteen seconds after Hull's second goal, the Blues' defense was caught sleeping as the Whalers' Brad Shaw passed the puck up the middle of the ice, a wide-open middle of the ice to a streaking Andersson, who netted his second of the game on a breakaway to extend Hartford's lead to 4-2.

Once again, the first period seemed to last an eternity. The Whalers scored four goals in a span of six minutes and 35 seconds, pummeling Joseph with 20 shots. After the period was over, Joseph should have gone straight to court and filed a lawsuit against the team, charging it with unfair labor practices. While his teammates were taking extended coffee breaks, Joseph was left to do all the work. Perhaps he had forgotten to pay his union dues.

In the last three games against Philadelphia, Detroit, and now Hartford, the Blues had been outscored 13-5 in the first period. For some reason, their batteries were low before the games even started. Perhaps they were so enamored and enthralled by the singing of the national anthem, that it took them at least a period or two before they could settle down and focus on the game at hand.

The Blues did come to life in the second and third periods, outshooting the Whalers 25-16. But they only managed one more goal, by Brett Hull in the third, to give him his first hat trick of the year. Hull's early-season slump appeared to be over as he was leading the league in goals with 15 in 17 games.

But as Hull's personal stats continued to climb, the Blues as a team continued to slide. Their 4-3 loss to Hartford brought their losing streak to three games, the longest of the year. And none of the teams that beat them was setting the league on fire. They were mediocre at best, hovering at or below the .500 mark. Joseph's personal 8-game unbeaten streak also came to an end, as he lost for the first time since the second game of the season, the 3-0 shutout by the Maple Leafs.

The Blues were definitely a team in trouble. The season was still very young, but the early signs were quite disturbing. They had won only four of eight at home, two of nine on the road, and perhaps most importantly had just two victories in seven games against Norris Division foes.

The Blues had a chance to improve on the last figure just 24 hours after losing to Hartford. Unfortunately, they were traveling to the worst place on the entire planet to break out of their slump. Thanks to the sadistic tendencies of the schedule makers, the Blues had to visit the "Pizza Capital of the World" once again. That's right. Just three days after being buried there 10-3, the boys in blue were forced back to Detroit for further punishment and humiliation.

Few would have been surprised to see the Blues knocked silly once again. But unlike their last visit, the Blues shot out of the gate with renewed confidence. Perhaps the Red Wings were a little too cocky after the last game and relaxed a bit. Or maybe the Blues figured they had nothing to lose and came out firing on all cylinders. Either way, this was a Blues team that had been dormant since their eight-game unbeaten streak ended the week before. Here they were flying around Joe Louis Arena, knocking people down, creating scoring opportunities, and limiting the Wings to only a few good chances of their own.

Unfortunately, a bad bounce of the puck gave the Wings the first score of the game a little more than eight minutes into the first period. Standing in his own end, Garth Butcher tried to clear a pass to Dave Lowry, who had just started to head up-ice. However, Lowry didn't see the puck, and it bounced off his skate back toward the area between the circles. An area where Bob Probert just happened to be located. Probert had been knocked to the ice, a rare sight indeed when the Blues were in the same building. Big Bob jumped to his feet, scooped up the loose puck, whirled and shot all in one motion. Before Curtis Joseph knew what was happening, the red light was on, and the Wings had a 1-0 lead.

A few minutes later, Detroit forward Kevin Miller welcomed Blues defenseman Dominic Lavoie to the NHL with a move that must give him nightmares to this day. Miller cruised through the neutral zone with only Lavoie standing in his path to the Blues' net. While skating backward, Lavoie had his head down looking only at the puck. That's when Miller made his move. At the blue line he faked to his right, switching the puck from his forehand to his backhand. Lavoie took the bait and crossed over to his left. Suddenly, the man he was guarding was nowhere to be seen. Miller had pulled the puck back into his forehand and scooted around the Blues' rookie defenseman. The move was made with such lightning speed, it's surprising Lavoie's shadow wasn't permanently burned into the ice. Miller raced in alone and lifted the puck over Joseph's glove for a 2-0 advantage.

The Wings and Blues exchanged goals the final few minutes of the first period, Ron Sutter scoring short-handed, and Gerard Gallant scoring on the power play. St. Louis had played extremely well, a marked improvement over its last three games. The Blues limited the Red Wings to 11 shots in the opening period and made only one major mistake, that by the inexperienced Lavoie.

But the Blues had nothing to show for their improved play except a 3-1 deficit. For the fourth game in a row, they had given up at least three goals in the first period. You would've sworn the Blues were in command most of the first 20 minutes until you looked at the scoreboard. It was disheartening to say the least.

Just when the Blues thought it couldn't get any worse, Dave Christian cut Probert's face with an inadvertent high-stick 18 seconds into the second. Christian was assessed a five-minute penalty and tossed out of the game.

Then, just 18 seconds later, Lowry was thrown into the penalty box for getting his stick up a bit too high on another Detroit player. The Blues suddenly found themselves down two men for a full two minutes. The visitors were in danger of being blown out once again.

But Bob Bassen, Rich and Ron Sutter, Jeff Brown, and the others built an impenetrable wall around their own net. Despite having two extra guys, Detroit could only muster a couple of decent scoring chances. The Blues penalty killers played with reckless abandon, killing off not only Lowry's two-minute minor but also Christian's five-minute major.

As is so often the case when a team kills a two-man advantage, the Blues' motors shifted into overdrive. They were so busy in the offensive zone, it looked like they had all 20 guys out there. Nelson Emerson and Ron Sutter each scored his fifth goal of the season just 40 seconds apart to tie the score at three. The Blues' new-found enthusiasm had put them in a position to actually win the game and stop this festering slump.

Still, you had the uncomfortable feeling that the Wings weren't finished putting the puck into the back of the net. Not counting the two-man advantage when they looked ridiculously inept, Detroit had started to create quite a number of scoring opportunities, only to be snuffed out by another fine performance by Joseph.

Besides, the Red Wings had to win this contest; it had been so ordained by the hockey gods of Detroit. In ceremonies before the game, the numbers of former Red Wing greats Ted Lindsay and Alex Delvecchio were retired. The two Hall of Famers are in the top five in games played, goals, assists, and points in Detroit's all-time record book. The last thing the home team wanted to do on a special night like this was to send the fans home hanging their heads. The Wings were given extra incentive to add two points to the standings.

So before the Blues could rejoice about coming back to tie the score, Paul Ysebaert and Shawn Burr scored two minutes apart to give the Red Wings a 5-3 lead after two periods. This time the Blues could not recover. Hull netted his league-leading 16th halfway through the third, but that was quickly followed by Probert's second of the game, which ended the scoring at 6-4.

The Blues' losing streak had climbed to four, the team's longest in two seasons. They fell back below the .500 mark with a record of 6-7-5. The Wings had leapfrogged the Blues into second place, and the fourth-place North Stars were just two points behind the sinking team from St. Louis. The only positive outcome over the last week was Brett Hull's being named the NHL player of the week after scoring eight goals in those four losses. However, Hull was unimpressed.

"I get player of the week, and we lose all four games," Hull said with dismay. "How brutal is that?"

About as brutal as the Blues' schedule. No one was making excuses, but this team was one worn-out bunch of hockey players. They had played their last 10 games in just 18 days, a dizzying pace. Now they were getting three days off before their next game, the first time in nearly three weeks they were allowed to have consecutive days off. But finding a player in the locker room willing to admit he was tired was impossible.

"Sometimes when you try too hard and press too hard, you forget what you should be doing," explained Bob Bassen, trying to come up with reasons for the Blues' slump. "We've been ready for the games. We just have to work through this."

"No one's hanging their heads," said Coach Sutter, defending the team's character. "They're concerned and that's the way you've got to be. You've got to have that concern all the time."

The next day at the Arena, Sutter gave that line to his players in the form of a written message. On the chalkboard in the dressing room, he scribbled, "When you're concerned, you end up having fun."

Sutter got the quote from Magic Johnson just a couple of days earlier, when Johnson announced he had tested positive for the AIDS virus. Sutter watched him intently during his news conference, listening not so much to what he was saying, but how he was saying it.

That's a favorite pastime of Sutter's. The Blues' head coach is constantly listening to people he admires and mentally noting the things they say. It's not uncommon to hear him blurt out, "Bill Walsh said this," or "Pat Riley said that," or "Vince Lombardi once mentioned this."

Brian Sutter is a student of such men. His admiration of their success is so great he literally feels it an honor to quote them. Their messages strike at Sutter's very soul. When those kinds of sports personalities appear on television, the first thing Sutter does is turn up the volume. When they speak at a dinner banquet, Sutter lets his food grow cold so as not to miss a syllable. If a man has had success molding others into champions, Sutter is a captive audience.

Recently, the St. Louis chapter of the Baseball Writers Association of America held a dinner honoring the 1942 world-champion Cardinals. Sutter was one of hundreds in attendance that night and was in awe listening to the likes of Stan Musial, Whitey Kurowski, Terry Moore, and Enos Slaughter.

"I realized they all had the same values I have," Sutter said. "Everything they said made so much sense about what it takes to be a winner."

Unfortunately, Sutter's team hadn't been doing any winning lately, and he again had become the target of Sutter-bashers across the city following the Blues' four-game losing streak. There were more calls for his resignation. Fans started to question his coaching ability. They again pointed to last March's trade with Vancouver and the more recent trade with the Flyers as reasons for the team's demise.

But the biggest complaint of all? You guessed it. The old Scott Stevens controversy was dragged out of the closet, dusted off, and proudly displayed by team critics. If Blues management hadn't been so foolish in dipping into the free-agent market, they said, we'd still have Stevens and the leadership he brought to the team. We'd still have toughness. We'd still intimidate other teams. We'd still do this and still do that.

Suddenly, Scott Stevens had been elevated to god-like status. He was now the greatest player ever to lace up a pair of skates. However, many fans had forgotten that Stevens was prone to making blunders like anyone else. He occasionally gave up the puck in his own end, making bad passes that led directly to goals. He also got caught up-ice from time to time, trying to help out offensively and forgetting about his role on defense. In other words, Stevens was human.

There's no question the Blues missed Stevens. They also missed the leadership of Harold Snepsts and Rick Meagher, both of whom had retired. But Sutter knew that it all came down to wins and losses. When the Blues were riding their eight-game unbeaten streak following the Riendeau-for-Zombo trade, hardly an unkind word was spoken. But now during their slump, Sutter and the boys were the biggest piece of horse manure in the league.

"If I win, I'm God," Sutter observed. "If I lose, then I deserve to be fired, and I don't deserve to be in this league. That's part of the profession. You can't get too high when there are good times. You have to understand why they're good, because they're not always going to be that way."

Didn't I hear Mike Ditka say that once?

*   *   *

Wednesday morning, November 13, 1991, Hartford, Connecticut. The Whalers vice-president and general manager, Eddie Johnston, strolled into the team's locker room and approached one of his players who was tirelessly pedaling the stationary bike. It was about the only action this guy had seen all year. He had become a spare part to the team. The 31-year-old veteran had a couple of nagging injuries, mainly a sore hip, but it didn't really matter. The Whalers weren't high on him, and he had no future in Hartford.

"Hey, Lee, when you got a second I need to see you," Johnston said.

"Sure, I'll be done here in just a bit," Lee Norwood responded.

Norwood wasn't quite sure what the big boss wanted, but he figured it couldn't be good. After all, nothing about his six-week stay in Hartford had been positive.

The 6-foot, 190-pound defenseman had been used sparingly by the New Jersey Devils the year before and asked to be traded. He got his wish on October 3, 1991, and was sent to the Whalers just before the season started. However, the change of scenery did little to improve his happiness. Hartford had as much use for him as a broken hockey stick. He skated in only six of the Whalers' first 16 games. It seemed that after stops with six teams over a span of ten years, including a productive one-year stint with the Blues in 1985-86, the career of Lee Norwood was coming to an end.

Norwood toweled off his face and walked into Johnston's office to get the lowdown.

"I got a call from Ron Caron," Johnston said. "He's looking for a veteran defenseman, and I figured you might be just the guy. I would only get future considerations for you, but that's about all I can ask."

"What are my options?" Norwood questioned.

"Well, you can go play in St. Louis or you can stay here," Johnston answered.

In other words, Norwood could continue to ride the stationary bike, or he could go to one of his old stomping grounds and try to resurrect his career. The choice was easy. Norwood was going to St. Louis, which meant he was going back to the Norris Division.

Norwood had spent the majority of his career in the Norris, the one year in St. Louis and more than four seasons in Detroit, where he had been a real pain in the butt to the Blues. He loved the style of play in the "Chuck" Norris Division, as it was sometimes called. It was bump-and-grind hockey at its best. During the time he played in the division in the mid- to late 1980s, there were few skilled, finesse players on any of the five teams. The Norris was better known for its rugged, hulking forwards and defensemen who loved to bang and brawl. It wasn't a pretty style of hockey, but for the fans who liked the physical side of the sport, there was no better division to watch. And Norwood couldn't wait to get back and get his knuckles dirty.

"I played with Brian Sutter for a year, and he watched me play in Detroit for a while after that," Norwood said after being traded. "He knows what kind of hockey player he's getting. He said I have nothing to prove. Just go out and play the way Lee Norwood is capable of playing."

And that's all Sutter was asking for. His defense was about as thick-skinned as a fresh peach. Sutter desperately was in need of some added toughness at the blue line and figured the return of Lee Norwood could only help.

Norwood was hardly Hulk Hogan. But he was a cocky son of a gun who was willing to take on all comers, and that included pucks. Norwood had established quite a reputation as a shot blocker, throwing his body to the ice and into the path of 90-mile-per-hour slapshots. The guy had more bruises than anyone after the final horn sounded. But there he was in uniform at the very next game, stopping shots again with every part of his body.

Norwood also brought to the team a left-handed shot, something the Blues sorely needed. The departed Scott Stevens, Glen Featherstone, and Robert Dirk were all southpaws. So was the injured Paul Cavallini. Their absence forced righties Jeff Brown and Mario Marois to play out of position over on the left side.

"The acquisition of Lee Norwood is going to give us stability, because he's played the game a long time," said Rick Zombo, a former teammate of Norwood's in Detroit. "He's a very tough competitor. He's a checker and very strong in front of his own net."

Norwood arrived in St. Louis just in time for a home game against Winnipeg on November 14. No one was putting the savior label on him, but he knew his job description. He had the task of strengthening the fifth-worst defense in the league. Only the Sharks, Oilers, Islanders, and Penguins had allowed more goals than the usually defensive-minded Blues. Watching a Brian Sutter-coached team crumble on defense was like watching Darin Kimble score a hat trick. It just wasn't supposed to happen.

"There's too much talent on this team to be struggling like this," said Norwood, sitting in the Blues' locker room for the first time in five-and-a-half years. "You get away from the little things that make a team win consistently like St. Louis has in the past.

Once that starts happening and little things start clicking again, the Blues will get right back on track. There's too much hard work and pride at stake."

The Jets flew into town with a mediocre 7-7-4 record, 10 points behind the Canucks in the Smythe Division. In their first meeting just 11 days before in Winnipeg, the Jets and Blues had skated to a 3-3 tie thanks to a dramatic goal by Jeff Brown with 28 seconds remaining. It was the third time this year the Blues had tied a game in the final minute with the goalie pulled.

Winnipeg was a nondescript team with no real superstars. Ask a random sample of fans in the Arena to name more than one or two Jets players and they were likely to suffer brainlock. Phil Housley was the only "name" player on the squad. He was a defenseman with a lightning-quick shot, one of the best point men on the power play in the NHL. He led the Jets in scoring in 1990-91 with 76 points. However, those stats elicit only yawns from Blues fans used to seeing Hull and Oates reach that total by the end of January.

The Jets also possessed a fine young goalie in Bob Essensa, who attended the same Toronto high school Paul Cavallani went to. He was to Winnipeg what Curtis Joseph was to St. Louis, a skillful netminder who was improving by the hour. Just like Joseph, Essensa was looked to as a building block for his team. In fact, the two goalies matched each other save-for-save in the earlier 3-3 tie, kicking out 32 shots apiece. Even more remarkable for Essensa, however, was that 13 of the pucks he faced came off the stick of Brett Hull, a personal high for Hull. Not one reached the back of the net. Advantage Essensa.

The second go-around proved to be no different. With Brian Sutter routinely mixing his lines to throw the opposition off-balance, the Blues stormed Essensa early and often. They threw 12 shots at the Jets' net in the first period, most of them quality chances. But Essensa stopped each one, including three slapshots from No. 16. Essensa must have started questioning all the fanfare surrounding this guy Hull.

Despite the Blues' fine play in the opening period, the Jets struck first. Which, of course, seemed only appropriate the way the puck had been bouncing for the Blues the last week. With six minutes left in the first, diminutive rookie Stu Barnes was left wide-open in front of the Blues net. He took a pass down low from Ed Olczyk, tried to poke it past Joseph once and was stopped, but successfully nudged it underneath him the second time to give Winnipeg the 1-0 lead.

The second period had "Blues" stamped all over it. It was one of the best 20 minutes of hockey St. Louis had played all year. Every line swarmed into the Jets' zone, creating a continuous wave of attack that made the defensemen dizzy and Essensa busy. Incredibly, ten Blues had at least one shot on goal in the second period. Seven had at least two shots. But Essensa continued to prove immortal, blocking every puck shot in his direction. The guy must have been hiding a puck magnet somewhere.

The Blues began to grow frustrated. The usually mild-mannered Oates even slammed his stick to the ice after one productive shift produced nothing but another Essensa highlight film.

Finally, at 12:27 of the second period, Oates scored what appeared to be the tying goal. Dave Christian let go a shot from the left circle, which, of course, was stopped by Mr. Essensa. The rebound shot high into the air and was whacked into the net by Oates as the puck fell to about waist-high. Immediately, referee Mike McGeough waved off the goal saying it was put in by a high-stick. Oates and Hull surrounded McGeough, demanding a replay. However, McGeough elected to use his eyes and not any piece of videotape. The call stood. No goal.

Fans, as frustrated as the players, started tossing paper cups and other garbage to the ice below. They had watched the Blues skate their hearts out, trying desperately to end their four-game losing streak, only to see a couple of guys named Essensa and McGeough shut them down. If this were a boxing match, the Blues would be way ahead on points. But the scoreboard showed a 1-0 advantage for the visitors, and the home crowd was growing restless.

Finally the Blues solved Essensa with just under two minutes left in the second. It was the rediscovered checking line of Lowry, Bassen, and Rich Sutter that finally found directions to the back of the Jets' net. After taking a pass from Bassen, Lowry skated in alone and wristed a shot that Essensa stopped. But Lowry stood his ground and poked in the rebound to give the Blues a well-deserved 1-1 tie.

With the fans jumping wildly up and down, Lowry pumped his fists into the air and joined the cries of celebration. Lowry had finally scored his first goal— first point for that matter—in the season's 19th game. For a guy who had scored 38 goals in the last two years, the season-long drought seemed like an eternity.

"You go that long without scoring a goal, it's a big relief," said Lowry. "I just have to keep going and hope the bounces start coming."

Bassen and Sutter got the assists, perhaps sending a message to their coach that the old checking line that had been the heart and soul of the team the year before was finally returning to its old form. Brian Sutter had split up the trio earlier in the year and had just put them back together the game before in Detroit to try and stir things up.

"We're just happy to be back together," said Lowry. "We all play the same way. We just get the puck in and get some hits and create chances."

The second period ended with the score tied at one, but the shots on goal were ridiculously lopsided. The Blues pelted Essensa for 19 shots, four coming off the stick of Hull. Joseph, meanwhile, was trying desperately to stay awake. He faced nine shots, most of which came early in the period and were from the safe locales of the perimeter. It was a cruel injustice that the Blues had to enter the game's final 20 minutes staring at a 1-1 score.

The third period was pared down to a battle between Hull and Essensa, with the Jets goalie coming out on top. One had to forgive Blues fans for suffering nightmarish flashbacks to the second game of the season, when Toronto's Grant Fuhr shut the door on Hull in a 3-0 victory by the Maple Leafs. On this night, Hull's nemesis was wearing blue and red instead of blue and white, and was now a left-hander instead of a righty. But the results were the same. Hull from the slot. Hull from the point. Hull in deep. Hull from the rafters. It didn't matter. Essensa took the best shots Hull had to offer and casually tossed them aside like peanut shells.

"I'll have nightmares about this guy," quipped Hull. "I'd like to think he was at his best. If not, I'm in trouble."

He ain't a-kiddin'. If every goalie treated Hull the way Essensa did, the Golden Brett would be sitting home wondering what to do with his life. Hull tallied four more shots on goal in the third period to give him 11 for the game and 24 in two games against Essensa. Not one of those shots ever slid across the goal line. That had to be one of the most incredible statistics in Hull's short, but illustrious career.

At the end of regulation, the score was still 1-1. Essensa had faced 41 shots and had been beaten only by Lowry. Joseph, hit with 31 shots, had given up only Barnes' first-period goal. Seventy-two shots and seven power plays, four for the Blues, but into overtime they went with just one goal apiece.

The Jets would have liked nothing better than to escape the Arena with a point. They weren't about to take any offensive chances and blow an important road game. Instead, they bottled up the middle and dared the Blues to take their best shots from the perimeter. As long as they gave Essensa a clear shot, the Jets figured a tie was in the bag.

With two minutes gone in the extra five-minute period, Coach Sutter sent out his checking line, along with the new defensive pairing of Lee Norwood and Jeff Brown. Norwood's arrival allowed Brown to move back to his natural position at right defense, and the duo had performed remarkably well in its first game together.

With Norwood and Brown taking their positions just inside the Jets' zone, Bassen and Lowry were fighting for control of the puck in the corner to Essensa's left. Lowry emerged with it and fired a shot from a difficult angle deep inside the right circle. The shot was way off-target, missing the net by at least ten feet.

Then everything seemed to move in slow motion. It was as if everyone in the building knew what was about to happen as they carefully watched the puck hit the endboards and bounce out to the top of the left circle. The puck started to lose speed and nearly came to a complete stop before the new guy stepped into the picture.

Lee Norwood, the man who had been given up on by every team but the Blues, the man who seemed destined to ride a stationary bike the rest of his career, coasted in from his spot just inside the blue line. As he approached the puck, Norwood wound up like Nolan Ryan about to fire a 100-mile-per-hour fastball. He cocked his stick high over his head, then let it recoil in blazing speed down toward the ice and through the puck. It shot off his blade like a cannon ball but appeared smaller than a pea.

Essensa had finally met his match. After stopping the league's most prolific goal scorer two games in a row, he could not stop

Norwood from recording only his 53rd career goal. The puck whizzed past Essensa's right leg and into the back of the net. When people talk of storybook endings, they talk of games like this.

Norwood thrust both arms high into the air, while the crowd of 16,924 created a deafening roar of approval. If not for the mob of Blues players piling on him, Norwood probably would have been able to fly right through the top of the roof.

It seemed like forever before the men in blue finally made their way off the ice and into the locker room. For the first time in a long while, the Blues' dressing room had a party atmosphere to it. KSHE-95, the self-proclaimed "real rock of St. Louis," was blaring throughout the room. It was loud. It was raucous. And it sounded so damn good.

"He comes right in here and gets the game winner in overtime," shouted Joseph of his new teammate. "The fans gave him a good reception even before the game started. I think they're happy he's here."

Dave Lowry could barely wipe the smile off his face. He had finally scored his first goal of the year and was named the game's number-three star. But he was much happier talking about the new guy who was awarded the number-one star.

"That's a big goal for Lee," the Blues' left winger said. "It takes a lot of pressure off him. He played a very solid game tonight. I think they knew what they were doing when they went out and got him."

Blues Chairman Mike Shanahan wasn't involved in the deal that brought Norwood to the Blues. But he felt obliged on behalf of management to welcome the ex-Blue back to his old workplace. As soon as Shanahan stepped into the locker room, he located Norwood and gave him a firm handshake and a pat on the shoulder.

"Some guys sneak into town and some come in with a bang," said Shanahan. "You got here just in time."

"I hope they're not expecting that every overtime game," Norwood laughed loudly over the sounds emanating from a nearby speaker. "It's nice the way it happened. I'm happy about tonight, but I still have to come back and work hard tomorrow."

As did the other defensemen on the team. With Paul Cavallini's return just a week away and Norwood's strong showing in his debut, at least one and probably two defensemen were about to lose their jobs.

*   *   *

"Excuse me, sir. Can I look at your program for a second?"

"Sure, here you go."

"Mmmmmm. It's not a mistake. There really is a guy on the Blues who wears No. 14."

"Yeah, I noticed that too. Must be some new guy who had to borrow one of Gino's jerseys. Notice the last name on his back?"

Okay, okay. The above conversation didn't exactly take place, at least that I know. Call it writer's embellishment. Or journalistic license. Or just an outright fib. But there's no question the sight of "14" skating around the Arena ice did seem a little strange. After all, it had been missing for 30 days while the man wearing it recovered from a strained ligament in his left knee.

Yes, Paul Cavallini returned to the lineup on November 20 for a home game against the Maple Leafs. His arrival spelled the end for Dominic Lavoie, who was sent to Peoria earlier in the week. The team still had eight defensemen, which meant another one was sure to follow. Since Rob Robinson hadn't played in the last two weeks, he seemed the obvious choice to head north.

In Cavallini's 13-game absence, the Blues went 4-5-4, roughly the same record as the year before when Cavallini was out with his finger injury. In fact, every statistic imaginable proved Cavallini's worth to the team.

During the four weeks he spent rehabilitating his damaged knee, the Blues' offensive output dropped from 3.4 goals a game to 2.9. The defensemen contributed just 1.5 points per game, down from 2.5 when Paul was playing. The power play, of which Cavallini was an integral member, fell from a success rate of 18.6 percent to 17.1 percent. And on defense, the Blues allowed 3.7 goals per game with him out of the lineup, and 3.4 with him in it.

Cavallini admitted he was a bit nervous before the game. But Coach Sutter didn't let him think about it on the bench. He sent Cavallini to the ice for the first shift, reuniting him with Butcher. He got in a hit or two, released the butterflies from his belfry, and returned to the bench with every part in working order. Now he could just concentrate on playing the game instead of worrying about the strength of his knee.

The Leafs, who came in with only five wins and the third-worst record in the league, scored the game's first goal, Bob Rouse netting his first of the year on the power play at 2:31 of the first period.

However, just three minutes later, the Blues tied it up with a series of crisp passes. Hull skated across the blue line down the right side, leaving the puck for Norwood. The Blues' new defenseman scooped it up and raced into the right circle. There, he quickly fired a pass across ice to Jeff Brown at the left post, who easily redirected it between Grant Fuhr's pads. Bang, bang, bang. It was 1-1.

The Blues then took the lead thanks to hard work by Adam Oates behind the Leafs' net. The play started innocently enough when Rick Zombo dumped the puck in. Toronto's Bob Halkidis skated back to retrieve it but was bumped off the play by Oates. His aggressive forechecking jarred the puck loose, allowing Oates to gain control of it and pass out to the slot to.... need I say? Hull wristed it over Fuhr's glove to give the Blues a 2-1 advantage. It was Brett's first goal against Fuhr in three games this year.

For the rest of the first period and all of the second, the Blues resembled a team gearing for the playoffs. They played smothering defense, not letting one Leaf float untouched into the Blues' zone. By far, it was the most outstanding display of defense all year.

That perhaps is the most important message Brian Sutter imparts to his players. If you only think about scoring goals, you'll invariably get burned the other way. But if you play solid in your own end first, the offensive chances will follow. As that famous French hockey player Rene Descartes once said, "I think (defense), therefore I am (scoring)."

Sure enough, the Blues' defensive game plan opened the doors into the Leafs' zone. The Blues outshot their opponents in the second period 15-3, by far the widest margin of any period this year. Cavallini's presence made his fellow defensemen play much more solidly in all three zones. His return also enhanced the team's transition game, helping move the play quickly from one end of the rink to the other. The team was in sync. It was in tune. And it was hitting on all cylinders.

Paul's brother, Gino, also shared in the spotlight. Late in the second period, Hull and Giant Gino tore down the ice on a two-on-one-break. Hull had the puck down the right side, and everyone in the building figured he'd try to work it in on net. However, the Golden One let off the pedal, coasted into the circle, and waited for Gino to crash the net. Once he was there, Hull passed ahead to Gino, who flipped it over Fuhr's right shoulder. It was a beautiful top-shelf goal, the 100th of Gino's career.

"It's a nice achievement for a slug like myself to get 100 goals," said Gino with self-deprecating humor. "I just put my stick on the ice, and I was ready for it. I guess all those thousands of pucks in practice finally paid off for me."

He wasn't exaggerating. Cavallini may be the hardest worker on the team. Long after practice is over, Gino is still on the ice flipping pucks into the net. Many times he'll lay a couple dozen pucks right near the goal crease, get down on his knees, and start whacking them into the net. Then he'll jump to his skates, take a few strides back, and start slapping in another batch of rubber disks. It's a tiresome process that Gino repeats almost daily.

"Where I get most of my goals is around the net," he said. "Usually there's a big pileup, and the goalie is on the ice flopping around."

In the "Cavallinis on Ice" show, the Blues went on to beat the Maple Leafs 5-2. Gino finally hit number 100, and brother Paul helped improve the team's ailing defense. For the first time in over a month, the Blues held the opposition under 30 shots on goal.

Afterward, Paul was almost in awe of the entire performance. He felt like a little kid again, just happy to be playing the game of hockey. He sounded like a mountain climber who had just scaled Mt. Everest.

"When I first skated out there I felt chills through my body," said Cavallini in almost a whisper. "It's so great to play on the Arena ice and be a Blue. It makes you think about the injuries that keep players out for their careers. It's exhilarating to get out there and play."

"It was a great game," said Hull. "Paulie played really well after missing so many games. He's a tremendous asset to our hockey club. He gives us a little spark."

Was it a mere coincidence, or did Paul's return really have that big an impact on the team? The Blues would find out three nights later against the New York Rangers. Shutting down the Leafs was one thing. But stopping Mark Messier and the gang was quite another.

The future Hall of Famer had been traded from the Oilers to the Rangers on October 4, the day after New York opened its season with a loss to Boston. His arrival instantly gave the Rangers a legitimate shot at their first Stanley Cup since 1940. In his first two games, he assisted on three of the team's four goals as the Rangers won a couple of 2-1 overtime thrillers against the Canadiens and Bruins. The 30-year-old center had already given the Rangers what they so desperately needed to push them over the top. Leadership.

"You won't find a guy who wants to win more," said Rangers' center Adam Graves, who played with Messier for two years in Edmonton. "He'll do anything to win."

And New York had been doing plenty of that in the early going. Coming into St. Louis, the Rangers were 13-9-1 for 27 points, fifth best in the league.

The Blues' outstanding defensive work in the Toronto game spilled over into this contest as both teams played tight, defensive hockey. The first real scoring opportunity for either team came 15 minutes into the first period, when Hull blasted a shot from the slot into what appeared to be an open net. But Rangers goalie Mike Richter came from nowhere to make a sweeping glove save on the league's top scorer.

Just three minutes later, the Rangers capitalized on their first chance, which started with the Blues in control of the puck in their own end. As the Blues started up-ice on a rush, Derek King intercepted a clearing pass intended for Brendan Shanahan and immediately passed down low to Messier, still in the Blues' zone. The home team was now out of position, with its forwards up-ice and its defensemen trying to cover for them. That proved impossible. Messier gave the puck to Joey Kocur, stationed in front of Joseph. There wasn't another blue jersey within miles. Kocur got three whacks at it before finally squeezing it past Joseph to give the Rangers the 1-0 lead.

The second period was a fan's nightmare. The game was played entirely in the neutral zone, as both sides refused to give any free passes into their territory. Like two boxers feeling each other out in the first round, the Blues and Rangers lined up at their respective blue lines and dared the other to strike the first blow.

"Red rover, red rover, send Hullie right over." The Blues obliged, but to no avail. In what seemed an impossibility, the Rangers actually prevented Hull from getting one shot on goal after he sent three on net in the first period.

"Red rover, red rover, send Messier right over." Same story, only better. Not only did Messier fail to shoot on goal in the second period, he was shotless in the first 20 minutes as well.

Incredibly, the two teams combined for only six shots on goal in the second frame, four by the Blues and two by the Rangers. The six shots were just one more than the all-time Blues record of fewest shots in a period, set in 1969 at Pittsburgh and equaled in 1974 against the Sabres.

The two shots by New York were the fewest the Blues had allowed in one period since the Canadiens managed only a single shot in the second period on January 3, 1985.

Unfortunately, the Blues made one mistake in their near-record-breaking second period, and it cost them. Brian Leetch held in Rick Zombo's clearing pass at the left point. The Rangers' high-scoring defenseman skated in a few strides and slapped a shot that beat Joseph over his glove. After two periods, the Blues were outshooting the Rangers 15-1, but trailing 2-0.

The third period was unmistakably similar to the second, much to the disappointment of the 17,617 in attendance. The tempo was agonizingly slow. That couldn't have been ice they were skating on. It must've been glue. The Rangers stuck to Hull and Oates, effectively taking them out of the game. What resulted was Mike Richter's first career shutout, as New York whitewashed the Blues, 3-0. Mike Garnter added an empty-net goal with 34 seconds left to finish the scoring.

On a positive note, the Blues limited the Rangers to 19 shots on goal, the fewest since giving up 18 to the Messier-less Oilers in the Blues' first win of the year back on October 10. It was the second game in a row in which the team had allowed fewer than 30 shots. Between coincidence and causation, you had to pick the latter when talking about Paul Cavallini's return and the sudden frugality of the defense.

However, the players were naturally disappointed with the game's outcome. The only two mistakes the Blues committed resulted in goals, while the team had several good opportunities to score a few of their own but couldn't connect.

"We could have easily won that game 3-2 or 4-2," said Joseph, whose personal record fell to 6-4-5. "We just have to keep plugging away. The good thing about it is we were there tonight. We're playing good hockey right now. Hopefully, it'll continue."

Joseph's coach agreed, but in a less positive tone. "We played well. No question about it," said Sutter. "But the bottom line is we lost. The two goals they scored were because of our mistakes."

Sutter has always preached that the game of hockey is a game of mistakes. It's a simple philosophy, but it rings true. The team that commits fewer errors generally comes out on top. The Blues had just completed one of their better efforts of the season. But two ill-advised clearing passes cost them two points.

The Blues fell back to the .500 mark at 9-9-5, six points behind the surging Red Wings, who were coming to town next week riding a ten-game unbeaten streak. For several reasons, particularly inconsistency and lack of on-ice leadership, the Blues just couldn't put a streak of their own together.

The truth couldn't be denied any longer. Many players, fans, and journalists, including yours truly, kept waiting for the Blues to snap out of their early-season funk. We were convinced the team would eventually wake up and start steamrolling its opponents. But after 23 games, there wasn't a shred of evidence that was ever going to happen. It pained us to admit it. But the Blues were barely a shadow of the 1990-91 team that seemed just a step away for the Cup.

"Whenever we take a step ahead, it seems like we take a step back," said Ron Sutter, one of ten new faces who wasn't on the team 365 days earlier. "It's just a matter of pushing each other a little bit more to get over that hump. We're just not going through with it."

And for a Sutter, that was unacceptable behavior.

Chapter Eight

SUTTER HOME

As steam rose from the hot asphalt and beads of sweat trickled down their faces, Tag Miller's road crew laboriously worked to repair the city streets of Red Deer, Alberta. Miller was old enough to be a grandpa to most of his young workers. And he certainly cared for them as if they were indeed his own relatives. But on this particular day, Miller closely watched only one of his employees, largely ignoring the others.

Nineteen-year-old Brian Sutter tirelessly shoveled asphalt onto the road, carefully maneuvered it into place, then returned to the truck for more while wiping the sweat from his eyes. It was May 27, 1976, and Sutter tried to treat this as a normal day. But everyone knew better, especially the foreman.

Miller couldn't help but smile while watching young Brian. This was a big day in Sutter's life, and Miller was grateful to be a part of it. Despite their age difference, the two men had forged a special relationship. Miller enjoyed the young Sutter's work ethic. With so many kids complaining about having to lift a finger, it was indeed a pleasure to witness a youngster work so hard. What's more, he actually enjoyed it. Strange kid, this Sutter.

Meanwhile, Brian was equally impressed with his boss, who also served as his baseball coach. Sutter respected Miller as much as his own father. In fact, Sutter respected all his elders. After all, they were the only people the Sutter kids knew.

While growing up on their farm in Viking, 120 miles northeast of Red Deer, the seven Sutter boys befriended people older than themselves. It was difficult to find seven boys their age in a town of only 1,900, especially since they lived nine miles outside the city limits. For the most part, the only visitors were neighboring men and women who stopped by to say hello or help with the chores. When the boys were old enough to play sports, they either competed against one another on the farm or went into town to battle older kids, sometimes men. Growing up on the 960-acre Sutter farm meant growing up fast.

"We were doing a man's work when we were kids," Brian recalled. "I was driving tractors and grain trucks before I was ten. The older kids, Gary, myself, and Darryl, had responsibilities of men because there was work to be done. The work was never, ever something we were told to do. It was just a part of normal life."

As Brian continued laying down asphalt, Miller turned on the radio. It was draft day in the National Hockey League, an event as important as any holiday in Canada. Miller knew in a matter of moments he would lose his prized worker to the NHL.

"What team are you going to?" shouted Miller.

"I'm not going anywhere," Sutter snapped back. And he really believed that. Or at least he made himself believe that to avoid being let down if his name wasn't called today.

"The Washington Capitals select Rick Green from London of the Ontario Hockey League," blared the radio announcer. The draft had started, with Green grabbing the honor of being the league's top draft choice.

The next couple of hours would be excruciating for Tag Miller and the boys. Where will Brian go? Will his name even be called? That's silly. Of course it would. He had established himself as one of the premier two-way players in western Canada. He had just tallied 92 points and 233 penalty minutes for Lethbridge in the Western Canadian Hockey League. There were players who were much more potent offensively, and others who were bigger and stronger and logged even more time in the penalty box standing up for their teammates. But few combined offense with toughness the way Brian did.

"We now move to the seventh pick," said the announcer as the draft continued. "The St. Louis Blues select Bernie Federko from Saskatoon of the Western Canadian Hockey League."

That was no surprise. Sutter knew all about Federko. They played on a line together in the WCHL All-Star game. Federko had just turned 20 two weeks earlier, and there weren't many, if any, kids who could handle the puck like Federko at such a young age. During the past season, he had banged in 72 goals and dished off 115 assists in only 72 games. His 187 points were the most of any Junior A player in Canada and broke the WCHL scoring record set by Bobby Clarke in 1967-68. And just look at the success Clarke was achieving in the pro ranks. As captain of the Flyers, Clarke had led the Broad Street Bullies to two Stanley Cup titles.

As the draft wore on, a few names were mentioned that put a smile on Sutter's face. All the doubts he had about being drafted faded away. He knew his name would be called anytime now.

"As I was listening to the first round, I heard a couple of guys mentioned who I knew I was a better player than," Sutter said. "I knew then I would be drafted, and I knew I would be drafted fairly high."

However, as the first round ended, the name of Brian Sutter had yet to be called. The 18 teams had made their first choices, and every general manager felt there was at least one player better than the tough-nosed teenager from Lethbridge.

"The Penguins start round number two by selecting Greg Malone of the Oshawa Generals," said the voice on the radio.

Brian acted oblivious to the sounds emanating from the black box. He wasn't about to stand there and listen to it. That was the worst thing he could do. He continued to shovel asphalt to help relieve the nervous tension.

"With the 20th pick," the announcer continued, "the St. Louis Blues select Brian Sutter."

Shouts of joy could be heard in various locations throughout Alberta. In a small, four-room farmhouse outside of Viking, the Sutter clan whooped and hollered. In Lethbridge, where Brian had starred the previous two seasons, residents started asking one another if they had heard the good news. And in Red Deer, where a certain road crew had put down its shovels to offer congratulations to one of their fellow workers, a woman was frantically calling city officials. She had to find Brian Sutter.

"It was my landlady," Sutter remembered. "She called the city yards and found out where I was. The city of Red Deer is a fairly large city, but she still managed to find me on the paving crew. We went out and had a few draft beer, that's for sure."

(Author's note: the word "beer" is never pluralized in Canada. You can drink all the beers you want in the States, but north of the border, do as the natives do and drop the "s.")

Like most kids growing up in rural western Canada, Brian knew very little about St. Louis. He had heard about the Plager brothers and knew a little something about Gary Unger and Red Berenson. But his knowledge of the city itself was hazy. He wasn't even sure where the place was.

When he reported to camp later that summer, Sutter felt awkward. That's a normal reaction, of course, for any rookie, but Brian felt especially out of place. And it was more than just the fact he was in another country, far removed from home.

Always intense, even at play, the Blues' second-round pick observed in amazement how some of the veterans handled themselves. Many of them seemed unenthused, unimpressed, and largely uninterested in the job at hand. Guys who had worked so hard to get to the NHL now approached the game with little fanfare.

How can this be? wondered Sutter. How can they coast through their careers like this, working just hard enough to get by? Has the money of a professional career in hockey spoiled some of these players? Sutter loved to have fun as much as anyone. But not when there was work to be done. And with guys fighting for jobs, there was plenty of work out there.

Sutter was dazed and confused. He began to doubt the values that had been instilled in him the last 19 years. Was his approach to hockey too intense? Was he going to burn out of the sport about which he was so passionate? The first few days of training camp were a time of soul-searching for young Brian Sutter.

"I felt I was very different," said Sutter. "I was much more strict and disciplined than most guys were in terms of preparation for the game."

But as camp wore on, Sutter noticed his values were very similar to at least one member of the Blues. Brian watched this man intently from the second he arrived at camp. The 5'11", 175-pound defenseman with thick, jet-black hair controlled the ice as if it was his domain. He barked orders, he demonstrated drills, and most of all, he commanded respect from everyone. No exceptions.

But this 35-year-old player from Kirkland, Lake, Ontario, still found time to put his arm around a teammate and discuss matters outside of hockey. And to a young, impressionable kid like Sutter, those visits were infinitely important in learning not just how to become a better player, but a better person.

"This guy had the exact same values I had," said Sutter. "He reaffirmed that I wasn't wrong in the way I felt. He was a lot like my dad."

That man was Barclay Plager. He proudly carried the title of "heart and soul of the Blues," a label that would be passed on to Sutter in a few short years.

Plager was traded to the Blues just six weeks into their inaugural season in 1967. It didn't take long for him to give the fledgling organization some character. Plager wore the "C" on his jersey for five years and directed the Blues to Stanley Cup appearances in their first three seasons. As a left-handed defenseman, Plager solidified the team's blue line corps and made St. Louis one of the most respected defensive squads in the NHL.

His values were not complicated. Live every day to the fullest and enjoy life. Attack every job as if it was the most important responsibility ever undertaken. And don't ever do anything half-assed. People fail not because of ability, but from the misuse of that ability. In the world of Barclay Plager, it was that simple.

Brian Sutter never questioned himself again. He observed Plager's every action. He listened to his every word. Their developing friendship was just another example of Sutter's respect and admiration for older men who shared his father's values.

"His attitude was, if you're going to do something you might as well do it all-out," said Sutter. "Otherwise, it's lost. And that had always been my attitude. That's why he was very special to me."

Plager didn't stick around camp very long. The Blues sent him to Kansas City that fall to coach their minor league affiliate in the Central Hockey League, his first head coaching job. It didn't take long for Plager to find success in his new line of work. As a player/coach for the Kansas City Blues, he led his team to the regular-season title and the Adams Cup championship, the CHL's version of the Stanley Cup. Plager narrowly missed an unheard of double sweep when awards were given out following the 1976-77 season. He was named the league's most valuable player and finished second in the voting for coach of the year.

The Kansas City franchise moved to Salt Lake City the following season and changed its name from the Blues to the Golden Eagles. Plager was retained as the head coach and was enjoying another successful year until an unexpected call came on February 16, 1978. Blues president and general manager Emile Francis told Plager to pack his bags and hop on the first flight to St. Louis. Francis had just fired Leo Boivin and named Plager to succeed him as the organization's 11th head coach.

Brian Sutter was ecstatic. The man he worshiped was coming back to St. Louis. Plager's presence paid dividends immediately for second-year players Sutter and Federko. "Sudsy" had struggled under Boivin, scoring just two goals in 52 games. His ice time plummeted as much as his confidence. Federko was equally discouraged. This alleged scoring phenom had pumped in only four goals in 54 games playing on the fourth line. Media and fans alike were wondering if the 1976 draft had been a bust.

But Plager's arrival erased all doubts. In Barclay's very first game as head coach, Federko scored two goals, and Sutter added a goal and an assist to lead the Blues to a 4-3 victory over Vancouver. That kind of production continued during the final six weeks of the season. Sutter went on a rampage, busting opponents with new-found rage and knocking in seven goals in the season's final 26 games. Federko was also given a more prominent role and promptly netted 13 goals and tallied 10 assists down the stretch. The two young men became linemates for the better part of the next ten years.

But two players do not a team make. In Plager's first full season as the Blues' head coach in 1978-79, the 22-year-old Sutter led the team in goals with 41, and Federko tallied a then-team record 95 points. Those two, however, were the only bright spots in a dismal season. The Blues lost 50 games, a franchise record that still stands.

Unfortunately for Plager, the team's ineptness flowed into the following year. After winning just eight of his first 24 games, the organization's "heart and soul" lacked the heart to proceed any further. On December 8, 1979, Plager voluntarily stepped down, switching places with assistant coach Red Berenson.

"I just can't motivate the team any longer," Plager said.

With the redhead now in charge and Barc allowed to become personally involved again with the players, something that is taboo for a head coach, the Blues were about to embark on one of the greatest rags-to-riches-to-rags stories in hockey history.

After stumbling along as one of the worst teams in hockey the previous four-and-a-half seasons, the Blues suddenly took off under the new coaching arrangement. They went 26-20-9 the remainder of the 1979-80 season to finish a respectable 34-34-12.

Almost overnight, the Blues became one of the league's elite teams. With an influx of talented new stars, including left wingers Jorgen Pettersson and Perry Turnbull, right winger Wayne Babych, and goalie Mike Liut, the Blues lost only four of their first 17 games in 1980-81 en route to a season-long battle with the New York Islanders for the NHL's top spot.

The Blues tired a bit at the end, winning just five of their last 13 games to finish second to the streaking Islanders. But their overall record was a remarkable 45-18-17 for 107 points. The team had gone from 50 losses to 45 wins in just two years. And with a majority of their stars 25 years old and younger, the Blues were set to blossom into a dynasty.

However (why does there always seem to be a "however" with this franchise?), the Blues meteoric rise gave way to an equally rapid decline. After being ousted in the second round of the playoffs by the New York Rangers, St. Louis suffered through injuries, ill-advised trades, and new coaching techniques that Berenson had picked up at the Canada Cup in the summer of 1981.

The redhead couldn't wait to try out his "innovative" drills when training camp started the following September. But the change in Berenson befuddled some of his players who couldn't understand why there was a sudden instructional overhaul following the best regular season in team history. Some guys started to question their coach's new-found philosophy. The plan backfired.

The destruction was complete. This once-promising team had been gutted. On March 8, 1982, following an embarrassing 8-1 loss in Minnesota that gave the Blues a 28-34-6 record, Berenson was given a one-way ticket out of St. Louis. Plager stayed on as an assistant, and Emile Francis added the position of head coach to his already cluttered list of titles, including team governor, president, and general manager.

But the damage had been done, and the Blues never recovered. Over the next four years, three different owners controlled the city's hockey team, and three different men coached it. But through all the turmoil, Barclay Plager remained as a coach, Brian Sutter retained the "C" on his jersey, an honor first given to him in 1979, and Bernie Federko continued to lead the team in assists and points. That triumvirate formed the core of the St. Louis Blues that lasted until the late '80s. They were the most recognizable figures on the team for more than a decade.

Federko respected Plager as a mentor and a close friend, someone who was more than willing to share a few pointers about the game of hockey and the game of life. Plager taught Federko about the honor of wearing the Bluenote. He told him the jersey was to be respected as if it were the Canadian or American flag. It wasn't to be thrown down on the floor or stepped on. When he wasn't proudly wearing it on the ice, Federko was instructed to carefully hang it in the locker room. The Blues' star center learned to associate Plager with everything great about hockey.

"He was like a big brother to me," says Federko. "He could rip me up and down if he didn't feel I was playing well. But at the same time, I could yell right back, and he'd always listen."

While Barc was a brother to Federko, he was more like a father to Sutter. Every time Brian looked into Plager's eyes, he saw his own dad back in Viking. He saw the same values, the same philosophy of life, and the same system for success. Every word Plager uttered left an indelible impression on the team captain. The two shared a special relationship that was seemingly unbreakable.

In the late '80s, that bond became stronger than steel. It had to be. Life would soon deal a cruel and vicious blow. Their world was about to fall apart.

*   *   *

"It's better to give than to receive." That line best describes one person. Barclay Plager.

Barc always assumed that the most unimportant person in the world was himself. He never felt compelled to bore others with stories of his illustrious hockey career. Nothing pleased him more than helping others achieve success. Look up the word "humble" in the dictionary, and you'll find a picture of Barclay Plager next to it.

On March 24, 1981, the Islanders invaded the Checkerdome, as the Arena was then called, for a game that would be watched by hockey fans across North America. The Blues were atop the NHL standings, three points ahead of the visiting Isles. A win would put St. Louis up by five points with just five games remaining, almost guaranteeing the club a first-place finish, an unprecedented feat. This game was one of the most significant in team history.

But this contest was also special for another reason. It was Barclay Plager Night. Before the first puck was dropped, the Blues honored Plager for his contributions to the franchise as a player, scout, head coach, and assistant coach. Taking part in the ceremony was New York Coach Al Arbour, one of the original St. Louis Blues. Before taking the Islanders to four consecutive Stanley Cup titles from 1980 to '83, Arbour played alongside Plager from 1967 to '71. Arbour then moved behind the bench and coached Plager for parts of three seasons in the early 1970s.

Barc had every reason to gloat on this night. But that would've been out of character. In fact, he felt a bit embarrassed about all the fuss being made over a mere assistant coach. As he was about to take the microphone, Plager turned and told those around him, "This is such a big game. I feel bad about the players having to wait for me to be honored before they can start the game."

Too bad Rickey Henderson wasn't there to hear that.

It was that kind of unselfish behavior that made Plager a winner. He never complained. He never bitched. And he hated it when others felt compelled to do so. If you had a few aches and pains, he didn't want to hear about them. He had them too. Plager's nose had been turned into mush after blocking pucks for 13 years with his face. His snout had been broken 15 times. His body showed the scars from hundreds of stitches.

But those injuries paled in comparison to the pain Plager began feeling after his playing days were over. He started to suffer from dizzying headaches that felt like someone was drilling a jackhammer into his head. In the fall of 1979, entering his second full year as the Blues' head coach, he was finally persuaded to see a doctor. After a few tests, Plager was diagnosed as suffering from "head trauma." Physicians told him it was from scar tissue that had developed after an earlier hockey injury.

Plager told the public that he would step down as head coach because he couldn't motivate the team. But many of his players knew better. They had watched his health deteriorate through the course of the season. In fact, he had missed four games because of his illness.

Plager started to take medication that lessened the frequency and severity of his headaches, but he was far from a picture of health. Over the next several years, he started to experience seizures that would shake one side of his body. He occasionally fell down for no apparent reason. His powerful body was slowly weakening. His strength was betraying him.

Plager didn't bother anyone about his worsening condition. Was he really that proud? Or was he afraid of what the doctors might find? Probably a little of both. He finally decided to go back to the hospital for further tests during the first week of November in 1984. The results were devastating.

Plager had inoperable brain cancer. Doctors were brutally honest, telling him he would be dead within a year. They immediately began chemotherapy and radiation treatments in a last-ditch effort to prolong his life.

"Barc the Spark" valiantly fought back. He sneered at his cancer, treating it like a pesky center iceman trying to sneak past him. Plager met the deadly disease halfway, and the two went at it, each landing a few solid blows. Occasionally the tumor would shrink, allowing the doctors to hope they were getting a handle on it. Then it would suddenly enlarge, and Plager's life again was in immediate peril.

A year came and went, and Plager was still swinging away. He remained the Blues' assistant coach, and he wasn't about to be stripped of that title by an uninvited disease. He continued to travel with the team, still keeping his seizures as secret as possible. Everyone knew he had cancer of the brain, but few realized the awful pain and misery he was forced to live through every day.

However, one player was very much aware of Plager's sickness—his good friend and soulmate, Brian Sutter.

On January 16, 1986, Sutter fractured the scapula in his left shoulder in a game in Minnesota. The injury was so serious the Blues captain appeared in only 16 of the next 118 games. During that time, Sutter visited the same group of therapists and doctors that was treating Plager. The two clients and their physicians, along with the Plager family, were the only people privy to Barclay's condition.

"No one else really knew," said Sutter. "Management, players, nobody. Barclay would make the doctors not tell anyone.

"There were times I took him to his room, undressed him and put him to bed. And then you'd have to get him up in the morning."

In the late summer of 1986, Dr. Alexander Marchosky of St. Luke's Hospital in St. Louis asked Plager if he would volunteer to undergo a new, untested treatment of tumors. In hyperthermia treatments, holes would be drilled into the skull and heated probes applied to the tumors. Dr. Marchosky was looking for a test group of 20 people who had inoperable brain cancer. The side effects could be life-threatening. That's why he wanted to find volunteers who had no hope of surviving their cancer.

Barclay Plager had every hope of living to be an old man. But he was willing to give the experiment a chance. Not because he wanted to prolong his own life. But because he thought his being a "guinea pig" might someday save another life.

"If going through these treatments helps someone else," he told Dr. Marchosky, "then let's do them."

Incredible. Here was a man who stared at death every day but was still thinking about the welfare of others.

The hyperthermia treatments caused mild damage to Plager's brain. He had to learn to walk and talk all over again. It was excruciating for loved ones to watch this proud and humble man struggle for survival.

Plager's visits to the rink grew infrequent, and he stopped going altogether after the 1986-87 season. He had lived years longer than any doctor had thought he could. But even Barclay knew he had only delayed the inevitable.

Plager remained hospitalized through the fall of 1987. Virtually every day, the three senior members on the team, Sutter, Federko, and defenseman Rob Ramage, visited their dying coach. They felt helpless watching this former hulk of a man reduced to a living skeleton. His cheeks were hollow. His eyes were sad and unfocused. It was impossible to believe this man was only 46 years old.

On January 26, 1988, Plager made a decision that would be his last. In an emotional farewell, he gathered his relatives and closest friends to his hospital room. He told them he was done fighting. He had informed his doctors he was through taking treatments. It was time to give in to this insidious disease. For the first time in his life, Barclay Plager admitted defeat.

Twelve days later Plager finally found peace. Mercifully, his pain disappeared as he quietly passed away. Newspapers across the United States and Canada carried the news. The sport of hockey had lost one of its true heroes.

Unfortunately, Barclay Plager never got to see Brian Sutter coach a hockey game. Just four months after Plager died, the man he helped mold into a fierce competitor and loyal team player was named the Blues' 15th head coach.

To this day, Brian Sutter can barely muster the strength to talk about the last few days of Plager's life.

"He never changed until the time he left us," recalls Sutter with great sadness. "I was with him that day. It was very tough. I'll never forget what he whispered to me."

Sutter pauses. His eyes fill with water. He looks to the ceiling as if to gather strength. He looks back down and clasps his hands together on his lap. Sutter just can't do it. Try as he might, the memories of that day are too painful to recall.

What was it, Brian? What did he whisper to you?

Again, only silence. He stares at his desk, his eyes red and tearful. He tightens his lips and shakes his head.

"He just brought to life something you can't explain," Sutter answers softly.

End of conversation.

Sutter is reminded of his former coach every day. Plager's picture hangs in the Blues locker room and in the coach's office. Looking at his eyes, one gets the eerie feeling he's keeping a close watch on the place, making sure the current Blues coach is giving it his all.

*   *   *

Flyers center Ron Sutter hopped on the team bus and took a seat near the front. Philadelphia had just beaten the Capitals 4-1 and was now 5-2-1 on the season.

The Flyers had something to prove during this 1983-84 season. They had won 49 games and finished with 106 points the year before, second only to Boston's 110 points. However, they were impolitely dumped in the first round of the playoffs by the Rangers, who swept the Flyers in three straight, including a humiliating 9-3 defeat in the final game. It marked the second year in a row that Philadelphia had been eliminated in the first round. Changes were not only expected, they were promised.

Head coach Bob McCammon sat near Sutter and flashed a Cheshire smile.

"Hey, Ronnie. Talked to your twin brother lately?" asked McCammon.

"Not in a couple of days. Why?" questioned Sutter.

"Oh, just wondering," said McCammon, still grinning from ear to ear.

Sutter sat back in his seat. What was that all about? he wondered. Is the coach just playing games or has Richie been traded somewhere? Perhaps here?

Flyers all-star Billy Barber saw what was happening and leaned over to Sutter.

"I heard your brother might be traded," he said.

"Do you know where?" Sutter asked.

"Here, I guess."

Ronnie couldn't believe it. Was his twin brother, Richie, really going to be traded from Pittsburgh to Philadelphia? That would be a dream come true. The two of them used to fantasize about playing together in the NHL. But for the dream to become reality, well . . .

As the bus pulled out of the Capital Centre, Sutter had a chance to reflect on the days when he and Richie played together in the juniors. Just like their older brothers before them, the twins played two years at Red Deer in the Alberta Junior League, then traveled to Lethbridge in the Western Hockey League for another two-year stint.

And again, just like their four older hockey-playing brothers, Ron and Rich opened a few eyes during their last full season at Lethbridge. In 1981-82, Ronnie totaled 92 points in only 59 games while serving 207 minutes in the penalty box. Richie was less productive offensively, but more feisty. He recorded 69 points and amassed 263 penalty minutes.

Because the Sutter reputation was already firmly established in the NHL, the twins were considered top prospects in the 1982 draft. Sure enough, Ronnie was the fourth player chosen overall, the highest pick of any Sutter brother. Richie had to wait only six more selections before the Penguins grabbed him.

The two were overjoyed with being drafted so high, but were also surprised by the teams that selected them.

"I was thinking Washington," said Ron. "They even faxed me a newspaper article that said they were going to draft me. I wasn't disappointed that I was picked by Philadelphia, but I have to admit I always hated them when I was growing up. Those were the bully days of the mid-'70s, and I didn't respect that style of hockey."

"I thought I was going to Calgary," said Rich. "They had taken me out to dinner before the draft. I even took physicals for them. But when their time came up at the draft, they took a timeout and made a big trade."

Next thing Richie knew he was heading to the city of steel. He and Ronnie parted ways for the first time in their lives. They had never been split up in their 18-and-a-half years. They were as inseparable as, well, twins. And now, just 16 months after being forced apart by the draft, it appeared they were about to be reunited once again.

After arriving back home in Philly late that night, Ron was dozing off when the phone suddenly rang. He looked at the clock: "2:00." Two o'clock in the damn morning? Who the hell could this be?

"Hello?" a groggy Ron Sutter answered.

"Hey, Ronnie. Were you sleeping?"

"Richie?"

"Yeah. I know it's late, but I had to call to see if you had heard what happened," said Rich.

"No. What's up?"

"I'm coming to Philadelphia! Can you believe it? I'm coming to Philadelphia!"

"No way," Ron said in disbelief. Sure, he had heard the rumors on the bus, but he refused to acknowledge them. Trade rumors abound in the NHL, and most rumored deals never materialize. Why would this one be any different?

"I'm serious!" said Rich, barely able to hold back his enthusiasm. "My plane gets into Philly in the morning, and I need you to pick me up. I'm supposed to be dressed for tomorrow night's game."

Just like kids on Christmas Eve, Ronnie and Richie were too excited to sleep very soundly that night. But the twins were so pumped-up about becoming teammates once again, their rush of adrenaline more than made up for any loss of shuteye.

As if writing their own fairy tale, the Sutter brothers each scored a goal in their first game together in the National Hockey League, as the Flyers beat the Maple Leafs 8-5. For Richie, it was a bonus because it was his first NHL goal. The very next game, Richie scored the game winner in leading the Flyers past the Quebec Nordiques 4-2. The story line was syrupy beyond toleration.

The twins enjoyed moderate success during the 1983-84 season. Ron racked up 19 goals and 32 assists, while Rich tallied 16 goals and 12 assists. The two established themselves as grinding, hard-working players who took great pride in skating back to help out in their own zone. Indeed, they proved worthy of the Sutter name.

However, the playoffs were disastrous once again. The Flyers were eliminated in the first round for the third year in a row. With nine consecutive losses in playoff games, the Flyers were quickly developing a reputation as postseason flops. In a sport where the regular season means virtually nothing, Philadelphia had become one of the worst teams in the league. The Broad Street Bullies had become the Broad Street Bambies.

In 1984-85, the Flyers again tore through the regular season, winning 53 games and finishing with 113 points. It marked the

12th time in 13 years that Philadelphia had accumulated at least 95 points.

This time, though, they didn't stumble in the playoffs. They cruised to the Stanley Cup finals where they ran into the defending champ Edmonton Oilers. Unfortunately for Philly, the Flyers' defense was no match for Gretzky and Company as the Oilers averaged more than four goals a game in beating the Flyers in four of five contests.

The next season proved to be another postseason disaster. After finishing the regular season with 110 points, second only to the Oilers' 119, the Flyers inexplicably lost again in the first round of the playoffs. Despite being one of the NHL's elite teams, at least during the regular season, Philly had been unable to advance past the first round in four of the last five years.

Richie and Ronnie returned to their homes in Lethbridge for the summer. Like their teammates, the twins were frustrated over the team's ineptness in the playoffs. Was there something about the month of April that caused the Flyers to go into hibernation? While nature was coming to life again, why were they always turning cold and dying? Even Mike Keenan, the team's fiery and obstinate second-year coach, proved unable to solve the Flyers' annual April swoon.

However, the Sutter twins could take pleasure in at least one bright spot from their first-round departure in 1986. The two were lined together with Rich Tocchet, a bruising second-year forward who had racked up 284 penalty minutes during the regular season. In the playoffs, their line was the top-scoring trio on the team.

"Our line did very well," said Ron. "We couldn't wait to get back and start the year again."

Sorry, but that wasn't going to happen. Just weeks after retreating to his farm north of the border, Rich was informed he was no longer needed in Philadelphia. He was now the property of the Vancouver Canucks. The same Canucks who had skated to just two winning seasons in their 16-year history. The same Canucks who weren't even invited to the playoffs for seven of those years. The same Canucks who advanced past the first round of the playoffs only once.

Sure, the Flyers couldn't seem to get past the first round, but at least they were given a fighting chance. The Canucks, on the other hand, were perpetually stuck in neutral with no other gear apparently available.

"It was really, really tough," remembers Rich. "It was so disappointing because we were so set on getting back to Philadelphia."

The twins were pried apart once again. They had been fortunate to play together in the NHL. But to join forces again in the future seemed doubtful. The chances of it happening the first time had been slim, but a second time? Forget it.

Over the next several years, Richie languished on a team that continued to be the doormat of the Smythe Division. Vancouver qualified for postseason play just once in Sutter's stay there. In 1988-89, the Canucks nearly became the surprise team of the playoffs, taking the Calgary Flames to overtime in the seventh game of their first-round series. However, the Flames squeaked by with a 4-3 win on their way to the Stanley Cup. The upstart Canucks had played valiantly against a much more talented team, but their rare appearance in the playoffs still lasted only seven games.

The following year, the Canucks again were mired in last place and heading toward another no-show in the playoffs. Trade rumors abounded. And it seemed the name that kept popping up was Rich Sutter's. His offensive production had taken a nosedive from 42 points in his first year with Vancouver to 18 in 62 games during the 1989-90 season.

"I had heard so much about a trade for two months," said Rich. "I didn't know where I was going to go or if I was going to go."

On the morning of March 6, 1990, Rich's wife, Rhonda, was listening to the radio when a stunning announcement was made.

"The Canucks have made a deal with the St. Louis Blues," said the sportscaster. "Vancouver sends forward Rich Sutter, defenseman Harold Snepsts, and a second-round draft pick to St. Louis for defenseman Adrien Plavsic and two draft choices."

Rhonda couldn't believe it. Why hadn't her husband called her? Why did she have to hear it on the radio first?

Simple. Someone in the Canucks' front office leaked the information to the media before Richie was even informed of the trade. Sutter was pulled out of morning practice and told of his departure to St. Louis well after his wife had heard it on the radio.

Reporters flocked to Pacific Coliseum to get reaction from Sutter about ending his nearly four-year stay in Vancouver. What they saw was a stunned hockey player. He was dejected. He was virtually speechless. He had tears in his eyes.

The media quickly went to work, writing and broadcasting that Rich Sutter was unhappy with the trade. Some reporters opined that Rich was unwilling to play for his older brother Brian, the second-year coach of the Blues.

As it turned out, Richie was indeed upset. Not with the trade, but with the reporting of the trade. He said he was not unhappy going to St. Louis, especially since his good friend, Harold Snepsts, was going along for the ride. Sutter explained the media misinterpreted his feelings.

"The media don't understand when things like that happen, and that's what really pisses me off," said Rich. "How would you like it if you were traded, and ten minutes later people were sticking cameras and microphones in your face and asking, 'How do you feel?' You don't even give a guy a chance to sit down and think about it a little bit."

Meanwhile, Brian Sutter was forced to answer his own critics back home, many of whom accused him of nepotism. Richie was considered a hard-working player with marginal offensive skills. Wasn't there someone better the Blues could've acquired? Probably, scoffed Brian's antagonists, but he just wanted one of his brothers here.

Rich Sutter probably wished the trade had not been made, at least in the beginning. Brian treated his younger brother like his worst enemy. He yelled and screamed at him. He pointed accusatory fingers at him. He worked him like a mule.

The reasons were simple. Reporters, fans, and even players were watching very closely how the two brothers interacted. Brian wasn't about to coddle Richie. One glancing smile or arm around the shoulder could spell mistrust in the locker room.

"It's definitely harder on one of my brothers being here that it is on me, because there are assholes pointing fingers," Brian said. "I don't spend any more time with them than I do with any other player. I don't go out to bars with my brothers. I don't go out to eat with them. I don't have them over for supper.

"I was harder on Richie because, as a family, we expected more of ourselves than anyone else. We expected a lot of each other."

But Brian went a little overboard, expecting a bit too much from his younger sibling. Harold Snepsts, one of Brian's chief antagonists during Sutter's playing days, couldn't bite his tongue any longer. Shortly after Harold and Richie were traded to the Blues, Snepsts marched into the coach's office to give his former foe a chewing out.

"You leave him alone!" barked Snepsts, pointing a finger at Brian's face. "You leave Richie alone, and just let him go out and play hard for you, because he'll always be there for you."

Message accepted. After suspicions faded away and people began to tolerate a team with two Sutters, Richie was allowed to go out and play without the coach tanning his hide at every turn.

In his first full season with the Blues, 1990-91, the right winger was teamed with center Bob Bassen and left winger Dave Lowry. The three grinders formed one of the most respected and exciting checking lines in the league. That line itself was worth the price of admission. They became the Blues' trademark of good old-fashioned, hard-nosed, "in-your-face" hockey. Richie scored 16 goals that year, the third-highest total of his career, and added six points in the playoffs, double the number he had tallied in any previous playoff year.

However, just when everyone thought the Sutter-bashers were safely locked away, they re-appeared with a new vengeance on September 22, 1991, when another Sutter took up residence at the Arena. The critics were given even more fodder when the new guy was awarded an "A" as the team's alternate captain.

But when Ron Sutter arrived in St. Louis, he brought with him an understanding of how some people would react. He was prepared for it, and let the criticism roll right down his No. 22.

"I really didn't have any problems when I came here because Richie helped me prepare," said Ron. "Even before I was traded, Richie gave me an idea what the relationship was like between the players, himself, and the coaches."

Sounds good. But don't the players privately grumble about the abundance of Sutters on the team?

"I haven't heard anything. If there are guys who are uncomfortable about it, then they're insecure about their own jobs. I've played in the NHL for nine years. You can't tell me I don't know how to play this game. I didn't get traded here because I'm a

Sutter. Richie and I got traded here because we're ingredients the Blues hope will help them win."

Fair enough. But what about playing for your older brother? Doesn't he single you out when things are going bad?

"Sure, Brian's had to kick me in the rear a few times, and I obviously deserved it. He's always stressed to me, 'Don't be an example, set an example.' That's one of the nice things about having your brother as a coach. You know what's expected of you every time you come to the rink."

Contrary to what his critics think, Brian insists he would trade one of the twins in a heartbeat if it meant improving the team.

"If a trade came up where we felt we could upgrade our hockey club," explains Brian, "and we had to trade Richie or Ronnie, I would say yes without hesitation. It comes down to business. We have to win."

So the three Sutters have managed to dodge most of the poison arrows flung their way. Occasionally, a scathing newspaper article will penetrate their thick coat of armor and strike a nerve. They are not insensitive to criticism. But for the most part, the Sutter brothers have learned to put the blinders on, stare straight ahead, and bust their tails in an all-out assault on success. The lessons they learned growing up in Viking, Alberta, were still being put to good use in St. Louis, Missouri.

*   *   *

"Here we go, here we go! Let's go, boys! Here we go!"

Brian Sutter was yelling encouragement to his players at the start of the Thanksgiving night game at home against Quebec. Not counting an exhibition match against the USA Olympic Team, the Blues hadn't played in five days dating back to their 3-0 loss at home to the Rangers on November 23. Sutter was hoping to give thanks for an inspired effort despite the weeklong break.

Just two days earlier, the Blues had shed yet another member of the successful 1990-91 team. Mario Marois became the 15th player to leave St. Louis in eight months. Paul Cavallini's return from a knee injury and Lee Norwood's recent acquisition from Hartford left Ron Caron no choice but to find a new home for one of his defensemen. He sent Marois to Winnipeg for future considerations, ridding the team of a $225,000 salary and 33 years in age.

The Nordiques came to St. Louis lugging a dismal 5-16-2 record, second worst in the league to the expansion San Jose Sharks. But the Nords had suddenly turned respectable since general manager Pierre Page had fired coach Dave Chambers and taken his place. Quebec had lost only twice in five games under its new head coach.

For Brian Sutter, this was the scariest kind of contest. His team had not played in awhile and hadn't tasted victory in eight days. An offensive-minded squad with nothing to lose comes to town, hoping to take the home team out of its game plan. The next matchup is much more important, a game against the Red Wings, who have trounced the Blues in three previous meetings. There is always the danger of looking past an inferior team and ahead to a divisional rival, where the stakes are much higher.

The game against the Nordiques had all the ingredients of an upset. Sutter talked to his players until he was red in the face about the importance of this contest against Quebec. After playing the Nords and Wings at home, the Blues had to travel for six of their next seven games. They had to accumulate victories while they could.

"You talk to them, and you talk to them," said Sutter. "But sometimes it just doesn't register."

At first, it seemed as if both teams had gorged on a little too much turkey and dressing. The Blues and Nordiques were uninspired the first eight minutes of the game. The only excitement for the standing-room-only crowd of 17,960 came from the dance routines performed by the San Diego Chicken.

Ironically, it took a holding penalty on Rick Zombo with less than seven minutes to play for the Blues to finally come alive. The Blues' penalty-killing was ranked a woeful 18th in the league, succeeding just 79.9 percent of the time. But on this power play, they made the Nordiques look silly. Every time Quebec carried the puck into the Blues' zone, it was swatted right back down the ice. The penalty-killers barely broke a sweat. Curtis Joseph could have knitted himself a new jersey.

After Zombo emerged from the penalty box, the Blues launched an all-out assault on Quebec goaltender Ron Tugnutt.

Each line represented a different wave of attack. They knocked over defensemen and buzzed the net. Tugnutt's neck must have turned to rubber after watching the puck whiz by him time and time again.

With a little more than three minutes left in the period, Quebec defenseman Craig Wolanin took a pass in his own end and started backpedaling as Brett Hull rushed in to forecheck. Suddenly, Wolanin slipped and fell, allowing the Golden Brett to steal the puck and race unmolested to the net. He quickly wristed a shot that grazed Tugnutt's left skate before hitting the back of the net. Hull's 19th goal of the year put the Blues up 1-0.

A one-goal lead after the first period is usually nothing to celebrate. But for the Blues, it marked a milestone of sorts. It was the first time in 11 games they scored the first goal. Not since Hull put the Blues up early against Vancouver on November 1, an eventual 3-2 win, had St. Louis lit the red lamp first.

In the locker room following the first period, the players encouraged one another to keep up the effort. They had just played one of their better opening periods of the year but had only a one-goal lead to show for it.

Sure enough, the Blues continued the onslaught in the second. A little more than two minutes into the period, Ron Sutter coasted into the Quebec zone along the far boards. With no one on him, Sutter was patient, holding the puck while he slowly drifted into the right circle.

Suddenly, like a bolt of lightning, Nelson Emerson dashed into the picture, heading straight toward the net. Sutter coolly passed the puck toward the goal crease, where it was punched in by Emerson right between Tugnutt's pads. The lamp went on, the siren sounded, and Ernie Hays broke into his obligatory rendition of "When the Saints Come Marching In." For the first time since a 6-5 victory over the Bruins on October 24, a span of 15 games, the Blues had jumped to a 2-0 lead.

A couple of minutes later, the Chicken unveiled a poster of a beautiful model in a nearly-invisible bikini. The woman was breathtakingly gorgeous. Her air-brush artist didn't miss a stroke.

The Chicken was standing in the first row directly behind the Blues' goal, pointing the poster toward the ice. The Blues' feathered friend was obviously trying to distract the Nordiques, who were engaging in one of their few offensive assaults. The

Chicken had apparently used this technique before. Whether coincidental or not, the plan worked.

A second after Curtis Joseph pounced on a loose puck, Quebec's John Kordic, a tough-guy right winger playing for his fourth team in as many years, inexplicably forgot his brakes and ran into Joseph after play had stopped. (Was he perhaps looking elsewhere?) Without hesitating, Blues enforcer Darin Kimble dropped his gloves and lunged at Kordic. They punched, shoved, grabbed, poked, and tangled for fifty seconds, an enormously long time for a hockey fight. By then the two goons were so exhausted they just stood in an embrace, patiently waiting for a linesman to step in and separate them. Both were led to the penalty box as the holiday crowd gave thanks for the game's first and only fight. Meanwhile, an overgrown bird with large webbed feet rolled up his poster and quietly retreated to another section of the Arena.

Ten minutes into the second period, the Nordiques were handed their fourth power-play opportunity when Brendan Shanahan was whistled for slashing. The first three chances had been embarrassingly ineffective; this one proved even worse.

Thanks to a lack of forechecking, Quebec was unable to control the puck for long in the Blues' zone. A minute into the penalty, Bob Bassen grabbed hold of a loose puck near his own net and immediately skated up-ice. As soon as he crossed into the neutral zone, he fired the puck ahead to Rich Sutter, who had sneaked past a sleeping Dan Lambert. Sutter raced in alone. He quickly flipped the puck from his forehand to his backhand to his forehand before nudging it past Tugnutt to give the Blues a 3-0 lead on a short-handed goal.

"Yeah!!" Sutter yelled with his hands punched into the air.

"Great pass, Bass!" shouted Sutter as he and Bassen embraced for a post-goal hug. On the play, Joseph was awarded his fourth assist of the year, tying him with Mike Liut for the team record for goaltenders. With 56 games left, Joseph was a cinch to obliterate the eight-year-old mark.

The frenzied crowd had barely had a chance to sit down when the Blues struck again on the power play. It was a vintage Adam Oates set-up, the kind that every Blues fan had come to expect from their all-star center.

As Oates controlled the puck along the right boards, he looked at Hull, who had positioned himself in the slot. Closely watching Oates' eyes, Quebec's Mike Hough left his post in front of the net to block the anticipated pass to Hull. Still staring at the Golden Brett, Oates fired a no-look pass across the crease to Shanahan, who was expertly positioned at the near left post. He easily re-directed the puck into the net to give the Blues a 4-0 advantage. That's one great thing about having a guy like Brett Hull on your team. The opposition is so aware of his presence, it sometimes forgets about the other players on the ice.

After feasting on Quebec for two periods, St. Louis, a bit sluggish in the third period, was outshot 12-4 and outscored 2-1. But for a game that had all the trappings of a poor showing, the team was pleased with its 5-2 victory.

"We had a bad third period," said Hull. "But it was just one of those games where you come out with a win and you're happy."

Jeff Brown agreed. "We were flat in the third period," he said. "Against some teams we would've been in trouble. We were fortunate to be up by four."

However, pummeling one of the worst teams in the league is one thing. Beating the NHL's hottest club is quite another. Two nights after the Quebec game, the Detroit Red Wings came to town riding a ten-game unbeaten streak, their longest in 36 years.

The Wings were flying atop the Norris Division with 31 points, six ahead of the second-place Blues. Detroit was bigger, faster, and much more talented up the middle. They sported three of the game's best centers in Steve Yzerman, Sergei Fedorov, and Jimmy Carson. Under the tutelage of head coach Bryan Murray, the Red Wings were fast becoming one of the top two or three teams in the NHL. It was an incredible turnaround for a franchise rich in tradition, but poor in recent performance.

The Detroit Red Wings had joined the National Hockey League in its infancy, 1926. After struggling during their first decade of existence, the Wings won back-to-back Stanley Cups in 1936 and 1937, and added five more Cups over the next 20 years.

However, after losing to the Canadiens in the 1966 finals, the Red Wings suddenly collapsed. The next year they missed the playoffs for only the third time in 29 years. The early departure was rare at the time, but it was something the team would get used to over the next two decades.

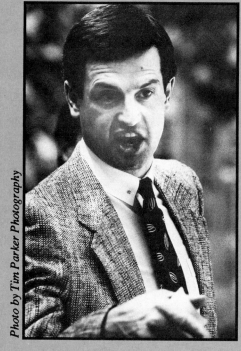

◄ **BRIAN SUTTER**
Brian Sutter did a lot of explaining in the end, but it wasn't enough to save his job.

BOB PLAGER ➤
Bob Plager has been given the task of coaching the Blues into their second quarter-century.

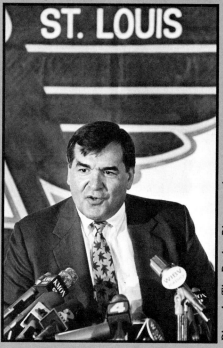

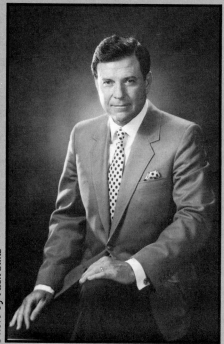

◄ **MIKE SHANAHAN**
Team chairman Mike Shanahan saved the team in 1986 and quickly became one of the most respected and revered citizens of St. Louis.

JACK QUINN ◄
A member of the Blues management staff since 1983, Jack Quinn has survived two ownership changes and four different coaches.

BARCLAY PLAGER ➤
His courageous battle with cancer stirred the entire community.

◄ **RON CARON**
One of the NHL's most successful wheeler dealers, Ron Caron's insight seems almost mystical.

Brett Hull ➤
Another 70-goal season, and the honor of wearing the "C" made Brett show off his million-dollar smile.

Photo by Tim Parker Photography

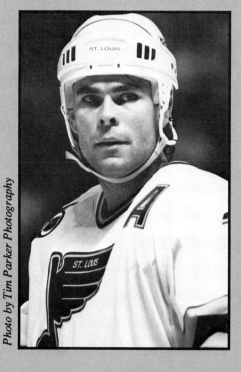

Photo by Tim Parker Photography

◄ Adam Oates
Adam Oates demanded more money from the Blues, but only got a one-way ticket to Boston.

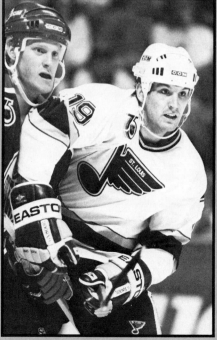

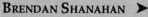

Brendan Shanahan ➤
Caught in the middle of the Scott Stevens controversy, Brendan Shanahan managed 33 goals and was "rewarded" with a multi-million dollar contract.

Photo by Tim Parker Photography

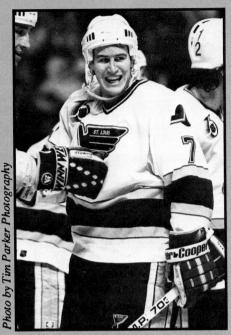

◄ **NELSON EMERSON**
With his blazing speed and dazzling moves, Emerson became a fan favorite and a symbol of the team's youth movement.

BOB BASSEN ►
Bob Bassen played with his usual intensity but, like his fellow Green Berets, couldn't capture the magic touch from the year before.

◄ **RICH AND RON SUTTER**
Rich and Ron were reunited once again, much to the displeasure of Sutter-bashers who cried nepotism.

CRAIG JANNEY ➤
Craig Janney was the center of attention after arriving in St. Louis, but he disappeared in the playoffs.

◄ **CURTIS JOSEPH**
Curtis Joseph made more saves than any goalie in the NHL, and could be on his way to superstardom.

BRETT HULL ➤
Even though he led the league in goals for the third straight year, Hull's season was one of frustration, losing two friends to Boston while losing the support of some fans for his outspoken candor.

▲ *Unfortunately, celebrations like this one were too few during the Blues' silver anniversary season (left to right: Murray Baron, Garth Butcher, Rich Sutter, Gino Cavallini, and Bob Bassen).*

GARTH BUTCHER ➤
As team captain, Garth Butcher took a lot of heat for not playing up to the standards of Scott Stevens.

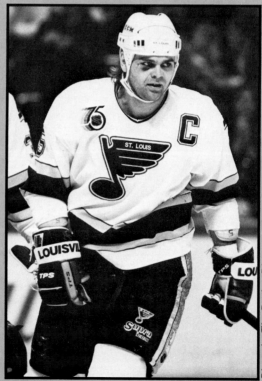

◄ **JUDGE HOUSTON**
Defending his decision on Scott Stevens, Judge Houston said Ron Caron didn't do his homework, calling Caron's presentation "not one of the best I've seen."

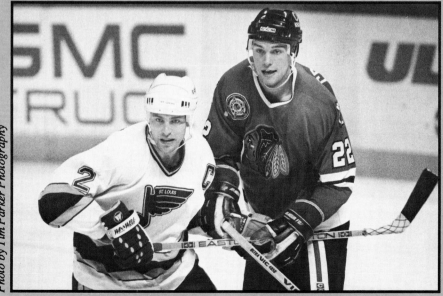

▲ **SCOTT STEVENS**
Guarding Chicago's Adam Creighton, now with the Islanders.

▲ *Close friends Brett Hull and Adam Oates enjoying a round of golf.*

▲ BRETT HULL
Showing the form that has made him one of the greatest scorers in NHL history.

From 1967 through 1983, a span of 17 seasons, the Red Wings made the playoffs only twice, and both of those years, 1970 and '78, they were retired after the first round. No other organization in history, not even the expansion teams, had such a long streak of futility.

The Red Wings had missed post-season play only twice since 1983, but they had been anything but world beaters. Since then, the Wings had finished with a winning record only once going into the 1991-92 season and had advanced past the first round of the playoffs just twice. In fact, when the Blues sent the Wings packing after the first round of the 1991 playoffs, there was no reason to suspect that the team from the "Pizza Capital of the World" would be any more powerful the following year.

Sure enough, the Wings were sluggish when the gates opened to begin the season. They won only six of their first 15 games, and most hockey observers figured they were headed for another uninspiring season.

But their 10-3 trashing of the Blues in game 16 started an avalanche of success that swallowed everything in its path. Suddenly, the Red Wings went from mediocre to magnificent, from awful to awesome, from uninspired to unstoppable. They jumped from fourth to first in just 12 days and forced every other team in the league to take notice.

When the Wings came knocking on the Arena door November 30, they brought with them a package of confidence and aplomb so large they could barely fit into the place. Not only had it been 25 days since the Red Wings had tasted defeat, they had thoroughly embarrassed the Blues in three previous meetings by a combined score of 22-10. The Peoria Rivermen would have been a tougher test.

Still, Coach Brian Sutter wasn't about to admit his team was inferior. Breaking down the three losses to Detroit, Sutter conceded defeat in only one.

"The first time we were in there, we certainly didn't play as well as we could have," Sutter said. "The second time, everything went into the net for them. Last time, they were on a roll. We played well enough to win the hockey game, but we didn't."

Fair enough. But a team doesn't get points for playing well. Only for scoring at least as many goals as the opposition. And so far, the final scores hadn't been close.

Detroit had scored the game's first two goals en route to each rout. Sutter knew that to beat the Wings tonight, his team had to score first, or at the very least keep the game close.

"We've got some ideas," explained Sutter before the game. "We're going to clog up the middle. We'll just have to see if we're ready to do it."

Indeed they were. It was as if trainer Mike Folga had secretly erased the past Detroit games from the Blues' memory banks. They forgot who they were playing.They obviously didn't realize they were supposed to fall flat on their faces again tonight.

After the Blues killed off two penalties in the game's first six minutes, they went on a forechecking rampage. They built a brick wall along the Wings' blue line, not letting the puck escape the offensive zone. Detroit was scurrying around its own end, desperately trying to catch the elusive piece of rubber.

The Wings got a bit frustrated, and at 8:32, Vladimir Konstantinov tripped Ron Sutter as he was skating behind the Wings' net. The Blues were given their first power play, and they wasted little time taking advantage of it.

Adam Oates and Kevin Miller battled for a faceoff to the left of Detroit goalie Tim Cheveldae. Neither could get his stick on the puck right away, so Oates used his left skate to kick it back to Brett Hull. The Golden Brett took one step around Steve Chiasson, took two more strides to the net, and fired a shot into the lower left corner. For the first time in four tries against the Wings, the Blues had netted the first goal.

Thirty seconds later, Chiasson was called for interference, and the Blues were on the power play once again. And just like the last one, the home team worked it to perfection.

Oates, who had assisted on the last goal, controlled the puck at the right point. Seeing no one open down low, he slid it across to Lee Norwood at the left point. Norwood, who possesses a rocket of a shot, launched a missile that beat Cheveldae on the far side. There was no one screening the goalie. The shot, plain and simple, outmuscled him.

The teams traded golden scoring opportunities the last half of the period. The difference was the goaltending: Curtis Joseph was sharp, Cheveldae was not. As in most games so far this year, the Blues were being outshot. But the outstanding work between the pipes by Joseph was the reason the Blues were up by two.

They made it three just as the first period was about to end. With less than thirty seconds left to play, Hull picked up a loose puck near his own blue line and raced down right wing. Dave Christian darted down the left side. Defenseman Brad McCrimmon was the only man standing in their way.

In the neutral zone, the two Blues crisscrossed, Hull changing direction toward the left boards and Christian heading straight toward the net. As McCrimmon started to float toward him, Hull passed the puck straight across to Christian, who backhanded it over Cheveldae's stick. The Blues were up 3-0 and well on their way to exorcising their past demonic performances against Detroit.

Thanks to an expertly-placed shot into the lower left corner by Detroit's Ray Sheppard, the Red Wings finally got on the scoreboard 2:30 into the second period. But for Blues' pessimists in attendance, there would be no breakdown tonight.

Halfway through the period, with the Blues on the power play, Adam Oates caught a Kevin Miller clearing pass. Oates immediately dropped the puck to his feet and slid a pass to a wide-open Hull in the left circle. Hull one-timed a shot that rocketed past Cheveldae, who never had a chance. The Blues had three power plays, and had scored three power-play goals. Perfect.

The Blues and Red Wings each scored two more goals in the second, including Hull's third to complete his eleventh career hat trick with the Blues, tying Bernie Federko's team record.

St. Louis iced the game in the third, thanks to tight checking, solid goaltending, and Rich Sutter's determination. With a little more than five minutes left in the game, Sutter tore down the ice on a breakaway. He had scored on a breakaway two nights earlier against Quebec and was looking for another.

However, Cheveldae made a wonderful, sprawling save by throwing his left leg high into the air. Sutter chased the puck behind the net, only to be squashed by Bob Probert and Dennis Vial. Nonetheless, Richie managed to stick the puck back out front, where Bob Bassen easily flipped it over Cheveldae's right shoulder.

Despite being outshot 40-30, a statistic that was becoming all too familiar, the Blues grounded the Wings 7-3. It didn't make up for the embarrassing trio of games earlier in the year, but it certainly gave the Blues confidence that they could not only compete with the league's hottest team, but obliterate them. The Blues stopped Detroit's ten-game unbeaten streak and moved within four points of first place.

With the close of November, the Blues finished the first two months of the season with an 11-9-5 mark. They were coming off two brilliantly played games in which they had dominated the opposition. Were they finally turning the corner after seven weeks of uninspired hockey? Or would this be nothing more than a blip in an otherwise dismal season?

The Blues were about to find out. The team was a dreadful 2-6-3 on the road, and the month of December was full of away games. Nine of the 13 contests in the upcoming month were away from that nice, cozy barn on Oakland Avenue.

"We can't use the excuse anymore that we have new faces," admitted Ron Sutter.

"Last year we always won the 2-1, 3-2 games because we were best at that," said twin brother, Rich. "There was always someone on the bench saying, 'I'm going to do it. I'm going to be the difference.' But the first month and a half this year, we were waiting to see who was going to step forward and do it first."

There was no time to wait anymore. With December overflowing with road games, the Blues were either going to start the New Year on a roll, or be forced to pick themselves up from the depths of the Norris Division standings.

Chapter Nine

THE GREEN BERETS

Dave Lowry just sat there. Motionless. Staring straight ahead. He felt his heart sinking to the lower depths of his stomach. He listened carefully to the words of Brian Sutter. And he felt numb. The words hit him like a puck between the eyes. Without mincing his metaphors, Coach Sutter informed Lowry he was playing like horse manure. He might as well pack his bags if he didn't improve. At best, he'd be banished to the pressbox; heck, there was a good chance he was going to Peoria.

For God's sake, Peoria? As in the minor leagues? Lowry suddenly felt about two inches tall. After starring for the Blues the last two years as one of the most talented checking left wingers in the league, Lowry suddenly faced the possibility of a demotion some 35 games into the 1991-92 season.

"He told me he wasn't happy with the way I was playing," said Lowry. "That sent a message. It hit home. It brings you back to reality."

And reality had been very unkind to Dave Lowry during the first two-and-a-half months of the year. After back-to-back 19-goal seasons, Lowry had put just two pucks into the net this year. There was no way Sutter would really send him to Peoria. Lowry would have to clear waivers first, and teams would be lining up to claim him. Still, the message was excruciatingly painful. The only thing lower than his stats was his confidence. It was Vancouver all over again. And the memories were depressing and tortuous.

Lowry was a sixth-round draft pick of the Canucks in 1983. He signed in the summer of '85 after two productive years at London in the Ontario Hockey League where he scored 196 points in 127 games. After inking his name to a contract, the 20-year-old Ottawa native made the Canucks in just his first training camp. Lowry never went to the minors, a rare feat indeed.

Canucks then-head coach Tom Watt was one of Lowry's biggest fans. He was enamored with Lowry's defense-minded approach to the game. The lanky left winger played tough. He played physical. And he played with unlimited emotion. He was a coach's dream and an opposing player's nightmare. It was hard to believe a guy with the nickname of "Pie" could be such a menace on the ice.

Lowry was given the name when he played at London and, no, it wasn't because he loved to devour home-cooked pies. It was just because he looked like he had.

"I had a little extra baggage, 16 percent body fat," said Lowry, now sporting a thin frame. "I played with Jimmy Sandlak at London when they called me 'Pieface.' We both ended up in Vancouver and he called me 'Pie' once there, and the name just stuck. It's followed me around since."

Pie, er, Dave, appeared in 73 games his first year with the Canucks, 1985-86, racking up just 18 points but establishing himself as a defensive forward with tons of potential. His job was to keep the opposing team's top line in check, and Lowry performed admirably. It was a thankless task, the kind that earned no headlines but plenty of respect from teammates and coaches.

Lowry scored only 18 points again in his second year, but increased his penalty minutes to 176. He was completely dedicated to the physical, defensive side of hockey. Tom Watt loved that about his young player. Watt's replacement did not.

After the 1986-87 season, the Canucks made wholesale changes at the top. The new management staff of Pat Quinn and Brian Burke told Watt to get lost and promptly hired Bob McCammon as the organization's tenth head coach in 18 years. The new alignment was the beginning of the end for Dave Lowry. He lasted only ten games into the '87-88 season before being sent down to Vancouver's top farm club in Fredericton, New Brunswick for his first taste of the minor leagues.

"They told me I was only a one-dimensional player, a defensive player," recalled Lowry. "They said if I wanted to stay and play in this league I had to go down and work on my offense."

And work on it he did. In 46 games at Fredericton, he tallied 45 points and earned just 59 penalty minutes. He had effectively increased his value as an offensive player, while lessening his image as a rugged, in-your-face defensive skater. But as it turned out, his change in play didn't mean a thing. Canucks management had already made up its mind about Lowry. He would never stick in the NHL. The only thing he was doing was taking up space.

At training camp the following season, McCammon called Lowry and several of his seldom-used teammates into his office.

"The waiver draft is coming up in a few days," explained McCammon. "We're going to leave you unprotected so any team can pick you up if they want. If no one selects you, be ready to report to Milwaukee (the Canucks' new minor league team)."

So it had come to this. After showing such promise under Tom Watt, Lowry was suddenly a piece of junk under Bob McCammon. The change of opinion on Lowry's playing ability had less to do with his talent than with a different coaching philosophy. It happens all the time in sports. One day, a guy is a team's most valuable player, and the next day under a new coaching staff he's worthless.

Perhaps the best example of this applies to Brett Hull. Under Terry Crisp at Calgary, Hull couldn't do anything right. He was lazy, pudgy, and soft. He didn't take himself or the game seriously, and that irked Crisp to no end. Hull appeared to have a scorer's touch, but Crisp wasn't about to waste his time on a kid with a famous last name and little else. He shipped him off to St. Louis (Ron Caron should be shipped to the Hall of Fame for this one), where, under the tutelage of Brian Sutter, he has only become the greatest scorer in the game today, and one of the best ever.

Lowry and four teammates were left home when the Canucks left on a five-game exhibition tour. They were told they had ice time at the University of British Columbia in Vancouver. It was a chance for the guys to stay in shape with the waiver draft coming up in a few days. They were either going to Milwaukee or to some other organization, but they were definitely going somewhere, and it was imperative to keep their legs fresh.

However, when Lowry arrived at the UBC rink, he couldn't believe his eyes. Had he made a wrong turn to get here? There, at one end of the rink, was a group of Japanese men trying to skate. It would have been funny if it hadn't been so dispiriting.

"We thought maybe we were going to share the ice with the University team," said Lowry. "But it was actually a Japanese exchange program. These guys were just learning to play hockey. We stayed at one end and they stayed at the other. I was thinking my playing days were almost over."

Unfortunately, the situation only worsened the next day. Lowry and his gang of vagabonds decided to let the Japanese have the college rink, instead skating at the Canucks' regular practice rink since the team was out of town.

There they found more unfamiliar faces. A group of big, burly men had invaded the practice facility, leaving Lowry scratching his head wondering what the hell was going on. He approached one of the men and asked if there was a chance they'd be leaving soon.

"Not for awhile," was the reply. "We rent this ice every Friday morning at this time. But you're more than welcome to share it with us."

Terrific. It was a group of longshoremen from the nearby docks, and they had complete control of the rink. Despite being professional hockey players, there appeared to be no place in town the soon-to-be-former Canucks could skate in peace and quiet.

Lowry went home that afternoon in a deep depression. The waiver draft was Tuesday, four days away. The way his luck had been going, the only calls he was going to get were from the Japanese Olympic team or a group of longshoremen wondering if he could join their Friday hockey league.

"I need to take a nap," Dave told his wife, Elaine, after he walked in the door. "You might as well unplug the phone. I'm pretty tired, and I just want to sleep."

Fortunately, however, Elaine did not unplug the phone. Just 20 minutes after Dave lay down, the phone rang. It was Pat Quinn, informing him he had been traded to the Blues for Ernie Vargas. He wasn't going to Milwaukee, and he didn't have to wait for next week's waiver draft.

"I was ecstatic," Lowry said. "I was so excited I was going

to throw the phone through the roof." The same phone that was nearly unplugged just 20 minutes earlier.

Lowry immediately placed a call to his new general manager to thank him for resurrecting his career. Ron Caron informed Lowry that he had been trying to get him out of Vancouver for some time. Caron told his new player that he liked his work ethic and his physical style of play. Caron said the Blues were trying to build a team of solid, gritty competitors who understood the defensive part of the game. In other words, Caron sounded a lot like Tom Watt. And that was good news for Dave Lowry.

"It was really a positive conversation," Lowry said. "It was amazing that he knew everything about me. He read off stats. I was amazed by his knowledge. I thought, 'Holy smokes, how does this guy know this?' He really knows his players."

Lowry's enthusiasm was tempered somewhat when he first arrived in St. Louis. He was introduced to his new teammates and coaches at a "Meet the Blues" banquet just before the start of the 1988-89 season. But after eating, Blues director of scouting Ted Hampson informed Lowry he wouldn't be making the trip to Minnesota to start the year. He was going to Peoria instead.

"I guess I didn't have a very good dinner," Lowry joked. "But looking back on it, it was probably the best thing. It gave me a chance to go down and play and get my game where I wanted it. I got the confidence back I didn't have."

At the midway point of the season, however, Lowry was still languishing in the minors. He was averaging more than a point per game while a couple of his good buddies, Cliff Ronning and Tim Bothwell, had been called up to St. Louis. He couldn't understand why he had been left behind. Just a few months earlier, he was so excited about going to St. Louis, but the trade had done little to further his career. This was no different from Vancouver, after all.

During the Christmas break, Dave, Elaine, and nine-month-old Sarah made the long trek north to Milwaukee to visit some friends. The drive gave the Lowrys a chance to reflect on their past and contemplate their future. Dave was only 23 years old, hardly a worn-out old veteran. But if he had no future in hockey, it was time to make a decision now, while he was still young enough to change professions and start from scratch.

"I'm just going to play as hard as I can during these last few months of the season," Dave told his wife while driving to Milwaukee. "I'll try and get some points and play as well as I can. And if things don't work out, I can honestly say I gave it my best."

Lowry's agent said there was a chance he could get him on a European team if his career fizzled in North America. Lowry said he'd be interested, but he wanted to give it one last shot stateside.

Playing with new-found fire, Lowry went on a rampage in Peoria. He skated like Paul Coffey, hit like Bob Probert, and scored like Brett Hull. Well, maybe not quite, but you get the idea. Dave Lowry held true to his word and played every game as if it were his last. On February 20, 1989, nearly eight weeks after that soul-searching drive to Milwaukee, Lowry was called up to the parent club.

He played in the Blues' final 21 games, netting three goals and adding three assists. He didn't exactly set the world on fire, but he had the chance to get his feet wet in St. Louis and get to know the team's system so he wasn't going in blind when camp opened next fall.

Sure enough, the 1989-90 season proved to be Lowry's rebirth. He scored a career-high 19 goals and 25 points. He became one of the Blues' most tenacious forecheckers, forcing turnovers and creating scoring opportunities for his fellow "muckers."

"It was an exciting year," Lowry recalls. "I wanted to convince people that I belonged and deserved to be here. There was a lot of satisfaction in being told I couldn't play in this league and then just going out and proving them wrong."

Not that the league needed any more proof, but Lowry was even better in 1990-91. He again netted 19 goals, but this time he added a career-high 21 assists while racking up 168 penalty minutes, nearly 100 more than the year before. He even received some votes for the Selke Trophy, which is given to the league's top defensive forward.

After failing in Vancouver and struggling to stay in St. Louis, Dave Lowry was now on top of the world. A couple of years before, he had contemplated an end to his hockey career. Now, it seemed, his hockey career was just beginning. He had fine-tuned his offensive skills at no expense to his defensive responsibilities. He had become a fan favorite, and one of his biggest fans was Brian Sutter.

The Blues' coach put Lowry on a line with center Bob Bassen and right wing Rich Sutter. Together, they became known as the "Green Beret" line. Whenever the opposition threw out its top snipers, the Green Berets threw on their assault gear and took off after them. The results were devastatingly one-sided. The three checkers combined for 51 goals and 101 points. Lowry was a plus-19, meaning when he was on the ice, his line scored 19 more goals than it gave up, not counting power plays.

That last statistic is perhaps the most remarkable of all when you consider the Green Berets' primary purpose was to prevent the other team from scoring. Because they performed that task so well, they were able to create their own scoring chances by forechecking with reckless abandon, forcing turnovers, and finding the open man near the net. They also found themselves on numerous breakaways and two-on-one rushes after gaining control of the puck in their own end and then racing back the other way. Hull and Oates made the most noise, but it was the Green Berets who quietly set the tone.

"Hullie scored his 86 goals and we all looked at him as our hero," said Lowry. "But he looked at our line as being just as important. It was a case of everyone appreciating what everyone else was doing. It was a fun year."

But here in December 1991, the fun had stopped. Dave Lowry had gone from the penthouse to the outhouse again. Inexplicably, his scoring touch had vanished. It took him 19 games to score his first goal and another nine to score his second. Even the defensive side of Lowry's game, his trademark, had virtually disappeared, and he found himself at the bottom of the team's plus/minus rankings at minus-11.

"For David to be successful, he has to bang in the corners and force the other team to make mistakes," said Brian Sutter, hinting that his left winger was performing well below expectations.

Sutter was trying to find the right combinations among newcomers Nelson Emerson, Brendan Shanahan, Dave Christian, and Ron Sutter, and the odd man out seemed to be Lowry. Christian occasionally found himself in Lowry's old spot on the left side of the checking line. The former 19-goal scorer was relegated to killing penalties and little else. He moved around from line to line like a lost soul trying to recapture his past glory. In mid-December, he even started three games on the first line with Hull and Oates, a spot he had occasionally filled with success the year before. But even that change of scenery failed to resuscitate the 26-year-old left winger. In the School of Hard Knocks, Dave Lowry was valedictorian.

Suddenly, the Green Berets were nothing more than a distant memory, an old black and white movie long on romance but short on realism. Sutter occasionally put the old line back together, but it seldom lasted more than a scene or two. Somewhere, somehow, the script had changed.

"If we knew what the problem was, believe me, we'd fix it," said Bassen, equally frustrated that his old checking line had been disbanded.

"Last year, we got the breaks and bounces," said Lowry, trying to come up with even the slightest of reasons for his individual demise, as well as the breakup of the Green Berets. "I find that people are pressing a little more. And when you lose hockey games the pressure builds even more. It just seems like there's a wall or something behind the goalie."

The harder Lowry tried, the thicker that wall became. He became so obsessed with trying to score goals, he completely forgot his defensive responsibilities. His whole game was now out of alignment. And perhaps the only way to fine-tune his play was a visit to Peoria. A move there would not only shake him up personally, but perhaps it would light a fire under the team as a whole.

The message was deafening.

"No one likes to hear those comments and no one likes to be put in that situation," said Lowry. "I'm not playing well and maybe I need something to open my eyes."

Lowry's biggest enemy during all this was not his coach. It was himself. And he knew it. He became his own punching bag. While some people are motivated by criticism, others sink in it. And Lowry was drowning in a sea of self-doubt and uncertainty.

The Blues' media guide lists Lowry at 6'1", 195. The man is bigger than that, if only they could measure his heart. This lanky left-hander is arguably the most sensitive individual on the team, compassionate and full of sincerity. He is quick-witted and quick to befriend. He wears his heart for all to see. That's why darts of criticism sting Lowry so painfully. They easily penetrate.

After the Christmas break, the Blues beat the Blackhawks in St. Louis 3-1 and lost to the North Stars on the road 5-2. Their worst fears going into the month were realized. They were world beaters in their own rink, roadkill away from it. They won all four home games in December, improving their Arena record to a league-best 13-3-2. However, of their first eight road games in December, they won only two, 6-3 over the Sabres on the 11th and a 4-2 struggle against Quebec on the 14th. The Blues road record stood at a dismal 4-10-5.

Unfortunately, their last game of the month had to be on the road. Fortunately, it had to be in Buffalo, where they had picked up one of their rare road wins earlier in the month. It was New Year's Eve, a perfect opportunity to ring in 1992 on a winning note. The Blues had been slowly losing sight of first-place Detroit. The red-hot Red Wings had lost only two of their last 22 games and had opened a nine-point gap over the second-place Blues.

Guy Hebert was handed his third NHL start in goal and second in Buffalo. He was the winning netminder there a few weeks back, so the superstitious Brian Sutter wasn't about to tempt fate.

However, there was something missing on this particular night. Something was terribly out of place. The answer came as soon as the Blues skated onto the ice. No. 10 was absent.

Dave Lowry had been banished to the pressbox for the first time as a member of the St. Louis Blues. Pressbox now, Peoria later? Brian Sutter wasn't kidding around. When he told Lowry he wasn't happy with his play, he meant it. And sitting in the rafters wearing a suit and tie was proof of Sutter's displeasure. It was one thing to sit with a group of athletic wanna-bes when you're injured. It's quite another to sit up there when you're healthy. And Dave Lowry was very healthy, at least physically. His emotional makeup was taking a real beating, however.

"Your mind is such a powerful element," said Lowry. "You start doubting yourself. You're sitting in the pressbox for a reason, and it's because you're not playing well. You feel that maybe the team's losing confidence in you, and you start to lose confidence in yourself."

The Blues played extremely well against the Sabres, one of their best road games of the year. They returned to their tight, defense-minded style of hockey and led Buffalo 2-1 after two periods. Lowry's fellow muckers, Gino Cavallini and Richie Sutter had the goals.

But the Blues were unable to put their opponents away. The Sabres scored three unanswered goals in the third period for a 4-3 win. The Blues' road woes had reached a new low. For the first time all year they had blown a third-period lead.

From a distance, Lowry experienced what Blues fans had been force-fed for 38 games. This was a team with tons of talent, but it also possessed a frustrating inability to win the close ones on the road. The Blues seemed to lack direction and focus. Their vision was perfectly clear at the Arena, but somehow blurred away from home. Earlier in the year, players had talked about getting over the hump. Well, that hump had grown into Mt. Everest, and it now seemed insurmountable. They would have won a game like this in St. Louis. But here in Buffalo, they took their loss and quietly retreated home.

Two nights later at the Arena, the Blues pounded the North Stars 6-1. It was a special night for a couple of the team's tough-guys. Kelly Chase scored his first goal of the year, and Gino Cavallini netted his eighth, equaling last year's output. It came just hours after Gino's wife, Katia, gave birth to the couple's first child, a 9-pound, 4-ounce boy named Aidan John Cavallini.

"I could have run a marathon today," said an excited Giant Gino after the game. "It's something that maybe one day we'll remember. But what I did tonight is nothing compared to the work Katia and Aidan did yesterday."

"I don't think he's had any sleep," said Curtis Joseph. "He's just going on emotion. He's probably going to shut it down for about 48 hours."

Joseph should know. Just a week earlier, his wife, Nancy, gave birth to their first child. Madison Joseph weighed in at 7 pounds, 5 ounces. And just four days before that, on December 19, Joseph earned his first NHL shutout, a 4-0 whitewashing of the Sharks. He also set a team record that night by contributing his fifth assist of the year, the most ever by a Blues goalie in one season.

"When a goalie gets an assist, it's kind of lucky," a modest Joseph explained. "I may never get another assist this year. But I'm certainly happy to get it."

Yes, the month of December was certainly a time of personal achievements for several of the players. But one man not taking part in any celebrations was Dave Lowry. He had been scratched again for the Minnesota game. Or more like knifed. While his teammates were giving each other high-fives, he was high above the rink watching in silence. He wasn't in the corners being crunched, banged, and bruised, but sitting in the pressbox hurt much worse.

The last time Lowry had gone through similar adversity, he passed the test with flying colors. That was the memorable drive to Milwaukee with his wife and baby daughter when he convinced himself he would give it one last shot to make it to the NHL. The shot scored, and he thrived for two solid seasons with the Blues.

It was now time to stand tall again. He was faced with the task of stepping up his game or taking it elsewhere. He decided to tackle the challenge head-on.

"I have to look at myself and say, 'I'm not doing what I'm supposed to be doing, and I'm one of the reasons why we're not winning as many hockey games,'" explained Lowry. "I try to look at it personally."

Lowry may be a sensitive man, but he's also a proud man, unwilling to give in to defeat. By sitting him in the pressbox for two games, his coach had given him an ultimatum to improve his play. Once again, Dave Lowry had to prove he belonged.

*   *   *

The rookie couldn't believe his eyes. Was he dreaming? He had to pinch himself to make sure he was wide awake. If there was ever a hockey heaven, the youngster had found it.

It was September 1985, and Bob Bassen was attending his first camp with the New York Islanders. He wasn't just some no-name rookie being ignored by Coach Al Arbour. No, Bassen was actually playing on the top line with Bryan Trottier and Mike Bossy.

That's right. This little left-hander from Calgary, Alberta, with a boyish face and childlike enthusiasm was actually playing left wing next to two future Hall of Famers, two hockey greats who had helped lead the Islanders to four consecutive Stanley Cups.

This was no mistake. The 20-year-old Bassen didn't have to sneak into the rink. He didn't have to slip the guards any money to get into the locker room. He didn't need fake identification with Denis Potvin's or Billy Smith's picture on it. In just a few weeks of training camp, Bassen had earned a spot on the number-one line alongside his idols.

From the first day of camp, Bobby Bassen made sure everyone knew who he was. He used his small, 5'10" frame as a battering ram, pounding his teammates into the boards and generally making a nuisance of himself.

"I wasn't really well-liked," said Bassen. "I had nothing to lose so I went in and banged. I was hitting some of the main guys there, like Bobby Nystrom."

And Nystrom was one of Bassen's favorite players. Imagine what he did to the guys he didn't like.

Bassen's style of play was a perfect fit for the Islanders' top line. His job was to forecheck like a runaway freight train, running over his opponents and clearing the way for Trottier and Bossy to work their magic. Bassen also displayed a scorer's touch, making him doubly valuable to the team. He was about to show the rest of the league it had made a big mistake ignoring him during his playing days at Medicine Hat in the Western Hockey League.

Bassen tallied 58 points and 93 penalty minutes in his first full year at Medicine Hat in 1983-84. But because he was tiny by NHL standards, few scouts seemed to notice. He was bypassed in the 1984 draft, much to his surprise and disappointment.

"People with a lot of hockey knowledge said I would be drafted," Bassen said. "When I wasn't, I almost quit. I thought, 'I'm done. I didn't get drafted.' Teams just don't like to take chances, especially on small guys like me."

The Islanders, the only team that had shown even the slightest interest, gave Bassen a tryout following the '84 draft. The Isles were impressed enough to offer him a free-agent contract. Bassen signed and then promptly returned to Medicine Hat for one more year of seasoning.

Bassen showed New York it hadn't made a mistake. In seven fewer games than the year before, he scored three more goals, added 21 more assists, and amassed 50 additional penalty minutes. He carried that success into his first Isles camp in 1985 where he ran over everyone in sight and earned a spot on the number-one line next to the two most prolific scorers in Islanders history.

Bob Bassen could almost taste the champagne. The Isles had won four Cups in a row in the early '80s. They nearly made it five consecutive titles following the 1983-84 season, Bassen's first full year at Medicine Hat. But the Gretzky-led Edmonton Oilers defeated the Isles in the finals that year, ending their dynastic run. Bassen was now hoping to be an integral part of New York's return to the top spot after a two-year hiatus.

However, disaster struck in the first game of the season in Los Angeles. As always, Bassen was racing around like an uncaged animal trying to open up the ice and create scoring chances for his line. The Kings' Jay Wells smashed Bassen into the boards. Bassen not only was knocked cold, suffering a concussion, his left knee buckled under him as he fell to the ice.

Bassen missed nearly the entire first month of that '85-'86 season. When he returned, he wasn't the same player the Islanders had seen in training camp. Wearing a knee brace, he was unable to play with the same aggressiveness. The team shipped him to Springfield, Massachusetts, the site of its top minor league affiliate.

Bassen continued to struggle. In 54 games at Springfield, he managed only 12 goals, hardly the numbers he was used to putting up. He was left to think of what might have been. After starting the season on the top scoring line for a Stanley Cup contender, he was now skating around minor league rinks on a bum knee. The world of sports can be so humbling, and Bob Bassen was suddenly among its most humbled victims.

But instead of growing frustrated and shaking an angry fist at the heavens, Bassen quietly prayed to the Lord and asked for strength and courage to help overcome his struggles on and off the ice. This was not a desperate man turning to religion for the first time. He was no panicked soldier in the trenches, suddenly shouting to God for help and promising to go to church if He would just get him home alive.

Bassen came from an extremely religious family. His father, Hank, an ex-NHL goaltender who had played for Chicago, Detroit, and Pittsburgh in the 1950s and 1960s, instilled the word of God in his children when they were very young. At a church camp when he was 12, Bobby confessed his sins and became a born-again Christian.

"Religion was such a positive influence," said Bassen. "I wouldn't have made it without that support. Some kids look for other means of support which can be destructive. Religious faith builds character."

Drawing upon that faith, "Bass" returned to the Islanders the following year with a healthy knee and a burning desire to make up for lost time. Al "Mr. Islander" Arbour had left after 13 seasons, handing the reigns over to Terry Simpson. Under his new coach, only the third in Isles history, Bassen produced relatively small offensive numbers. In 77 games, he netted just seven goals and added 10 assists. The Isles won only 35 games that 1986-87 season and were eliminated in the second round of the playoffs.

Bassen and his teammates coasted through another unspectacular season in '87-88. Bobby tallied only 22 points, and the Isles were unable to survive the first round. The team was quickly dropping to the depths of the NHL, a neighborhood the organization hadn't seen since its expansion days of the early 70s. The shining glory of the New York Islanders had been eclipsed.

The team finished in last place the next season, the first time in 16 years the Isles had missed the playoffs. Bob Bassen managed to play in the postseason, however; he just had to do it with a different team. On November 25, 1988, Bassen, along with defenseman Steve Konroyd, was traded to the Blackhawks for Gary Nylund and Marc Bergevin.

The Hawks were in a similar situation to the Isles'. They were struggling to make the playoffs under first-year coach Mike Keenan. As in New York, Bassen was given the "grinder" label and sent immediately to the checking line. The Hawks were not a very talented team, but they battled to the point of exhaustion every night. The team's fiery head coach expected nothing less.

The Norris Division's last playoff spot came down to the last game of that 1988-89 season. The schedule makers deserved a bonus for this one. Chicago and Toronto, vying for that final spot, battled one another in game 80. The Maple Leafs held a one-goal lead in the third period and appeared to be heading to the playoffs for the fourth year in a row. However, a 23-year old kid named Bob Bassen rifled in just his fifth goal of the year to tie it up. The Hawks then went on to win the contest and keep their playoff-appearance streak alive at 20 consecutive years, second only to Boston's 22.

Having struggled through the regular season and needing a win on the final night to make the playoffs, the Blackhawks enjoyed an incredible run during the month of April. They ousted the first-place Red Wings in the opening round and dumped the second-place Blues in the following series. They were finally extinguished in the Campbell Conference finals by the Calgary Flames, who went on to beat the Canadiens for their first NHL title. But Chicago had certainly raised some eyebrows around the league for its impassioned drive toward the Cup.

Bassen had a tough time enjoying the playoffs, however, despite his team's surprising success. No matter what he did, he couldn't seem to please his head coach. Bobby played in only 10 of the Hawks' 16 playoff games. The other six he found himself in the pressbox watching his teammates make an improbable run at the Stanley Cup. He played his heart out when he had the chance. That was the only way Bassen knew how to play. In fact, Mike Keenan didn't have a more loyal, team-oriented subordinate. But for a large chunk of the playoffs, Bassen had to shout encouragement from the rafters instead of the bench.

The next season was even more discouraging. Bassen wasn't even given a chance to strut his stuff in Chicago. He played in parts of only six games for the Hawks, spending the majority of the season in Indianapolis, Chicago's minor league team. Here was a guy willing to jump off a cliff if his coach demanded it. But there was no cliff high enough to please Mr. Keenan. As long as he was the head coach, Bob Bassen wasn't going to see any ice time at the NHL level.

"That hurt more than anything," said Bassen. "Being sent down to the minors hurts more than being traded. When I see guys being sent down, I know what they're going through."

When a player is traded, he at least feels wanted by the team acquiring his services. For many, it's a positive move, a step forward in his career. But when he's told to pack his bags for the minors, he doesn't feel wanted by anyone. He feels he's taking a giant leap backward. He's being told he's not good enough to play with the big boys. It's a crushing blow to the ego, and it forces scores of players each year to contemplate retirement.

But Bob Bassen kept his chin up and enjoyed a whale of a season at Indy. Not only did he score 22 goals and add 32 assists, but he spent 179 minutes in the penalty box, by far the highest number in his professional career. He was in a perpetual state of irritability. Every opponent must have looked like Mike Keenan to him.

Indianapolis went on to win the 1989-90 International Hockey League championship, as Bassen racked up 11 points in 12 playoff games. The team was coached by Darryl Sutter, a man Bassen would grow very close to, and one of the six Sutter brothers Bobby would either play with or be coached by in his career.

"That was the one positive about being in the minors," Bassen said. "We had a great team and we had a great coach."

But as exciting as it was, Bassen was ready to say good riddance to Indianapolis, Coach Sutter, and the minor leagues. He was ready to return to the NHL and felt confident he would be a member of the Chicago Blackhawks when the 1990-91 season opened. Not only did he have a great training camp, but there were several jobs open. During the off-season, Al Secord and Duane Sutter had retired, and Denis Savard was traded.

As it turned out, though, Bob Bassen wasn't going to play for Mike Keenan if he was the last player on earth who knew how to skate. Days before the Hawks opened the season at home against the Rangers, Bassen was informed he had been put on waivers. In other words, he was absolutely useless to the team.

Darryl Sutter, who had moved up to the parent club as an assistant coach, put his arm around Bassen and told him everything would work out just fine. The gesture was appreciated, but it couldn't save Bassen's job. His future in hockey was now in question. He felt fairly certain some team would pick him up. But then again, he had been pretty confident he would start the season as a member of the Blackhawks.

To this day, Bassen refuses to publicly badmouth Keenan. When asked about his former head coach, he usually shrugs his shoulders and mutters, "Well...you know...," and that's about the end of it. Many other ex-Hawks have roasted Keenan to a crisp, some even suggesting the man is insane the way he handles his players. But Bassen has kept his lips sealed. Few would blame him for joining the others in making disparaging comments about Keenan, but it would be completely out of character for

Bassen to lambast another human being. It's not his style. He's one of the most positive people you'll ever meet. If a conversation turns negative, Bassen wants no part of it.

Bobby's confidence about being picked off the waiver wire proved true. Brian Sutter, a man looking for a few good men, wasted little time in getting Bassen to St. Louis. Over the past several seasons, Sutter had enjoyed watching the pesky little gnat bang heads with players twice his size. He saw a young man short in stature but tall in grit and fortitude. If Sutter could assemble a team of one Curtis Joseph, one Brett Hull, and 17 Bob Bassens, he'd take his chances.

When Bassen first put on the Bluenote, he couldn't help but think back to his first NHL game with the Islanders when he filled a spot on the top line. Five years later with the Blues, Bassen again found himself on the number-one line, this time at center with Sergio Momesso to his left and Hull on his right. The Blues' regular top center, Adam Oates, was experiencing discomfort in his lower rib cage, a problem that would plague Oates through the first three months of the season.

Bassen's stay alongside Hull was short-lived. Coach Sutter felt he could better utilize Bassen's skills on the checking line. It wasn't long before he, Dave Lowry, and Rich Sutter began making a name for themselves. The "Green Beret" line quickly established itself as one of the premier checking lines in the league. Bob Bassen had finally found hockey heaven. He was having the time of his life. He shattered his NHL career highs with 16 goals, 18 assists, and 183 penalty minutes. And equally important to a man who checks for a living, Bassen turned in a plus/minus rating of plus-17.

"We had a bond between us. We were very tight on and off the ice," said Bassen of the Green Berets. "We got our share of goals and that was our trademark. We could keep the opposing top lines from scoring, but we could also put the puck in the net. It was a very exciting year."

In just his first year with St. Louis, Bassen had become an instant celebrity, the most popular of the Green Berets, quick as a deer and tough as nails. It seemed impossible that this young man with a pubescent face and high-pitched voice could play like such a ruffian on the ice. But that's what made him so endearing to fans. It was like watching your kid brother pummel the neighborhood bully. You pulled for him. You cheered for him. At 5'10", 175 pounds, Bassen is physically "average." But we fellow "average" men know our limits. We're not about to skate head-on into the Bob Proberts of the world. That's why so many fans felt such a bond with Bassen. They lived vicariously through him.

It was an absolute joy to watch Bassen glide around the rink in his patented crouch position, resembling Pete Rose with a hockey stick, and then level an opponent with such force that the guy probably thought of wearing an air bag the next time out. Bassen single-handedly broke every law of physics. When two bodies of mass collide, the larger one is supposed to come out unscathed. But when Bassen gets involved, the larger body usually has to pick his teeth up off the ice.

"That's the way I'm always going to play, working as hard as I can," said Bassen, endorsing a philosophy from which we can all learn. "Strong people work hard, and that's how I play. Hard."

Toward the end of that '90-91 season, Bassen's face resembled a roadmap with lines and crevasses all over it. You didn't have to ask what he did for a living. You could literally see it on his mug. Stitches, cuts, scars, bumps, and bruises covered what was once such a delicate face it took weeks just to grow a 5 o'clock shadow. An oceanful of Rogaine wasn't going to grow hair on his cheeks.

When camp opened the following September, Bassen's face had healed, but the memories of the Blues' early playoff exit had not. An enjoyable year had been ruined by a lackluster performance against the North Stars. But when pressed on what the Blues could do differently in '91-92 to avoid a similar collapse, Bassen had little to say.

"Well, we just have to be that much better to prepare for the playoffs," Bassen said the first day of camp, on September 8th. "But it's too early to talk about that already."

Sure enough, Bassen had other things on his mind at the start of the season. It became apparent early on that with so many new faces, the Green Beret line was in jeopardy. Dave Christian and Brendan Shanahan spent considerable time on the checking line as Brian Sutter tried to find the perfect fit for his new arrivals.

It didn't help matters that Bassen and his ex-linemates were struggling offensively. Just like Lowry, Bassen grew frustrated with his inability to put the puck in the net as consistently as he had the year before. He scored his third goal of the year on December 3 against Minnesota, and it took him another month to net his fourth against Winnipeg.

As his offense went south, so did his defense, the part of the game that Bassen had to constantly improve upon to be an effective hockey player.

"I've always had offensive skills," he said. "The thing I try to work on is my defense."

The demise of the Green Berets could be linked directly to the Blues' failure to win on the road. Teams don't suddenly become less skilled when they leave the confines of their own arena. Road games are a test of character and confidence. And because the Green Berets had an abundance of both the year before, their enthusiastic play had spilled over to the rest of the team, as it recorded a league-best road record of 23-13-4.

Three guys with different backgrounds, but all sharing the same values, had joined forces and friendships to lead the Blues to their second best season in 24 years. The three men were throwaways from other teams, but in St. Louis, they became part of a system that utilized their talents and cultivated their work ethic.

The three checkers still possessed an enviable amount of character in their second season together, but their confidence took a beating as they were unable to put any points on the board game after game after game after...

It was now up to the others to take charge on the road. There was no one player or one line to set the tone any longer. The Blues had a chance to show their true colors in December with so many games on the road. It was time for each and every player to step forward on his own, to lead instead of follow. As Brian Sutter always preached, it was time to "set an example, not be an example."

The Blues set an example, all right. They demonstrated how not to play on the road, winning only two of nine away from home in December. The results were inexcusable for a team that had been road warriors just a season ago. The Blues were still playing hard. They were still playing to win. But they were losing the close ones, games they could have put in their hip pocket the year before.

To make matters worse, an insidious black cloud began filtering into the Blues' locker room. It spread subtly about the room, infecting the players in different ways. It seemed harmless at first, but as weeks passed the acid cloud began to eat away at the team. A star player, a man who wore an "A" on his jersey, a guy who was supposed to help lead the team, suddenly shifted his interest away from the ice and pointed it upstairs to the Blues' executive offices. At a time when the Blues needed him most, he was about to unwittingly turn the Arena into a three-ring circus.

Chapter Ten

SOWING WILD OATES

"How close are you? . . . mmm . . . yeah . . . Well, what's going to happen? . . . I see . . . uh-huh . . . So you're not backing down? . . . Interesting."

KMOV sports director Zip Rzeppa was on the phone talking to Lou Oppenheim, a sports agent based in New York. It was midafternoon January 7, 1992, an uneventful day. At least until now.

I was sitting at my sports desk just a few feet to Zip's right, mulling over some statistics from St. Louis University's big basketball upset of Southern Illinois the night before. Freshman forward Ryan Grant had netted a short jumper as time ran out to give the Billikens an improbable 73-71 win, only their second victory of the year.

But at the same time, I was keeping an ear to the conversation next to me. Oppenheim was Adam Oates' agent, and Zip was getting the very latest on their demands that Oates' contract be renegotiated.

Rumors had started to circulate at the beginning of the season that the Blues' star center was extremely unhappy with his contract. Oates never talked about it publicly, but others inside the organization said Oates and Oppenheim had made it very clear to Blues president Jack Quinn that if he was a fair man, he'd tear up Oates' current deal, sit down at a typewriter, and begin fashioning a brand new one immediately. Adam Oates the hockey player had become Adam Oates the businessman. He suddenly seemed more interested in the bottom line than the blue line.

On the surface, Oates had every right to feel cheated. He was the most talented puck handler in Blues history, shattering a number of team assist and point records. In 1990-91, he recorded an amazing 90 assists in just 61 games. He also scored 25 goals to give him an average of 1.9 points a game, second only to Wayne Gretzky's 2.1.

Oates was the perfect complement to Brett Hull; the two shared a magical relationship on the ice. It didn't matter if Hull was hiding in the stands, Oates would get the puck to him. His uncanny ability to pass the rubber disk to No. 16 never ceased to amaze. It was as if he had a string on the puck, threading it through traffic to the Golden Brett, who would invariably bury it in the back of the net. Arena announcer Tom Calhoun ran out of breath yelling their names so frequently he finally got wise and made a recording. Hull scored again? From Oates? Okay, put the tape in and press "play."

"Blues goal scored by No.16, Brett Hull!!!"

Press "pause." Let the crowd cheer for a few seconds. Okay, "play" again.

"Assisted by No. 12, Adam Oates!!!"

Eject and store in a convenient place. It'll be needed again in a few minutes.

Off the ice, Oates was just as committed to detail. While some of his teammates read the *Hockey News*, he scanned the *Wall Street Journal*. While they mulled over statistics, he fixated on salaries. And what he saw was very displeasing. Under the heading "St. Louis Blues," Oates had to move five notches down the list before he saw his name. Above him were Dave Christian ($475,000 a year), Brendan Shanahan ($625,000), Garth Butcher ($700,000) and Brett Hull (about $1.5 million). He could stomach Hull's name being at the top; he obviously deserved to be there. What he couldn't swallow were the other three names. When Oates looked up, he saw the backsides of those three players and they were sporting big, fat wallets, much bigger than his own. At about $420,000 for the '91-92 season, Oates felt grossly underpaid.

"I just want to be second on the team, which is where I assess my value," Oates said. "We sold 14,000 season tickets this year. They come to see the Blues win and Brett score 100 goals. I'm a big part of that, and I just want to get my equal billing."

No question. The point was undebatable. Adam Oates deserved to be the second-highest-paid player on the team, right behind his soulmate, Hull. Even Blues management acknowledged Oates' importance to the team and surely felt that in a fair and just world, their all-star center would be closer to the million-dollar mark. However, there was much more to the story than dollars and cents. It wasn't black and white, or in Oates' case, green and white.

When Oates was traded to the Blues in June, 1989, he and Oppenheim politely marched into Quinn's office and told him to do the right thing: trash Oates' current contract, the one he signed a couple years earlier with the Red Wings, and design an original one that would make his new player happy. In other words, fork over some extra cash. Citing company policy (business executives are so good at doing that, aren't they?), Quinn said that was impossible. He could, however, "rework" the existing contract by giving Oates extra goodies that would fatten the deal.

"Oates' contract was a typical Red Wings contract, which is laden with personal incentives," said Oppenheim. "So we traded those incentives for an extra year on the contract. Adam felt a little insecure about his future so the extra year was important."

However, just a year later, in the summer of '90, Oates and Oppenheim felt insecure again. They marched into Quinn's office for the second time and asked the Blues' president, if he would be so kind as to please "rework" Oates' contract once more. Player salaries around the league had begun escalating in unprecedented fashion, and Oates was unable to cash in. He was locked into a three-year deal with the Blues, and the only way for him to take advantage of the current market was to persuade Quinn to add more money to those three years. Citing company policy again (cough-cough), Quinn restated his position on renegotiating contracts. Instead, he extended Oates' deal by yet another year while giving him a hefty signing bonus spread over the life of the contract.

By now, the last couple of years of Oates' contract were overflowing with big bucks. According to well-placed sources, he was set to earn about $1.15 million in 1993-94 and $945,000 the following season, which would be his option year. He obviously had no problem with those figures. But the first two years of his contract still reflected relatively small numbers in comparison with others of equal ability. After making a little more than $420,000 in 1991-92, he would make a small jump to $530,000 the next season. The total package was worth $3.2 million, with the bulk of the money to be released the last two years. Oates, though, wasn't content to wait that long to become a millionaire. He wanted to be compensated now, not later. As an athlete approaching 30, he knew time was running out.

So barely a year went by when, guess what? Yep, Oates and Oppenheim decided two contract extensions still weren't good enough. The market continued to skyrocket upward while Oates was left behind to smell the fumes. The odor of money was intoxicating, and Oates wanted more than a whiff. He and Oppenheim could stand it no longer, so they took a stand from which they would not back down. In the fall of 1991, just two months after signing the second contract extension, they gave Jack Quinn an ultimatum. Pay Oates what he's worth, or find another team that will.

It wasn't long before the story became public, forcing Oates and Oppenheim to explain themselves.

"I've proved to the fans that I can play to a certain level," Oates said. "That's the reason I'm doing this. I really don't think I'm asking for that much. The salaries went up drastically this year, and I just want my due."

"We didn't have a problem with the Blues when they signed Hull and Stevens to those big contracts in 1990 because they were free agents," explained Oppenheim. "But then they changed the rules of the game on us. They started signing Garth Butcher and others to big deals, and Adam was left out."

True. But the Blues didn't renegotiate, rework, or extend the contracts of Butcher and some of his lesser-paid teammates. Their contracts ran out, and it was time to sign new ones. If Oates' contract had expired, then he would've become a millionaire overnight. Instead, he was chained to a contract that seemed to have no end because he kept agreeing to one-year extensions. Still, when Oates found out Butcher signed a new deal worth $700,000 the first year, he felt used and abused.

"I never really discussed the money part with Adam. I had my own contract that was up," said Butcher, defending his salary. "I signed with what I was happy with and to me that's what each guy has to do. I don't believe in talking about a contract unless it's done. There have been times in the past where

I signed longer contracts, and I obviously felt I was underpaid. But you play that out and hopefully you benefit from it later on."

Meanwhile, Quinn said he was tired of pulling out his desk drawer, opening the Adam Oates file, and trying to figure new ways to please his disgruntled star. In no uncertain terms, Quinn said Oates would have to live with his current deal, while general manager Ron Caron entertained trade offers from other teams.

So on the afternoon of January 7, 1992, I casually listened to Zip's conversation with Oppenheim, wondering if there was anything new on the situation. Oates and his agent still held out hope that Quinn would soften his hard-line stance and upgrade the first two years of Oates' contract. But after what he was about to tell Zip, there was no way in hell that was going to happen.

With Zip forechecking over the phone, trying to pin the agent down on what he planned to do if Quinn didn't reopen the contract, Oppenheim finally blurted it out. Oates would walk out of the Arena in less than two weeks, literally quit the team, if the Blues didn't satisfy his contractual demands or trade him. Oppenheim pointed to the All-Star game on Jan. 18 as the deadline. If nothing was done by then, Oates would pick up his toys and go home.

"You won't believe what they're going to do!" exclaimed Zip as he hung up the phone. It's not difficult to excite the Zipster, but he was especially jumpy after this conversation. "Lou Oppenheim says Oates is walking by the All-Star break if the Blues don't renegotiate or trade him!"

You've got to be kidding, I thought. Has it really gotten this far?

"Can we go with it?" I asked.

"Well, I don't know," Zip answered. "I guess we can. He didn't say it was off the record."

"Well, there you go," I said. "We've got to go with it. That's major stuff."

Of course, it wasn't my neck on the line. If Oppenheim meant for his conversation to be off the record and Zip shouted it across the airwaves for all to hear, he was in deep doo-doo, not me. We discussed it for awhile, retracing his conversation with Oppenheim. After determining Oppenheim never asked that his comments be sequestered, Zip decided he would break the story that night during his 6 o'clock sportscast. He asked the station's hockey analyst, Bernie Federko, to join him on set to talk about Oates' latest threat.

Meanwhile, I put in a call to Jack Quinn to get his response. I didn't expect to get through right away. In fact, I really didn't expect to hear from him at all. I don't know if other St. Louis reporters experience the same problem, but for some reason the guy avoids me like the plague. In the most memorable incident earlier in the season, I needed to talk to Quinn about a story relating to the Scott Stevens controversy. Instead of waiting by the phone for his return call, I grabbed a photographer and headed to the Arena. His car was outside his office so I set up shop near his back bumper and waited for him to emerge.

However, after about 30 minutes of pacing across the parking lot, I saw a tall, thin man with lots of hair, definitely not Jack Quinn, emerge from the office door, hop into the car I thought was Quinn's, and drive off toward the back of the building. I just stood there, dumbfounded, as if somebody had just stolen my lunchbox. I looked at my photographer, Scott Thomas, and shrugged my shoulders.

"I bet they're switching on you," said Thomas, an award-winning cameraman who has won numerous Emmys for his investigative work. "Quinn's probably jumping into the car at the back door."

No way. Why would he go through all that trouble? All he had to do was tell me he couldn't say anything as he got into his car and sped away.

I walked inside the Blues' administrative office to call back to the station and tell Zip that Quinn was hiding somewhere. Unbelievably, right in the middle of the conversation, the guy who had just jumped into Quinn's car walked through the office right past me. It was Jerry Jasiek, the Blues' director of finance. And yes, I had been duped, the 'ole switcharoo trick. Ever since then, I've never expected Quinn to be completely straight with me on anything. That is, if I can even get through to him in the first place.

However, on the day of Oppenheim's revelation, Quinn didn't ignore me. Must have been my lucky day, I guess.

"Jack, what can you tell me about Oates' threat to quit the team if you don't trade him by the All-Star break?" I asked.

"Who told you that?" Quinn demanded to know.

"Well, I don't think I can really tell you. But it's from..."

"I know, I know," he interrupted. "Let me guess. A certain Channel 4 sports director calls his agent in New York and gets the latest scoop."

I had to laugh because I knew that was coming. Zip's agent just happened to be Art Kaminsky, the head of Athletes and Artists, the agency for which Lou Oppenheim works. Quinn was implying that Zip had an "in" and was being kept abreast of everything that was going on with the Oates situation. However, in defense of Zip, his personal ties to the agency didn't help him in this particular case.

Over the last couple of months, Oppenheim had given every reporter the same information. He played no favorites. He was as open and honest as he could be, and the media soon became very attracted to his candor and sense of humor. He was a sound bite machine. To suggest he was slipping Zip inside information was completely off-base. To this day, I'm convinced another reporter would have broken the story first if he or she just happened to call Oppenheim on a whim and started pressing him for information the way Zip did.

"Jack, you might be right," I said, not wanting to debate how we got the story. "I'm just curious if you know anything about it."

"Honestly, I haven't heard this latest threat," Quinn responded. "That's a new one. I guess I really can't comment on it, because I haven't talked to Lou about it."

"But if it's true, what are you going to do? Just let him walk?"

"Adam Oates has a standard contract of performance. To get paid, he has to perform. If he decides not to perform, he doesn't get paid." It was that simple.

Over the next couple of days, the story snowballed into an avalanche of controversy. The sports call-in shows were dedicated almost exclusively to the Oates threat. Virtually every other subject matter was temporarily shoved aside. The *Post-Dispatch* began printing daily updates on the situation. KTVI, St. Louis' ABC affiliate, even sent a reporter to New York, where the Blues were playing when the story first became public. KTVI reporter Bill Davis did an excellent job tracking down Oates to get his comments, the first to air on network television. Oates was also besieged by New York and national sports journalists during the Blues' four-day stay in the New York area. By the time

Oates returned to St. Louis the following week, he would be in a surly mood, refusing to talk to local reporters.

In the meantime, fans split into two camps, debating the merits of Oates' threat. Some felt Oates was just another overpaid, spoiled athlete who somehow felt cheated for making such a "measly" salary. These fans backed Quinn 100 percent and demanded that Oates shut up and play hockey. You don't know how good you have it, they shouted. Try living in the real world, pal.

Many others, however, couldn't understand such insensitivity. The Oates backers had a tough time fathoming how one of the premier hockey players in the league was barely making $100,000 more than Rich Sutter. Where's the fairness in that? they asked. Oates is the second best player on the team and should be paid accordingly.

"I'm still not asking for what the top 20 players in the league make," said Oates. "I'm just hoping the Blues see my side a little bit more."

Once again, peace and tranquility proved fleeting for the 25th anniversary Blues team. The year had started on a sour note, and now it seemed it would end that way, too. First the Scott Stevens controversy. Then the trade for another Sutter. Then the acquisitions of Zombo and Norwood, a residual effect of the loss of Stevens. That was followed by the road woes in December that pushed the Blues farther behind the Red Wings. Judge Houston tipped the first domino in September, and they were still falling in January.

That was doubly frustrating because the month of January appeared so promising. The Blues played seven of 13 games at home. And of the six on the road, only two were against teams with winning records, the Rangers and Devils whom they played back-to-back on the 8th and 9th. Perhaps there was finally an end to the Blues' string of bad luck and off-ice problems. Just maybe the Blues could get down to playing hockey again without any more distractions.

But just when the clouds seemed to break, just when everyone started to feel upbeat about the second half of the season, a new controversy threatened to destroy team morale and keep the players buried under a mountain of self-doubt and in-house finger-pointing. With so much attention focused on Adam Oates and his squabbles with management, there seemed a genuine fear that the Blues would never acquire the family atmosphere needed for a run at the Stanley Cup.

At first, however, the suspicions of a team collapse seemed greatly exaggerated. The day after the pay-me-or-trade-me-or-I-walk threat was aired on KMOV, the Blues had to visit Madison Square Garden, the home of the New York Rangers. In the Blues' 25-year history, they had won only five times in that famed building, the fewest road victories in any NHL arena for the Blues. The game was aired live on KPLR, and you can bet a majority of viewers were carefully watching the play of Adam Oates, looking for any sign that he was dogging it. The sideshow had officially begun.

Throughout the controversy, none of his teammates would ever accuse Oates of languid play. He proved from the very beginning he wouldn't let his business interests interfere with playing hockey. Seven-and-a-half minutes into the Rangers' game, Oates raced behind the New York net, bumped James Patrick off the puck, and fed it to Dave Christian standing nearby. Christian then slid it out to Hull between the circles and WHACK!—it was in the net. The Blues had the early lead thanks to Oates' aggressive play.

In the third period, with the Blues clinging to a 3-2 lead, Brendan Shanahan, working the left point on a power play, passed to Oates, positioned between the circles. With his back to the net, Oates quickly turned and rifled a no-look shot over Mike Richter's right shoulder to give the Blues a two-goal advantage over the second best team in the league.

Later in the period, after the Rangers had cut the lead to 4-3, Oates and Hull teamed up again to ice the game. The Rangers had control of the puck at center ice until Sergei Nemchinov and Jeff Beukeboom collided, coughing it up to Oates, who just happened to be cruising by the area. Oates simply backhanded the puck forward to Hull, who broke in alone. The Golden Brett went from his forehand to his backhand to his forehand again before sliding it past Richter to end the scoring at 5-3. The Blues, thanks to Oates' goal and two assists, exited the Garden with a rare win, only the fifth road victory of the season. The Oates antagonists watching the game had to be extremely disappointed with his performance. In the wake of his agent's explosive announcement the day before, Oates had just turned in one of his finest performances of the season.

"We went into New York and played outstanding hockey against a good team," said Brian Sutter. "We've played pretty darn good hockey on the road going back to November. We just haven't had results. We're not as bad on the road as people think."

"I think we played very, very well," said Hull, who extended his goal-scoring streak to ten games with his fifth hat trick of the year. "I almost get a feeling that we're coming together as a unit."

Really? Is it possible that the players were actually growing closer because of, and not in spite of, their disgruntled teammate? Professional athletes do stick together when one of their own is battling management for more money. They're usually right there with him knocking on the boss' door. In matters of the pocketbook, few ever denounce a fellow athlete for trying to add a couple of extra zeroes to his paycheck.

"We feel for Oatsie," said Rick Zombo. "We understand his point. We're behind him all the way."

"Adam Oates is a great hockey player, and the fans should respect the way he plays," explained rookie Nelson Emerson. "He's a hell of a talent, and I think they realize that. I'm behind Adam because I know what he does for this hockey club."

"He's such a valuable part of this team, far more than I would ever be," said Hull modestly, too modestly. "He's such a good leader and does so many other little things that you just don't see. It'd be a shame to lose him and I'll do my best to make sure that doesn't happen."

After the impressive win over the Rangers, the Blues traveled to the Meadowlands to take on the Devils. There were some very painful memories in that building. The frustrating season started there with a 7-2 thrashing by New Jersey. But on this night, the Blues had a chance to exorcise the season's demons along with the Devils. In a game heaped with symbolism, all it took was a win for the Blues to purge their sins.

The teams traded quality scoring chances the first half of the opening period until New Jersey's Alexei Kasatonov scored at 9:47. Just 36 seconds later, Stephane Richer scored on a wraparound between Guy Hebert's pads to give the Devils a 2-0 lead. This game was frighteningly similar to opening night, when Jersey scored three goals in 5 1/2 minutes to put the game away. The demons seemed to be alive and well three months later.

Unlike that first game, however, the Blues roared back in the second period and cut the lead in half on Brendan Shanahan's 18th goal of the season. The Devils got their two-goal lead back later in the period when Claude Lemieux ripped a shot from near the blue line that beat Hebert on the far post.

Leave it to Shanahan, though, to burn his old teammates. Nearly nine minutes into the third period, Hull gained control of a loose puck in the neutral zone and slid a no-look, behind-the-back pass ahead to Shanahan, who then skated in alone across the blue line. As he entered the left circle, Shanny wristed a shot that eluded Devils goalie Craig Billington on the far post. It was Shanny's fourth goal in two games against his ex-mates, and Billington didn't appreciate it. As Brendan skated by with his arms raised in the air, Billington reached out and gave his former teammate a poke in the back. Shanahan quickly whirled around to go after the Devils' goalie. However, the linesmen and several players stepped between the two men, and Shanahan settled for shouting a few choice words.

"Last year I used to always tease him that I owned him in practice," said Shanahan of Billington, not making a big deal out of the confrontation. "But he's a good guy. He's fiery and competitive. Our friendships are there off the ice."

But on the ice, Billington owned the Blues, at least on this particular evening. After Shanahan's score, Billington allowed only Ron Sutter's power-play goal late in the third period as the Devils held on for a 4-3 win. Oates was a non-factor in the loss that not only dropped St. Louis 11 points behind Detroit and into a tie with Chicago, but also stopped Hull's goal-scoring streak at ten games, three short of the record he set the year before.

Forty-eight hours later, the Blues soundly whipped the New York Islanders 6-3, as the curtain went up early for the Hull and Oates show. Just 39 seconds into the game, Gino Cavallini roared behind the Isles' net and smacked defenseman Bill Berg so hard the only thing left intact was the puck itself. Oates, who always seems to be around every loose puck, scooped it up and fed a backhand pass to Hull between the circles. The Golden One blasted a shot over Steve Weeks' left shoulder to give his team a 1-0 lead, and the Blues never trailed from that point.

Oates scored the game's final goal, his ninth of the year and second in the three games since his latest threat went public. Oates skated into the offensive zone and left the puck for Zombo.

The Blues' defenseman wasted no time in slapping a shot on net. Goalie Mark Fitzpatrick, who replaced Weeks early in the third period, stopped the shot but let the rebound slide out in front of him. Oates was in perfect position to flip the rebound past Fitzpatrick to end the scoring and push the Blues back into sole possession of second place. It was the franchise's 800th victory in 24 1/2 years.

Oates' critics had every right to condemn the all-star for what they saw as a selfish and greedy demand for more money. But they had no evidence to rip him for playing poorly. After all, that's the last thing Oates wanted to do. If he shirked his duties on the ice, he didn't stand a chance at gaining anything but disdain from even his most ardent supporters. But as long as he played well and the Blues continued to post impressive wins, especially away from the Arena, perhaps a groundswell of support from the fans and media could persuade Quinn and Company to satisfy Oates and Oppenheim.

However, when Adam returned to St. Louis following the Islanders' game, it didn't take long for him to realize that the only groundswell of support so far was for his departure. Media members in a position to voice their opinions generally came down on the side of management. As for the fans, the ones who paid Oates' salary, they would have their chance to speak the night of January 14, the Blues' first home game since Oates threatened to walk. Get out your earplugs. This one was going to be loud.

*   *   *

"Okay, here he comes," I told my cameraman. "Go ahead and roll tape."

It was January 13, and Adam Oates had just stepped off the ice at the Brentwood practice rink. He was heading in our direction to the locker room, and I firmly believed he would stop and talk to us. Only once had a member of the Blues ever refused my request for an interview. During the playoffs the year before, the North Stars had just ripped the Blues 8-4 to take a three-games-to-one lead in the series. When I asked Rick Meagher if he could spare a minute or two, he took his gum out of his mouth, rifled it into the trash can, and promptly whirled around and headed to the shower. Yikes.

Looking back on that incident now, I completely understand Meagher's reaction. He was set to retire at the end of the season after 11 years as one of the most pesky, pain-in-the-rear centers in hockey. He shadowed Gretzky, smothered Lemieux, suffocated Yzerman. After a career of shutting down the league's most prolific scorers, Meagher wanted nothing more than to go out a winner. But sitting in that Minnesota locker room the night of April 24, 1991, he realized there would be no championship rings, no memories of carrying the Stanley Cup around the ice. When he looked back on his career, he would remember how it ended. He would recall how an upstart team no one paid any attention to during the regular season suddenly sprang up and knocked the Blues out of the playoffs. His one last shot at winning it all was about to end with a thud. The last thing he wanted to do was to sit down and talk to a pesky, pain-in-the-rear reporter.

I could tell right away that I was about to be turned down for the second time. As Oates approached us, he kept his head down and his eyes focused on the ground. The message was subtle but clear: Don't bother.

"Hey, Adam. Can I talk to you?" I asked.

"No, I have nothing to say," Oates said as he hurried past. That little encounter would be the only "interview" we'd have to show our viewers that night. But even though it lasted only a blink of an eye, it was as poignant as any 20-second sound bite.

Oates was a troubled and discouraged man. He didn't have any regrets about asking for another contract extension. He was frustrated, however, that his demands were up for public dissection. He never meant for his behind-the-door negotiations to become a matter of debate for the entire city of St. Louis. The videotape couldn't lie. The attention heaped on Oates was beginning to take its toll.

I should have left Oates alone at that point. But then again, I'm not the smartest guy in the world. I figured that after a shower he might feel a bit more relaxed and ready to talk. I went outside the rink and waited for him to exit to the parking lot.

Oates emerged from the locker room to a throng of autograph seekers. This was actually a pleasant sight to witness.

Despite the overwhelming response against him on the radio call-in shows, there was still a large contingent of fans willing to greet Oates with smiles, pats on the back, and requests for his signature. Surely, Mr. Oates would be Mr. Happy now.

"Adam, has an extra 15 minutes changed your mind?" I asked, grinning from ear to ear as if that would help.

"Fuck, I've talked to everyone already!" he said loudly, quickly brushing past me for the second time.

"Everyone but Channel 4," I answered back.

No response. Oates continued walking to his car and quickly sped off to find some peace and quiet.

I really thought my last comment would make him stop and talk to us. After all, KMOV was the only major media outlet in town that had come down on the side of Oates. And there was good reason for that. His name was Bernie Federko.

Channel 4's hockey analyst, the man who coincidentally was traded for Oates three years before, did little to mask his support for the Blues' center. Federko suggested that Oates' request for more money was a private matter and nobody else's business. Bernie stopped short of speaking out against Blues management, but his was definitely the only pro-Oates media voice in town.

"Adam knows who's saying what," said Lou Oppenheim. "Believe me, he's aware of all that."

That's why I thought a quick reminder of who I worked for would persuade him to utter a few syllables beyond, "Fuck, I've talked to everyone already!" I guess I was wrong.

The next night, Oates would learn who his true friends were. And he would learn he didn't have very many outside the dressing room. The Blues hosted the Washington Capitals, who came in with the second best record in hockey, behind only Montreal. The Caps were also second in goals scored with 196, trailing only the high-flying Penguins' 200.

But on this evening, no one outside of either locker room seemed to really care about the impending matchup. The question was, How would the 17,000 fans greet Adam Oates? The issue became bigger than the game itself. I'm sure Las Vegas was even taking odds on it.

"You want $100 on the fans booing Oates? Okay. Now, do you want to bet they'll boo only at the beginning of the game, or do you think it'll get louder as the game progresses? At the beginning, fine. And how loud do you think it'll be? Just a smattering of boos, about half and half, or an arena-filled chorus of boos? An arena-filled chorus. Okay, thank you, and here's your stub."

Brian Sutter didn't give the boo-birds a chance to sing at the beginning of the game. He elected to sit Oates on the bench so when the starting lineups were announced, the fans had no opportunity to heckle the embattled center. They'd have to wait until Oates took his first shift a minute or two into the game.

Sure enough, a little less than 60 seconds had elapsed when Oates, Hull, and Gino Cavallini jumped onto the ice. At first, there were only a few isolated boos from the hard-core haters, the fans who probably had rested their voices for a week just for this contest. Otherwise, the majority of the crowd was more interested in the game at hand.

One major reason for the lack of negative reaction was the fine play of the Blues' top line on its first couple of shifts. Hull and Oates buzzed goaltender Mike Liut, threatening a barrage of goals in the first period. Ten minutes into the game, the Blues held an incredible 8-0 advantage in shots on goal. For a while, the fans forgot that the man wearing No. 12 was threatening to walk out on the team. To them, No. 12 was the guy continuously crossing the blue line with the puck and getting it to his right-hand man.

However, the mood of the fans quickly changed after those first ten minutes. Their shift in opinion coincided with the shift in momentum on the ice. With the Blues on their first power play, Oates tried to get something started by dumping the puck into the far corner. However, Caps defenseman Kevin Hatcher beat Ron Wilson to the puck and immediately fed it up-ice to a streaking Mike Ridley. The Washington center broke in on Curtis Joseph, who reverted to his bad habit of going down too early. Ridley cut over to the left post and easily slid the puck in the net for a short-handed goal.

Just 38 seconds later and the Blues still on the same power play, Jeff Brown scored his eighth of the year to even things up. Unfortunately, the tie didn't last long. Later in the period, with the Blues on their second power play, Dimitri Khristich scored the Caps' second short-handed goal to give his team a 2-1 lead.

The Blues outshot their opponents 13-7 during the opening period but had been outscored on their own power play. The fans were growing restless. They needed to vent their frustrations. And they had their perfect whipping boy.

The Blues started the second period on the power play, but it looked as though they were the ones at a disadvantage. They absolutely could not get the puck across the blue line. The fans had seen enough. The isolated boos turned into a cacophonous chorus of contempt for Adam Oates. Every time he touched the puck, a thunderous roar of disapproval echoed throughout the building.

The Blues wilted after that as the Capitals must have felt like they were playing a home game. They scored one goal in the second and three more in the third to humiliate the Blues 6-1. It was St. Louis' worst home loss of the year, and it couldn't have come at a worse time. Oates and his teammates had a chance to win over the fans' hearts, but they had failed miserably. The Blues gave the home crowd every opportunity to boo and it took advantage.

The fans' irritability seemed to subside in the third period. It was as if many of them grew embarrassed by the behavior of those around them. A small minority of fans even cheered Oates to let him know that some of them, while they didn't necessarily agree with his stance, appreciated his efforts on the ice. But the cheers were no match for the jeers. Most of the fans were sending a loud and unmistakable message to Oates: Don't let the Arena door hit you in the ass on the way out of town.

"I don't give two shits what they think," snapped Oates after the game. He hurriedly dressed to get out of the place that had suddenly become enemy territory. It was difficult for him to bite his lip, but after making that first statement he was able to compose himself and talk about what might have been.

"When we got those chances right off the bat, it got me feeling good," he said. "Two goals and three assists would have made it a lot easier. It's just bad timing."

The Blues' dressing room was like a morgue. It was bad enough to be totally dominated on home ice. But playing in front of an unforgiving crowd made for an especially unforgettable night.

"We have to put it behind us," said Dave Lowry. "It's disappointing because of what Adam has done. He's still out there working hard. His first priority is with the hockey club. On the ice, he gives it everything he has."

"The fans are entitled to their opinions because they pay good money to come to the games," conceded Nelson Emerson. "But it's too bad because of everything he's done for this team."

"It makes it tough on him," added Dave Christian. "Everyone can feel for him. It's not the first time in my career I've seen the fans react negatively to a player and it's always tough."

And did the booing have a bearing on the outcome of the game? No question, said Oates' best friend and biggest supporter.

"I can guarantee it had an effect on everyone," said an irate Hull after the game. "You don't think a guy touches the puck and he's getting booed that he doesn't want to bear down and do a little more than he should? It's unfortunate. It had a big bearing on the game."

All everyone talked about the next day was the booing of Adam Oates. It was the centerpiece of discussion at every office water cooler. It was the topic of conversation over lunch. And it was debated on radio and television. St. Louis fans hadn't booed one of their own in this manner since Garry Templeton flipped off the Busch Stadium crowd nearly 12 years earlier. A few months later, Templeton was shipped west to San Diego for some guy named Ozzie Smith. Where would Oates go, and was there some young talent out there that could grow into a superstar like the Wizard?

Two nights after the game from hell, the Blues hosted the top team in the NHL, the Montreal Canadiens. The schedule makers couldn't have picked a worse time to bring those guys into town. Trying desperately to put the last game behind them and hoping to quiet the Oates antagonists, the Blues had to battle the league's top defensive team.

Montreal plays what the average fan might call "boring hockey"; defensive, deliberate, tight, and responsible. And it has won the Canadiens a Cupful of victories over the years. Unfortunately, it's the kind of hockey that can easily bore non-students of the game. That's not to suggest St. Louisans don't know hockey, but like most American audiences, they like to see the red light get a workout. They want the goaltenders to be busier than the beer concessionaires. An 8-5 score with a couple of brawls is the perfect hockey game. A 2-1 game with only hard checking spells restlessness. Not a good sign for Oates.

Speaking of signs, there were about a half-dozen of them in the crowd on this night. "Hull and Oates/You've lost that loving feeling," and "Hull and Who?" were among the more negative messages. Not to be outdone, the pro-Oates contingent made its presence known. One sign read, "Roses are red, St. Louis is blue, Without Oates, What will we do?"

There was a good chance they'd find out soon. This was the last game before the All-Star break. If there was no movement in Jack Quinn's office and Oates was true to his word, this game was his last hurrah for awhile. He was scheduled to play in the All-Star game in two days in Philadelphia. After that, it looked quite likely that Oates would clean out his locker and stay home for an indefinite period of time.

As it turned out, the Blues and Canadiens engaged in one of the most high-flying, wide-open contests of the year at the Arena. In the first seven minutes, the teams combined for nine shots on goal. If they continued at that offensive pace, the fans would witness a total of 77 shots. It was the perfect pacifier for a potentially surly crowd.

Montreal got on the scoreboard first after the Blues overcommitted in their own end. With a little more than ten minutes left in the first period, Garth Butcher, Murray Baron, and Dave Lowry raced behind Curtis Joseph to clear out a loose puck. Unfortunately, there were only two Canadiens back there, leaving three out in front of the net. Oates had one tied up along the boards while Hull, uh, well, Hull didn't seem too interested in this particular play. He stayed out near his blue line hoping his teammates could gain control of the puck and feed him on a breakaway. That left Mathieu Schneider and Sylvain Lefebvre feeling a bit lonesome on the points.

Sure enough, Montreal won possession of the puck and fed Lefebvre at the right point, no one within 20 feet of him. The defenseman glided in a few feet, sized up Joseph, then beat him just inside the far post. That was the only score in the first period, in which Montreal outshot the Blues 13-10.

But the open style of play wasn't the only surprise on the night. The boo-birds forgot to buy tickets. They were conspicuously absent. There were anti-Oates signs, yes, but the lack of vocal disdain was deafening. Instead, Oates was actually being cheered when he touched the puck. It wasn't exactly a standing ovation, but it must have sounded like it to him after his reception two nights earlier.

The change in support wasn't exactly a major surprise to native St. Louisans. It's difficult for this city to stay adamantly upset with one of its heroes. The fans suddenly felt remorseful for their behavior at the last game. They begged for forgiveness. They wanted to kiss and make up.

It's like an older brother who beats up his younger sibling. The bigger kid is so angry he can't hold back. He belts his younger brother to settle the issue. But after a period of time, he falls victim to moral anguish. His heart feels like it weighs two tons. With his head down and tears in his eyes, he apologizes to his kid brother and repents for his past misdeeds (usually at the strong urging of Mom and Dad). If the younger brother doesn't suddenly try to swing back, then all is forgiven.

That's exactly what was happening here. The fans had taken a shot at Adam Oates and they couldn't live with themselves. After a 48-hour cooling-off period, the majority of the crowd regretfully acknowledged its poor behavior and asked to be pardoned.

The offensive shootout continued in the second period. Only this time the puck kept getting past the goaltenders. There was only one more shot on goal, but seven pucks hit the back of one net or the other, five of them ending up behind Patrick Roy. Suddenly, the Blues found themselves on top 5-3.

It was their fourth goal that sealed the fate of the anti-Oates crowd. With less than two minutes remaining in the period and the score knotted at 3-3, Oates was directing the power play from the right point. The Canadiens were doing a masterful job covering everyone near the net, so Oates had no choice but to rifle one at Roy. Somehow the puck threaded its way through a maze of players and flew past Roy's right leg into the net.

The crowd went absolutely nuts. Not only had the Blues come from behind to take the lead, but villain-turned-savior Adam Oates had scored the go-ahead goal. When the announcer shouted Oates' name, it had to have been one of the loudest receptions in Arena history. The poor old building did every-thing it could to withstand the decibel level. Somehow the walls stayed intact and the roof kept its place. I thought I had been to some loud rock concerts in this place, but nothing compared to the ear-splitting noise after Oates' goal. The only thing missing were fans flicking their lighters.

However, a collective groan suddenly filled the Arena. The play was being reviewed. It seems that Oates' shot had indeed hit something on the way to the net, and that something was Ron Wilson's stick, which he was waving around in midair. However, the replay judge ruled there was no conclusive evidence that Wilson's stick was above his shoulders; the goal stood. Montreal coach Pat Burns was livid, banging the plexiglass around his bench and yelling obscenities at the officials. His tirade cost him a two-minute bench penalty, and Hull scored on the subsequent power play.

After the judge's ruling, announcer Tom Calhoun had to explain the scoring again to reflect the change in names.

"Blues goal, his third of the year, scored by No. 18, Ron Wilson!!!"

Again, the fans shouted their approval. But it was nothing compared to their reaction to the following name.

"Assisted by No. 12, Adam Oates!!!"

I didn't think it was possible, but the crowd was even louder this time around. I began to look at the roof, expecting it to crash down at any time. I looked behind me for the nearest fire exits. There's talk that the Arena will be torn down when the new Kiel Center is erected downtown. I'm not so sure about that. The city better think about purchasing weapons from the Pentagon. This place would probably put up a better fight than Saddam Hussein.

The third period proved just as wild as the first two. After Montreal's Brent Gilchrist scored to make it 5-4, Brett Hull restored the Blues' two-goal lead with his second goal on the night and 47th of the year. The play was set up by none other than Adam Oates. He had the puck behind the Montreal net and waited for Hull to break clear. However, the Canadiens' defense again protected its territory expertly by knocking Bluenotes out of the crease area. Oates got tired of waiting and slowly skated to his right and into the far corner. Finally, he just shot the puck through a pile of players fighting for position in front of the net. The puck hit Hull's stick and deflected past Roy to give the Blues a 6-4 lead with a little more than 12 minutes to play.

Again, the fans went into a frenzy when the names were announced, proving Oates' point from the game before. If the

Blues had played this way against Washington, the boos would've been kept to a minimum. But with the fans having a change of heart and the Blues playing solidly against the league's best team, Oates could've run for mayor on this night and won in a landslide.

Unfortunately, the home team gave up its chance to win convincingly, letting its opponent back in the race. The Canadiens scored twice in a span of 2:30 late in the game to salvage a 6-6 tie. The one point was extremely disappointing for the Blues, who had lost a chance to gain some ground on first-place Detroit. A distressed Brian Sutter was outraged over his team's lack of discipline on defense.

"Some of you guys think I'm off my rocker in everything I stress," he said. "I hear people tell me, 'You worry too much about defense.' We get the goals to win every night, believe me. Anyone who says defense doesn't matter doesn't know shit from wild honey if he thinks we don't have to play defense in this league to win."

But on the subject of the fans, Sutter smiled for a second and changed the tone of his voice. The difference in fan support between the last two games didn't surprise him in the least.

"Each fan that walks in this rink, you have to stand up and pat them on the back because they've supported us," said Sutter. "When I started coaching here four years ago, there were 7,800 season ticket holders. Now, there's over 15,000. We draw more than New York City and the hockey hotbed of the world, Montreal. That's a credit to our fans, and we owe a hell of a lot to them."

Others who hadn't been in St. Louis for very long were perplexed about the crowd's sudden turnaround in support.

"It's hard to believe how you can boo a guy one night, and then two nights later show that kind of support," said Ron Sutter. "It's really mind-boggling."

The most-asked question circulating around the dressing room was, do you expect to see Adam next week? No one was positively sure either way. But most expressed hope. They wanted nothing more than to walk in the building next Monday and see Adam Oates lacing up his skates.

"We expect to see him," said Curtis Joseph. "We just wished him luck and hopefully he'll play well in the All-Star game and have a good time there."

"I plan on seeing him here," chimed in Hull, flashing his pearly whites. "I'm hoping like hell to see him here Monday."

Oates, meanwhile, avoided the media immediately after the Montreal game. He hid in the "Wives Room," which is across the hall from the locker room. Every time the door opened, one could see Oates sitting in a chair, looking into the hallway to see if the reporters had gone home yet.

Not a chance. They were going to stay all night if they had to. The story was too important. Not only did they want his reaction to the fans, but this was the last opportunity to talk to him before the All-Star game in two days. Was this your last game in a Blues uniform? Were you still prepared to walk? Or would we see you back here at practice Monday? Not one journalist left the back hallway. Sooner or later, he had to come out.

And sooner, he did. Either he got tired of trying to outwait the media, or one of his teammates convinced him to just go out there and answer questions for a few minutes. Either way, he emerged from the "Wives Room" and instructed the throng of reporters to follow him back into the locker room where there would be more space to accommodate everyone.

"I'm not sure what happened in two days, but it was definitely nice," said Oates, referring to the standing ovations he received after his two assists. "Two nights ago was very hard. It was the first time I had ever been booed. I have certain values that I place on myself, and one of those is coming out and working hard every night. What happens on the ice shouldn't matter to them."

Will you return to practice at the Arena Monday?

"I don't know," he shrugged. "I guess that's up to the Blues right now. We haven't had any significant talks in the last couple of days. I'm pretty optimistic something is going to happen this weekend. Hopefully, I'll be staying in St. Louis. That's what I want to do."

Do you think you're being a bit selfish? Aren't your actions disrupting the team?

"My intentions were never to distract the team," Oates said tersely. "I've talked to almost all the guys individually. Some people think I'm selfish. But I place a value on myself, and most of the guys understand that."

Notice how Oates used the words "some" and "most" when referring to his teammates? He was well aware that not everyone backed him. Oates' contract demands weren't necessarily destroying team morale, at least not yet. But they were most definitely leading to back-biting and mistrust. While telling the public what it wanted to hear, that the team was still one big happy family, some players privately groused about Oates' greed.

"I would never bitch about my contract," said one. "I like it here in St. Louis, and I wouldn't do anything to screw it up."

And if Oates returns to St. Louis after the All-Star game, will the fans boo him?

"They better," another one said.

Chapter Eleven

SLIP, SLIDING AWAY

Journalistic license. Those two words are a reporter's shield. The media are free to say or write just about anything they want, then hide behind that phrase.

"Hey, what gives you the right to report that?"

Journalistic license.

"Didn't you even get it confirmed?"

Didn't have to. Journalistic license.

In general, news reporters are responsible enough to take time and effort to get the facts straight and verify every bit of information before presenting the story to the public. Any copy editor or television news director worth his salt checks each story carefully before approving it for mass consumption. Respect, dignity, trust, and credibility are on the line each time a newspaper rolls off the presses or a newscast is beamed across the airwaves.

But then there's the wild and wacky, wonderful world of sports, as one local sports anchor likes to refer to it. The sports media never met a rumor they didn't like. I was a news reporter for six years and have been a sports reporter for the last two, and the one thing I still can't get over is how some so-called sports journalists print or broadcast stories that have no basis in fact, the kind of stuff that would get news people fired or sued or both. The information titillates, but it has no real merit or substance.

Never were there more unsubstantiated sports stories than during the Adam Oates controversy. Journalists were even taking unfair and baseless shots at each other to try and gain the upper hand. In his *Post-Dispatch* column on January 18, 1992, Bernie Miklasz wrote, "Speaking of Oppenheim, did you know that he works for Art Kaminsky—the same Kaminsky who represents Zip Rzeppa of KMOV, Channel 4? Hmmm."

So what? That line served no purpose other than to get readers to interpret a variety of hidden messages. Did Bernie mean that Zip first broke the pay-me-trade-me-or-I-walk story because of his association with Kaminsky and Oppenheim? And that any other information Zip gets has to be attributed to that connection?

"Cocaine was found in a first-floor room of City Hall today. Just so happens the mayor was in an adjacent room telling co-workers how he needed a 'Coke.' Hmmm."

Can you imagine what would happen if that appeared on the front page of the newspaper? Apologies wouldn't cut it. The paper would be forking over large sums of cash for that one. But when you turn the page to sports, or the anchors pitch to the sports desk, anything and everything goes.

Obviously, the world of sports affords greater latitude in the manner in which stories can be reported. Ethical boundaries are flexible when the world of sports takes center stage. After all, few athletes are seriously damaged because of rumors that are printed or reported about them, especially in St. Louis where its heroes are generally treated with kid gloves. Seldom are their personal lives highlighted in a negative fashion unless, as in the case of Mike Tyson, their actions become public record.

But there was something about the Adam Oates story that made some sports reporters forget about their journalistic code of ethics. When it came to possible trades, rumor after rumor after rumor was being reported without proper verification.

First, Oates was heading to Los Angeles for a combination of Tony Granato, Marty McSorley, Rob Blake, and Tomas Sandstrom. Then he was shipped to the Rangers for Sergei Nemchinov and an unnamed defenseman. Then he was traded to Hartford for John Cullen. Then he was told to switch places with Boston's Joe Juneau, who was playing for the Canadian Olympic team and hadn't even been signed yet. Oates was also rumored to be going to the Flyers, Jets, Oilers, and Islanders.

But the rumor that wins the top prize is the one that had four teams involved in the same trade. It went something like this: the

Flyers would ship Rick Tocchet and some other player to Edmonton for Dave Manson and Martin Gelinas. Manson, in turn, would be sent to the Blues for Oates, who would then be traded by the Oilers to the Kings for a variety of players mentioned at the top of the previous paragraph. Confused yet?

I kept waiting to hear the rumor where the league would finally step in and take over the mess, allowing every team to borrow Oates through the remainder of the season. "Let's see, you Kings can have Oates this Friday against the Canucks, but you have to let him go immediately after the game. After all, Hartford needs him for its game Saturday against Boston."

It didn't matter where the rumors were originating. If they were juicy enough and had the name Oates attached to them, then, by gosh, the public deserved to know about them.

"Where did you hear this trade rumor?" a reporter's boss might ask.

"From the guy who cleans the locker room," the reporter would answer.

"What the hell are you talking about? We can't report that."

"Hey, the guy's worked there for two decades. How can we question the accuracy of a 20-year veteran?"

Of course, we'll never know how truthful any of the trade rumors were. No reporter was ever allowed access to the executive offices when possible deals were being discussed. But it seems unlikely that any of the talked-about trades were actually close to being pulled off.

"Everyone talked about proposals," Brian Sutter would later say. "There was one. And at another time there was a second one. But that was it." During the week leading up to the All-Star break, in fact, Ron Caron was in Florida for a general managers' meeting, hoping to be flooded with offers for his disgruntled center. However, despite all the rumors to the contrary, Caron said there was little interest in Oates, mainly because his unhappiness had become public. Few teams were willing to give up quality players for a guy who had never been satisfied with any of his contracts.

"The Blues maintain their position that, yes, we would trade him in the right trade," said Caron after returning from the Sunshine State. "But there hasn't been a right trade. We talked to some teams, but all answers are negative."

So now the Blues were truly in a bind. They weren't going to give Oates another red cent. And yet they couldn't find anyone else willing to do so either. If they traded Oates, it was doubtful the Blues could get anyone of equal value in return. It was like trying to get rid of a player with bad knees. No matter how talented the player had been in the past, you just weren't going to get much for him because of his physical condition. With Oates, it was a financial condition.

And that too scared away prospective employers. No general manager wanted to trade for Oates and then have him barge into the office saying, "Look, I appreciate you saving me from those tightwads in St. Louis. But it's come to my attention in the three weeks I've been here that I'm grossly underpaid. What are you going to do about it?"

There wasn't a team in the NHL who wouldn't have wanted Oates strictly for his skills on the ice. He was one of the top two or three playmaking centers in the league. But his poor-mouth reputation was also common knowledge to each of the 22 teams. This would prove to be one of Ron Caron's greatest challenges.

There was no doubt the Blues general manager had a mandate to get rid of Oates. But to do so without depleting the team's talent or destroying its chemistry would test Caron's well-earned reputation as a successful wheeler-dealer.

*   *   *

Brett Hull was having the time of his life. With a nationally televised audience looking on, Hull skated up and down the Spectrum ice next to his idol, a man known simply as the Great One. Hull was on Cloud 99, realizing a dream he had fantasized about his entire career. On this January afternoon in Philadelphia, Brett Hull was playing alongside Wayne Gretzky.

It was a sight to behold. The two greatest goal scorers in the game today, perhaps ever, playing on the same line for the Campbell Conference All-Stars. With the Kings' Luc Robitaille taking care of business on the left side, the three men combined for three goals in the game's first 32 minutes to lead their team to a 10-6 win over the Wales Conference.

Hull's face must have hurt for days after the game. He flashed his million-dollar grin from the moment he arrived in Philadelphia to the game's closing ceremonies when he was presented with a new truck as the game's MVP. Hull scored two goals, both assisted by Gretzky, while adding an assist of his own on a goal by, you guessed it, the Great One.

"I've wanted to play with Mr. Gretzky now for a long time," said Hull. "And I don't think I'm the only one. There are a lot of people who don't get that opportunity. I was just having the time of my life. It was fun out there. It felt good out on the ice."

In the same locker room, just a few feet away, sat Adam Oates. He, too, had delighted in playing alongside the game's greatest stars. Oates chipped in an assist on a second-period goal by the Flames' Theo Fleury.

"It was a great day," Oates said after the game. "It's been a lot of fun."

Still, one couldn't help but think about Oates' predicament. Here he sat, perhaps sharing a locker room with Brett Hull for the last time. While reporters swarmed Hull to ask about his MVP performance, others gathered around Oates to ask him about his plan to quit the team Monday. Oates said he was going through with his threat, but admitted it would be extremely difficult to part ways with No. 16.

"I would hate to leave him not just because of hockey, but because he's a good friend," said Adam. "It's not too often you get to spend that much time with a buddy. That weighs heavily on my mind. He understands my situation, and he's behind me. I really appreciate that. That's what friends are for."

Hull and Oates were the only members of the Blues contingent still left in the building when the final horn sounded. While the all-stars were racking up the score past a beleaguered group of goalies, the Blues' top three executives, Mike Shanahan, Jack Quinn, and Ron Caron, left the rink to catch an afternoon flight back to St. Louis. That the team's top brass exited before the second period ended was not a good sign for Oates and Oppenheim, who didn't attend the game at all. Oates had hoped to meet with his bosses at an All-Star party following the game. But now, any chance of a last-minute deal to keep Oates in St. Louis seemed remote.

Oates did run into Quinn at a party the night before the All-Star game. It was a rather awkward and uncomfortable meeting as the two men, along with Oates' dad, David, tried to socialize. In fact, one of the announcers of the All-Star game mentioned how David Oates and Jack Quinn were somewhat argumentative.

"That's garbage," snapped Adam Oates after hearing those comments. "We just walked by and kind of bumped into them. It certainly wasn't the easiest situation in the world. But I was with my family and friends and introduced them all. My dad and Jack talked for awhile."

However, those would be the last talks between the two sides for some time. The attention now shifted to Oates and whether he would go through on his threat to stage a one-man strike. Several reporters met Oates at the airport when he returned Sunday afternoon, but he had absolutely no comment, not even a "get lost." To find the answer, you had to go to the Arena the next morning and learn on your own what Oates was going to do.

As it turned out, however, no one had to wait quite that long. As St. Louisans picked up their morning paper on Monday, January 20, hours before the Blues were scheduled to skate, they turned to the sports page to find a headline that told the story.

"Oates Awaits Blues' True Colors.
Center Says He Will Practice Today"

Dave Luecking did it again. All it took was one little phone call to Oates' house Sunday night and— voila!—he had the answer before anyone else. (Is it possible that Luecking once had lunch with Art Kaminsky—the same Kaminsky who employs Lou Oppenheim, who represents Adam Oates? Hmmm.)

Needless to say, every sports reporter besides Luecking felt a bit depressed and deprived driving to the rink that morning. Depressed because the beat writer beat everyone else to the story once again. Deprived because the story took away the uncertainty of what was going to happen. Would we find Oates cleaning out his locker? Would we see him telling his teammates good-bye? Would we see him at all? We had the answer now. There would be no surprises. Oates was staying. At least for now.

As usual, Hull and Oates arrived together for the morning skate. "He's baaaaack," quipped Hull as the two players stepped out of Oates' Chevy Blazer. The rest of the morning became a game of follow-the-leader with Oates being the pied piper and the media tagging along like mice. Reporters stayed glued to his heels, hoping to find out why he had backed down. I half-expected some of them to lace up a pair of skates and follow him to center ice.

Oates had nothing to say until practice was over, when he motioned everyone to follow him into the locker room. It was a hilarious sight, as more than a dozen people with an assortment of pens, pads, tape recorders, microphones, and cameras followed Oates into the dressing room in single file. At the end of the line was Hull singing, "Should I stay or should I go now?" The note on his jersey definitely didn't symbolize a talent for singing.

While the throng of reporters fought for position around Oates' stall, he suddenly sat down on the bench, forcing everyone to get on their knees and fight for position all over again. I almost started laughing as I forced a microphone through someone's armpit just to get it close to Oates' mouth.

I looked over my shoulder at Hull, who was just staring in disbelief. "Holy mackerel," he said, wide-eyed.

Just being seen in a Blues' practice jersey would certainly be construed as a weakening on Oates' part. Quinn and Oates had drawn lines in the sand, stared at each other for a couple of weeks, and Oates blinked first.

However, Quinn wasn't treating this as a game of I-won-you-lost. He applauded Oates' appearance, even telling him after practice that he "took a step in the right direction," but that the Blues' position had not changed. Oates would have to honor his current contract while Caron looked around the league for a potential buyer.

So why did Oates have a change of heart? Why did he back down from his threat to walk? It seems Oates thought that perhaps there was a chance that Mike Shanahan might get directly involved in settling the matter. Oates had heard through the grapevine that Shanahan wanted to see him.

"I was told Mr. Shanahan wanted to talk to me at his convenience," said Oates. "I respect that. I've been waiting by the phone ever since."

Adam must have grown bored waiting for the phone to ring. Shanahan had no desire whatsoever to appease Oates' demands for a new deal. According to Quinn, Shanahan only wanted to congratulate Oates for making the All-Star team.

Nothing more. But having heard the team chairman wanted to talk to him gave Oates the perfect alibi to break his threat and report to practice.

It was clear that Oates did not want to sit out. He was trying to show management he was willing to do anything to work out a deal. I didn't quit the team, he was saying.

Despite his denials, it appeared that something indeed was happening behind Quinn's closed door. And it wasn't just the possibility of a trade. Several signs pointed to a potential new deal that might let both sides save face.

After establishing himself as the media's best friend, Lou Oppenheim had suddenly grown quiet. He was still picking up his phone in New York. He just wasn't saying anything.

"I wish I could say something," Oppenheim said. "You know how much I like to hear myself talk. But I just can't discuss the matter right now."

Can we take this as a positive sign? Is something happening?

"I just can't get into that," he said. "I wish I could. We're still hopeful things can be worked out."

The Golden Brett was also laying down a trail of hints. Just read between the lines here.

"After talking with people, and people talking with Adam...well, I don't know what he's told you so I'm not going to elaborate on it," Hull said. "Let's just say some good things have been said between the two parties. You show a sign of good faith like that (Oates reporting to practice) and it just makes everything a lot easier."

Meanwhile, life on the ice was anything but easy for Hull, Oates, and the Blues. In their first game after the All-Star break, the Blues wore their road jerseys even though they were playing at home. The jersey switch was being repeated across the NHL to commemorate the league's 75th anniversary. Up until the early 1970s, teams wore their dark jerseys at home, so this move was to call attention to the "glorious past" of the NHL.

Of course, the Blues had shown a penchant for playing poorly when wearing their road uniforms. Their 6-13-5 record away from The Arena was a testament to that. Sure enough, despite holding a 5-1 lead over the Buffalo Sabres with less than 13 minutes to go in the game, the Blues must have finally noticed what jerseys they were wearing. They panicked as their four-goal lead slowly slipped away.

Dale Hawerchuk scored on a power play at 6:47 of the third period to cut the lead to 5-2. That seemed harmless enough. But at 18:24, Pat LaFontaine scored from the crease area to pull the Sabres within two goals. Still, there was no way Buffalo could score two goals in the final 90 seconds to tie it up. Was there?

Just 41 seconds later, at 19:05, LaFontaine did it again. He poked in the rebound of a Ken Sutton shot, and, just like that, the score stood at 5-4 Blues. A collective groan filled the Arena. A delightfully one-sided affair had become unexpectedly close.

Actually, the fans should have felt fortunate. They were on vacation without spending an extra cent. They were watching in person how the Blues performed on the road. The fans didn't have to watch the game on TV and hear over and over how Rick Meagher checks for a living even though he retired the year before. It was as if they were in Buffalo, witnessing the men in those dark blue jerseys find another way to lose on the road. And the fans didn't even have a three-hour flight back to St. Louis.

The Sabres pulled their goaltender in the final 45 seconds of play, and it nearly worked. LaFontaine, trying to score his third goal in 96 seconds, broke across the blue line and headed straight toward Curtis Joseph. Just as he was about to get the shot away, Paul Cavallini hooked LaFontaine down from behind and was sent straight to the penalty box for an indiscretion that probably saved the tying goal.

With their goalie still on the bench, the Sabres had a 6-4 man advantage with 16 seconds left. With the crowd on its feet and the bench players on the edge of their skates, the Blues' Ron Wilson won a huge faceoff in his own end and cleared the puck to the other end of the rink. The Sabres could not recover in time to get a shot away, and the Blues held on for the 5-4 win.

Once again, St. Louis was outshot by a large margin, 40-27. Oates could cry all he wanted, but Curtis Joseph was the most underpaid man in hockey, if not in all of sports. Joseph had silenced much of the talk about Scott Stevens. Sure, it would have been great to have Stevens still in a Blues uniform. But if that meant Joseph would be in a Devils jersey instead, where would the Blues be without their star goaltender?

They learned the answer two nights later at home against the Kings. Still wearing their road jerseys, the Blues raced to a 3-

0 lead in the first 18 minutes of play. L.A.'s Luc Robitaille scored with one second left in the first period to cut the lead to 3-1, but the Blues got the goal back early in the second period on Nelson Emerson's 19th goal of the year. That's when the Kings made their comeback. And unlike 48 hours before against Buffalo, the Blues were unable to hold on.

Los Angeles scored five goals past Guy Hebert in the final 31 minutes of play to beat the beleaguered Blues 6-5. Hebert was not sharp, but several of the Kings' goals were the direct result of breakdowns in the Blues' defensive coverage. You can make a few mistakes on offense and get away with it. Commit a few errors on defense, and it'll cost you the game.

"I'm very concerned," said Blues captain Garth Butcher. "When you get a lead you can take care of your job defensively. Then chances will happen for you because the other team is taking chances to get their goals. But we seemed to take our chances at inopportune times, and they were able to score on them."

The bill had finally come due. The Blues had gone into debt earlier in the year by counting on last-minute heroics to avoid defeat. Now the balance sheet was evening out.

The next day, the Blues were put through a long and arduous workout. But not with their legs, with their brains. Just before the morning skate at the Brentwood ice rink, Ron Caron shut the locker room doors and preached to the players for nearly 40 minutes on how to play hockey, just in case they had forgotten. Then, after the Blues buzzed around the ice for about an hour and a half, Caron ordered the players to the Arena for the premiere of a new movie called, "This Is Your Life, And You Ain't Gonna Like It." The setting: the Arena. The actors: the Blues. The plot: how a hockey team manages to win only one of its last three home games despite holding comfortable third-period leads in all of them.

The movie was actually a videotape replay of their loss to the Kings the night before. Caron shuttled through the tape frame-by-frame, sometimes replaying a particular moment over and over again. The group sat in the locker room all afternoon, re-learning the game of hockey and what it takes to be successful. Little emphasis was put on offense. The majority of "the professor's" lesson centered on defense and the lack thereof.

"Oooh, boy, it wasn't fun, and it wasn't pretty," said one player. "But we deserved it. We needed it. We haven't been playing very well lately."

However, others were a bit bored, even confused, by Caron's message.

"He would ramble off into tangents," said one. "He was hard to follow sometimes."

"He wouldn't answer certain questions directly," said another.

Admittedly, Caron can be difficult to understand at times. His brain works much faster than his mouth, and there are occasions when the message somehow gets scrambled along the way. Earlier in the year, Caron tried to compare Hull's goal-scoring drought to the demise of the St. Louis football Cardinals. He left this author in a state of brainlock for weeks trying to figure out the comparison. There probably is a brilliant, analytical analogy on the subject stored in Caron's noggin. But formulating his thoughts into words, while at the same time translating them from his native French to English, can prove to be a formidable task.

But on the subject of team defense, the professor's profundities somehow got through, as evidenced by the Blues' following game against Vancouver, the final contest of a five-game home stand. The Blues looked almost terrified of venturing into the offensive zone. They assumed a goal-line stance along their blue line and dared the Canucks to cross it. The result? Vancouver managed only seven shots on goal in the first period, five in the second, and six in the third, as Joseph and his defensive-minded mates shut out the Canucks. The 18 shots were the fewest the Blues had allowed in regulation play since giving up 16 to the Oilers way back on October 10, the third game of the season.

However, there was one problem. One BIG problem. The Blues apparently forgot that to win a hockey game, you generally need to score a goal or two. Vancouver also shut out the Blues, as the two teams battled to a rare 0-0 tie after 60 minutes of play. Ron Caron had apparently made himself clear. Perhaps too clear. His team was so concerned about bottling up the middle and playing good, sound, positional hockey, it slipped the players' minds that they should, every once in awhile, carry the puck to the other end and maybe shoot it at the opposing team's net.

In the extra period, the Blues immediately retreated to their own zone in an attempt to blank the Canucks for five more minutes and earn a point for the scoreless tie. They hadn't shown much of a propensity to score in the first 60 minutes, and they weren't going to change their game plan now. The message—just hold on for 300 more seconds and the shutout is ours.

Unfortunately, there was no game plan for a bouncing puck, the kind of bouncing puck that eludes everyone's stick but the guy standing near the net wearing an enemy jersey. A little more than two minutes into the extra period, the Canucks' Jim Sandlak sent a pass from behind the Blues' net to just below the left post. The puck hopped over Lee Norwood's stick to Tom Fergus. The Canucks center had trouble controlling the knuckling puck and just slapped it toward the net. As he always does, Norwood fell flat on the ice to block the puck. It bounced off Norwood's midsection, deflected over to Brown where it promptly bounced off his knee and right back to Fergus. With the puck still fluttering around as if drunk, Fergus managed to get enough wood on it to sneak it between Joseph's skates. Sixty-two minutes and 12 seconds after the first puck was dropped, the first goal was scored.

For three periods and then some, the Blues were more defensive than a politician in trouble. They were tighter than a speedo on John Goodman. And yet, because they couldn't follow the bouncing puck, they managed to find yet another way to lose. No matter what they tried, no matter what they did, the Blues were coming out on the short end of the hockey stick. They had just completed their most unsuccessful home stand of the year, one win in five games. And in that one victory they had to hold on for their lives, as the Sabres and Pat LaFontaine nearly pulled off a miraculous comeback.

But instead of hanging their heads after losing to Vancouver and crying over the game's only goal, the boys in blue pointed to their defensive work as something to build on. If they continued to suffocate their opponents like they had the Canucks, the goals would eventually come, and so would the wins.

"This was a good game. I don't know how entertaining it was, but it was a good game," said Joseph. "I think our guys played very well positionally and kept the mistakes to a minimum."

"It's kind of unfortunate that it was a bouncing puck there at the end that determined the hockey game," observed Coach Sutter. "I'm disappointed as hell at the outcome of the game, but I can't be disappointed with the effort. There's been a lot of pressure on us lately to tighten up and play better defensively. We have to continue to do that."

"Mr. Caron talked so much about playing defensive hockey, and then we come out and play so solid," Oates added. "We kept the shots down and minimized the chances. It's just that their only goal hurt us."

Oates and the Blues now had to embark on a four-game, coast-to-coast trip that would start in Los Angeles and end in Philadelphia. However, for Oates, the end could come even sooner. There were so many rumors floating around that he was heading to Los Angeles, he wasn't about to be caught out there empty-handed. He packed extra sticks and other belongings for the trip west. He had a sneaking suspicion he was about to play his last game as a member of the Blues. After all, if there was anyone who could afford to make Oates a millionaire, it was Kings owner Bruce McNall.

*   *   *

"Oates stick handles through a crowd at center ice, across the blue line. He'll stop just inside the left circle and look for Hull in the slot. But wait! What's this? Oates has dropped his stick and is taking off his jersey. That's right, he is taking off his jersey right there on the ice! And look at this! Tomas Sandstrom is also taking off HIS jersey and the two are exchanging their uniforms while play is still going on! This is unbelievable!! Now, Oates picks up his stick and starts moving the puck the other way. I can't believe what I'm seeing!! Now Jeff Brown is taking off his sweater. And so is Paul Cavallini. Oh my, Rob Blake and Marty McSorley have jumped off the Kings' bench to go join Brian Sutter! Go crazy, folks, go crazy!!"

The rumor mill was churning so rapidly, I kept expecting an Oates trade package to develop right in the middle of a game. An on-ice swap had never occurred in the 75-year history of the game, so why not now? That's how crazy the whole Oates affair had become. It seemed that every member of the Blues organi-zation was now being mentioned in trade rumors with the exception of the office receptionist, Pam Barrett, and that's only because she had a no-trade clause in her contract.

"Rumors are just something the press likes to make up," said Brown, a man frequently mentioned as the guy to be sent packing with Oates. "Everybody knows the Oates situation and people are making up different names and stuff. Mr. Caron has assured us that there's no substance to any of the names being mentioned. If management wants to make changes, then that's their decision. But nobody knows what's going to happen."

Perhaps. But Coach Sutter was already preparing for life without Adam Oates. Sutter threw out his first line to start the game in Los Angeles, and Oates wasn't a part of it. As many expected, and even feared, Ron Sutter was the new number-one center, with Hull to his right and Shanahan to his left. The Sutter bashers were given additional material with which to build their case of nepotism. A man who had set a number of Blues assist records was being replaced with a guy who had never scored more than 60 points in a season.

Oates, meanwhile, was dropped to the second line with Christian and Emerson. That was it. The evidence was over-whelming. Sutter knew something that the rest of us only assumed. Oates would be traded in a matter of days, perhaps hours.

The contest was very one-sided in the first period, and, surprisingly it was on the Blues' side. They continued to play smothering defense, but now added an offensive assault to the game plan. The Blues fired 13 shots at the Kings' net while giving up only five at their own. Unfortunately, the only goal scored in the opening period was by L.A.'s Corey Millen on a power play with under a minute left to go. Once again, the Blues had nothing to show for their strong effort on the road.

The second period was lopsided again, only this time it was the Kings who were doing all the work. They scored twice in the first four minutes to extend their lead to 3-0. The deficit forced the Blues to abandon their defensive shell and start taking some offensive chances, exactly as the Kings had in coming back from three goals down to beat the Blues in St. Louis.

Leave it to the Golden One to get things started. With less than two minutes to play in the second period, he scored his 50th of the year, becoming only the second player in NHL history to score 50 goals in 50 games more than once. The only other player to achieve the feat was sitting on the Kings' bench, Wayne Gretzky.

"That's one of the things I'm very proud of because I'm in a category with a guy like that," Hull said. "It's quite an achievement. It was a big thrill."

A big enough thrill that it inspired the rest of the team to come out flying in the third period. They were even more dominating than in the first, pinning the Kings in their own zone and firing away at Kelly Hrudey. Halfway through the period, Oates picked up a loose puck near the left post and slid a no-look, backhanded pass across the crease to Dave Christian standing near the right post. Christian easily redirected the puck into the net to cut the Kings' lead to one. If Oates was hurt by being moved off the top line he wasn't showing it. Like the rest of his teammates, he was playing an outstanding game.

Four minutes later, with the Blues trying to kill a penalty, Joseph came out of his net to clear the puck down the left boards. Richie Sutter got behind the Kings' point men, picked up the rolling puck, and was off to the races. As soon as he skated into the right circle, he let go a slapshot that Hrudey stopped. However, the puck rebounded straight up the middle. Paul Cavallini, trailing the play, put the puck right back on net. Hrudey was still on the ice after his first save and was unable to stop Cavallini's open-net shot. The Blues' 11th short-handed goal of the year, tops in the league, tied the score at 3-3.

Both teams had excellent chances to score in the remaining few minutes of the third period and in the five-minute overtime. But Joseph and Hrudey each came up with some spectacular saves to preserve the tie for their respective teams.

The Blues once again played Scrooge on defense, limiting the Kings to 24 shots, four of those in overtime. Caron's message was firmly entrenched in their brains. At the same time, they were able to get the offense untracked, pummeling Hrudey with 37 shots. Still, the Blues managed only a single point for their effort. They had won just once in their last six games and only three of their last 12. With a record of 21-20-9, the Blues trailed second-place Chicago by five points. Worse yet, they were only five points ahead of fourth-place Minnesota which had just beaten Hartford 4-3.

Two nights later, the Blues got past the San Jose Sharks 4-2 for their first victory in ten days. On the ice for St. Louis was none other than Adam Oates. The Blues hadn't left him behind in Los Angeles for a bundle of broken sticks and box of hockey pucks to be named later. His trip to San Jose could only mean one thing. A trade with Los Angeles wasn't going to happen. Otherwise, it would've been made when the Blues were still there. The black cloud of uncertainty was still hanging over the team.

Blame it on the Oates fiasco, or point fingers at the grueling coast-to-coast schedule of four games in six days, but the Blues were horrendous in Pittsburgh and Philadelphia. Against the Penguins, the Blues suddenly forgot how to play defense, allowing 26 shots on goal. Uh, that's not 26 shots for the game; that's 26 in the first period! That broke the team record of 25 shots allowed in one period, which had been reached three times, most recently in 1981 against Toronto.

The Penguins scored four times in that opening frame and held on for a 4-1 win. The Blues' only goal was scored by defenseman Jason Marshall, who had just been called up from Peoria to replace the injured Lee Norwood. It was Marshall's first goal in just his second NHL game.

The very next night, February 2, things went from bad to worse. Against the last-place Flyers, a team playing without injured stars Rick Tocchet and Pelle Eklund, the Blues were absolutely lifeless, giving up five goals on 33 shots and falling 5-1. For the second game in a row, Hull and Oates were held without a point; Dave Lowry scored the Blues' lone goal.

A mini-slump had dropped its prefix and turned into a full-blown maxi-slump. The Blues limped home with only two wins in their last nine games, four in their last 14, five in their last 17. Players were grumbling. They were pointing fingers. They were trying to come up with excuses for their pathetic play over the last six weeks. Though they wouldn't do so on the record, many were pointing to the locker stall of No. 12.

Was the excuse merely convenient? Or did it have some merit? It didn't seem to matter. Whether real or perceived, the Oates controversy seemed to be taking its toll. That's all the media wanted to talk about, continuously forcing the players to discuss the matter. Some of the guys who had been against Oates getting any more money didn't seem to really care anymore.

Either sign him or trade him, they said. But for crying out loud, do something! The team was crumbling under the weight of the controversy, and it seemed the players had no stamina left to deal with the problem. For the most part, St. Louis hockey fans were unaware of the clubhouse dissension. They knew, of course, that not everything was rosy, but fans got a jolt of reality when they opened the sports page on the morning of February 4. Dave Luecking penned an in-depth analysis of the Blues and came up with several disheartening conclusions: the team was possibly heading toward its first no-show in the playoffs in 13 years; Brian Sutter had lost control of superstar Brett Hull, and some of the younger players were intimidated by Hull's brash, outspoken nature, especially in his stubborn defense of Oates. Luecking referred to the Blues as "Team Turmoil," a fitting title for a team on the road to nowhere.

"Appropriately, some players headed to the golf course Monday," Luecking wrote, "perhaps in preparation for early elimination from the National Hockey League playoffs."

At practice that morning, I had to ask Ron Caron about the article. The man was absolutely livid, referring to the piece as a bunch of unconfirmed hearsay.

"I want some fucking names," Caron said, referring to the unnamed players Luecking quoted. "There is no turmoil. You have all the turmoil you want. There are all kinds of ways of looking at reality. You can keep counting disappointment, but I don't look at things that way."

And what about the coach, the man who was behind the moves that so drastically changed the complexion of his team? Where did his responsibility lie? And did he fear being fired just one year after being named coach of the year?

"You've got to be concerned about that every day," answered Sutter. "I'm always looking to be better and upgrade myself. We're all in this together. Hey, things haven't gone the way we've wanted them to. It's everyone's responsibility to try and upgrade that."

And one possible solution to upgrade the situation was to finally solve the Oates dispute. Despite Caron's remarks, many players applauded Luecking's article, calling it "honest and truthful." Even Jack Quinn had had enough. Some of his front-office people remarked how they'd "never seen him so passionate about one thing" as over the Oates controversy.

The time had come to rid the team of a festering problem. Since Quinn had made it clear that he wasn't about to touch Oates' contract for the third time, the Blues had to trade him somewhere, somehow, for something. It was getting to the point where it didn't matter who or what they got in return. If the Blues were to have any shot at saving a rapidly decaying season, they needed to find a suitable buyer. And fast.

Chapter Twelve

THE CLOUD LIFTS

He looked larger than life. Like a character from a Far Side cartoon, he was grossly out of proportion. He was actually only 6'1", 215 pounds, but on this night, the man looked gargantuan. It wasn't his physical appearance that made him appear so colossal. It was everything he represented. For this one player carried the weight of all the Blues' troubles squarely on his shoulders. Everything that had gone wrong in the team's 25th anniversary season was written across his jersey. He was the symbol of all of their sins. And yet he wasn't even a member of the Blues' organization.

It was February 6, and Scott Stevens had returned to the Arena, wearing, fittingly, a Devils uniform. By no means was it his fault that the Blues were laboring at .500. But his forced departure five months earlier was just the start of a bedeviled season. His absence was indirectly blamed for every trade, every injury, every goal, every loss. Hell, he was probably at fault for Oates' current state of depression. If only Scott Stevens were still in St. Louis, many fans said, the Blues would be atop the division, the players would be joyously happy, and the world would be a perfect place.

Of course, reality tells quite a different story. No question, the Blues missed their former captain dearly. But for starters, Stevens' departure allowed Curtis Joseph to develop into one of the top goaltenders in the league. We'll never know if Vincent Riendeau could've withstood a nightly barrage of 35 to 40 shots. But we do know that Joseph routinely kicked out more than 90 percent of those shots, while Riendeau's best save percentage had been 89 percent the year before.

And don't forget that Riendeau had injured his knee just days after reporting to Detroit. Was that an injury just waiting to happen? If so, the Blues would have started the season counting on Pat Jablonski, with only 12 games of NHL experience, and Guy Hebert, who had yet to wear an NHL jersey, to lead them to the promised land.

It's an argument that will forever be debated among Blues fans. One camp firmly believes that Stevens' presence alone would have kept the shots on goal down to an average of 30 or fewer. No matter who was in goal, a lower shot count meant fewer goals.

The other side argues that Riendeau, even if he had stayed healthy, had proven his unworthiness in the playoffs. Who cares about the regular season? these fans demanded. Riendeau couldn't get the job done in postseason play and it was time, with or without Scott Stevens, to give the young kid, Curtis Joseph, a shot. Besides, it wasn't the lack of defensive talent that permitted so many shots on goal, they said. It was the lack of a defensive game plan that kept the Blues running around in their own zone wondering how the heck to get the puck out.

You could almost hear the thousands of conversations taking place inside the Arena as Stevens skated onto the ice. Everyone was offering his or her opinion on the subject. Some even cheered Stevens' appearance. And that's why Stevens looked so monstrously large as he moved around the rink. All eyes were focused squarely on his broad shoulders. Here he was. Back in St. Louis. Wearing red and green instead of blue and gold. This was more than just a game. The Blues, especially Brendan Shanahan, were determined to prove they could win without Scott Stevens. They were determined to beat him head-to-head.

In two previous meetings, both at the Meadowlands, the Devils had whipped the Blues 7-2 on opening night, and edged them 4-3 on January 9. But this contest was different. It was being played before the home crowd. The Blues had a chance to redeem themselves and quiet the pro-Stevens faction. A loss would only make the doubters scream that much louder.

With so much attention directed toward Stevens, many fans may have missed an odd sight at the other end of the rink. Brett

Hull, casually gliding around in circles wearing his familiar No. 16, was also wearing a very unfamiliar letter "A," as in alternate captain. For the first time in his five-year NHL career, Hull was given the honor of wearing a letter on his jersey, "borrowing" it from Ron Sutter who was out with a knee injury. The "A" symbolized leadership. It symbolized character. And it was long overdue. As many fans and media members pointed out, Hull should have been awarded the "A," if not the "C," at the beginning of the year.

"It's just a letter," Hull said as he shrugged off a suggestion that it was a source of honor and pride. "You get to talk to the refs, that's all. If that makes you change your game, I don't think you should be in the game."

But don't you think you should have been wearing a letter since game one?

"I can't comment on that," he was quick to answer.

So according to Hull, this was just another game. Which meant the Blues and Curtis Joseph would be pummeled with a multitude of shots early and often. Sure enough, the Devils surrounded the Blues' net and fired seven shots in the game's first five minutes. But it was the Blues who scored first, at 6:56, on their fourth shot. Oates cleared the puck ahead to Hull who was patiently waiting above his own blue line. The Golden Brett skated in alone, lost control of the puck for a split-second as Bruce Driver hacked at him from behind, but still managed to nudge it between Craig Billington's skates for a 1-0 lead. When Oates' assist was announced, the boo-birds returned. The mood of the fans had shifted once again.

Later in the period, Dave Mackey, just called up from Peoria the day before, scored his first goal as a member of the Blues on a backhander to increase the lead to 2-0. The team picked up the offensive pace after that and should've had at least two more goals. They outshot the Devils 13-12 and looked remarkably proficient, in contrast to their recent poor play.

Right as the horn sounded to end the first period, Stevens and Shanahan banged in the corner to control a loose puck. They eyed one another and, just like their last meeting a month before, grabbed each other's jerseys and started politely pushing back and forth. Two men who had involuntarily changed places were staring at the source of their troubles. Stevens never wanted to leave St. Louis, and he was looking right into the eyes of the person responsible. Shanahan, meanwhile, was staring at the man of whom he was so constantly reminded. Standing face to face, neither was going to back away. Although they weren't throwing punches, they weren't going to separate until the linesmen stepped in.

Or until Lee Norwood stepped in. A loyal teammate, Norwood wasn't about to let Shanahan get thrown out of the game for punching the man he certainly wanted to take a swing at. Without provocation, Norwood landed a few blows to Stevens' head. The only problem was, Stevens couldn't retaliate. His arms were tied up by one of the linesmen.

Stevens was furious. He tried desperately to escape the clutches of the linesman to get at Norwood, Shanahan, anybody. However, Stevens wasn't going anywhere but his dressing room. As the officials restored order and escorted both benches to their respective exits, referee Mark Faucette gave Stevens and Shanahan two minutes each for roughing and tossed Norwood out of the game.

In all, Faucette would call 70 minutes in penalties in a very physical, even dirty, game. The sticks and fists were flying everywhere. The Blues may not be the biggest team in the world, but they're as gritty and feisty as anyone, and they matched the Devils punch for punch.

Just 39 seconds into the second period, the home team extended its lead. Rick Zombo, another player indirectly affected by Judge Houston's decision, buzzed down the right side and wound up to shoot as he approached the circle. However, just as Billington eased over to cut off the angle, Zombo wristed a pass to Hull in the opposite circle. With a blink of an eye, Hull one-timed the pass just inside the left post to give the Blues a 3-0 lead.

Jeff Brown got involved in the scoring just before the period ended. With Hull fighting Laurie Boschman for position in front of the New Jersey net, Brown rifled a slapshot from the left point. Just as it left Brown's stick, Hull turned away and let the puck fly right past him. Billington was screened and never saw the puck until it hit the back of the net. Despite being outshot 25-18 after two periods, the Blues held a 4-0 advantage.

You'd think, conscious of their recent history of blowing huge third-period leads, the Blues would continue to muster some kind of offensive output against the Devils to avoid letting them back into the game. Wrong. Clinging to their four-goal lead, the Blues retreated into their own zone and played prevent defense. They basically stood aside and let Joseph make save after save. It was as if the Blues were asking the fans, "Who would you rather have now? Scott Stevens, who hasn't been much of a factor, or Curtis Joseph, who has single-handedly shut out the opposition?" If Judge Houston was watching this game back home in Ontario, what would his answer have been?

The Devils finally broke the goose egg at 13:26 of the final period on a short-handed goal by Tom Chorske. He skated alone down the right wing and slapped a shot that beat Joseph on the far post. No question, it was a shot Joseph should have stopped. He made at least a dozen saves of the spectacular variety. It was a crying shame to lose the shutout on a routine shot, and with the man advantage, no less.

The Blues were outshot by an incredible 18-5 margin in the third period, 42-23 for the game. And yet the final score showed a one-sided 4-1 victory for the Blues, only their third win in nearly four weeks. In a game that had so many individual and personal battles going on, the Blues came out on top on all counts. As he had been proving all season, Curtis Joseph was the team's MVP. And what a night to turn in one of his outstanding performances, against Scott Stevens and the New Jersey Devils, a team Joseph would be playing for if Judge Houston had only made the "right" decision.

At the conclusion of the game, public address announcer Tom Calhoun shouted out the game's three stars.

"The number-three star, stopping 41 of 42 shots, No. 31, goalie Curtis Joseph!"

With the crowd giving him a standing ovation, Joseph returned to the ice for an obligatory wave before heading to the dressing room.

"The game's number-two star, with three assists, number 12, Adam Oates!"

This time, no one emerged to be greeted by the fans. Amid a mixture of cheers and jeers, No. 12 was nowhere to be seen. Despite having been told he was one of the game's stars, Oates declined to stick around and wave to the crowd. Instead, he had already retreated to the privacy of the dressing room. He had been roundly booed in two of the last three games, and he wasn't about to give the fans another opportunity to shower him with Bronx cheers.

Hull waved to his adoring fans after his name was announced as the game's number-one star. But many were still outraged at being snubbed by Oates. They saw Oates as a guy who had already quit on his teammates. Now he was quitting on them. There was absolutely no chance Oates would ever be cheered again at the Arena.

Meanwhile, up in the executive boxes sat two gentlemen who could barely hold their anger. Mike Shanahan and Jack Quinn were furious at what they had just witnessed. It was one thing for Oates to quarrel with team officials. But deliberately turning his back on paying customers would not be tolerated.

Adam Oates had just pulled his last stunt.

*   *   *

Something wasn't right. As I sat in the locker room at the Brentwood ice rink following practice, the players seemed unusually quiet. Looking around, I suddenly realized the reason for the silence. Brett Hull was nowhere to be seen.

Hull is the life of every party. He's a bit more reserved before and after games, but catch him in the morning after practice and watch out. He's always jabbering, singing, yelling, and cajoling. Usually all in one breath. The man's mouth is like the Energizer rabbit. It keeps going and going and going and going...

But on the morning of February 7, the day after the 4-1 win over the Devils, Hull disappeared after practice. Even stranger, Adam Oates was missing too. There was no way they had already left the building. Practice had just ended minutes ago. The two were usually the first ones off the ice, but they didn't exit the rink THAT early.

"Jack Quinn told Brett to give him a call," one of the guys softly told me in the dressing room. "He's back in the coach's office."

The source didn't know exactly what was going on. But we both speculated it had something to do with Oates' being traded.

As Oates' best friend, Hull had become so intertwined in the contract dispute that Quinn wanted Hull to hear the news directly from the top and not secondhand from some reporter. Without a doubt, Quinn also strongly recommended that his superstar not talk to the press about the trade. Dangerous in its candor, Hull's mouth had gotten him in trouble before. The last thing Quinn wanted to see on the nightly news was his million-dollar player spewing derogatory sound bites about Blues management.

Convinced I was on to an exclusive story (little did I know John Kelly was about to break into KMOX programming with news of the trade), I hurried to my car to get over to the Arena as fast as possible. As I was shuffling across the parking lot, I noticed Hull right in front of me with a crowd of autograph seekers following him. As soon as I saw his face, I knew his good buddy had been sent packing.

Hull was in a daze. His head was in a cloud so thick his eyes needed fog lights. He barely acknowledged the people around him, signing an autograph or two as he continued to walk to Oates' Blazer. He didn't even notice a youngster politely tugging at his jacket to get his attention. Hull's body was on that parking lot, but his mind was somewhere else. He jumped into the passenger seat and waited for his soon-to-be-ex-teammate to join him. After Oates filtered through the crowd and took his place behind the wheel, the two men quickly sped off to the Arena together for the last time.

The news spread quickly through Brentwood that Oates was gone. No one quite knew where, but the rumors were too strong to ignore. Reporters and photographers hurriedly gathered their belongings and raced over to the Arena to get the scoop.

The reception area outside the Blues' main office rapidly filled to claustrophobic capacity. The word hadn't been made official yet, but that didn't stop every man, woman, and child with a media credential from showing up.

"Here you go," said public relations assistant Jeff Trammel, as he handed out press releases.

There it was in black and white. Adam Oates had been traded to the Boston Bruins for center Craig Janney and defenseman Stephane Quintal. Ron Caron had done it again. How he managed to pull this one off will forever remain a mystery. Not only did he get another talented playmaking puck handler who was five years younger than Oates, he also picked up a bruising 23-year-old defenseman who would help solidify and strengthen the defensive corps. Simply put, the trade was a steal. At least on paper. If making one-sided deals were a crime, Caron would have a lengthy criminal record. He was the Charles Manson of hockey general managers.

Ron Sutter walked into the administrative office a short time later, trying to make his way through the crowd of reporters and photographers. Sutter was still out with a knee injury and hadn't practiced that morning at Brentwood. In other words, the guy had no idea what all the fuss was about.

"Ronnie, did you hear about the trade?" I asked.

"No. What is it?"

He grabbed my press release and started scanning it, his eyes moving rapidly across the paper.

"Wow," he responded. "That's the first news I've heard of it. Hopefully, things will work out for Adam. I admire him a lot, and I think he's a really good hockey player. I hope nothing but the best for him."

For the first time, players started talking on the record how Oates' contract dispute had indeed affected the sanctity of the dressing room. They didn't find it appropriate to discuss the matter while Oates was still a part of the team. But now that he was gone, many of his former teammates breathed a heavy sigh of relief, satisfied the squabble had been squared away.

"At times, it was a little unsettling in the locker room," admitted Ron Sutter. "It was starting to get to that point."

"Mr. Caron obviously saw that as well," added team captain Garth Butcher. "It's something you can put aside for a small length of time and put it out of the room. But it had gone on for some time, and it was time for something to happen for both sides."

Coach Brian Sutter adamantly stated he had never been angry with Oates during the controversy. He may not have agreed with him, but Sutter opined that Oates' play on the ice didn't suffer during his off-ice disagreements with management. However, with that said, the Blues head coach acknowledged that his team was under a lot of strain, partly due to Oates' problems. A number of other players were continuously looking over their shoulders, wondering if they were in some kind of a trade package with Oates.

"To say it hasn't affected the hockey club is wrong," said Sutter. "This did affect the guys. There's no way you were going to block that out on the ice. It was frustrating for us as coaches because we have to deal with winning and losing. The idea is to win every day, every day, every day. Well, that wasn't the first contention when people came to the rink. The questions were, 'Was Adam going to be there? Who's he getting traded to?' And who did I have to deal with that day when his name was mentioned in the media?

"It's (the trade) good for everybody. I've said since the beginning that I only wanted one thing for Adam and that was for him to be happy with the Blues or someplace else."

However, Oates was anything but happy. With a long face and downcast eyes, he met the media for an impromptu news conference in the same room where Vincent Riendeau had told everyone good-bye nearly four months earlier. Someone should put a skull and crossbones over the door. Every time a player entered that room it usually meant bad news.

Oates was relieved it was finally over. No question, he wanted to stay with the Blues. But he had pushed his demands to the point of no return. He gave the team's top brass no choice but to move him elsewhere.

"In fairness to the rest of the guys on the team, they can regroup a little bit here and refocus," said Oates. "I obviously didn't want to leave. I never thought it would get to this point until a while ago, when I realized there was no turning back. I'm glad it's over for the rest of the team and me and my family. It's now time to move on for the Blues and Adam Oates."

As his agent, Lou Oppenheim, would admit a few weeks later, there was a "tinge of regret" that Oates had backed the Blues into a corner, giving them no choice but to trade him. The all-star center wanted nothing more than to end his career in St. Louis alongside Brett Hull. They were primed to break every Blues scoring record imaginable, pushing guys like Bernie Federko, Brian Sutter, and Gary Unger down the charts.

But Hull and Oates, one of those perfect name combinations, had played its last show. Half of the group had split, leaving the other half to go solo. For arguing on principle, Oates had argued himself out of town.

"I didn't think I was asking for anything outlandish, although a lot of people did," he said. "They're entitled to their stand and that's fine. But now it's over and hopefully both parties will do well."

Oates caught a flight to Boston later that night where the Bruins would host the Devils the next afternoon. The talented center fit right in, assisting on two power-play goals to increase his league-leading total to 61 "helpers." However, another ex-Blue, Scott Stevens, scored a couple of goals himself to lead the Devils over the Bruins 6-4.

Over time, Oates' pain over leaving the Blues will disappear. Scott Stevens was certainly depressed when he left for New Jersey. But you can bet he rarely gives it a thought anymore. Same with Oates. He'll fit in nicely with his Bruins teammates, make new friends, and continue piling up the assists.

But his plight in St. Louis is proof positive of the lure of money. It's a powerful, sometimes destructive, drug. Everyone is looking for a quick fix. For some, that fix is so intoxicating they're willing to give up so many things that are dear to them. Adam said good-bye to his best friends, temporarily to his fiancee, who was from St. Louis, and to one of the best locations a professional athlete can do business in. Dozens upon dozens of sports personalities settle down in the Gateway City, no matter how long they worked here. From Dan Dierdorf to Stan Musial to Bernie Federko to Bob Costas, the city is loaded with famous people who were raised all over North America but decided to settle in the middle of it.

"This place is the best-kept secret in the NHL," said Garth Butcher.

But Oates made up his mind to leave this little secret behind for a bigger pot of gold elsewhere. He decided to stand up for what he believed was right, and for that he must be praised. It was one of the hardest decisions of his life, but he stuck to his guns, took abuse from fans and the media, and never backed down. The man deserves all the credit in the world for his unwavering defense of principle.

However, his move east did not guarantee financial happiness. Even though Bruins officials hinted they were willing to restructure Oates' contract, they refused to even talk about it until late September, 1992.

*   *   *

Craig Janney was playing ping-pong at the Boston Garden when he was interrupted with an important message. The big boys wanted to see him upstairs.

No big deal, he thought. These kinds of meetings happen all the time after a morning skate. But he soon realized this particular get-together had nothing to do with strategy. It had nothing to do with the team's play. It had everything to do with saying good riddance.

"Steph (Stephane Quintal) came up to me and said, 'Hey, they want to see me up there too,'" recalled Janney. "I said, 'Oh, I guess we're probably traded.' "

Even though his insides were churning, Janney's outward appearance reflected a devil-may-care attitude. He's a man who seems unfazed about anything. No matter the news, it bounces right off him.

For the most part, Janney is one of the more well-adjusted, confident people you'll meet, and that came in handy during his last few months in Boston. Janney possesses a pair of soft hands and keen eyes, a deadly combination for a passing center, but the Bruins brass demanded him to throw his weight around a little more. They wanted a combination of Wayne Gretzky and Bob Probert.

Sorry, but that wasn't going to happen in a million years. Despite his 6'1", 180-pound frame, Janney is tossed around like a rag doll. When constructing Craig Janney, God was generous in so many ways, except when it came to muscle.

"From a hockey point of view, they weren't happy with me," Janney said, referring to his former bosses. "They wanted me to play a bit more physical. I don't play that way. I try and pick passes off and do stuff like that. But they weren't happy with that."

The unhappiest of all was Mike Milbury, Boston's assistant general manager. As a former Bruins tough-guy, Milbury spent 1,552 minutes in the penalty box during his career, second in Bruins history to Terry O'Reilly's 2,095. To Milbury, the "B" on the Bruins' jersey stood for "brawl." Anyone wearing the black and gold was supposed to punch first and ask questions later.

Janney had proven his skills as a passer/playmaker. Like Adam Oates, Janney seemed to have eyes in the back of his head, and he always found a way to put the puck on Cam Neely's stick. He was the principal assist man for Neely when he scored 55 goals in 1989-90 and added 51 the following year. It may not have had the same ring to it, but Neely and Janney were Boston's version of Hull and Oates.

But that wasn't good enough for Milbury. He wanted Janney to bang a couple of guys in the corner and THEN put the puck on Neely's tape. The rink at the Boston Garden was too small for finesse players, Milbury said. But Janney never could display the kind of grit Milbury expected. So after four years in Beantown, C.J. was sent packing to St. Louis for another finesse player, but one who showed more of a physical side. Oates averaged twice as many penalty minutes as Janney.

"Mike Milbury and I didn't see eye to eye," Janney said matter-of-factly. "He was in charge of the trade, and he made the trade. That's why I think I'm here. But that's fine."

That's fine? The Hartford, Connecticut native was being uprooted from the New England area for the first time in his life and that's fine? Once again, Janney shrugged off something over which he had no control. He was going west, and that was that.

"I think anytime when this happens, whenever there's a major upheaval in your life, be it for the better or for the worse, it's a shock to your system," Janney admitted. "But this is a part of our profession. It's a part that we don't control. It's a part you have to deal with, and we're dealing with it as best we can. We just want to come here and help out and basically just win."

Janney was a local hero who starred at Boston College, leading the nation in scoring in 1986-87 when he tallied an amazing 83 points in 37 games. The following year, he accumulated 72 points in 54 games playing for Team USA. After the '88 Olympics, Janney signed with the Bruins, who had drafted him two years before. Ironically, only St. Louis had interviewed Janney before draft day. However, when their pick came in the first round, the Blues bypassed Janney and took Jocelyn Lemieux, whom they soon traded to Montreal for lack of production. Three selections later, the Bruins nabbed the future Olympian.

"I was definitely very excited," acknowledged Janney, who was able to stay close to home. "It was a great day for me, my family, and my friends."

It didn't take long for C.J. to be teamed with Neely and form one of the more potent combinations in the league. But 1991-92 proved to be the toughest year in both men's careers. Neely played only nine games due to a major knee injury he suffered at the end of the previous year. Without Neely, Janney's offensive production was still commendable—he accumulated nearly a point per game— but it wasn't up to his first three years in the league when he averaged more than 1.1 points per contest. Lower numbers, combined with his lack of toughness, made the local product expendable. After 283 points in 262 games, Craig Janney changed addresses for the first time.

The new Blues arrived at Lambert Airport the morning after the trade. Janney walked off the plane with his sticks, a thick Boston accent, and his girlfriend, Cathy Hooley. Stephane Quintal made similar traveling arrangements, packing his sticks, a thick French-Canadian accent, and his girlfriend, Carole Trembley. But just in case they got lonely, "Steph" also brought along his parents, Roland and Therese Quintal, along with his aunt and uncle, Yolanda and Andre Quintal. This was truly a family affair.

The contingent was greeted by Blues representatives Jeff Trammel and Mike Caruso who quickly whisked the players into a side room to meet reporters. Both men appeared upbeat, which wasn't surprising. Janney, like Oates, had been hearing trade rumors in his sleep. He couldn't escape them. He claims he rarely reads hockey articles, but if he had, he would have seen his name being moved to every roster in the league. Interestingly, the rumors finally subsided just weeks before the actual trade.

"It's funny. When the rumors die down, that's when it happens," Janney said. "That seems to be the way it always is in professional sports."

As for Quintal, his name was hardly ever mentioned in any trade rumors. In fact, his name was seldom mentioned, period. Languishing in the shadows of other Bruins defensemen, namely Ray Bourque, Quintal hadn't seen much ice time until very recently. He averaged only 36 games and four points his first three years with the Bruins. He was seeing more action in this, his fourth NHL season, but was still considered nothing more than a raw young player who was filling a spot. Going to St. Louis, a team desperate for a defenseman his size no matter the age, meant filling a much more important role. This was an opportunity for Stephane Quintal to finally establish himself in the NHL.

"The Blues have a good club," said Quintal minutes after arriving in St. Louis. "I talked with Brian last night and he said they were struggling a little bit. But it only counts in the playoffs. That's where you want to get it going."

Quintal and Janney got it going immediately. Not only did they play their first game in St. Louis just hours after flying in, the two players and their new teammates were battling the Blackhawks for a game that had important ramifications in the standings. With a win, the Blues would move within a single point of Chicago. The Blackhawks had kicked the Blues out of second place 25 days earlier, and the boys in blue were bidding to regain their old spot.

As expected, Janney took Oates' old spot on the top line between Christian and Hull. Everyone assumed C.J. would be inserted there, but with Brian Sutter at the helm, you always expected the unexpected. After all, Janney and Hull had played together on Team USA before the season and they hadn't exactly clicked. One time, Janney failed to get Hull the puck in a rush up-ice. A disgusted Hull threw his arms up in the air and promptly skated to the bench. When Janney returned to the bench, one of his teammates asked, "Did you feel the knives in your back?"

But five months later, Janney seemed unconcerned about what happened at the Canada Cup. Craig knew there was only one star in St. Louis, and he knew what his job description would be here.

"He demands that you get him the puck," Janney said of Hull. "He wants to shoot it every time. I just hope we find the chemistry and get along on the ice. And I hope he keeps scoring. I don't want him to skip a beat at all."

Janney and Hull looked remarkably solid together against Chicago. Although Hull didn't score, Janney showed he was more than capable of controlling the puck in the offensive zone and getting it to the open man. Oates had nothing on this guy. He handled the puck the way Michael Jordan handles a basketball. In the second period, Janney expertly threaded the puck between two Hawks to Shanahan, who beat Eddie Belfour for his 21st of the year, his fifth against Chicago. It took but a few minutes for the fans to start asking, "Adam who?"

Quintal also surprised a lot of people with his play. The scouting reports described him as something of a lumbering oaf, slow and unsure of himself. Well, the scouts must have been watching a different Stephane Quintal. The one who showed up at the Arena looked like a seasoned veteran. Teamed with Jeff Brown on his very first shift, Quintal absolutely creamed Jocelyn Lemieux (yes, the same guy the Blues selected in the first round six years ago ahead of Janney). It was one of the better open-ice checks of the season. Lemieux picked his head up off the ice and slowly retreated to the bench.

Unfortunately, the debut of the new players was spoiled by a 3-1 loss to the Hawks, moving the Blues five points behind second place. The power play was especially off-balance with Hull moving to the point to take Oates' place, and Janney setting up shop down low.

"We didn't get a lot of time to practice it," said Coach Sutter. "But it's not something totally foreign to Brett. When we did get the puck low, we had opportunities, but there weren't very many."

"With the new guys and people in different positions, it made it a little difficult," said Hull, who questioned his coach's strategy. "I think we have to utilize my shot by throwing me in the slot and having Craig on the boards. They usually put two guys on me, and that just opens it up for everyone else when I'm in the slot."

But the power play was about the only negative conversation in the locker room. The players were generally pleased with the effort and were extremely thankful that the black cloud had dissolved.

"Before the game it seemed like we all came together," said Nelson Emerson. "Because of the new guys, I think it'll take another couple of games before we're a team. But it feels really united, and that's important."

"It's a very positive locker room," added Joseph. "It's very energetic and enthusiastic. Even after the loss, it's very upbeat."

Indeed. All the evidence needed was found in the coach's office. Usually after a loss, reporters tiptoe into Sutter's quarters with great trepidation. Invariably, Sutter leans back in his chair, carefully surveying each person who has the guts to enter his domain. Every muscle in his face is working to form one of the most pronounced and painful frowns you'll ever lay eyes on.

On this night, Sutter was wearing his "victory" expression. He occasionally broke into a smile, extraordinarily rare after a defeat. I felt an urge to call back to the station and have them interrupt programming for a special report.

Sutter had only praise for his team and the hard work it had displayed. He could tell instantly his boys were a different lot. The weight of the world had been lifted off their shoulders.

Without mentioning Oates by name, Sutter remarked how the team looked much more relaxed without HIM around.

"Individuals can now be worried about their jobs and not be concerned about other people," he said, obviously referring to the since-departed Oates. "They can do their own jobs, plain and simple."

Even Hull was remarkably upbeat. Somehow he had managed to bite his lip in the 36 hours since the trade. You kept waiting for him to explode and start ripping every person who had ever worked for the organization. But to his credit— and at his employer's urging— Hull took a vow of silence until after the game. Other than his frustration with the power play, he had nothing negative to say. Perhaps Janney's play surprised him a bit, leading Hull to believe the transition wouldn't be that difficult after all.

"We're going to miss Adam a lot. But you go ask Cam Neely what he thinks about Craig Janney, and he won't say a bad word about him," explained Hull. "We're going to play some good hockey. You saw the pass he (Craig) gave to Shanny tonight. I'm looking forward to it."

So was Janney. After 60 minutes in a Blues jersey, the New Englander realized he would fit in nicely alongside Hull. He was disappointed with the loss, but optimistic about the future.

"Hopefully if I keep playing with him, we can get it going," Janney said. "With Cam, I try and set up behind the net. But now the surface is a little bigger, there's more ice to get it to Hullie. Hopefully, I can get him 10 shots a night, and we'll see what happens."

Standing about five feet to Janney's left, Stephane Quintal slowly tucked in his shirt and wrapped a tie around his neck. Wearing a broad smile, Quintal remarked in broken English how the butterflies were swirling around his stomach at the start of the contest.

"I was a little nervous before the game," he said. "But after I got my first shift out of the way, I felt pretty good."

And why not? After leveling Lemieux, Steph instantly became Brian Sutter's best friend. That's the kind of toughness the Blues had been missing all year, and it was a welcome sight to see a defenseman throw his weight around like that.

Three nights later, the Blues edged the Kings at home, 3-2. Janney and Hull collaborated on a goal for the first time late in the second period. Janney was cruising down the right side through the neutral zone when the Kings' Pete Ahola knocked him on his fanny. However, despite sitting on his derriere, Janney stayed with the puck and nudged it across the blue line, where the Blues other Olympian picked it up. Dave Christian quickly passed the puck to his left, where Hull, standing in his favorite slot position, rifled a shot between Kelly Hrudey's pads.

But perhaps the most outstanding performance of the night was turned in by the checking line of Bob Bassen, Ron Wilson, and Rich Sutter. Not only did they smother Gretzky, who never even got a shot on net in the final period, but Sutter and Bassen assisted on the Blues' second goal scored by Butcher, and also assisted on the third goal scored by linemate Wilson. In a truly remarkable statistic, Bassen led both teams in shots on goal with seven. A checker firing more than a half-dozen pucks at the net? You betcha. Bassen and Sutter just had a feeling it would be their night.

"It's funny. For the first time in a long time, the three of us came to the rink and just had that feeling that we were going to do it," boasted Richie after only his second multiple-point game of the year. "It's not a matter that we're fortunate or we're lucky. It's just a matter that we kept believing in our system and the team's system and stuck with it."

"We all just looked at each other and said, 'We're going to do something tonight. Let's get something done,'" said Bassen, who also recorded only his second multiple-point game of the season. "We knew it. We just looked at each other and could see it was going to happen."

That was the kind of confidence that the ex-Green Berets had been lacking this year. Maybe, just maybe, they were starting to regain the self-assuredness that had made them such a success the year before.

The win enabled the Blues to move back to three points behind idle Chicago and ten points behind the Red Wings. With a pair of new faces and a new-found enthusiasm, the Blues were about to embark on their most successful stretch of the season, winning five of their next six and eight of eleven. By early March, their winning ways would propel them ahead of Chicago for the all-important home-ice advantage in the first round of the play-offs. Without it, the Blues were unlikely to see the second round.

*   *   *

Three years.

That's how long it had been since Adam Oates had to walk in the Arena's rear entrance as a member of the visiting team. He remembered this route from his days with Detroit. But after racking up the points in St. Louis, he never thought he'd be denied access through the front door for the remainder of his career.

But here he was, six days after being traded to the Bruins, getting off the bus and walking in the back way with his new teammates. It was the morning of February 13, about nine hours before the Bruins would battle the Blues. It would be an awkward game for several players. Oates, Janney, and Quintal had to compete against their former teammates and current friends. With the trade less than a week old, the wounds hadn't healed yet.

Looking stylish in his brown overcoat, khaki pants, and blue shirt, Oates put his hands in his pockets and strolled to the visiting locker room. He was in a rather chipper mood, glad to be back and anxious to get the game over with.

"I'm not too sure how it's going to be tonight," Oates said. "I've got a lot of nerves. But a couple of other guys on the other team are going to be just as nervous."

Oates was fitting in extremely well in Boston. Despite not having a pure goal scorer to pass to anymore—Neely was still sidelined with a knee injury—Oates had racked up four assists in his two games with the Bruins.

"I missed a few goals like normal," he laughed. "My job is a feeder, and I'm not going to change that."

Oates was uncharacteristically talkative that morning. A quiet and reserved man, Oates enjoyed the camaraderie of a few select friends and nothing more. He shied away from crowds and didn't care for the media attention afforded star athletes.

At the same time, Oates was an extremely level-headed and easygoing person. In that respect, he was very much like the man for whom he was traded, Craig Janney. Both stuck to business and let the outside world's problems roll off their backs. That's why Oates was able to stand up to a month of scrutiny before the trade. Because he firmly believed in what he was doing, Oates had the mental makeup to deal with the invective directed at him.

"I think we're fortunate the media's not following me around or following someone else around," said Rick Zombo, implying that other players might eventually snap under a similar microscope.

When Oates returned to the rink later that night for the game, he was much less talkative and much more nervous. He could deal with a few old familiar reporters. What concerned him were the nearly 18,000 fans who were waiting to get their two cents in. Oates was bitter about the reaction of Blues fans after his contract dispute went public. Now, as a member of the Bruins, he was hoping the crowd would just forget about the past and watch the game without feeling the need to shower him with boos.

"I'm not sure how the fans are going to react," he said, standing outside the visitors' locker room. "As far as I'm concerned, I played hard for them every night, and I think they should respect that."

With the crowd starting to trickle in and the teams ending their pregame skate, Oates slowly glided through the Blues' end toward the visitors' exit. All eyes were on No. 12 for they knew what was about to happen. Hull had boasted about it the day before.

Brett just stood in his own end and waited for his old buddy to skate behind him. As if watching a re-run for the upteenth time, Oates picked up a loose puck and fed it to Hull who was standing about 10 feet to his left. As soon as the puck got near him, Hull rifled it into the open net. Hull and Oates had been reunited for one final encore. The few thousand fans who had already taken their seats cheered loudly. Oates to Hull. One goal, one assist. Just like old times.

During the game, however, the crowd wasn't nearly as friendly. A little pre-game sideshow was fine. But this was business, and the fans returned to the business of booing, at least in the second period. The Blues' checking line of Bassen, Wilson, and Rich Sutter did an exceptional job of shutting down the Bruins' top line, centered by Oates. The ex-Blue was a non-factor, barely getting a chance to touch the puck in the first period which meant the fans barely had a chance to boo him.

Finally, about eight minutes into the second period, with the Bruins on their first power play, Oates couldn't hide any longer. Working the point, it was the first time he had held the puck for any length of time. Not about to waste its first opportunity, the crowd made its displeasure known by booing its former all-star. A few seconds later, those jeers turned to cheers as Richie Sutter nailed Oates with a body check along the boards. This was not the kind of homecoming Adam Oates had hoped for.

Meanwhile, the Blues offense was clicking. Dave Lowry and Michel Mongeau netted goals in the first period, Jeff Brown scored his twelfth in the second, and Bob Bassen, who effectively smothered Oates all night, found the back of the net in the third period for his fifth goal of the year. At the other end of the ice, Curtis Joseph kicked out all 34 shots he faced. It was his second shutout of the season, lowering his goals-against average to 2.95.

The 4-0 whitewashing made the recent trade look even more one-sided. While Oates was being hounded into submission, Janney and Quintal played their second strong game, Steph assisting on Mongeau's goal, his first point in a Blues' uniform. Janney played well, despite not having a right winger to pass to. Brett Hull was largely indifferent to the game, cruising the ice with little emotion as if conducting a one-man protest. After all, his old friend was in town, and he wasn't about to show him up. Hull completely disappeared in the third period, unable to muster even one shot on net and refusing to skate back into his own zone to help out defensively. That "A" on Hull's jersey stood for "apathetic." Usually he was a joy to watch, but on this night he was an embarrassment.

After the game, Hull ducked into the Wives' Room to avoid the media. That was fine. No one was going to get anything out of him anyway. Watching him mope around the ice, every reporter in the building knew he was going to be a terror in the dressing room. It was best just to let him go on this night.

On the other side of the Arena, Oates hurried out of the locker room to answer a couple of questions.

"Can we make this one quick, guys?" he asked.

No problem. Were you more nervous than you expected?

"Yeah, very nervous. It was hard playing against the guys you had played with every day. But a couple of guys on their team had to go through the same thing. Everyone's done it in this league."

Is the crowd reaction what you expected?

"Yeah, I guess so. I was obviously disappointed with the results. I wish I had played a better hockey game. The Blues played solid."

And that was that. After shaking hands with a couple of people, Oates left the old barn for the last time of the year. He would be back next season, but the circumstances would be different. The nerves would be a bit calmer. The fans' wrath wouldn't be as noticeable. And Brett Hull might actually come to play. "The Return of Adam Oates: The Sequel" wasn't going to get near the advance billing the following fall. Most fans will have forgotten about Oates. And after watching him for nearly three years turning in one dazzling play after another, that was perhaps the saddest part of all.

Chapter Thirteen

BRETT BEHAVIOR

Sweat was pouring off his face. He was desperately trying to find his breath. Just three days before the season opener in New Jersey, Brett Hull was working his tail off in preparation for the start of the 1991-92 season. Hull is a man who never takes anything for granted. Just because he led the league in goals the previous two years didn't mean he could start lying back and just will the puck into the net.

"My biggest nightmare is going to the rink and never being able to score again," he said.

Hull had been back from the Canada Cup less than two weeks but had already scored plenty. Not with his stick, with his mouth. He had spouted off against everything imaginable. The summer was a drag. There were too many demands on his time. He hated the Canada Cup. And Judge Houston sold the Blues down the river by sending Scott Stevens to Jersey.

That last subject was Hull's sorest spot. After he suggested "the fix was in," the league scolded Blues officials and strongly suggested they have a nice little chat with their superstar. Hull had to publicly apologize or else.

That brings us to the morning of October 2, 1991. Just before practice, a fax was sent to various media outlets detailing Hull's "apology." Few reporters bought it, assuming the statement was fashioned by someone in public relations and signed by Hull. Most broadcasted or printed it with a wink, wink, nudge, nudge. The approach was to submit the apology for mass consumption and let the fans evaluate its sincerity.

After reading the fax at my sports desk, I just smiled and shook my head. Who were they kidding? There was no way Hull was apologizing for his critique of Judge Houston and the NHL. One of the great things about Hull is that he speaks his mind and doesn't give a hoot whom he might offend. He's a reporter's dream. They must have tied him to a chair and tortured him into signing this piece of paper.

I doubt Blues management was trying to pull a fast one. They likely figured everyone would read the fax and laugh. But the league had directed the Blues to make one of its employees say he was sorry, and team officials had no choice but to oblige. I couldn't wait to hear Hull's explanation.

The Golden One wiped his face as he made his way off the ice. As always, he stopped to talk to a television reporter demanding yet another minute of his time. After asking him about the upcoming season opener, I casually inquired about the fax I had received back at the station. I wasn't prepared for his response.

"I wasn't apologizing," Hull said. "I was doing what I thought was right, and what my representatives thought was right instead of causing a big hoopla. I just decided to do whatever they wished. Unfortunately, I had to do that, because I stand behind what I said."

Wow. I knew Hull could be brutally honest, but I didn't think he would look right into the camera and thumb his nose at the league. I had to make sure I was hearing this right, so I didn't cause a big stir when we aired this interview. I asked him again. Was this your decision?

"Someone told me to apologize," he continued, not about to back down. "It was definitely from the league office. I was advised by Mr. Quinn and Susie Mathieu, along with my lawyer and my agent that it's not worth the time or the effort to stand up for what you believe in. Just rescind what you said, and that's what I did."

And if you didn't, what would happen?

"I honestly couldn't tell you. That's why I did what I did."

Double wow. Inside our news camera sat a videotape with the potential of creating a major controversy. Not only would it send shock waves through the city of St. Louis, but the major hockey cities in North America would also pick up on it. Not that he cared, but I was certain Hull had just gotten himself into some major trouble with the league.

After leaving me in stunned silence, Hull continued walking to the locker room. As he approached the steps, he looked up to find Susie Mathieu leaning on a rail overhead.

"I hope I said the right thing," Hull shouted to the Blues vice-president of public relations.

"Why, what did you say?" she asked.

"I just retracted my retraction."

"What! You can't do that!"

The two exchanged a few more words before Hull finally disappeared into the locker room. No doubt about it. The Blues superstar was creating a super mess. It bothered him that he was forced to apologize for something he felt so strongly about. He was getting in the last dig. He wanted the whole world to learn of his anger and frustration.

Susie wasted little time making her way down to us. She had lost control of Hull. Perhaps somehow she could control us.

"You can't use that," she said matter-of-factly. "He wasn't supposed to say any of that."

"I'm sure he wasn't," I said. "But you can't ask us not to use it. He said it on his own. I didn't make him say anything."

"I'm serious. You can't use that." Susie turned away and walked toward the locker room to give Hull a piece of her mind. She must have felt he'd lost a piece of his.

In all honesty, I felt badly for Susie. She was in charge of a loose cannon named Brett Hull. A few minutes later, she marched back out with orders that only escalated the controversy.

"If you use that, Brett will never talk to you or anyone else at Channel 4 again," she said.

"What? You can't make a demand like that."

"I'm just telling you what Brett told me. He'll never talk to you again if you use that interview."

"Susie, you know that's a bunch of bull. You can't tell the media what they can or can't report."

She just shrugged her shoulders as if transferring all of the responsibility onto my shoulders. I could hear all my old college journalism professors yelling about principles. I didn't need an ethics manual to tell me I had every right to broadcast the interview.

Believe me, I'm one of those people who keeps their mouth shut, but Susie Mathieu had just struck a raw nerve. Principles or no principles, no one had the right to demand that we destroy the videotape because it might cause problems. It was one thing if we coerced Hull into retracting his apology or secretly taped one of his conversations. But Brett freely and honestly answered my questions regarding the fax I had received, and now I was being made to feel guilty about his candor.

I strolled into the locker room to hear it from Hull himself. I had to find out if he was being forced once again to say something he really didn't mean. Brett was sitting on the bench in front of his locker stall, looking down and fiddling with the laces on one of his skates. After a couple of seconds, I finally found the courage to confront him.

"Is it true that you're never going to talk to me again?" I asked.

"Yep. If you run that interview, I'll never talk to anyone at Channel 4 the rest of the year."

Hull still didn't look up as he continued to play with his skates. However, Kelly Chase was looking at me with a stunned expression wondering what on God's green earth was going on. He was standing next to Hull, his eyes shifting from me to Hull. This was great. All I had to do was say the wrong thing, and Hull would just give a little nod to Kelly, who would proceed to extract my tongue.

"Brett, I know you're in a corner here," I continued, trying to show some diplomacy. "But this is a bunch of bull. I didn't make you say any of that."

"I'm just telling you," he answered back, looking up for the first time. "If you use that tape, don't ever expect another interview with me."

"Well, this is over my head now. I'll take this tape back and let Zip decide what he wants to do with it."

"Fine. Then, it's in Zip's corner."

I couldn't wait to relay my story to the boys back at the station. Little did I know they were already well aware of what was taking place. Jack Quinn heard about the incident and quickly phoned KMOV general manager Al Cohen to express his concern. Suddenly this thing had turned into a major incident.

My news director, Al Holzer, was waiting for me as I walked in the newsroom. He motioned me into his office, where Cohen, assistant news director Michael Castengera, and program manager Jim Rothschild were holding court. They wanted to hear my story before deciding what to do. Like me, Cohen was incredulous.

"When I get backed into a corner like this," he said, "the hair stands up on the back of my neck."

We discussed the options. We stand up for our rights, broadcast the interview, and face a backlash not only from the Blues, but from many of their fans. Think about it—the league hears Hull's comments and promptly fines the team, perhaps even suspends Hull for a game or two. It's suddenly KMOV's fault that the town's hockey star is sitting in the pressbox because we had the audacity to cause him trouble. This would only help feed the misconception that the media is an evil industry, unconcerned with other's rights and personal liberties.

Or we could decide to eat the interview out of a favor to the Blues. And that's the decision we ultimately made. Cohen called Quinn back and made it clear that this would not be tolerated again. It wasn't worth creating a storm of controversy over a player's comments made in the heat of the moment. This wasn't a life-or-death issue. We decided to let it slide.

In reality, athletes take back comments all the time. Postgame interviews are full of retractions such as, "Scratch that. I didn't mean it that way." Or, "I take it back. I shouldn't have said that." And my favorite, "Don't write that! What are you trying to do, get me in trouble?" Invariably, the reporter backs off, understanding that emotions are still running high after a game. There's a general understanding that if an athlete blasts someone and then quickly requests that his statement not be printed or broadcast, the reporter usually obliges. Forever ruining a working relationship over an athlete's spur-of-the-moment remarks isn't worth the trouble.

The Hull incident, however, was a different story, and that's why it was so troubling. If he had come back out of the locker room and asked that we not air his comments because we'd get him into trouble, there's no doubt I would have agreed to his request. Then it would have fallen into the category of, "I take it back. I shouldn't have said that." But threatening an entire television station with an interview blackout was like using a bazooka to kill a mosquito. There was absolutely no need for it.

As it turned out, KMOV and the rest of the media outlets around town would have plenty of other opportunities to publicize controversial remarks made by Hull. In a season full of tumultuous events, Hull was a walking time bomb. His mouth was more dangerous than his stick. Susie Mathieu would earn every cent of her salary in the upcoming season.

*   *   *

Arguably Brett Hull's most enjoyable experience in the fall of 1991 didn't occur on the ice. It happened on the diamond. On the night of Sunday, October 27, the Minnesota Twins were crowned champions of the world after a thrilling 1-0, 10-inning victory over the Atlanta Braves at Minneapolis. It took a masterful pitching performance by Jack Morris and a dramatic pinch-hit single by Gene Larkin to bring home the Twins' second World Series title in five years. A native of Duluth, Hull was as ecstatic as any Twins fan that night.

But on the ice, life was anything but enjoyable for Brett. After 10 games, he had netted only six goals, a pace that would give him 48 at season's end. That's a career year for most hockey players. In fact, neither of the Blues' all-time leading goal scorers ever approached that mark. Bernie Federko's career best was 41 goals during the 1983-84 season. Brian Sutter scored 46 the year before.

But Hull was a notch above anyone else who had previously worn the Bluenote. He had averaged a goal a game his last two years. He was the game's newest superstar and the city's newest sports idol. To finish the season with fewer than 50 goals seemed almost sacrilegious. And yet here he was, sitting on a half-dozen goals three weeks into the season.

"The more fun I have, the more goals I score," he said. By his own admission, Hull was not a having a particularly good time. Not only was he missing from his customary position atop the NHL goal-scoring race, he was tied with two of his own teammates. Newcomers Dave Christian and Brendan Shanahan each had lit the red lamp six times.

A week after the World Series ended, Hull finally regained his scoring touch, with seven goals in a three-game stretch. The sudden explosion propelled him to the league lead with 15 goals in 17 games. It was a position he would not relinquish the remainder of the season. There was only one problem, however. The Blues lost all three games, by a combined score of 18-9. That's right, the Golden Brett accounted for seven of the team's nine goals. So much for the extra scoring punch the Blues were counting on.

Hull learned to stay relatively quiet during the first couple of months, when the Blues were struggling to keep their heads above water. There was no blasting management, no chiding teammates. Instead, Hull adopted a strategy of making reporters think for themselves. Instead of pointing out the deficiencies of the team himself, he dropped little hints to the media so they could draw their own conclusions. Call it Hull-speak.

The best example came after a tough loss to the Kings. Carefully read between the lines, and you'll hear Hull complain about all the recent personnel changes that had disrupted the team's chemistry and underminded its chances of success during the first half of the season.

Any answers on tonight's loss?

"Were you watching the game?"

Yep.

"Then you tell me."

I want the guy on the ice to tell me.

"I'm not going to say. I'm not pointing fingers. I'm going to let you guys figure out what could have been done. Because I think you know. I'm not allowed to say. What do you think of that?"

Hull paused for a second as he dressed himself. Before a reporter could follow up, he continued.

"I don't think it's a matter of what needs to be done. It's a matter of what WAS done. What shouldn't have been done."

Hull started chuckling as he threw his tie around his neck. There's no question he was enjoying this kind of one-sided banter. By looking at the different expressions, he could tell who understood and who didn't.

"You guys try to figure it out," he finished. "You guys try to answer my questions."

There's no doubt Hull would have loved to have just come right out and say, "Here it is, folks. I'll lay it on the line for you. This player should be here. That guy shouldn't be there. This will work. That won't work." But to his credit, Hull kept a lid on it and opted to drop hints instead of bombshells. Sometimes his answers lent themselves to a variety of different interpretations, further confusing reporters and further distancing him from any controversy.

But Hull reached the boiling point in January. When the Adam Oates controversy started to garner headlines, he could no longer hold back. It was like trying to cap a volcano with Saran Wrap. When he learned that the Blues were contemplating trading Oates instead of paying him more money, Hull made it very clear he was in Oates' corner, even suggesting he would transfer some of his salary to Adam's pocketbook just to keep him in St. Louis.

"Brett and I talked about it," said Oates at the time. "What a tremendous friend to do something like that. Whether I could accept it or not, I'm not sure. He's showing the Blues how adamant he is about me staying."

Meanwhile, some media members started to criticize Oates, which makes Hull furious to this day. They suggested Oates was a whiner. They told him to shut up and play hockey. And they hinted that if he had any class, he'd drop his demands because of the locker room disruptions he was causing. Hearing and reading those comments, Hull fired back.

"It's unfortunate that some of the media around St. Louis don't think before they talk," he said. "They've embarrassed themselves. It's unfortunate because Adam Oates is a class guy. To demean him is unfair to say the least."

After hearing those comments, *Post-Dispatch* columnist Bernie Miklasz returned fire.

"We know Hull is honest," he wrote. "And we applaud him for that—even if, based on his media attacks, Hull disapproves of First Amendment privileges when an opposing view is expressed. Sticking up for a pal is a nice, brotherly thing to do— even when your homeboy is dead wrong."

So what started as an internal matter between Oates and management had escalated into a full-scale war of words that now included Hull and the media. And to make matters worse, the war would soon by joined by the fans themselves. When a sellout crowd booed Oates with such utter disdain on January 14, Hull finally exploded. He dropped his gloves and went after paying customers.

Hull saved his cruelest shot for a fan by the name of Steve Truetken of Florissant. A rather sizeable figure at 6'2", 225 pounds, Truetken fashioned a sign that became the symbol of the Oates squabble. It read, simply, "AdiOates." It was ingenious. You can bet every sports reporter and editor in town was trying to come up with the perfect word or headline to describe the controversy. And here it was in the stands, being held by a loyal Blues fan who had the right to express his feelings. Of course, Hull had the right to express his own, and he didn't waste the opportunity.

"That fat, bald bastard," Hull said in anger after the game. "I'd like to crawl up there and rip his head off."

As far as the rest of the fans, Hull didn't have much nice to say about them either.

"I took it for granted that we had a lot of classy people coming to watch us play," he said. "Obviously, I was mistaken. It disgusts me. I never thought it would come to that. It's so unfortunate. It just makes me sick. Did they come to watch hockey, or did they come to make fools of themselves?

"I expected St. Louis fans to take a look at what he's done and how he's entertained them over the last few years. If you don't know all the facts and you don't know enough about it, keep your mouth shut and watch the game."

Ouch. Hull had now turned his back on the very people who revered him so dearly. They didn't have a problem with the Golden Brett. They had a problem with his partner, who they felt was unfair in asking for a new contract for the third time in three years. So the fans made their feelings known through the only vehicles at their disposal, their posters and their voiceboxes. But Hull had reached up and slapped everyone who had the audacity to boo. It was time for Susie Mathieu to put on the hard hat once again.

After hearing Hull's comments secondhand, she immediately called the Wives' Room, where Hull and Oates were relaxing after the game. Mathieu lit into Hull like a mother scolding a misbehaved child. Still seething, Hull lashed back, telling her, "I'm going to say what I feel!"

The next day, many fans called the Blues' switchboard, complaining of Hull's comments after they became public. How could a man of such grace, of such high standards, become so vile in his outrage against the fans? they asked. What gives him the right to get involved in the crowd's displeasure with Oates? Let Adam fight his own fight, they said. Would Stan Musial ever act this way? Would Ozzie?

The fans were hurt, and Hull knew it. Feeling a deep pang of guilt, Brett called the *Post-Dispatch* the next day and bared his soul to Dave Luecking. There's an obvious tendency to assume Hull was forced into an apology, as he was earlier in the year when he ridiculed Judge Houston, but Hull categorically denied Blues management had anything to do with his phone call to the newspaper. He said it was his idea to kiss and make up with the fans who pay his million-dollar salary.

"My comments were made in the heat of the moment, and I'm sorry about that," Hull told Luecking. "The fans ill-perceive how we feel. Every player here and players who have been here in the past will tell you there's not a better place to play because of the fans. They're the greatest. I love it here."

It sounded like a major case of sucking up. But it didn't matter. An apology was all the fans wanted to hear. They could fall back in love with their hero once again. Even Steve "AdiOates" Truetken wrote the newspaper, saying there were no hard feelings.

"Let's forgive Brett Hull," he wrote. "This incident aside, I think he is one of the classiest players to ever wear the Bluenote. In a time when overpaid athletes have become arrogant, believing they are bigger than their sport, Brett Hull is a breath of fresh air."

How bad do you think Hull felt after he read that? One thing about the Golden Brett. He's accommodating to a fault. He can't stand the thought of upsetting even one hockey fan, even if they show up on his doorstep. On one afternoon during the past season, Susie Mathieu was at Hull's house when the doorbell rang.

"It's some kids who want your autograph," said Susie. "Do you want me to tell them to go away?"

"No, you can't do that," answered Hull. "I'll sign them."

"Brett, you can't allow this to happen, kids just ringing your doorbell expecting your autograph."

"If they took the time and trouble to come all the way out here, the least I can do is sign my name."

Hull is also accommodating when it comes to media commitments. As many local hockey fans know, Brett does a radio show on KMOX from his restaurant after each Saturday night home game. After showering, dressing, and racing out west, he rarely gets there by 11 p.m., the ideal time for his arrival as far as the station is concerned. It's usually a 20- to 25-minute trip. Hull was making it in 15.

"You're going to have to push the time back," Mathieu told KMOX's Randy Karraker just weeks after the show started. "Brett's driving 85 miles per hour out there. He's going to kill himself."

All in the name of satisfying the desires of others. Much to the displeasure of Mathieu, Brett is quick to please. He finds it difficult to just say no. He has to be forcibly removed from a crowd of autograph-seekers. He can't—and won't—leave on his own accord. Hull admits the hardest thing to do is tell a little kid that he can't sign that hockey card right now. So when people started to question Hull's commitment to St. Louis after he blasted its fans, he quickly zipped it. "Silence is golden" became the Golden Brett's new motto.

He continued to be honest about his team's play. That'll never change and every journalist in St. Louis is thankful for that. If he thought his teammates were dogging it, he said so. If some of the guys were outstanding, he wasted no time in praising them.

Hull never, ever talked about himself unless asked. It was always, "Curtis played great again," or "What a terrific job Bassen's line did," or "We wouldn't have won without Butchy and the other defensemen."

But Brett, what about that fancy goal you scored to win the game? "Couldn't have done it without Craig," he might say. Like the rest of his teammates, he is as humble as a schoolteacher. That's the most amazing feature of Brett Hull's makeup. The guy is simply the most gifted hockey player in the world today, and yet his lifelong friends will tell you the only thing that's changed about him is his wardrobe. In an era of mediocre athletes making themselves out as modern-day Babe Ruths, Hull is a pleasant reminder that superstars CAN be unpretentious, willing to show a little humility instead of a lot of pride. Hull's lack of vanity is constantly noted by out-of-town reporters who meet the Golden One for the first time. "Man, that guy is really nice," is often heard around the Blues' locker room.

From a reporter's standpoint, that's the best part about covering hockey. Unlike other sports, you'll be hard-pressed to find a hockey player willing to beat his own chest and demand the rest of the world notice him. Even Oates, who some accused of being arrogant, was very down-to-earth and unassuming. The guy never felt comfortable talking about himself. That's why the contract dispute got to be so bothersome down the stretch. Virtually every day Oates was forced to scrutinize himself publicly, something that made him extremely uncomfortable.

The official end of Hull's uncontrolled outbursts came on the very day Oates was traded. Everyone was expecting a tornadic tirade of expletives directed at management. After all, he had shown little fear of superiors so far this season. He'd blasted Judge Houston. He took a shot at the league itself, and at President John Ziegler. He was openly critical of Blues officials during the entire Oates dispute. So what would he say now that his good buddy was told good riddance? Would we even be able to use it on the air? Surely, Hull would finally lose it. This was going to be fun.

Instead, Hull quarantined himself. He locked himself away from the media until he could think straight. I happened to catch him walking out of Coach Sutter's office about an hour after the trade and tried to pry a quick comment out of him.

"Hey, Brett, got a second?"

"Nope. I don't want to get in trouble."

And that was that. He quietly walked out the back door without muttering another syllable. Hull had obviously been "advised" about commenting on the trade. He had a well-documented history of making controversial remarks in the heat of the moment, and it wasn't going to happen again. Jack Quinn made sure of it. So did Brian Sutter.

"Brett's disappointed," said Sutter after Hull left his office. "I played 12 years, and I had a couple of very dear friends traded. It's not an easy thing. But in sports, these things happen."

After the infamous Boston game on February 13 when Hull was accused of lackadaisical play during Oates' return to the Arena, Hull's stock as a leader suddenly took off. It was as if he had to get that one game of protest out of his system. Now, it was back to business. Without hurting his offensive production, Hull started to show more interest in the defensive part of the game, back-checking more proficiently and going deep into the corners to gain control of the puck. Locker room pundits started talking about Hull's "new-found maturity."

"No question, Brett's a more complete player since Oates left," said one teammate.

Some said Brett had to be. Oates was more willing than Janney to bang bodies in the defensive end of the rink. With Adam gone, Hull had to sacrifice himself a bit more in both ends of the rink.

Others said it was just a matter of Hull's taking his leadership role more seriously. After pouting over the Oates controversy and being lambasted by the local fans for the first time, Brett decided to bear down and become the team leader everyone expected him to be. After all, he was the engine that made the Blues run. With him churning along at full speed, there was no telling how far this team could travel.

"As Brett goes, so goes this team," said one Blues executive. "I'm sure Brett has watched Mario Lemieux take control of the Penguins and lead them to the Cup. He can score all the goals he wants, but until he wins a Cup, he won't be considered one of the great players."

After the Boston game, Hull and Janney went to work. Against Calgary two nights later, Craig scored a hat trick, his first goals as a member of the Blues. Hull added a goal and an assist as his team blew out the Flames 7-2. Especially noteworthy was the uncharacteristic success of the power play. The Blues were two for five with the man advantage, Janney netting both of them.

"We're starting to get used to each other," explained Brendan Shanahan, who assisted on one of the power-play goals. "Power play is just confidence and puck movement, and knowing where your teammates are going to be, so you don't have to look before you pass."

"There are a lot of talented guys on that power play," said Janney, the game's number-one star. "Everyone in the barn knows our main weapon is going to be Brett. That's the person we're trying to get it to in the right area to shoot. If he's tied up, then we're going to move on to other guys."

So what was Hull's opinion of the power play? Only hard-core fans will understand this explanation.

"With Shanny down there, we've got a lot of strength down low and in front," he said. "And he can move to the slot, and I can move down low. Or I can move to the slot, like what happened tonight, and you've got Shanny down low and you've got Craig going to the net, and you've got the outside 'D' coming down the back door."

I think I liked the controversial Hull a lot better. At least he didn't sound like John Madden on the CBS chalkboard.

Hull, the critic-turned-choreographer, enjoyed a successful February, beginning with that game against the Flames. Over the remaining eight games of the month, he netted eight goals and added nine assists to retake the overall NHL scoring lead with 99 points, surpassing Kevin Stevens and Wayne Gretzky. When Ron Sutter returned after a 10-game absence from a knee injury, he reacquired his "A" from Paul Cavallini, not Hull. When they sewed the letter on Hull's jersey at the beginning of February, it was there to stay.

Reports of Hull's demise were greatly exaggerated. After he'd popped off against the fans and media, then disappeared during the Bruins game, it seemed entirely plausible that Hull would remain in a funk the rest of the year, taking the team down with him. The Blues were sinking fast, and it appeared their superstar was in no mood to save them.

But Brett suddenly became recharged. Knowing the team could go only as far as he would take them, he decided to lead instead of follow. He wasn't the rah-rah sort, telling inspiring "win one for the Gipper" tales. His locker room antics still consisted of singing off-key and poking fun at teammates.

"He's still as obnoxious as ever," said one.

But his on-ice leadership was unmatched. Seeing him race up and down the ice was unprecedented. Watching him stay in his own end for more than two seconds made you want to give him the game puck. Hull was becoming the complete player Brian Sutter had longed for. He was now a dangerous penalty killer (he scored five short-handed goals for the season, four in the last half), he remained the league's top threat on the power play, and he was now running interference near his own net, a place he barely knew existed before.

"It was an absolute joy to watch how Brett matured throughout the year," Coach Sutter observed.

Thanks to the Hull-led resurgence after the Oates trade, the Blues went into the final month of the regular season with a 30-26-9 record and 69 points, good for second in the Norris Division and seventh overall. Only the Rangers, Canadiens, and Red Wings had a better home mark than the Blues' 21-9-3.

However, the team still had trouble winning on the road. In the 12 games since the Oates trade, the Blues had played only four away from The Arena, winning two and losing two. Their road record of 9-17-6 was ahead of only the Flyers, Nordiques, and Sharks. For the team to have any shot at finishing high in the standings and advancing in the playoffs, it had to start showing some character on the road.

The Blues would get their chance during the very first week of March. They were scheduled to travel through the Smythe Division, playing in Vancouver, Edmonton, and Calgary. They had been playing their best hockey of the year, and this trip yielded the perfect opportunity not only to start a winning streak on the road, but to start the season's final month on a bang.

This was the time of year teams started to rev up for the playoffs. They were in the back stretch now, kicking it into overdrive while fine-tuning all their parts. A team's success in the playoffs is usually reflective of their success during the last month or two of the regular season. A slump now could mean an early departure in the postseason. Brett Hull and the boys were determined to avoid such a collapse.

*　　　*　　　*

As many friends and admirers as he had, it was inconceivable this man was leaving St. Louis alone. But on the afternoon of February 27, Gino Cavallini walked through Lambert Airport with only his sticks and a suitcase. The senior member of the Blues was departing after six years.

"Life goes on," Giant Gino professed as he stood at the TWA ticket counter.

Cavallini's longevity in St. Louis allowed him to creep up the Blues' all-time scoring charts. Not known for his delicate scoring touch, Gino ranked 16th in goals with 91, twentieth in assists with 120, and twentieth in total points with 211. An iron man during his stint in St. Louis, Cavallini played in 454 games for the Blues, ninth on the all-time list.

But life with the Blues hadn't been much fun for Cavallini the last few weeks. While the club was finally turning things around and notching victory after victory, Gino was sitting in the pressbox, relegated to watching instead of playing. Their heaviest player at nearly 220 pounds, Cavallini's role was to crunch the opposition and spring the puck loose to his linemates. But Coach Sutter felt Gino had abandoned his responsibilities, so he banished him from the ice. The last time he had seen any action was nearly four weeks earlier, on February 2 against the Flyers.

"I don't question Brian's decisions," said Cavallini. "He's the coach. He has to ultimately live with those decisions. I respect him because he wants to win as badly as anyone else. I just wanted continued success for the team and hopefully an opportunity to get back in there. As it turned out, I never did get that opportunity. It got discouraging."

Cavallini's sudden fall from grace was extraordinary. He went from playing on the top line with Hull and Oates during the first half of the season to not playing at all. How in the world did that happen?

"It was a tough responsibility playing with them," he explained. "They were such good offensive threats that sometimes I got caught up in that part of the offense and forgot to play solid defense. And that was my role."

So Ron Caron did the most humane thing possible. Instead of letting the 29-year-old forward rot in the pressbox and possibly cut short his career, Caron put Cavallini on waivers, which allowed a team to pick him up at minimal cost. He obviously had no future with the Blues. It was only fair to see if any other team was interested in his services.

Caron put Gino on waivers on February 25. Teams had 48 hours to claim him or he remained the property of the Blues. If that happened, he still wouldn't have stayed in St. Louis very long. The team likely would have sent him to Peoria so he could get back into playing shape.

As the deadline approached, no team had made contact with the Blues. But that was not surprising. According to the rules regarding irrevocable waivers, out of all the teams interested in picking up such a player, the one with the worst record gets the first shot. In other words, if Toronto makes it official it's interested in signing Gino, all other teams with a better record—and that's most of them—are automatically eliminated. Only teams with worse records are still eligible to sign him. That's why teams wait until the last minute. No team wants to tip its hand. It's a game of wait-and-see.

Just two minutes before the 48-hour period expired, at precisely 10:58 a.m. St. Louis time, a team finally flashed on the computer screen in the Blues' office where Gino was patiently waiting. It read, "Quebec Nordiques." Only the San Jose Sharks had a worse record, but they were uninterested. It was official. Gino Cavallini was the newest member of the Nordiques.

It usually costs a team around $20,000 to claim a player off waivers. But to make Gino more attractive, Caron lowered the asking price to $5,000, another saintly gesture for which the general manager should be commended.

When I met Cavallini at the airport a few hours later, I expected him to be depressed and spiritless. Not only was he leaving his home of six years, he was going to a French-speaking city, whose hockey team had been the laughingstock of the league the last several years. Instead, Gino was radiant. By no means was this a trip to purgatory. This was a chance to resurrect his career.

"I've met a lot of great people, a lot of good friends," Cavallini said. "But people have to realize this is to better my career. I wasn't having very much fun the last three weeks. It was great that the team was winning. But I wasn't any part of the streak they're on right now, and I wanted to be badly."

And with that, Gino jumped on a plane to Los Angeles where the Nordiques were playing that night. He assisted on the game's first goal, an eventual 4-2 loss by Quebec. Cavallini would get used to losing there. The Nordiques would miss the playoffs for the fifth year in a row. And what probably came as a blow to his pride, Quebec left Gino unprotected at the end of the season for the two expansion teams to pick him up. However, Tampa Bay and Ottawa were uninterested and passed him by.

Chapter Fourteen

ON THE ROAD AGAIN

When I first discussed this book idea with Brian Sutter, he put a hand on my shoulder and said, "You've got to come on a road trip with us to see the other side of the players, to see how they come together as a unit." No question, that was something I had been planning, so it was a relief the coach invited me before I had to bring it up first. I had been on numerous road trips before to cover specific games—Hull's mile-stone fiftieth goal in Detroit in February of 1991, for example, and playoff games in Detroit, Minneapolis, and Chicago.

But I wanted to make this road trip different. I wanted to get a feel of what it was really like to be "one of the guys" away from home. I planned to leave my reporter responsibilities at home and just stick with the team wherever it went and whatever it did. Thanks to the graciousness of the coaching staff and the players, I was allowed to hang out with the team during its three-game trip in early March. I stayed with the guys from the moment we left St. Louis on March 1, to the second we arrived back home March 8. As it turned out, the trip would prove to be a major turning point in the season. The Blues would lose not only their team captain, but also their momentum heading into the playoffs. The next two chapters detail our trip.

"Please be seated. The pilot is ready to depart."

The flight attendant had repeated her request a couple of times, but several players didn't seem to notice. They were busy changing seats in preparation for their flying ritual of playing cards. Those who liked to gamble gathered in one section of the plane, tossing out the non-gamblers and sending them to a different section of the aircraft.

"Hey, would you sit down back there?" Rick Zombo demanded. "The pilot can't see out the back window."

I started to laugh until I noticed no one else was even smiling. I guess Zombo's one-liner was a standard road trip joke. We hadn't even left Lambert Airport yet, and the guys were already digging into one another. It was something I would get used to over the next seven days.

More than four hours after leaving an unseasonably warm day in St. Louis, we arrrived to fog and 53 degrees in Seattle. I couldn't wait to jump off that plane and stretch my weary bones. I don't travel much, and now I know why. Sitting on that plane for an entire morning, watching nothing but clouds and farm fields pass by, was enough to drive me absolutely nuts. I don't see how people do this for a living. Just driving 25 minutes to work every day is a strain for me.

"Hey, where's your tie?" Brett Hull demanded as we walked through the Seattle airport.

He was right.   The dress code for all members of the traveling team included a tie. And since I was part of the group, I was violating the rule. I was wearing a pair of Levi's, cowboy boots, and a double-knit sweater pulled over an Oxford button-down. I figured it was the perfect outfit for western Canada. I figured wrong.

"Who do you think you are?" asked Paul Cavallini as the guys continued to needle me. "Dave Luecking?"

"Oh, give the guy a break," Kelly Chase answered. "Don't compare him to Luecking for Christ's sake."

I knew there was a reason I liked Chase.

After an hour-and-a-half wait at the airport, we jumped on a United flight for the short trip to Vancouver. I had just settled into my seat near the back of the plane when someone behind asked a small favor of me.

"Could you move?"

It was Dave Lowry, one of the principal card players. Knowing that I earn a small fraction of what everyone else on the plane makes, he wasn't about to ask that I hang out and start tossing large sums of money around.

"Sure," I said. "Where do you want me to go?"

"Go trade places with Nelson if you wouldn't mind," Lowry replied.

What was I going to do, say no? They also tossed Hull to the front of the plane. If they could boot that guy out of his seat, I wasn't about to argue.

"Nelson, do you want to switch seats with me?" I asked after walking to the front of the aircraft. "They want you to go back there to play cards."

"You sure you don't mind?" Emerson asked.

"Nah, go right ahead. I'm not a card player."

The Blues' rookie went back there and promptly won $20. I should have asked for a cut.

Seated across the aisle from me were Hull and Garth Butcher. They were carefully flipping through pages of information sent to Butcher from the NHL players' union office. As the team's player representative (Gino Cavallini had held the title until going to Quebec a few days earlier), Butcher was studying the latest demands the union would make as the players and owners tried to hammer out a new collective bargaining agreement. There were rumblings that the players would walk if no settlement was reached by the end of the regular season. I found that hard to believe. Certainly, the two sides would settle the issue before it got to that point.

Minutes after leaving Seattle, we arrived in Vancouver, a place I had never seen. And that was my loss. As we started to fly over the city, I realized this was God's country. It had to be the most beautiful setting I had ever laid eyes on. The city was nestled into the base of the Coast Mountains, just west of the Rockies. With the sun reflecting off the Pacific Ocean—or, rather, Burrard Inlet, as the ocean water bisects Vancouver— I figured this must be what heaven looks like.

"It's a beautiful city, isn't it?" said John Kelly.

"Damn right," I answered, still gazing at the outlay below us. It was breathtaking.

After checking through customs, the players gathered around the luggage concourse to wait for their belongings. It didn't take long for the money to start flying around again. These guys actually bet on whose suitcase would come down the chute first. Everyone threw in a dollar with the winner taking the pot.

I never did find out who won the prize. I was too busy watching the people around us. We were now in hockey country, and the players had attracted quite an audience of star-gazers. As expected, most were staring at the guy with the golden locks. That's all the folks were doing for now, just staring; that quickly changed when we exited the airport to hop aboard the team bus.

There were a couple dozen kids waiting to pounce. Armed with pens and hockey cards, the youngsters quickly surrounded their idols. The players graciously signed autographs as they pushed through the crowd. However, one man was conspicuously absent. Brett Hull ran in a different direction to avoid a mob scene. And it didn't matter if the kids ran to the bus to catch him. They weren't going to find him there. Hull's mother, who lives near Vancouver, was waiting in the parking lot for her superstar son. Hull jumped in the car, and the pair quickly sped off. He had this down to a science.

As I sat on the bus and watched the players make their way through the group of autograph seekers (Upper Deck's new set of "sports reporters" wasn't out yet, so thankfully I wasn't recognized), I suddenly realized why so many athletes complain about signing their names. Some of these kids were beyond pushy, they were downright ravenous. What's worse, one adult was actually shoving his kid into the group to get a few autographs.

Meanwhile, one youngster, about 10 or 11, had positioned himself directly in front of the door to the bus. Every player jumping on the bus had to either sign an autograph or physically remove the kid from the entrance.

"That kid's pushy," complained Brendan Shanahan as he hopped aboard. "That kid. Right there. In the blue jacket." Shanahan was pointing out the road block to his teammates who had managed to slip past him.

With the crowd growing larger around the bus, one player was still missing. Bob Bassen. No, he hadn't been consumed by the large pack of autograph hounds. He was still in the airport, desperately looking for a bundle of hockey sticks he was going to present to his nephew in Calgary. Somewhere between St. Louis and Vancouver, the sticks had gone AWOL. Bobby searched through the concourse and asked airline personnel for assistance, but no one found even a trace of them. Bassen couldn't wait any longer. He turned the search over to the proper authorities and ran back out to catch the bus. No one ever did find the sticks.

With his teammates watching through the windows, Bassen made his way toward the bus, with Kid Aggressor blocking the way to the door.

"Watch out, Bass!" Shanahan yelled and laughed at the same time.

The players were howling in the back of the bus. They were about to watch a confrontation. Would Bassen stop and sign the kid's autograph, or would he push past like many of his teammates?

"Get him Bass!" Brendan continued to yell. "Get him!"

Bob Bassen isn't the type to turn down ANY autograph request. But he obviously had other things on his mind. He had a look of distress as he made his way toward the bus. He'd been looking forward to giving those sticks to his brother's kid, but now he had no idea where they were. In a daze, Bassen politely nudged past the kid and jumped aboard the bus. To the delight of his fellow players, Bassen had effectively beaten Kid Aggressor.

"Attaboy, Bass!" Shanahan yelled. Most of the guys were giving Bobby a standing ovation, patting him on the back as he made his way down the aisle. Of course, he had no idea what all the commotion was about. But when you're the recipient of a standing ovation, you don't ask questions.

As the bus finally started to move, Shanahan derisively waved at the kid as if to say, "Gotcha, you jerk." The youngster wasn't about to let it slide. With an angry glare, he promptly flipped Shanahan the bird. Brendan returned the favor, and that was that. The bus pulled out of the airport and headed to the Hotel Vancouver. I'll tell you one thing. The next time I hear how an athlete was rude to a an autograph seeker, I'll assume that maybe, just perhaps, there was another side to the story.

We checked into the hotel a little after 3 o'clock that afternoon. After throwing my stuff in my room, I went back down to the lobby to meet Richie Sutter. The Canucks were playing a Sunday afternoon game against the Flames, and Richie invited me to tag along to watch the final period. As a former Canuck, Sutter still had connections to get us in the building.

We thought the scoreboard was malfunctioning when we entered the place. It read, "Canucks 7, Flames 0." And that was after only 40 minutes of play. The home team was absolutely obliterating its Smythe Division rivals. The Flames had been struggling ever since trading Doug Gilmour to the Maple Leafs in a monstrous 10-player deal back in early January. But this was ridiculous. After finishing with more than 100 points the year before, Calgary was suddenly struggling to keep its head above water. Sound familiar?

Unbelievably, Richie and I witnessed four more goals that final period, and all were put into the back of the Flames' net. The 11-0 shutout was the most lopsided victory in Canucks history and the most one-sided loss in Flames history. And that meant only one thing. The Blues would win here tomorrow night. Guaranteed.

It happens over and over again. A team scores a ton of goals while romping over its opponent. The very next game, the same team comes out as flat as a pancake. Everything goes so perfectly, so easily in one game, that the players tend to relax a bit the next time out, forgetting that it took hard work and effort to achieve that lopsided win.

"You always have to be worried when you score a bunch of goals," Hull once admitted. "They're usually harder to come by the next time out."

After the blowout, Sutter and I made our way to the locker rooms so he could see some of his old friends and teammates. Lo and behold, there sat Mike Folga and Jim Pickard, the Blues' trainer and equipment manager, respectively. They were waiting for the Flames to clear their equipment out of the visitors' locker room so they could start moving their own stuff in.

While the rest of the Blues were out doing their own thing around Vancouver, these two gentlemen were already getting their hands dirty and working up a sweat. It was a sight I'd see throughout the week long trip. Folga and Pickard were the first ones to work every morning and the last ones to turn out the lights in the dressing room at night. They're the unsung heroes on the team, the true heart and soul who are responsible for just about everything short of scoring goals.

No matter what business you're in, we all know people like Folga and Pickard. They're the ones who are paid the least money, but do the most work. The ones whose hard work and dedication goes largely unnoticed by management, but is greatly appreciated by the people closest to them. In this case, that's the players. Folga and Pickard are the occasional recipients of tips handed out by the guys on the team. It's a show of thanks and gratitude for the effort put forth by these two men. Just like the "roadies" who work for a traveling concert tour, the show wouldn't go on without Mike Folga and Jim Pickard. And what's more, they were underpaid compared to others around the league. Pickard, who had been in the league for 20 years, including 17 with the Islanders, was earning a salary in the low $20,000 range. Folga, who was in his fourth year with the Blues, was paid $38,000 when the average salary for an NHL trainer was closer to $45,000. And most of those trainers were under contract while Folga was not. It was a sore spot for Mike, one that would come to a head at the end of the year.

After Richie said hello to a multitude of people, he and I caught a taxi back to the hotel, where I hooked up with the voice of the St. Louis Blues, John Kelly. It was dinnertime and we had a date with mass quantities of food. All that traveling from place to place doesn't afford an opportunity to sit down and eat. You wonder why there are very few fat athletes? It's not because they work out. They just never have time to fill their stomachs.

We settled on a seafood restaurant within walking distance of the hotel. As we entered, I saw it was a fairly popular place among the players, too. Nelson Emerson, Stephane Quintal, Craig Janney, and Dave Christian were sitting at one table. The Sutter twins occupied another table with some friends from back home in Lethbridge.

After dinner, John and I sat in the hotel lounge and just relaxed, having another drink or two. Brian Sutter and his two coaches, Bob Berry and Wayne Thomas, were at the bar, going over tomorrow night's game against the Canucks, no doubt. Brian sent over another round of drinks before heading off to bed around 10 p.m.

"What time does the bus leave for the rink tomorrow morning?" I asked John.

"It's supposed to leave at 10:15," he said. "But you'd better be ready to go by five after. That's Sutter-time."

"Sutter-time?"

"Yeah. The bus always leaves about five or ten minutes before it's supposed to. If you show up at 10:15, you might as well call a taxi."

Heeding John's advice, I walked down to the lobby the next morning at exactly 10:00. Most of the players had already gathered, which showed me there really was something to this Sutter-time. Sure enough, at precisely 10:08, the bus took off toward the Pacific Coliseum for the morning skate.

When we got to the rink, the players immediately went to the dressing room, and I took a seat in the empty stands. The Pacific Coliseum is a nondescript building that looks like an oversized gymnasium. The walls are a dingy gray, and the lighting is horrendous, creating shadows all over the ice. The Canucks are in the process of building a new downtown arena that will be ready for use in 1995, and I would think the players and fans are more than happy about that.

There was one young man who looked to be in his mid-20s already on the ice, taking slapshots at the empty net. He had a hell of a shot, too. The lefty was whizzing them from the blue line and the pucks were taking off like rockets and snapping the back of the net. He was wearing an old Blues jersey, but I had no idea who he was. He had to be more than just a fan, or he wouldn't be allowed on the ice.

"Who is that guy?" I asked a photographer sitting nearby.

"That's Bart Hull, Brett's brother," he responded.

Should've known. All those wasted years of biology in high school and college. Everything I needed to know about genetics was being demonstrated right in front of me.

Brett's mother was also in attendance for the morning skate. She had hired Jonathan Cruz Photography, a Vancouver-based company, to shoot pictures of the Hull boys. Most families take their portraits in front of some sort of goofy, finger-painted backdrop. Not the Hulls.

After a short practice, I entered the locker room to talk to some of the players about life on the road. We had left St. Louis only about 30 hours earlier, but it already seemed like an eternity. Not that I was homesick. I was actually enjoying myself. But I just couldn't fathom how players do this throughout the course of a season. Get on a plane, wait at the airport, hop on another plane, fight through autograph seekers, take the bus to the hotel, find a place to eat, get up the next morning and jump aboard another bus, practice for an hour, take the bus back to the hotel, try to get some shuteye, hop on the bus again to go back to the rink for the game, and so on and so on.

"It's always a grind," said Dave Lowry. "And it gets harder when the kids get older."

No matter the town, it's home to at least a few of the players and/or their relatives, and that makes the trip a bit more enjoyable. The night before, Lowry had dinner with his wife's parents, Peter and Cathy Dinsdale, munching on pasta, his favorite pre-game meal. Visits like that make the trip much easier to swallow.

Some players, particularly the single ones, actually relish hitting the road, with or without family members present.

"I love it," admits Bassen, a 27-year-old bachelor. "It makes the game easier sometimes. It's more structured. You have specific times to get on the bus, to eat, to arrive at airports. I think it's easier to become distracted at home."

In other words, the single guys don't have to pick up after themselves on the road.

After practice, a large crowd of fans had gathered outside the rink in preparation for an autograph feeding frenzy. However, they were going to go home hungry. The bus was actually inside the building, having driven through the service entrance where trucks unload supplies. The players were then able to jump aboard without incident. When the huge garage door swung open and let the bus emerge, many of the fans showed their disgust by flipping off the players. The Blues weren't making very many friends in Vancouver.

On game days, the players hit their rooms for an afternoon snooze. Some are able to saw wood immediately, others toss and turn worrying about the game, just hours away. But as Bobby Bassen says, it doesn't do any good to replay a contest you haven't even played yet.

"You can overthink the game," he says. "There's no reason to get too wrapped up in it."

"I never, ever had a problem going to sleep," said Bernie Federko, a 14-year veteran of afternoon naps. "That was something you train yourself to do."

The bus was scheduled to leave the hotel for the rink at 5:15 p.m., and amazingly it left at that time. What happened? Was Sutter-time running slow? Was the head coach softening his rules of departure? No, not at all. It seems that an appearance by a certain individual named Brett Hull created quite a mob scene. Dozens of fans, even more than we'd seen at the airport the day before, surrounded Hull outside the hotel as he tried to get on the bus. They had him pinned against the building. Hull was obliging, writing his name on everything handed to him. But if he was intent on signing autographs for everyone there, we weren't going to make the game on time.

"Honk the horn, driver," ordered Bob Berry.

That was the signal for Hull to stop everything he was doing and jump on the bus. The sound of the horn was Hull's alibi, his perfect excuse to the fans that he just couldn't sign any more autographs.

But Hull didn't emerge from the crowd. The driver honked again. Still no Hull. Had he been consumed by the growing number of hockey buffs who wanted a piece of the sport's most prolific scorer? I was absolutely stunned watching this unfold. Back home in St. Louis, Hull was besieged by autograph seekers outside the Arena, but it was nothing like this. I had the urge to jump through a window to rescue the poor guy.

"Hey Bobby, go save Hullie," said Ron Wilson to Berry. "They've got him pinned."

Just as Berry exited the bus to pull his star player out of the mass of people, Brett was finally able to break free and leap aboard. And to think he has to go through this wherever he goes. No thanks.

"Those kids don't listen!" complained Hull as he walked toward the back. "They won't get out of the way!"

As the bus made its way through downtown Vancouver and toward the Pacific Coliseum, the players were generally quiet. It was quite a contrast to the bus ride earlier in the morning, when everyone was much more talkative and outgoing. I wasn't sure whether they were a little more uptight or just fearful of acting like they were having a good time when Brian Sutter was sitting in the front seat about to have an anxiety attack.

I sat directly behind the Blues' head coach and observed him the entire 20-minute drive. He was a nervous wreck. He leaned forward, placed his elbows on his knees, clasped his hands together, and slowly tapped his feet up and down, up and down. After a few seconds of that, he leaned back, crossed his legs and began tapping his fingers on the arm-rest. In between he was letting out heavy sighs, "Whooooooosh." It sounded like air being released from a balloon.

As I watched this man struggle through his pregame tension, I started to wonder what he was like before an important game. Let's be honest. A road game in Vancouver wasn't exactly a home game against Chicago. Most hockey fans back in St. Louis weren't even going to watch or listen to this contest in its entirety since it wasn't starting until 9:35 Central Time. If he was this nervous before a Canucks game for crying out loud, what did he look like before a big divisional matchup?

But I could just hear Sutter snap if someone suggested this wasn't a big game. "Every game is important!" he would say. "Beating Vancouver is no less important than beating the Hawks. Two points are two points." And, of course, he would be right. Brian Sutter wanted to win EVERY game, no exceptions. What if the Blues lost this contest and ended up finishing a point behind Chicago for second place? This game carried as much weight as the other 79.

The bus pulled into the service entrance just like before to allow the players to walk to the dressing room in peace. I grabbed my media pass and headed upstairs to the press lounge, where I sat next to the two Blues play-by-play announcers, John Kelly and Ken Wilson, along with their producer, Tom McGlocklin. The three men were discussing who to highlight during the pregame show.

"I thought we'd show Ronning and Momesso," Kelly said to McGlocklin.

"You don't want to show Bure or Larionov?"

"Nah, I don't think so. Or maybe McLean. We could show him."

"Well, whatever. We could go either way."

"What do you think, Ken?" Kelly asked Wilson, tossing him the Canucks' roster.

"It doesn't matter to me. Bure and Larionov would be nice. But Ronning and Momesso are fine with me."

And so Cliff Ronning and Sergio Momesso were the two players who would be highlighted during the five-minute pregame show. It only made sense. They were the players Blues fans were most familiar with. They had been sent from St. Louis to Vancouver one year earlier in the deal known simply as The Trade. On March 5, 1991, the Blues sent forwards Geoff Courtnall, Cliff Ronning, and Sergio Momesso, along with defenseman Robert Dirk, to the Canucks in exchange for forward Dan Quinn and defenseman Garth Butcher. At the time, the Blues had the best record in the league and were considered among the favorites for the Stanley Cup. However, the Blues were ousted from the playoffs in just the second round and had been struggling along at .500 the majority of this season. Many people pointed to The Trade as the beginning of the end for any hope of a championship.

Quinn, of course, had been sent packing to Philadelphia back in September, but hockey buffs back home wanted to be kept apprised of the four ex-Blues' statistics in Vancouver, just to see if they had any more reason to hate Butcher. After all, the Canucks were racing to their best regular-season finish in team history and their first winning season in 16 years! Ronning already had 62 points, far surpassing his best totals in St. Louis, where Coach Sutter was not his biggest supporter. John Kelly and Ken Wilson were about to remind everyone in St. Louis that since The Trade, the Canucks had become the surprise team of the NHL, while the Blues had plummeted back to mediocrity, where they had spent the majority of their first 24 years.

I took my seat in the pressbox high above the rink. The shadows across the ice were even more pronounced from my birds-eye view. No wonder the Flames permitted 11 goals yesterday afternoon. They couldn't see the puck dancing in and out of the shadows. I've heard of home-ice advantage, but this was a bit much.

As it turned out, the shadows had no effect on the Blues. As predicted, the Canucks were lifeless in the early going. Less than 12 minutes into the game, the Blues had already scored three times on goals by Hull and the Sutter twins. When Ronnie and Richie score in the same game, you know things are going well. It marked only the second game of the year that the Sutter brothers had scored in the same contest, the first coming on November 16th in a 5-3 win over Minnesota. The twins would accomplish the feat a third time on March 19, a 4-1 win over the Bruins.

The Canucks got one of the goals back just before the period ended. With the Blues on the power play, Pavel Bure raced behind the Blues' net and stole the puck from Paul Cavallini, who had been struggling in recent weeks. Bure slipped around to the front of the net, where his first shot was stopped by Joseph. However, in his attempt to make up for his original error,

Cavallini tried to sit on the loose puck but knocked Joseph down in doing so. Bure managed to retrieve it from under Cavallini and promptly flipped it over the fallen Joseph.

The Blues got their three-goal lead back early in the second period, when Hull scored on a patented one-timer from above the left circle. Craig Janney won a faceoff, and kicked it back to Hull, who blistered a shot over Kirk McLean's right shoulder. The entire play lasted about a second.

Later in the period, Hull completed his eighth hat trick of the season to give the Blues a 5-1 lead and complete control of the game. The visitors were pummeling one of the top goaltenders in the game, a guy who had better stats than even Curtis Joseph. McLean came into the game leading the league in wins (33), was third in goals-against (2.69), and fourth in save percentage (.910). But thanks to a lackluster performance by his defense, the Blues were having no trouble getting the puck past him.

The Canucks' Jimmy Sandlak scored his team's second goal with 43 seconds left in the second period, causing Wayne Thomas to slam down his headphones in the pressbox. You never, ever give up a goal in the final minute of a period. It can change momentum going into the next 20 minutes and wipe out everything that's been accomplished so far. What was especially disconcerting was that the Blues had stopped playing since Hull's goal at 12:25. The Canucks fired off the last seven shots of the period and appeared to be regrouping after a lackluster beginning. No one, however, with the exception of Curtis Joseph, was quite prepared for the onslaught that was to occur in the third period.

Sandlak scored early to cut the lead to 5-3, and suddenly it was a different game. The home team started firing away, using Joseph for target practice. The Blues' goaltender was being abused more than a crash-test dummy. He stopped shot after shot after shot after shot. Halfway through the period the Canucks had outshot the Blues 16-0. Let me write that again so you know it's not a misprint; 16-0 halfway through the period. Add the final seven shots of the second period, and Vancouver had slapped the last 23 on goal.

The Blues finally ended the Canucks' streak at 26, when Brendan Shanahan wristed a shot on goal at 12:40. But that one shot didn't change the momentum. Vancouver simply scooped up the rebound and skated back to the Blues' zone, where they set up camp once again. With five minutes remaining in the period, the Canucks enjoyed a 23-1 edge in shots for the period. How the Blues enjoyed a two-goal edge in goals was a complete mystery. In the battle of two of the NHL's best netminders, Curtis Joseph was winning pads down.

Vancouver sent four more shots on goal the final few minutes of the game, but not one managed to find its way past Joseph. The final numbers were numbing. Twenty-seven shots on goal in the third period, breaking a Blues record that had stood for only a month, since the Penguins' 26. Fifty-four shots total, tying a team record set in 1974 by the Canadiens and equaled in 1980 by Pittsburgh.

Every reporter sitting along press row knew that the Blues were lucky to be escaping Vancouver with two points. Except for the first period, the visitors had been completely dominated by a quicker and seemingly more talented team. The Canucks were able to skate across the blue line with relative ease and fire away at will. But Joseph had one of those nights when the puck looked as large as a beach ball. He was in "the zone," a mindset an athlete refers to when everything seems to move in slow motion except himself. When an athlete is in "the zone," every swing connects, every pass finds its target, every shot hits the basket, and every puck, at least to a goalie, seems to trickle along the ice at half-speed.

"I was fairly busy," said Joseph, in the understatement of the year. "Games like this certainly keep you in it, that's for sure."

"He's been the MVP for our team," said Hull, trying to convince outsiders of a fact everyone in St. Louis already knew.

When Paul Cavallini walked by the group of Vancouver reporters, he couldn't resist getting in a dig.

"How does that Butcher trade look now, fellas?" he asked, almost daring any one of them to say something, which they didn't.

Cavallini was right. Momesso was the only ex-Blue to figure in the scoring, an assist on Sandlak's goal in the third period. Butcher, meanwhile, assisted on Hull's first goal while playing a strong, physical game in his own end, one of the few Blues defensemen to shine on this particular night. At least for one game, critics of The Trade had nothing to gripe about.

Another strong defensive effort was turned in by Jeff Brown, who took a face full of wood when he was high-sticked by Trevor

Linden late in the second period. After the game, Brown sat in front of his locker holding a towel full of ice to his injured mug. His bottom teeth had been pushed back a bit. His mouth was sore and swollen. Ten stitches were needed to sew up a gash under his lower lip. The guy looked like he had just been jumped by a couple of street thugs.

And what did his assailant get? Absolutely nothing. Referee Mark Faucette ruled Brown had grabbed Linden's stick and hit his own face with it. No penalty was called, sending the Blues' defenseman into a rage. A penalty was then immediately called. Two minutes for unsportsmanlike conduct on Jeff Brown.

"I'm not strong enough to injure my own face like this," mumbled Brown, barely able to form words with his badly damaged mouth.

"Hey, Brownie!" shouted Bob Berry from across the dressing room. "You better get married now, because you're not getting any better looking!"

Wow. Talk about hitting a man when he's down. These guys showed no mercy. Brown was in no mood to be cut down after being cut apart. He just stared at his assistant coach with disdain.

"C'mon, Brownie," said Berry. "Relax."

"Bobby," mumbled Jeff, "I wish we were alone in the room."

Meanwhile, outside the locker room, Brian Sutter was defending his team against suggestions that the better club lost. He bristled at a reporter when asked if the Blues went into the game assuming the Canucks would be flat after their 11-0 pounding of the Flames the day before.

"No way," snapped Sutter. "We didn't even talk about it. We knew they'd be high after a game like that. We took nothing for granted."

Question after question was shot down. No matter what it was, Sutter fired a defensive answer right back. He wasn't going to give the Canucks credit for anything.

"That son of a bitch hasn't changed a bit since his playing days," observed one reporter.

"Yeah, he's still wearing his game-face," agreed another.

The problem was they didn't know HOW to ask Sutter the questions. That comes after spending a considerable amount of time with him. I'm sure it's that way in every city. You get to learn a coach's personality and what buttons to push to elicit particular responses. Instead of asking Sutter if he thought the Blues were lucky to win, you turn the question into more of a statement that you know he'd agree with.

"Well, Brian, your team played awfully well against a very talented Vancouver team." That's the proper way to get Sutter to comment on the Canucks.

"You're right," he would say. "Vancouver is a very skilled team and they proved that again tonight. Curtis saved us once again."

And if you wanted a comment on the Blues' porous defense, you'd never ask, "Brian, why did your defensemen struggle so much tonight?" That kind of question would only antagonize a man who never rips his players in public. A better way to get a response would be to say, "Brian, the Canucks spent a lot of time in your end tonight. It seems there wasn't much you could do to stop them."

"Well, that's correct," he would answer. "Certain individuals on the hockey club didn't play up to their capabilities tonight."

After snapping at reporters, Sutter and Company hopped aboard the bus for the trip back to the hotel. Officially, the players have an 11 p.m. curfew on the road. Unofficially, it's rarely enforced in a strict sense. After all, the team usually doesn't arrive at the hotel until well after 11 p.m. on game nights. As adults, they deserve the right to visit with friends or have a few postgame drinks. The message was clear: Do what you have to do, but stay out of trouble. No one's coming to bail you out of jail at 3:00 in the morning.

I shared a few draft beer(s) with John Kelly, Tom McGlocklin and the three Blues coaches in the hotel lounge. We shot the bull for an hour or so before Sutter and his sidekicks decided to turn in. A few minutes later, I followed suit and headed up to my room. I had been in Canada barely 36 hours, but it seemed like 36 days already. My eyes were tired from observing, my hand exhausted from writing, and my liver...well, uh, my liver was being put to pretty good use so far. However, it was just a warm-up to the workout it was about to get.

Tomorrow morning, the team was heading to the mountain resort lodge in Banff, Alberta. The players were being treated to a three-day vacation there to unwind and let off steam. The next game wasn't until Friday the 6th in Edmonton, and the players couldn't wait to take advantage of their free time. In a season of rushing around from city to city at a dizzying pace, this was a wonderful opportunity for the guys just to relax and get to know each other a little better, especially important for a team that had undergone so many personnel changes in recent months. Unfortunately, the idea backfired. When it was time to return to business, the team's energy had been left behind in the mountains.

Chapter Fifteen

BANFF BLUES

"Seven million dollars?"

Ron Sutter shook his head. He couldn't believe what he was reading. Second baseman Ryne Sandberg had just signed a multiyear contract with the Chicago Cubs for a little more than seven million bucks a season.

"Seven million. Seven million."

Stephane Quintal repeated the numbers over and over again as if to make sense out of them.

Sandberg's record-setting contract was the talk of the team Tuesday morning, March 3. No question, the players were envious as hell that a fellow athlete was able to convince his bosses he was worth that kind of money. But realistically, some of them thought it was nonsensical that a team owner would fork over that kind of cash to anyone. They didn't care if he was Babe Ruth.

"That's what's going to destroy baseball," said one player. "You watch."

The Blues were relaxing at the Vancouver airport, ready to take off for Calgary, where they would catch a bus to the Banff resort lodge. The team was spread throughout the gate. Some were reading, others were talking, while a few were munching on breakfast snacks. One man trying desperately to force food into his stomach was Jeff Brown, he of the mangled face. He was in excruciating pain just trying to nibble on a muffin. Each bite was slow and deliberate as he tried carefully to keep his jaw from falling to the floor.

"I'm setting a record for the longest time eating a muffin," he said, also setting a record for the longest time getting out a sentence.

Jeff Brown was one of the most approachable members on the team. Whenever you needed a quick sound bite, one that cut to the core, Brown was your man. He was probably the most interviewed player on the team after Brian Sutter, Brett Hull, and Curtis Joseph. In many ways, Brown was like Hull. Both were carefree and easygoing young men who gave as much effort away from the ice as on it. Brown wasn't as boisterous as Hull, but he shared Brett's lust for life. Jeff came to St. Louis from Quebec on December 13, 1989, with a reputation for living life in the fast lane, a true wine, women, and song kind of a guy.

"Yeah, that about sums it up," admitted the 26-year-old bachelor.

And that's where the problem was. He had numerous run-ins with his no-nonsense head coach. Sutter saw Brown as a player with worlds of skill but little work ethic. Hull had a similar reputation but was largely left alone. When you score a goal a game and are adored by millions, you can get away with goofing off a bit more. When you're anyone else, like Jeff Brown, you have to skate the straight and narrow.

"I'm outta here by next week," Jeff said matter-of-factly.

He was referring to the trading deadline exactly one week away. He was convinced Sutter despised him so much that he would be skating for a different team before the deadline passed.

"Oh, bull. You're not going anywhere," I said. "They'd be stupid to trade you with the tear you're on now."

Simply put, Jeff Brown had been the team's best defenseman over the last month. He had tallied 12 points over the previous 10 games on five goals and seven assists. Only the dynamic duo of Hull and Janney had more points in that time span, 20 apiece. Brown was the most skilled defenseman the Blues had right now who could move the puck out of his own end and create offensive pressure. Paul Cavallini had similar abilities, but his stock, in the eyes of the coaches, had plummeted in recent months. On a team sorely lacking the talent to move the puck up-ice, Jeff Brown's job security seemed assured. But then, this was the St. Louis Blues we were talking about. Their team dictionary didn't include the word "stability."

Once aboard the plane, Brian Sutter and Wayne Thomas sat next to each other to watch a videotape of last night's game on a lap-top VCR. I had never seen such a gadget, and I don't think the flight attendant had either.

"I'm going to have to ask the pilot if that's okay to use," she told Sutter. "It could interfere with his radio transmission."

"No it won't," Sutter was quick to say. "We use this all the time."

"Uh, okay. I'll just go make sure."

She didn't return.

Sutter and Thomas logged the number of shots against just to make sure the official scorer was correct. The two Blues coaches came up with a figure less than 54, but the total was still lopsided in the Canucks' favor.

"You gotta stand them up at the blue line," Thomas said to the VCR. "Look at us backing in."

Across the aisle sat Bob Berry, whose mind was far removed from hockey. He was engaged in one of his favorite hobbies, a crossword puzzle. I was amazed and impressed watching Berry work through that thing as if it was designed for a second-grader. Peering through his glasses at the end of his nose, Berry looked more like your favorite grandpa than a hockey coach. He was known as a very wise and intelligent man, and he certainly looked the part.

After landing in Calgary, we waited and waited and waited and waited inside the terminal. Seems there was a new member of the team we were supposed to pick up, but his plane was late, making the players a bit irritable. Everyone passed the time by chewing on airport burgers and fries. Yum-yum. This new guy was going to have a tough time making friends after this.

Finally, after everyone had gone ahead and jumped on the bus to continue waiting, Curt Giles appeared. The 12-year veteran had been a free agent ever since the North Stars told him back in training camp that he didn't fit into their plans. Giles immediately caught on with Team Canada, helping to lead his country to a silver medal in the just-completed Winter Olympics. His strong defensive work showed the NHL that the 33-year-old's career was far from over. Quebec, Hartford, Minnesota (yes, the same team that had booted him six months earlier), and St. Louis expressed interest in acquiring his services. But the

Blues were the only team willing to sign him through the 1992-93 season, so Giles accepted and flew to Banff to meet his new teammates.

"Don't make this a habit!" yelled Hull as Giles boarded the bus more than an hour after he was scheduled to. Giles took a seat next to Dave Christian and, without turning around, waved a hand of acknowledgment to the back of the bus, where Hull was stationed. I seriously doubt the Golden Brett would make a very successful Welcome Wagon representative.

The Blues picked up Giles for one reason, and one reason only. He was being counted on to provide strength and leadership around the Blues' net, a place that saw more rubber than B. F. Goodrich. The 5'8", 180-pound fireplug was anything but an offensive threat. He had never scored more than six goals or 30 points in a season. He also had never accumulated more than 87 penalty minutes, proving he was no Butcher-like agitator. But Giles, a former North Stars captain, commanded respect. He had the unique ability to make his teammates listen and learn, a talent the Blues had been missing since the departures of Scott Stevens and Harold Snepsts.

"This is a classy organization with lots of character," Giles explained. "Everyone here works hard and never quits. I know Brian wants me to do the best job I can, and I'll do anything to help out."

The trip to Banff took us through some of the most majestic and awe-inspiring mountain scenery I've ever traveled through. For a man who grew up in a city where The Hill is considered high ground, this particular range of the Rockies was an imposing sight indeed. The snow-capped peaks seemed to reach to the heavens and pull strands of sunlight down upon themselves. The mountains appeared to have an ego, thrusting their chest out for all to see and admire. It's difficult not to believe in God when visiting a place like this. You could see His handprint everywhere.

After a two-hour trip from Calgary, we finally pulled into the resort area, first dropping off equipment at the Banff ice rink, where the Blues would practice the next couple of days. As if on cue, the players exited the bus to help Mike Folga and Jim Pickard unload the supplies and carry them inside the facility. John Kelly and I stayed seated until it was strongly suggested that we assist in the chores.

"What are you guys doing?" Richie Sutter demanded to know.

"You don't think you're going to stay on the bus, do you?" Butcher asked.

We didn't need to answer him. We quickly jumped off and began carrying bags and boxes full of sticks, skates, and other tools of the trade into the locker room. The whole exercise took about five minutes, which was about five minutes more than I had performed in years.

"That didn't hurt, did it?" Butcher poked in fun.

"So that's what work is?" I said. "I've never done it before."

As the players started to get back on the bus, Darin Kimble noticed a group of wild elk that had made its way down from the mountains and was now within about 50 yards of the bus. He and a couple of other players walked toward the animals, for what purpose I'm not sure. If they punched as hard as Bob Probert, Kimble was in trouble.

Suddenly and without warning, Kimble started making guttural "mooing" noises at the elk as if he expected them to walk up and start conversing with him.

"We've got some brainless guys on this team," said one player.

"He must belong to the Elk's Lodge," said Lee Norwood of the Blues' tough-guy.

Failing to get the elk to respond to his mating call, Kimble gave up and retreated toward the bus.

"I guess I've lost my touch," the Saskatchewan native said. "They're not responding."

Maybe he'd have better luck in town.

We arrived at the lodge in the late afternoon, allowing everyone to unwind for a couple of hours before going out to dinner. I jotted down a few notes, took a short nap, and then met John Kelly and Dave Luecking for dinner at a Banff steak house. The players, meanwhile, were having a private rookie dinner, an annual event where the veterans rack up the highest dinner tab they possibly can, and then turn the bill over to the rookies to pay. On this particular night, the players spent a little more than $1,000 on food and drinks and promptly handed the check to Nelson Emerson and Pat Jablonski.

The players later remarked what a terrible restaurant it was. The choice of food was limited, they complained. The place didn't carry the most expensive bottles of champagne. A thousand dollar tab sounded extremely high to me, but apparently it was modest compared to past dinners. As a rookie with the Canucks in 1985-86, Dave Lowry claimed he and two of his fellow newcomers were handed a bill for more than $3,000!

"I wish they would have asked me," said Hull. "I would have found a better place than this."

But picking the most expensive items on the menu wasn't the sole purpose for this particular rookie dinner. The players voted to unanimously support Bob Goodenow and the players' negotiating committee in their efforts to sign a new collective bargaining agreement with the owners. The players had been skating without one all season, as the old one had expired during training camp. For the first time in six months, the two sides had started talking again in a last-ditch effort to avoid the first full-scale strike in NHL history.

The poll wasn't a strike vote, per se. It was just to show solidarity, to back Goodenow if he decided a strike was necessary to force the owners to make concessions. The majority of the other teams had already taken similar votes, with the remainder to follow over the next several days. The players were demanding less restrictive free agency rules (ever hear of Scott Stevens?), a more effective salary arbitration system, and a larger chunk of playoff revenue, just to name a few of the issues. The potential for a strike and next week's trade deadline were the two hottest topics on the trip.

While the players were talking business, Kelly, Luecking and I paid our dinner tab, which was about $950 less than the players', and made our way to one of Banff's night-spots, the Rose and Crown. It was an English-style pub with hardwood floors, a couple of dart boards, and a live band. The Blues' coaches were already there, watching a game between Calgary and Pittsburgh on one of the many TV screens. After sharing a couple of beer(s), the coaches retreated to the lodge. I'm sure they knew the players were about to take over the town, and they didn't want to be anywhere near them.

Sure enough, just minutes after Sutter and Company left, a few of the players started to trickle in. And that's when I started to feel uncomfortable for the first time. These guys didn't know me from Adam. Sure, they were used to my face hanging around the Arena, used to my constantly sticking a microphone under their chin. They even took the time to discuss things outside of hockey, like hobbies, families, politics.

But they didn't know ME. They had no idea who Dave Simons really was and what his intentions were on this trip. Was I going to observe their every move? Was I looking to dig up dirt like the tabloids? Would I report that a certain player got so drunk he started ripping his clothes off in public? (No, no, that didn't happen. I'm just making a point here. All players' wives can relax.) More than a few of the guys were a bit wary of my presence.

After growing tired of trying to shout over a band that wasn't very good anyway, our little contingent of sports reporters, which now included Mike Folga, hoofed it to a more relaxed environment around the corner. This place had no live band, just a couple of pool tables and a few television sets. In other words, it was dead. But just as we were about to walk back out, we noticed a recognizable figure sitting at the bar watching the hockey game. Brett Hull was his name. His two traveling buddies for the night, Kelly Chase and Darin Kimble, were nearby waiting to get on one of the pool tables.

What amazed me the most was the fact no one was surrounding Hull. He was completely alone, just sitting there looking up at the television over the bartender's head. I guess there really is a place where Mr. Hull can go without being mobbed. I'm not sure whether it was because no one had any idea who he was or they were just too shy to say anything about it. Either way, he was certainly enjoying his rare public solitude.

"That guy has no idea what he's talking about," Hull said, looking at the screen.

"Who doesn't?" I asked, taking a bar stool next to Brett.

He named the television announcer. "He's terrible. He doesn't know what he's saying."

"So who does? Who do you think is a good hockey announcer?"

"People who have played the game before. Like Bernie Federko. He's a guy I respect because he knows the game, and he knows what's going on."

Hull had just summed it up perfectly. Athletes who have played the game before, and who possess even the smallest of on-air talent, have it made when their careers are over (I should make it clear I'm not referring to Bernie when talking about smallest of on-air talent. Federko is actually a very adept analyst). Not only are their opinions respected more by viewers, their opinions are typically shared by the players in the locker room. That's not to say they'll all be million-dollar sports anchors. Most won't be. And there will always be a place for non-athletes with reporting and anchor skills to make it in the business. But if you have had any success hitting a baseball, throwing a touchdown pass, sinking a jump shot, or putting the puck in the net, the door of TV opportunity will swing wide open for you (Sound like a case of sour grapes? Probably).

After listening to a period of the hockey game and watching Chase get his clock cleaned by a pool shark, our little gang climbed into a taxi and rode to the outskirts of town to a happenin' place called "Whiskey Creek." Finally, we found the spot we were looking for. The rock 'n' roll was deafening, the place was packed with young people dancing to exhaustion, and the beer was ice-cold. What more could you ask for? We were apparently the last people to find it. At least half the team was there, lined up against the back wall overlooking the dance floor. The decision was made. We would close down this joint.

Luecking, Kelly, Folga and I took a spot near the bar on the other side of the dance floor from where the players were positioned. We had a wonderful time observing everyone cuttin' a rug, while swapping a multitude of stories ranging from covering the Blues to stupid things we used to do in college. Hour after hour went by and no one budged, including the players who stuck to the back wall and tapped their feet to the music. Before I knew it, my watch showed 2 a.m. and Richie Sutter had made his way down to our end of the dance floor. He was the first player who dared to approach me. In other words, he was the first player who trusted me.

"This is the tightest I've seen the boys in a long time!!" he shouted over the blaring music.

"Really?!!" I shouted back.

"Yeah, this trip is exactly what we needed!!"

No doubt, the Blues were a team that had chugged along through the first 60 games in a veritable fog. There was no direction, no focus, little leadership, and only a tiny amount of team chemistry, much less than a season ago.

But the Blues had been playing their best hockey of the year in recent weeks, winning eight of their last 11. Coincidence or not, their success began as soon as Oates was booted to Boston. The Blues were now 31-26-9, two points ahead of Chicago and ten behind Detroit. That was certainly a large chunk of real estate to make up, but heading into the final month of the season, anything was possible. Perhaps this three-day get-together in Banff would provide that extra push toward the top spot in the Norris. The boys could let loose for a few days, become closer as a team, then ride their enthusiasm into the playoffs.

After a few minutes of shouted conversation, Sutter reclaimed his old spot next to his teammates and left the non-athletes to carry on with their previous topic, which for the life of me, I can't remember. Must have had something to do with the growing number of empty bottles along the top of the bar.

It wasn't long before I noticed a hand waving at me from the back of the wall. I peered across the dance floor to see Richie motioning for me to come up there to join the group. I politely gave a thumbs-down in return. I wasn't going to venture up there in a million years. That area was the players' sanctuary and I didn't feel right to disturb it, not until I got written permission from every man up there.

As a sports journalist, there is one unwritten rule I abide by. Never, ever try to become an athlete's best friend. There may come a time when you have to report on something controversial involving the player in question, or rip him for his poor performance. Becoming too close to an individual compromises your ability to be honest and straightforward. It's important to establish a relationship of respect, but it should seldom move beyond that. There's no problem sharing a beer, a conversation, or a round of golf during one of those celebrity tournaments. But inviting him and the wife over for dinner and a movie is a journalistic no-no.

Of course, Richie wasn't inviting the wife and me up for an outdoor barbeque. He was merely asking that I join him for a drink, which was fine. The problem was, I knew Richie better than anyone else on the team. And as an outsider, I didn't feel comfortable breaking into the players' circle just because one guy I knew said it was okay. If just my presence in the bar made them uneasy, imagine their anxiety if I took a seat right in the middle of everyone, listening to their conversations and watching what they were doing up-close. Nope, I had to decline Sutter's offer. Didn't work. Richie continued to wave for me.

"Just go up there!!" yelled John Kelly.

"No way!!" I shouted back. "I don't think I should!!"

"Why not?!! Just go!!"

Perhaps I was completely overthinking this situation. Perhaps if I moseyed on over there, no one would even notice. So I made my way around the dance floor and took a seat next to Sutter. Sure enough, a couple of the players just sat there stone-faced, staring at the dancers in front of them. While most of the guys didn't seem to give a hoot I was there, a few of them gave strong signals of being uncomfortable. The next morning, a couple of them told me directly they were reticent for a reason.

"Some of the guys were talking about it," said one player. "They're just not sure what you're after. But I don't think it's any big deal."

"I talked to Dave Luecking about you," said another. "We all know and trust him. We just had to find out about you, and he said you're all right."

I only sat amongst the players for a few minutes before heading back to more familiar surroundings. A few of us decided to head to the lodge and turn in for the night. It was about 2:45 a.m., roughly 15 minutes before closing time. We failed to keep our sacred vow of shutting the place down.

We weren't in the taxi more than 30 seconds when we heard the call from another taxi driver on the two-way.

"This is 16 to base. We've got a flat tire here, so we'll be tied up for a few minutes."

As it turned out, Rich Sutter, Brett Hull, and Jim Pickard were in that cab. It wasn't their vehicle that had suffered the flat, but another car. Being the Good Samaritans they are, the three men stopped to offer assistance. After using some of the taxi's tools to fix the problem, Hull and Sutter suddenly threw Pickard into the back of the trunk and promptly shut it. Poor Pickard would have to enjoy the rest of the trip looking at the top of a taxi trunk. Boys will be boys.

My head finally hit the pillow a little after 3 a.m. Practice was in less than seven hours. Of course, that meant nothing to me. All I had to do was drag my body to the rink and plop it down in a seat. As for the players, the ones who were close to watching the sun rise, it would be a different story. I would be in pain just watching them.

*   *   *

"C'mon, boys, c'mon, boys!"

Brian Sutter was shouting instructions to his players as he sent them racing around the rink, lap after lap after lap. It hardly seemed fair. The same coach who allowed his subordinates to stay out until the wee hours was now putting them through one grueling practice. It was as if he was saying, "I don't know what any of you guys did last night, but just in case it was something you shouldn't have been doing, I'm going to make you pay for it."

Actually, everyone who went out the night before had a marvelous, but extremely harmless, good time. They loosened their collars, had a few brews, and jammed to some good ole' fashioned rock 'n' roll. No harm in that. Until this morning.

Round and round they went, skating one sprint after another. Then they practiced for awhile, passing the puck back and forth while continuing to skate at full tilt. Then they did wind sprints. Then they returned to practicing. I was completely exhausted just watching them. Some of the players had the most pained expressions, bending down and putting their hands on their knees as they tried desperately to catch their breath. Their faces were red and their mouths wide open. Their insides were shaking an angry fist.

"It's hard the first couple of minutes," one player said. "Your legs are completely dead."

After practice, the players were in one of the most jovial moods I had seen them in all year. Maybe this vacation idea was a stroke of genius. The guys were spitting out one-liners, zinging them at anyone who dared to enter the locker room. No one was safe, not even a 12-year-old kid with a punk-rock haircut who was given permission to go back there for a few autographs.

"Do you want us to go find him and beat him up?" asked Rich Sutter.

"Beat who up?" the kid asked.

"The guy who cut your hair."

"It's a she."

"Awright. Do you want us to go and beat up the girl who cut your hair then?"

"No, I like it this way."

After grabbing Sutter's autograph, the youngster turned to Dave Lowry who scribbled his unique but largely indecipherable signature. The only way to tell it was Lowry's was by the number "10" he wrote next to it.

"What's this?" the boy demanded to know.

"Can't you read, kid?" Lowry asked.

"Yeah, I can read. But not this."

"Well, if you'd go to school, maybe you'd learn how to read it."

"I go to school."

"Yeah? Why aren't you there now?"

"Because."

Not having a suitable answer, the youngster left in search of a friendlier environment. Tough crowd in there.

Meanwhile, I went on my own tour of the dressing room. Not to collect autographs, but to collect thoughts. The players were in such a light-hearted and cheerful mood, I had to find out more about this trip and what it meant to everyone. So far it seemed to have the desired effects. The guys were coming closer together and having a raucously good time doing so.

"With so many changes, it's important to get the guys together like this," captain Garth Butcher explained. "It isolates us from the outside world. This team is very tight, and our play is starting to show that."

"A night like last night gave us an opportunity to just go out and have fun," Lowry said. "On other trips, you have friends and family you visit and go out to eat with. Here, you don't have those friends. It's just us. This lets us relax. We're close anyway, but this brings us together even more."

"Closeness has to be achieved," Paul Cavallini philosophized. "This team has gone through a lot of things, but we're finally starting to win. This is a perfect time for us to come together. The friendships keep growing and growing. The chemistry is coming together at the right time."

But would Cavallini stick around much longer to see those friendships continue to develop? His name popped up more than any other as the trade deadline approached. Playing for an organization that didn't believe in continuity and spit out players who were becoming too comfortable in a Blues jersey, Cavallini seemed a logical choice as the next guy to go. With over four years and 313 games of service in St. Louis, Paul was the most tenured member of the team. And that's the last title you wanted on this club. That's like being the fattest turkey on the farm the day before Thanksgiving.

But as we leaned against a wall outside the locker room, Cavallini pleaded his case. With so many young defensemen on the team, and with strong rumors the Blues would soon sign a 21-year-old Olympian, Bret Hedican, Cavallini was adamant in his argument for veteran leadership in front of the Blues' net.

"Defense is the toughest position to play," he pointed out. "You can't make a mistake there or you're pulling the puck out of your net. You can make a mistake in the other end, but not your own. It's much easier for a defenseman to play a forward position than it is the other way around."

Cavallini was entirely correct about the need for veterans on the defensive line. That was the primary reason the Blues picked up Curt Giles, who appreciated the fact that he didn't have to jump right into a game situation and prove his abilities immediately. He was allowed to hang out with the team away from the ice first.

"I'm very fortunate to come now," he said. "It's a nice time to relax and get to know all the guys."

Another new player also joined the team for the morning skate by pretty much sneaking in the back door without anyone noticing. The man's name was Philippe Bozon, a 25-year-old native of France who had just completed a tour with the French Olympic team. The Blues had to set a record for the most Olympians in one organization. They had Christian and Janney from the USA, Giles and soon Hedican from Canada, and Bozon from France. If anything, this team had tons of international experience.

No one on the Blues knew a lick about the French forward. He came to the Blues carrying the typical European label. Good speed, great puck-handling abilities, and an aversion to the physical side of hockey. In other words, he seemed to be the exact opposite of who Brian Sutter was looking for. While other teams had begun stockpiling European players, Bozon was the first from across the Atlantic whom the Blues signed in Sutter's tenure as head coach.

Interestingly, Bozon had been the property of the Blues since Ron Caron first signed him as an undrafted free agent way back in 1985. He went to training camp the next year, spent some time in Peoria, and eventually returned home to France. However, Ron Caron never gave up hope that Bozon would develop into an impact player and therefore never took him off the Blues' reserve list. Now, more than five years later, Philippe Bozon was coming back to the only NHL team that had given him a chance.

"I just want one more shot at it," said Bozon in broken English. "If it doesn't work, I'll go back home. But I just have to see if I can make it."

Bozon was extremely reluctant to make the trip stateside for a very personal reason. His girlfriend, Helene, was expecting their child within the next couple of weeks, and Philippe hated the idea of leaving her at such a crucial time.

"But I will go back when it happens," he said.

It didn't take long for vacationers to learn that a professional hockey team was in town. A small crowd, mainly kids, gathered outside the rink to get autographs from the players as they exited. One youngster got Hull's signature and was done for the day.

"Aren't you going to get anyone else?" his friend asked.

"Nope," the kid responded. "There are hockey players, and then there's Brett Hull."

Fair enough. But most of the others were desperate for anyone they could get their hands on. Even a very non-athletic-looking journalist. For the third time in as many days, a kid asked me for my autograph. Each time I explained I wasn't a player and just walked on. It worked the first two times, but not the third.

"I don't care if you're a reporter," said the kid. "I've got Don Cherry and he's a broadcaster."

How could I argue with that? If he was putting me in the same class as Don Cherry, I wasn't going to turn him down.

After the players cleared out of the rink, Luecking, Folga, Kelly and I walked to the Rose and Crown for lunch. This is where it had all started the night before, and I wasn't about to start it again. I decided a light lunch and one beer would be enough. I needed to get back to the lodge and catch up on some of my writing. After all, I was supposed to do SOME work while I was here. The publisher was paying for the trip.

Just as we were about to leave, Craig Janney and Dave Christian, who were sitting at a table with Ron Wilson next to us, invited all takers to a game of darts. Folga gave a thumbs-up. Luecking and Kelly respectfully declined, which is exactly what I wanted to do. But there was no way I was going to pass up this opportunity.

Christian and Janney, former teammates on the Bruins, were two of the most quiet and reserved members of the Blues. They were very difficult to get to open up. While it was relatively easy to sit next to most of the players and shoot the breeze about any subject imaginable, Christian and Janney never seemed interested in discussing much of anything. But here, outside of the rink, I was being asked to throw a few darts and chug a few brews with guys I knew nothing about. I had to say yes. If anything, I had to prove to Janney I wasn't the ogre he made most media types out to be.

"I think the biggest egos in the world belong to reporters," he said with no hesitation. "If you don't want to talk, they take that as a sin. I think the people who are the most standoffish and rude are reporters. I just don't like that part of it (doing interviews). I know it's a part of it, so I do it. But I'm not going to do it and be happy about it."

Folga walked to the chalkboard and divided the four dart throwers into two-man teams, Wilson deciding to be a spectator. On one side of the board, he wrote, "80 Team," on the other, "88 Team." The Olympic references were clear. Christian was on the first team and Janney on the second. Folga assigned himself to Dave while pointing me over to Craig. At the time, I figured we'd be there an hour or two and then head our separate ways. Little did any of us know we'd be tossing those damn things for the next eight hours!

Folga and Christian won the first two games, but Craig and I came back to grab the next three. I guess it took us awhile to develop team chemistry.

"Do you believe in miracles?" I asked. "Noooooo. The '88 team is kicking the '80 team's ass!"

Janney and I then proceeded to lose about every game after that. That's what I got for opening my big, fat mouth.

Losing all sense of time, I was surprised to see Luecking and Kelly return to the Rose and Crown later in the day. I had no idea it was now 7 p.m., some five hours after we had thrown the first dart.

"Have you guys really been here the whole time?" an amazed John Kelly asked.

I'm afraid we had been, tossing dart after dart and beer after beer. My elbow had seen more action than Curtis Joseph's glove. And yet we kept going. The game was just so addictive. Just like golf, you were convinced you would better your score the next time around. Just give me those darts, I'm finally going to hit the bull's eye on my first throw.

Luecking and Kelly formed a third team, and then there was no end in sight. As the night wore on, and the crowd grew larger around us, there was a certain group of six men hogging one of the two dart boards. It didn't matter that pestering patrons continuously asked when we'd be finished. Our hands had become permanently attached to the darts, our eyes permanently affixed to that round board with numbers on it.

I have no explanation for why we glued ourselves to one corner of a pub for an entire afternoon and evening. Was it fun? Sure. Was I glad I didn't go back to my room? You bet. Did I know why we were still there eight hours later? Not really. I hadn't exactly learned anything earth-shattering about Janney and Christian, other than they were as normal as you or I.

Finally, a little after 10 p.m., everyone decided enough was enough. Sore arms and constant harassment from dart-throwing wannabes finally forced us out. Craig Janney and Dave Christian—not to mention Ron Wilson, who deserved the Ultimate Spectator Award—went their separate ways. Luecking and Kelly headed up to the Whiskey Creek while Folga decided to stay put. I stuck around with him for a while before heading to the Whiskey Creek myself.

However, the action there paled in comparison to the night before. The dance floor was less crowded, and the music just didn't seem to be as appetizing. I shared a pizza with Dave and John and finally headed to my room for the night. I could get away with this kind of behavior back in college. But my body was becoming a bit too old for this. Even the players who hit the town for the second consecutive night were much more laid back and much less interested in cuttin' loose.

"Last night was our night," explained one Blues forward.

"It's not the next day that hurts you. It's two days after partying where you really feel it."

As I sat alone in the taxi heading back to my room for one last night, I reflected on the marvelous time I had enjoyed here. Our three-day jaunt to the mountains would come to an end in about 12 hours. The next day the players would skate through morning drills, then pack up the bus and head northeast to Edmonton for a game Friday night. In a way, I was relieved that it was time to get back to business. And so were the players.

Many of them complained that there was nothing to do in Banff but sit around and drink. They weren't allowed to ski, and that's really all the resort town had to offer, outside of its pubs and hot-tubs.

"This was stupid to come up here," said one player. "We're probably going to be flat as shit when we start playing again."

"Why didn't we stay in Vancouver?" asked several others. "At least we could play golf there."

When the players jumped on the bus the next afternoon after practice, most were relatively quiet and subdued. As with most vacations, this one sucked quite a bit of energy out of them. Fortunately, their next game wasn't until tomorrow night. Unfortunately, this bus trip took five hours before rolling into Edmonton, pushing the guys closer to the brink of exhaustion.

Halfway through the trip we traveled through Red Deer, the city where all six Sutter brothers began their professional hockey careers as teen-agers in the 1970s.

"This is a great place," said Richie as we stopped for a quick snack.

"They're supposed to be building a new rink here," mentioned Ronnie.

The other Sutter wasn't around to offer his comments. Brian had left Banff on his own to visit his farm just down the highway from Red Deer. While he was there, he helped his father-in-law bring a few calves into the world. This man didn't know what the word "rest" meant. As far as he was concerned, the only thing a rocking chair was good for was firewood.

Finally, just before 7 p.m., we drove into Edmonton and went straight to the Northlands Coliseum, where we helped Folga and Pickard unload the equipment. After that, the bus dropped us off at the hotel to let everyone collapse in their rooms. For the first night of the week, I actually put the "Do Not Disturb" sign on my doorknob before 10 p.m. The vacation was over. It was time to get back to work.

*   *   *

"That's what we're trying to accomplish in St. Louis," said Brian Sutter.

The Blues' head coach was looking at the rafters. Hanging from them were 21 banners that listed everything from "82-83 Smythe Division Champs" to "89-90 Stanley Cup Champs." There were five of those Cup banners, an amazing feat when you consider this was only the Oilers' 13th season in the NHL. Only the Canadiens (22), Maple Leafs (12), and Red Wings (seven) had their names engraved on the Cup more often. And they were three of the original six teams that first began playing for Lord Stanley's top prize in 1917.

While the Blues engaged in their morning workout, I looked around the ice and pictured Wayne Gretzky crossing the blue line and feeding Jari Kurri for the goal. Then I saw Mark Messier dance around a defender and put the puck in the back of the net. I turned to find defenseman Steve Smith tossing players out of the crease while fellow defenseman Paul Coffey put on a speedskating clinic rushing from one end to the other. Between the pipes I saw the shadows of Andy Moog and Grant Fuhr combining for one of the most dynamic goaltending duos in the history of hockey. I could hear the deafening roar of the crowd as a group of future Hall of Famers skated around the Coliseum hoisting a big, silver cup over their heads.

This place didn't have the aura of the Montreal Forum, but over the last decade there wasn't a building in the league that had witnessed more success than the Northlands Coliseum. It was creating a storied past of its own that was already making newcomers dream of hockey legends.

Such illustrious history is not lost on rookie players making their first tour of the league's most famous facilities.

"The first time I went into Montreal it was so exciting," said Nelson Emerson. "All the history in that building and the Maple

Leaf Garden made me think, 'Holy cow, I'm playing in these arenas.' You admire how they won all those championships."

"The Forum is a great old building," agreed Pat Jablonski. "All the old buildings have so much atmosphere. It'd be great to bring some of that back to the Arena."

"I remember the first time in the Islanders' Nassau Coliseum," said Murray Baron. "I remember thinking, 'Wow, I'm playing where all the greats used to play.' And then there was my first home game in Philadelphia. When Kate Smith sang 'God Bless America' it sent shivers down my spine." Of course, by then, it was just a taped recording. Ms. Smith passed away in 1986.

After a brief but brisk workout, the players returned to the hotel for their afternoon snooze. I, on the other hand, had to check out this place that everyone was demanding I visit. Some structure called the West Edmonton Mall, supposedly the largest mall in the world.

I understood the immensity of the structure when my taxi driver gave me some much-needed advice.

"When you call for a taxi to pick you up," he said, "tell the dispatcher what entrance you're at. Otherwise he'll never find you. For example, see this entrance I'm letting you off at? It's No. 60."

Sixty?!! You've got to be kidding. I was hoping the entrances were numbered by the tens instead of ones. As I paid my $15 fare, the driver asked me one last question.

"How much time do you have to spend here?"

"Oh, about an hour and a half or so," I answered.

"That's barely enough time to get in the door," he laughed. "Obviously you won't be able to see everything. I'd recommend spending your time down by the rides."

Rides? Was this a mall or an amusement park? Sure enough, at one end of this gargantuan block of concrete was an entire area filled with rides and games. Six Flags had nothing on this place. There was even a roller coaster called the "Mindbender," which was very similar to the "Ninja" at Six Flags. For $18.95 you could buy an all-day pass to every one of the 20 rides. And in case you're wondering, yes, this park was under one roof, the same one that covered the rest of the mall.

There was also a huge water park similar to Oceans of Fun in Kansas City, as well as a submarine ride, a car dealership and, get this, bungee jumping. That's right. In one corner of the mall, the roof is so high that patrons can bungee jump at their own risk. The cost is a mere $90. The future had come to, of all places, the town of Edmonton, Alberta.

Of course, the building had its share of mall-like clothing stores, record and tape outlets, and fast-food restaurants. But who wanted to venture into those places when you could tell your friends you fell off a ledge inside a mall with an elastic cord wrapped around your waist?

"That's quite a place, isn't it?" Bob Berry said as everyone boarded the bus later that afternoon to return to the Coliseum.

"You ain't a-kidding," I said. "You can buy a car and bungee jump all in the same place. That's what I call living."

But now it was time to return to the task at hand, playing hockey. Or in my case, observing hockey. This game would tell a lot about what the trip to Banff meant to the players. They would either come out of the gates fired up and take the play to the Oilers, or they would limp onto the ice and run out of breath after their first shift. With just 14 games left and an outside chance at catching the Red Wings, the Blues couldn't afford to be tired.

While Philippe Bozon was told to sit out this game, Curt Giles was given his first start as a member of the Blues, taking the place of Rick Zombo, who was feeling pain in his left foot. Lost in the defensive shuffle once again was Lee Norwood, one of the team's most consistent and solid defensemen since scoring his dramatic overtime goal to beat the Jets on November 14th.

Norwood was in a deep depression. No one seemed to have a logical explanation for his absence on the ice. There was strong speculation that Brian Sutter just didn't like the man for some reason. At the end of the year, Sutter would give this response.

"Lee still thinks he's 25 instead of 35," Brian said (he was actually 32). "He just can't catch up to the play as quickly as he used to. His body has taken a real beating over the years, and it's catching up to him."

Perhaps. But for a team needing some added grit around its net, there seemed to be little justification for telling Norwood to take a hike. After being informed he wasn't playing for the 13th time in 15 games, Norwood sat in solitude at center ice following the morning skate. While the players were showering, he plopped himself down in the middle of the rink and stared into space. He just sat there in silence with his legs extended and his helmet between his knees. One could only imagine the thoughts dancing around his head as he wondered what he had done to piss off his head coach.

"Oh, man," said one guy who emerged from the locker room to find Norwood still sitting in solitude. "It's time for a suicide watch."

Once the game started, the Norwood-less Blues got some unexpected offensive help from the slowest man on the team, Garth Butcher. Six minutes into the contest, the team captain let go a shot from the right point that somehow sneaked between Bill Ranford's pads and trickled in to give the Blues a 1-0 lead.

After the Oilers scored twice to take the lead, Butcher tied it with a slapper from nearly the same spot as his first goal, only this time the shot sneaked past Ranford's right skate just inside the post. Both shots should've been stopped. But Butcher and the Blues didn't complain as they went to the dressing room tied at 2-2.

The score should have been at least 4-0 Oilers. The Blues were given two gift goals while running around like lost kids in their own zone. The defensemen seemed to be a half-step slower than their opponents and were continuously being knocked off the puck. Was the uninspired effort a result of the break in Banff, or just a carry-over from the third period of the Canucks game, when the Blues had given up a record number of shots?

Whether they deserved it or not, the Blues took the lead early in the second when Jeff Brown scored his 17th of the year, a goal the Blues finally earned. On the power play, Hull ripped a shot that just missed the left post. The puck hit the endboards and bounced to Janney, stationed atop the right post. As Ranford stopped Janney's weak shot with his chest, the Oilers' goalie lost his footing and fell back into his net. Brown skated in and easily banged in the loose puck to give the Blues a 3-2 advantage. The Oilers were outshooting the visitors but still found themselves trailing on the scoreboard. This was turning into a typical Blues contest.

However, their slow feet finally caught up with them. The Oilers scored three goals in an 11-minute span to take a 5-3 lead. The trio of goals was the result of poor defensive work, the Blues' agonizing inability to catch up to the puck around their own net.

"The Blues' 'D' is terrible," observed one man from the press box. "They're brutal."

"Maybe they kept Gino by mistake," another reporter quipped, referring to Paul Cavallini's poor play.

However, the Blues came out firing on all cylinders in the third period. Just when you were convinced they were suffering the ill effects of the long trip, they buzzed the Oilers' net non-stop. They fired off 15 shots in the period while giving up only five. The fans sitting behind Pat Jablonski, who was making his sixth start of the year, had every right to ask for a refund. The only action they saw was Jablonski's occasional drink from his water bottle.

But just as the Blues had won a game they should've lost four nights earlier, they fell to the Oilers 5-3 in a game they very easily could have won. Their strong third period gave the Blues a 32-25 advantage in shots on goal. It marked only the seventh time all year they had lost a game in which they outshot their opponents. To put that in perspective, the Blues had won 17 contests in which they were outgunned by the opposition. Incredibly, the Blues had been outshot in eight of their last 11 wins. A team can do it with smoke and mirrors for only so long. With the playoffs just around the corner, their porous defense could be exploited to embarrassing consequences.

"Don't look at Jablonski," an angry Brian Sutter told reporters after the game when asked about his team's giving up five goals. "We left guys open in front of the net. We played much too loose in the first two periods. And they did too. The score could've been 9-8."

"Look to us if you're pointing fingers," answered Butcher. "I thought Jabber played pretty well."

"We need to protect Jabber better than that," agreed Rich Sutter. "We should've been fired up after that long break, but we weren't."

Even the presence of Curt Giles did little to change the complexion of the Blues' defense. Giles was solid but unspectacular, a description he was used to hearing after 12 years. He was a man who made hits, not headlines.

"I had lots of butterflies, but it wasn't difficult to get back into the flow of things," he said. "I was hoping for something positive. We're here to win hockey games, and we didn't do that tonight."

After the game, the players walked outside to the bus to find something we had expected throughout the week. Snow. The white stuff was gently falling from the sky and slowly accumulating inch by inch. Everyone had remarked how lucky we were with the beautiful weather we had been experiencing. Every day was gorgeously sunny, with temperatures reaching well into the 60s. At the same time, St. Louis was hitting record highs in the 80s. A summer-like weather pattern had descended across most of North America, including the western provinces of Canada. But with about 24 hours left in our trip, March-like weather had returned to the Edmonton area, blanketing the landscape in an ocean of white.

As the snow continued to tumble from the night sky, the bus unloaded its occupants at the Edmonton hotel to give them one final rest in Canada. In the morning, the team would fly to Calgary for a game at the Saddledome before heading south to home, sweet home. And, if the truth be told, I couldn't wait until that aircraft touched down at Lambert. I was tired of living out of a suitcase. I was exhausted from riding bus after bus, making sure I abided by Sutter-time. I had seen more of God's green earth than the folks at Rand McNally. I just wanted to go home to my wife and curl up in my own bed.

And yet, the only thing I had exercised was my drinking hand. I wasn't skating up and down the ice. I wasn't banging bodies in the corner. I wasn't sitting in the locker room so sore I could barely move. The players traveled every inch I did, but still had to earn their money playing hockey. I never realized the kind of the shape these guys were in until this trip. They deserved the title of "athletes." By the time we headed home, I suddenly felt very old and out-of-shape. Thanks, guys.

*   *   *

"So what is his stepbrother doing these days?" Dave Luecking asked.

"He's an accountant with a fire extinguishing company," I said.

"And he's supposed to meet his real dad this summer?"

"That's what he told me."

Luecking and I were discussing the personal side of Curtis Joseph. The *Post-Dispatch* scribe had written an article about Joseph and his adopted family a couple of years before and wanted an update.

For the first time during the trip, I separated myself from the team. Instead of flying to Calgary with everyone else, I took up Luecking's offer to make the nearly three-hour drive from Edmonton to Calgary in Dave's rented vehicle. Because he had a number of articles he was working on, Luecking wasn't able to make the flight and was looking for a passenger to sit shotgun alongside him later in the day. Just as I couldn't pass up the opportunity to play darts with Dave Christian and Craig Janney, I wasn't about to waste the chance to talk hockey with the Blues' beat writer.

If anything, I wanted to clear the air. I wanted to make sure there weren't any hard feelings that I, a mere TV sportscaster, was crossing over into his territory. Print people do it constantly, appearing on the radio and television to express their viewpoints on every topic known to mankind. But very rarely does it work in reverse, where a member of the electronic media dares to undertake a task without his face or voice attached to it. I felt I was exploring virgin territory and just wanted to know if that was going to cause any ill will. After all, a member high up in the Blues' organization told me to watch out for the "jealousies of the print media when writing this book."

I don't know about the other writers, but I soon learned I had nothing to worry about with Dave Luecking. Egos wouldn't get in the way.

"If there's anything I can help you with, let me know," he said as we made the drive south. "If you need a fresh pair of eyes I'd be more than happy to read over any material you have."

I thanked him for his offer, but even though I never told him this, I couldn't accept. We had our own styles, our own way of looking at things, and our own spins on what we observed with the hockey team. His offer was greatly appreciated, but I privately declined it. I'm sure he would have done the same thing if the roles were reversed.

Luecking and I arrived at the Westin Hotel in Calgary just as the players were gathering in the lobby to board the bus for the arena. They were extremely quiet and sedate. The weeklong trip had taken a lot out of them. One player pointed out that on a normal road trip the enthusiasm might have been a bit more pronounced. But the trek to the mountains and all the activities associated with it proved to be a mistake.

The Saturday night game was scheduled to start at 6:05 Mountain Time. However, in a special pregame ceremony, the Flames honored Jim Peplinski for his 10 years of service to the organization, longer than other player in team history. It was a touching tribute to a long-time favorite of Flames fans, but it droned on entirely too long. The entire ceremony lasted nearly 30 minutes, making the boys at KPLR scramble to find something to fill the unexpected half-hour hole before televising the actual game.

The worst part about it was the players didn't get a chance to loosen up before the game. While Peplinski was being honored for everything but building the Saddledome, the Blues were forced to stay in the locker room. When the event finally ended, the team rushed onto the ice only to stand still for the two national anthems. Before they knew it, the puck was dropped and the game had started.

During the first couple of minutes, I noticed once again how silent the crowd was. In all three Canadian venues on this trip, the fans were extremely hush-hush. They don't cheer hockey. They watch it. To most of the fans north of the border, the sport deserves their undivided attention. It's as if they're in an art museum, admiring the great works by the masters of their profession. The crowds were less rowdy but much more attentive. I'm not saying that's good or bad. Ask the players, and most will say they prefer playing before a rowdy, boisterous crowd. It's just that Canadians tend to take the sport much more seriously, and the low decibel levels prove it.

It didn't take long to realize the Blues' defense was in trouble once again. A little more than two minutes into the game, the defensive pairing of Curt Giles and Paul Cavallini was losing a game of keep-away in their own end. It looked as though the Flames were just toying with them as they kept circling Curtis Joseph, looking for the perfect shot. Sure enough, Sergei Makarov raced behind the Blues' net with the puck and passed it out to Gary Suter at the left point. The Flames' defenseman quickly sent it down low to Joe Nieuwendyk who faked Joseph down before flipping it over him. Giving Nieuwendyk that much time in front of the net to juggle the puck was inexcusable. But it was a sight that was becoming all too familiar.

Later in the period, Calgary defenseman Al MacInnis, who possesses the hardest shot in the game, rifled the puck from the left point but hit Joseph straight on. The rebound fluttered to the slot, where Joel Otto wasted no time sliding it underneath the Blues' goalie to give the Flames a 2-0 lead after the first period of play.

It was much more of the same in the second. Gary Roberts scored with one second left in a power play, and Theo Fleury netted his thirtieth of the year by skating around the Blues' net (was there some sort of league mandate that the visitors weren't allowed back there?), stopping in the left circle, and whacking the puck just inside the right post. After 40 minutes of play, the Flames held a 4-0 advantage and had outshot the Blues by a ridiculous margin of 28-11.

The Blues were making one of the worst teams in the league look like world-beaters. The Flames had fallen on extremely tough times in recent weeks, failing to win a game in their last five. Their pathetic play, including that record 11-0 loss to the Canucks earlier in the week, had forced Doug Risebrough to vacate his coaching seat on the bench and concentrate solely on his general manager duties.

The move failed to pay any immediate dividends. Right after the coaching switch was announced, the Flames lost to the Penguins 6-3 and tied Toronto at home 5-5. The Leafs game, just 48 hours before the Blues came to town, was the ultimate in frustration and discouragement. Calgary was cruising to an apparent 5-3 win with under a minute left to play. But Toronto scored twice in the game's final 47 seconds to earn a point against a very troubled team. It seemed the perfect time for the Blues to visit. It was a chance to kick 'em when they were down.

But the only ass-kicking on this night came when Stephane Quintal, in his first major fight for the Blues, obliterated Paul Kruse with a series of non-stop blows to the head that floored the Flames' rookie thug. It was like a ball of granite ramming into a block of concrete. Quintal had to leave the game with a fistful of bloody knuckles, but his first professional knockout was a memorable one.

Unfortunately, that was the only bit of life the Blues exhibited against a team they should have pummeled. Ron Wilson saved his team an embarrassing shutout by scoring a power-play goal nearly midway through the third period. Feeling a bit sorry for their visitors (they had actually found a team in worse shape than themselves), the Flames eased up a bit in the third and didn't feel the need to bury the puck anymore. The final score of 5-1 was a final lesson in scheduling. Don't plan any more retreats to the mountains during the season, especially so close to the playoffs.

"I don't think those three days off in Banff did us any good," Hull said. "We were playing well up to that point."

"You can't have guys dragging their feet," snapped Coach Sutter, refusing to let his players use their vacation as an alibi. "Some guys are just standing around. The travel and the vacation and all that stuff, that's no excuse."

"We certainly didn't look very good," said Joseph, whose goals-against average rose barely above 3.00 for the first time in a month. "I can't put a finger on it. You can't attribute our trip to it."

Really? Was it merely a coincidence that the Blues, winners of seven of their last nine, cut loose at a resort lodge for a few days before coming out flat in Edmonton and then rolling over and dying in Calgary? So what WAS the reason? It certainly wasn't the level of competition. And it definitely wasn't the remnants of any kind of a slump. The Blues hadn't been in one since before the Oates trade.

There was no denying the trip to Banff had a major impact on the team's performance. As professional athletes, the Blues weren't going to head for the mountains to find excuses. Except for Hull, Mr. Honesty, no one was going to blame the team's sluggish play on the snow-capped peaks of the Rockies. But without a doubt, the layover there, along with the subsequent five-hour bus ride to Edmonton, had sent the Blues into a deep sleep from which they never fully regained consciousness.

A weary band of travelers climbed aboard a chartered TWA flight for the trip home. The players were fairly loose, perhaps realizing this road trip was finally nearing its end. In fact, the Blues had only one more trip left in the season, a four-game swing back east in mid-March. The rest of the schedule, except for one game in Minnesota on April 2, would be played in the friendly environs of the Arena.

Meanwhile, from the back of the plane, a gruff-sounding voice was demanding immediate attention.

"Hey, Folga. I need you back here."

It was Garth Butcher calling for the team trainer. Butcher had taken a blistering shot by Gary Suter off his left foot. But instead of leaving the game, he hobbled around the ice as best he could despite the throbbing pain. He also refused to take off his skate to look at his damaged foot for fear of its swelling so large he couldn't put his skate back on.

"I had tightened the skate up on it to keep the swelling down so I could keep skating," Butcher said. "When I opened it up, it bruised right away right in front of my eyes. Then and there, I was concerned about it."

On the plane, where he could afford to be a little less macho, Butcher couldn't ignore his injury any longer. He asked Folga for a couple of aspirin and a pack of ice. The foot indeed had swollen, turning black and blue in the process. No one cared to speculate on the seriousness of the injury. Hopefully, it was just a deep bruise and not a broken bone. X-rays would have to be taken in the morning.

As it turned out, the month of March would prove extremely costly for the Blues. The players they could least afford to lose to injury were felled by a variety of ailments that would keep them out the remainder of the year. Someone, somehow, somewhere had put a curse on this team. In some dark corner of some league office, there sat a couple of voodoo dolls of Jack Quinn and Ron Caron with pins through them. There seemed to be no other realistic explanation for it.

Chapter Sixteen

PURPLE HEART BLUES

With play stopped, Brett Hull cruised over to the bench. But instead of taking a seat on the pine, he stayed on the ice and rested his elbows on top of the boards as if trying to catch his breath. He mouthed a few words to Coach Sutter, who immediately pointed him off the ice.

What was this? Why was the Golden Brett leaving right in the middle of the first period with the Blues and Red Wings tied at 1-1? He didn't appear to be hurt. Must be equipment problems. Yeah, that's it. Has to be equipment problems. Please God, let it be equipment problems!

"Brett Hull has suffered back spasms," Susie Mathieu announced to the press corps, minutes after Hull retreated to the locker room. "He is expected to return."

Whew! That last sentence was soothing, to say the least. All the Blues needed right now was their star player lying on some operating table having his back torn into. Just three days before, on March 9, Garth Butcher learned he'd be out for the rest of the regular season with a broken tarsal bone in his left foot after stopping Gary Suter's slapper in Calgary. The Blues already possessed one of the most non-intimidating defenses in the league. The loss of Butcher made it that much weaker. And that may have saved Paul Cavallini's job.

The trade deadline came and went without one player leaving St. Louis, the first time in three years that Ron Caron ignored the deadline. Cavallini was thankful for the reprieve but bitter about all the rumors he and his family had been forced to hear. His name had been traded so many times they were thinking of putting it on the New York Stock Exchange.

"It's been a tough year," Cavallini said. "You have everyone telling you, 'Keep it out of your head, keep it out of your head.' But when you make a mistake in a game—boom!—the first thing that pops into your mind is, 'They're going to trade me now.'"

Meanwhile, the Butcher/Hull-less Blues were engaged in an exciting battle with the Wings before 17,736 screaming fans. Late in the first period, Rick Zombo broke the 1-1 tie on a beautiful goal set up by Janney. The Blues' center held the puck in the slot, where he quickly passed it down to Zombo at the bottom of the right circle. Uncovered, Zombo raced across the goal crease where he deked Tim Cheveldae with a nice head fake before sliding it under him to give the Blues a 2-1 lead.

However, Detroit regained the lead with three unanswered goals in the first half of the second period. After playing extremely well the first twenty minutes, the Blues inexplicably lay back in the second. They were outshot 13-2 after the Wings' three-goal outburst to start the middle frame.

But as only the Blues could do it, they scored on their next two shots to tie things up. Rich Sutter scored from a difficult angle as he sped down the right side, and Dave Christian redirected a Janney pass into the net to bring the Blues back to 4-4. The Wings' Steve Chiasson scored on the power play less than two minutes later to break the tie, but the Blues had to feel fortunate they were down only a goal as they skated off at the end of two periods.

However, there was something much more disturbing than the way the Blues were playing. No. 16 was nowhere to be seen. He was conspicuously absent during the second period. When Susie said Hull was supposed to return, did she mean this game or sometime this season?

"The latest on Brett Hull," Mathieu announced, "is that he will not return after suffering muscle spasms in his back."

Oh, boy. This obviously wasn't some minor discomfort. Hull had pulled something in his back, and there was no telling how serious it was. Not taking any chances, the team decided to leave Hull in the locker room, where he'd be safe from cross-checks. For the first time in his career, he would go on the injured list, joining Butcher.

Suddenly, the captain's "C" appeared as treacherous as the Hope Diamond. Wearing the "C," Butcher breaks a bone in his foot and is sidelined for several weeks. He passes the letter on to Hull, who wears it for the first time on March 10, a 5-2 victory over Minnesota. But here in his second game as team captain, Hull pulls a muscle in his back and is forced off the ice for an indefinite period of time. Torch that letter. It was definitely jinxed.

Ron Sutter was fortunate. His brother/coach had been primed to take the "A" off Ron's jersey and replace it with the "C." That is, until team officials stepped in and said, "Don't you dare." The city of St. Louis would have burned the Arena down if Brian had given the captaincy to his brother instead of the player who deserved it, Hull. The man with the golden locks had shown so much poise and maturity since the Oates trade that it would have been a crime if he had been bypassed for Ron Sutter. No question, Ronnie was a team leader on and off the ice. But when you have a guy who puts the puck in the net an average of once a game, while single-handedly bringing thousands of paying customers to the rink, you give him the "C." No questions asked.

When the Blues returned to the ice for the start of the third period, they obviously forgot to tell Curtis Joseph the intermission was over. Instead of going to his customary position between the pipes, he stayed behind to keep Hull company while Pat Jablonski took over the goaltending duties for the final period.

What in the hell was going on here? Don't tell me: After the second period, Hull gave his "C" to Joseph, who promptly tripped over his stick and broke his leg. The dreaded curse had claimed its latest victim.

Seriously, no one quite knew why Joseph had been taken out of the game. No announcement was immediately made. But the situation had to be serious. The Blues were down by a goal against the front-running Red Wings. If they could come back and win this thing, they'd be just seven points out of first with ten games left. If the Blues lost, you could forget any fantasies of catching the Wings for the top spot. The fact that Joseph was missing for the third period of such a pivotal game was not a positive sign.

The Butcher/Hull/Joseph-less Blues showed tons of character in the third period, playing without their three stars. Led by

Jablonski's stellar goaltending, the Blues shut out the Wings the final twenty minutes while putting tremendous pressure on Cheveldae. However, when the final horn sounded, the injury-stricken team had nothing to show for its efforts but a 5-4 loss. The Blues had so many opportunities that you had to wonder if Hull would've been able to put just one of those pucks across the goal line.

"He gives you that extra nudge on the power play, no doubt," said Ron Sutter. "And we had a lot of power plays tonight, especially in the third period. We missed Brett. We definitely could've used him."

"Any time you have a sniper like Brett," Brendan Shanahan explained, "not only is he always a threat to score, but he commands a lot of attention. And that leaves a lot of other guys open to shoot the puck."

Mathematically, the Blues were still alive in the hunt for the division title. Realistically, there wasn't a snowball's chance. The Blues had to concentrate on catching the Blackhawks, whom they trailed by three points. And they had to do it without arguably their three most important players.

After the game, Hull was walking with such delicacy it looked as though he was stepping on eggs without trying to break them. No question, he was in some pain.

"It's not good," Hull said as he disappeared into the Wives' Room. The Blues were scheduled to play the NHL-leading Rangers at home in 48 hours, but based on preliminary observations, Hull would be watching that one from the press box.

As would Joseph. The team's star goalie was suffering from tendonitis of the ankle, which would force him to miss his first game of the year due to an injury. In my scientific opinion, Joseph must have accidentally rubbed his foot on Butcher's jersey when he was still wearing the "C." That damned curse had struck again.

Think I'm kidding? When the Blues skated onto the ice for the start of the Rangers game on March 14, not one player was wearing it. Ron Sutter, Jeff Brown, and Ron Wilson each had an "A" attached to his jersey. That's right. Brian Sutter had three alternates but no captain. After watching their teammates fall by the wayside every time they even looked at the "C," the rest of the players suddenly found no pride in being asked to wear it.

Okay, okay. So I'm taking this superstition thing a little far. Coach Sutter obviously felt the only players worthy of the captaincy were Hull and Butcher. And Ron Sutter, of course, until he was overruled. But Brett and Garth were injured, and Scott Stevens was in Jersey. No choice but to suit up a C-less team.

The problem was, the Blues played like they had no leaders. The Rangers toyed with their opposition like a cat toys with an injured mouse before finally killing it. New York pounded Jablonski with 36 shots, a figure Joseph was used to, but his understudy was not. Making just his seventh start of the year, Jablonski had faced 196 shots coming into the game, or 1,691 fewer than Joseph. The Toledo native allowed six pucks to sneak past him, while his counterpart, John Vanbiesbrouck, kicked aside every one of the 27 shots he faced. The 6-0 loss was the Blues worst defeat at home since falling to the Devils 8-2 way back on March 24, 1988.

There wasn't one player in the Blues' dressing room willing to publicly admit the team's horrendous showing was attributable to the absence of Hull, Joseph, and Butcher. But Blues critics had every right to snicker after the worst home loss in four years. There was an assumption by many that this team was nothing without Hull and Joseph. Despite numerous deals, trades, and acquisitions, the Blues suddenly looked woefully inept without their two most valuable players. Would the Red Wings have looked this helpless without Yzerman and Cheveldae? Probably not. Would the Blackhawks have played so poorly without Belfour and Roenick? Doubt it.

But without their two big guns, the Blues looked extremely defenseless and harmless. Was the team really that weak without Hull and Joseph? Or was this just one of those games that should be tossed aside as an aberration rather than a realistic barometer of the Blues' talent? We would find out during their last road trip of the year, to Washington, Boston, Montreal, and Toronto. This was a trip that, at least on paper, was their most formidable of the year. What perfect timing.

*   *   *

"Hey, Chief! Could you go grab me a Diet Coke?!"

Jamming to the Beach Boys, watching a soap opera, and working out on the Stairmaster all at the same time, Brett Hull found the strength to ask a reporter to fetch him a drink. This guy had more talent than I ever imagined.

As Brett swayed his hips while working the pedals up and down, Garth Butcher was seated in front of him using an arm-rowing machine to build his upper body strength. More than two million dollars' worth of talent had stayed behind at the Arena to work their injured bodies back into playing shape.

This was a picture in contrasts. The man on the Stairmaster was in his glory except for the fact he had to work out. In Hull's opinion, the only fun exercise is stepping out of a golf cart. But he was jamming to the oldies, his favorite kind of music, while keeping up on the latest soap opera plots. With a television camera rolling, he was also able to show off the Diet Coke can, making his sponsors proud.

Directly in front of Hull was a man who was working his machine so frantically I expected smoke to start pouring out of it. It was as if Butcher was challenging the machine to see who would quit first. He seemed oblivious to the blaring music surrounding him and the pictures emanating from the television above him. Judging by their outward appearances, it looked like Hull was enjoying this little get-together much more than Butcher.

"What did you think of last night's game?" I asked Hull as I handed him his Diet Coke.

"What about it?" he asked back.

"I was just wondering how you thought the guys played."

"We lost."

"Yeah, but they played pretty well."

"We lost."

Hull can never be accused of side-stepping an issue. Didn't matter how they played, he was saying. The Blues lost. Period. Plain and simple. End of conversation.

But it was a crying shame the team hadn't been able to leave Washington with at least a point. They outshot the Caps 38-29, a remarkable feat considering they were without the league's shots-on-goal leader and were playing the NHL's third-best team in its own building. Every line played exceptionally well, creating one scoring chance after another. Playing without the injured Hull, Craig Janney picked up the slack by scoring two goals and playing one of his better games in a Blues uniform.

Unfortunately, Pat Jablonski played one of his worst. With Curtis Joseph watching from the Capital Centre press box, Jablonski's first mistake came four minutes into the game, when he sleepwalked to near his own blue line in an attempt to swat away a loose puck. Todd Krygier beat him to it, side-stepped the wayward goalie, and shot it into the open net. For Jablonski, it didn't get much better than that. He allowed five goals, pushing his GAA to 4.87. It would be his last appearance of the season.

The Caps scored an empty-netter with 19 seconds left to finish off the Blues, 6-4. The loss dropped their record to 32-31-9, still three points behind the Hawks, who had a game in hand. The Blues had wasted their terrific streak after the Oates trade and were now down to a .500 team again. They had lost five of their last six, and the trip from hell was just beginning.

"That was tough to watch," said Butcher, the next day. "It's easy (to watch on television) when the team does well, and it's a lot harder when it doesn't. Last night was a tough night for the boys."

"You see the good things, and all of a sudden you see the bad," agreed Hull. "You just wish you were out there helping. This is the first road trip Garth has ever missed. Same with me."

Meanwhile, the disabled list continued to grow. Rick Zombo had been bothered by a bruised left foot for some time and had missed games in Edmonton and Calgary because of it. He came back to play in the next three contests, but the pain resurfaced just before the Blues made the trip east. Zombo, whose sore foot turned out to be a broken foot, went with his teammates, but would not see a second of playing time in any of the four games. Taking his place was Lee Norwood, finally given a chance to play after sitting out 15 of 17 games.

Hull stepped off the Stairmaster, wiped the sweat off his face, and took a last guzzle from the soda can. *Too bad the folks from Coca-Cola weren't here filming this. If that scene wasn't the perfect advertisement, I don't know what is.*

Brett was still listed as day-to-day with the hope he could join the team sometime on its East Coast swing. He had been receiving daily therapy for his back while working the rest of the body to stay in shape. Team doctors ruled that Hull had simply pulled a few back muscles after taking a constant beating in front of the net.

"The doctors have come to the conclusion that all those cross-checks in the Minnesota game had a part," Hull said. "And then the morning of the Detroit game I went out a little early, and took a couple of hard shots before I was really loose, and I felt something."

The play that finally sent Hull to the showers came halfway through the first period, when Jeff Brown took a shot from the point that missed the net wide and headed in Hull's direction along the boards. With Steve Yzerman directly in front of him, Hull tried to side-step the Wings' center to steal the puck and keep it in the offensive zone.

"But going from one direction to another without being able to pivot my hips," explained Brett, "I just pulled all the muscles."

After putting the Stairmaster through a grueling workout and grooving to the oldies, Hull walked into the locker room and slowly put on his skates. He had been given permission to skate for the first time since hurting his back six days ago. He wasn't allowed to shoot the puck, but this was Brett Hull we're talking about, a man who never met an order he liked. He grabbed a stick and a puck and headed onto the Arena ice.

Rick Meagher came down from his office upstairs and joined Hull in a leisurely skate around the rink. The two former teammates passed the puck back and forth, a sight one bystander didn't exactly cherish.

"He's not supposed to be using his stick," Susie Mathieu said, her arms crossed and her eyes fixed on Brett's every move. She figured it'd be okay for Hull to lightly move the puck across the ice, but one windup for a slapper and I guarantee she would have raced across the rink and tackled her hard-headed star.

"It's starting to feel good," said Hull as he skated off. "A couple more days, and I think I'll be ready to go."

Meanwhile, Hull's injured teammate had dressed and was limping out of the locker room to go home for the day. Even though he was nowhere near ready to play, the prognosis for Butcher's return was promising. He had been scheduled to wear his ankle cast for at least a couple of weeks, but it had already been taken off after only nine days.

"It's still a little sore," he admitted. "But there's been a lot of progress the last couple of days. It's coming along good."

When he wasn't working out at the Arena, Butcher was busy attending to his player representative duties. His co-rep, Craig Janney, was obviously involved with other matters out east. So Butcher used his idle time to keep himself abreast of the latest contract negotiations between the players' union and the owners. If the two sides couldn't hammer out a new collective bargaining agreement by the time the playoffs rolled around, it seemed certain the players would walk.

"As of right now, I don't think things have gone that well," Butcher said. "Both sides have dug in their heels. We haven't heard a great deal because there hasn't been a great deal happening."

In fact, about the only thing that was happening was a bunch of posturing on John Ziegler's part. The NHL president was starting a public relations poor-mouth campaign. He felt it was imperative to let hockey fans across North America in on a little secret. The league was going to lose millions of dollars over the next couple of years, while these greedy players were demanding the owners make concessions to them that would further destroy the future of the game.

"We told the players, 'This business is now at risk. This business is now fragile,'" Ziegler said. "These owners are not going to enter into an agreement that locks in the destruction of the league."

Ziegler claimed that as many as 16 teams were on a course toward financial ruin, while the league was set to lose $20 million for the season. He pointed out that players' salaries had increased 56 percent over the last two years, so he found it difficult to understand how they were being cheated.

The players and union chief Bob Goodenow scoffed at such dire predictions. Where did the $150 million go that the three expansion cities had put up to enter the league? And how was it that the first time in sixty years the players were getting tough with their employers, the league was suddenly in jeopardy of going under for the first time? Mere coincidence? Or negotiating ploy?

Many sports fans complain that the NHL is a garbage league living in the dark ages. Well, with a strike looming on the horizon, hockey was about to join those other great American institutions like baseball and football, which had seen work stoppages in their pasts. Yep, hockey had finally come of age.

Meanwhile, the Zombo/Butcher/Hull/Joseph-less Blues (how long was this damn title going to get?) had their own problems staying afloat on the ice. The team limped into Boston on March 19 trying to avoid falling to an even .500 for the first time since sporting a 22-22-9 record back on February 2. Hoping to fill one of the many gaping holes on defense, the Blues signed U.S. Olympian Bret Hedican to a four-year deal worth a little under $200,000 per season.

The 21-year-old St. Paul native had such blinding speed that he'd seen action at left wing while playing at St. Cloud State University. However, the Blues had no immediate plans to put the 6'2", 188-pounder up front. The team was in desperate need for a speedy defenseman who not only had the ability to play physically in his own end, but could also skedaddle with the puck from blue line to blue line.

"He could step in right now," Ron Caron predicted shortly before signing him, "and be one of our top three or four defensemen and one of our fastest skaters."

That's some heavy baggage to carry for a kid who hadn't seen the inside of an NHL locker room. But Hedican had made such great strides in the last few years that anything was possible. He was ignored by many NHL scouts and wasn't taken by the Blues until the tenth round in the 1988 draft. Very few players taken that far down in the draft ever get an opportunity to suit up with the big boys. But after a successful three-year stint at St. Cloud State and a tour with the U.S. Olympic team, Bret Hedican was ready and willing to take that next step to the pro ranks.

"It's something I've been looking forward to all my life," he said. "It's definitely a good feeling to see a lot of those guys. Their jerseys are hanging there, and mine's hanging there, too."

The wide-eyed rookie didn't get a chance to wear his jersey right away, however. He was scratched in Boston and Montreal before breaking into the lineup in Toronto at the end of the road trip.

With Hull and Butcher back home in St. Louis, and Joseph and Zombo nursing sore feet in the Boston Garden pressbox, the Blues picked up where they left off in Washington and played another strong road game. But this time, Guy Hebert was in goal, and the results were different, as the Blues skated past the Bruins 4-1. For the first time in their 25-year history, the Blues swept their season series with the Bruins, beating them all three games.

The only puck Hebert allowed past him was a fluke, as the puck ricocheted off Glen Wesley's skate and into the net. He stopped the other 34 shots he faced to earn the game's number-one star and improve his record to 3-3, while lowering his GAA to 3.04.

The team was showing remarkable character with two fine performances in a row. It would have been very easy, perhaps even expected, for the Blues to roll over and die after being blown away by the Rangers the week before. That loss proved to many people that the Blues, without their injured stars, weren't much better than the Peoria Rivermen. But Brian Sutter assembled a number of excellent line combinations to make up for the loss of Hull, and the team responded favorably.

The top line of Dave Christian, Craig Janney, and Brendan Shanahan had looked especially formidable the last two games, combining on three of the team's eight goals. The second line consisted of Nelson Emerson, Ron Sutter, and Kelly Chase. That's right, Kelly Chase, one of the Blues' appointed hit men, had been given an offensive role for the first time in his young NHL career.

Chase had proven in Peoria that he knew where the net was located. He scored 20 goals and 54 points at the minor league affiliate the year before. But with better offensive talent on the parent club, Chase figured the only way to stay was to use his fists instead of his stick. Despite standing under six feet and weighing less than 200 pounds, the 24-year-old had taught himself the finer points of boxing on skates. After all, Chase possessed intelligence, uncharacteristic of hockey thugs. His technique—clutching his opponent's jersey while throwing a punch, then ducking, throwing a punch, then ducking, throwing a punch, then ducking—had become a familiar sight to Blues fans. It didn't matter the size of his opponent, Mr. Chase rarely got the worse end of a confrontation.

But now playing alongside Emerson and Ron Sutter, Chase was given the opportunity to showcase his offensive talents, and he wasn't about to waste it. For the first time in his 86 NHL games covering three seasons, Chase scored points in consecutive games, assisting on Murray Baron's goal in Washington and Nelson Emerson's in Boston. His pass to Emerson was a thing of beauty. Stationed in the corner to the right of the Bruins' net, Chase worked the puck around a defender and threaded a perfect pass to Emerson in the slot, who banged it past Andy Moog. I replayed the videotape of that goal over and over again to make sure that was Kelly Chase I was watching. No doubt about it, he looked good on that second line.

"It feels good, too," Chase said.

The only question was, how long would he stay there? For various reasons, including a tendency to take unnecessary penalties at inopportune times, Chase was not one of Brian Sutter's favorite players. Against the Flyers back on February 2, Chase had run into goalie Ken Wregget and gotten his right skate tangled in the net. With his knee in extreme pain, Kelly hobbled off the ice and sat on a stretcher back to the dressing room. When Sutter saw that Chase needed assistance instead of trying to limp to the dressing room on his own accord, the head coach went berserk. He later scolded Chase for trying to "get attention," spouting off a series of expletives that would made a drill sergeant blush. Even though he was healthy enough to play, Kelly found himself in street clothes for the next couple of weeks.

But here he was in mid-March strutting his stuff, feeding the puck to Nelson and Ronnie. And since Chase was a favorite of the fans and media, it was a joy to watch him find some success at the NHL level. After all, how could you not love a guy who comes from Porcupine Plain, Saskatchewan? Now, if he only could stay away from those stretchers...

*   *   *

"In plain terms, a strike will occur unless a collectively negotiated agreement is reached by that deadline," said Bob Goodenow.

The players' union had finally done it. The strike deadline was Monday, March 30. If team owners couldn't hammer out a new collective bargaining agreement with the players in the next ten days, the first full-scale strike in the NHL's 75-year history—many players had staged an abortive holdout in 1932—would be called.

In typical negotiating banter, the union accused the owners of dragging their feet and misrepresenting the true financial condition of the league, while the owners accused union members of blindly asking for more money when there wasn't an additional red cent to give. The two sides were a world apart, and there seemed no doubt the players would walk on March 30.

That date was picked for two very important reasons. One, it came just after most players received their last paychecks of the regular season. And two, it was just a week before the playoffs were scheduled to start, a time when the owners made a large chunk of their revenue, as much as $600,000 per game. The players were kicking the owners right where it hurt the most. In the seat of the pants, where they carried their wallets.

The players' demands hadn't changed much since they were first made public back in training camp. They wanted less restrictive free agency, an increased take from playoff revenue, better benefits, and a cut in the draft from twelve rounds to six. That last request would mean more undrafted players who were eligible to be signed as free agents, thereby elevating the salary structure. The union originally had asked that the entire draft process be eliminated, which would result in a bidding war for all the young stars coming out of high school, college, Europe, and the former Soviet Union. But Goodenow backed off from that demand and was now asking the number of rounds simply be cut in half.

The owners, led by John Ziegler, continued to plead poverty. They argued that the recent increase in salaries was proof that the current system was working extremely well. Any additional strain on league coffers would put a number of teams out of business.

"No matter what kind of action they may wish to take," said Ziegler, "the ownership is not going to sign an agreement that guarantees that we are going to have teams lose a substantial amount of money."

So the line had been drawn. It was now just a matter of seeing who would blink first. The owners had never been put in this position before and found it difficult to believe the players would even think of quitting right before the playoffs. After all, the owners had had ex-union chief Alan Eagleson in their pocket. Under his leadership, the players were dragged around like blind mice munching on any morsel the owners felt charitable enough to hand out. But Goodenow, the former agent who represented Brett Hull when he signed his multimillion-dollar contract, was seen as the players' savior, a tough, no-nonsense negotiator, who would lead them to the promised land.

Though a strike deadline had now been set, the Blues adamantly denied it would have any effect on their play over the next ten days. We're professionals, they pointed out. When we hit the ice, we leave all that other crap behind.

"We come to the rink every day knowing we have jobs to do, and we're going to try our best to win hockey games," said Ron Sutter. "Once we get on the ice, it's the furthest thing from our minds."

"We can't do anything about it while we're out on the ice," agreed Brendan Shanahan. "We've elected representatives from every team and representatives for the entire league to take care of that type of business, so the rest of us can just worry about playing."

Meanwhile, the Blues' head coach was torn between the two sides. Brian Sutter wasn't about to publicly take a stand for either the players or the owners, since he had to work so closely with both of them. But this was just another controversy, another dispute that defined the Blues' silver anniversary season.

"It seems like the whole season's been one thing or something else," he deadpanned. "It'd be sad to play a whole season, and then not be mentally prepared for a couple of games because you're thinking about something else."

Sutter was quick to point out that his team had yet to show any signs that its attention had been diverted because of all the strike talk. He praised his players for staying focused on the task at hand when they came to the rink. But at the same time, Sutter acknowledged that all 22 NHL teams would eventually be affected one way or another by all the publicity surrounding the strike deadline.

"They're all human beings," he observed. "They're going to think about it, and it's going to bother them. But they're also professional players, and once we step on the ice they're paid to play."

Sutter and the Blues traveled to Montreal on March 21, hoping not only to ignore the strike controversy, but to continue the excellent road play they had exhibited in Washington and

Boston. Playing in the Forum would be a true test of their ability to compete without Hull, Joseph, and Butcher. The Canadiens had the third-best record in the NHL, 90 points, and the top home mark at 27-8-3. Of course, it didn't matter to the Blues what Montreal's record at home was. The team from St. Louis had a history of failure in this building, winning only eight times in fifty games.

The Canadiens also sported the stingiest defense in the league, yielding only 185 goals, the only team under 200. Goaltender Patrick Roy led the NHL in wins (36), goals-against average (2.26), and save percentage (.916). Those weren't exactly the kinds of numbers the Blues wanted to see when their top gun was sitting in the hangar.

Even though the Blues looked strong in the early going, Montreal took advantage of its first two power plays to sneak the puck past Guy Hebert. But before the first period came to a close, Jeff Brown scored on the power play, powering a slapshot from the left point past Roy. The Blues controlled play the first twenty minutes, outshooting the Canadiens 15-10, a remarkably high number of shots considering where and whom they were playing.

However, 13 minutes into the second period with the Blues two men short—Ron Sutter off for tripping and Norwood for instigating a fight—rookie Gilbert Dionne slapped a shot off Hebert's leg from close range to extend the Montreal lead to 3-1.

Jeff Brown came back to do it again. Ron Sutter won a faceoff in the Canadiens' zone and kicked the puck back to Emerson at the right point. The Blues' rookie immediately slid it over to Brown at the left point where he fired a rocket just inside the left post. Not only did Brown cut the lead to 3-2, he was also within one goal of tying the Blues' scoring record for defensemen. Larry Sacharuk netted twenty goals during the 1974-75 season, just the fifth defenseman in league history to reach that level. Of course, that mark has been surpassed numerous times since, including by Brown himself, who scored 21 with the Quebec Nordiques in 1988-89. But the Blues have never been a team known for its offensively gifted defensemen. At least until now. With 19 periods of hockey still to play in the regular season, Brown seemed a cinch to at least tie the Blues' mark and a good bet to match his personal record.

"That's not something I'm thinking about," said Brown. "I just want to help the team win. If I can get the 21st, that's great. It's not so much the record. It's the milestone of scoring 20 goals by a defenseman."

Don't let Brown's cool demeanor fool you. The record was so important he announced to his teammates that $100 would be awarded to any player assisting on the record-tying goal.

"He's hoping he'll score on an unassisted breakaway," kidded one teammate, claiming Brown had a well-earned reputation of being a bit tight in the wallet.

With the Blues trailing the Canadiens 3-2 entering the final period, the number-one line came out with a vengeance, pinning the defense in deep and buzzing the net. Their hard work paid off, when a bouncing puck ended up on Shanahan's stick above the right post, and he quickly flipped it past Roy to even the score.

The rest of the period was the Guy Hebert show. For some unexplained reason, the Blues stopped putting pressure on the Montreal net and lay back in their own zone as if trying to protect the tie. Hebert made save after save, gaining confidence with each puck he kicked aside. He was in goal for the second consecutive contest, the first time in his career he had backstopped back-to-back games. With two strong performances in a row, he had effectively overtaken Jablonski as the team's backup goalie to Joseph.

Just as they were apparently trying to do, the Blues escaped Montreal with a 3-3 tie but fell four points behind the Blackhawks, who beat the Maple Leafs. Nonetheless, the trip was shaping up as the best of the year. After being blitzed by the Rangers in their last home game, there seemed no way the Blues could go on their toughest road swing of the year without their most valuable players and even hope to compete. But they fell to the Capitals mainly because of poor goaltending, then earned three points in Boston and Montreal, two of the toughest buildings in which to play. If the judges were scoring this trip, the Blues would earn perfect marks for courage and character.

It looked as though the Blues would finish the road trip on a winning note in Toronto on March 23. Less than four minutes into the game, Janney skated behind the Leafs' net with the puck and slid it out front to Shanahan, who one-timed it past Grant Fuhr's left skate for a 1-0 lead. Unfortunately, that would be about the only highlight of the night for the road-weary and injury-riddled team. Three poor defensive plays, two in the first period, resulted in all three Toronto goals, and the Blues were never able to recover.

Bret Hedican, playing in his first professional hockey game, panicked a bit trying to move the puck out of his own end. With a player bearing down on him, Hedican tried to chip the puck off the boards and ahead to the neutral zone. But Doug Gilmour stole the loose puck and fed Glenn Anderson in front, who pushed the puck between Hebert's pads to tie the score.

"Definitely, it was a bad play by me," confessed Hedican, who made the mistake on only his second shift. "But I've just got to shake that off and keep getting better with each game and each period. You learn from your mistakes and go on."

A little more than a minute later, Stephane Quintal made a horrible error, trying to pass the puck up the middle as the Blues were breaking out. Bad move. Mark Osborne caught it at the blue line, skated in a few strides, and beat Hebert with a fluttering knucklepuck.

With the score still 2-1 Toronto in the third with 14 minutes left to play, the Blues were caught too deep in the offensive zone. Rob Pearson intercepted the puck and fed ahead to Wendel Clark, who broke in on Hebert. With Quintal draped over his back, Clark's shot was kicked out by Hebert. But Dave McLlwain was trailing the play and backhanded the loose puck between Hebert's legs. Shanahan scored late in the game to make things interesting, but the three errors proved too costly and the Blues fell 3-2.

The Blues' four-game road trip suddenly seemed very unproductive. After three strong games against better opponents, the boys in blue fell apart against a team that wouldn't make the playoffs. Out of a possible eight points, the Blues managed only three, and returned to St. Louis with very little chance at catching the Blackhawks for second place.

"We played twelve periods, and we probably had one bad one," said Brian Sutter, referring to the first period in Toronto. "I thought our guys showed a lot of character when you consider the people we have out of the lineup. It could've been one heck of a road trip."

"I think we had a pretty successful trip," said Guy Hebert, perhaps the most surprising star on the trip. "Maybe we didn't get as many points as we would've liked. But I think you could see the team playing good team defense, and that's going to carry the team a long way in the playoffs."

But first, the Blues had five more games left in the regular season. Since Chicago had six games remaining with a four-point cushion over St. Louis, it seemed a certainty the Blues would open postseason play in Chicago Stadium. It wasn't exactly the scenario that made Blues fans start dreaming of a Stanley Cup. The Blues and Blackhawks had faced each other seven times in playoff competition, and the Blues had advanced to the next round only once, in 1988, when the series started in St. Louis. Overall, the Blues were 4-14 in Chicago Stadium during the playoffs. How's that for a confidence builder?

The Blues returned to St. Louis with two games left before the strike deadline. With both sides still unable to agree on much of anything, the final three regular-season games and the subsequent playoffs were in jeopardy. On March 25, the day before the Blues hosted the Hartford Whalers, the players held a ten-minute, closed-door meeting to watch a videotape sent them by Bob Goodenow. The union boss outlined the latest offers by both sides and kept the players abreast of how the contract talks were moving along.

The night before, in a Toronto hotel, the two negotiating committees met for the first time in more than two weeks, and very little was accomplished. But, at the very least, they agreed to meet again the next day to continue disagreeing. And that was a major departure from the last time they talked, March 9 when the two sides screamed and yelled at each other, until the players got up and walked out.

The second day of negotiations still didn't bear any fruit, but players and owners alike remarked how the talks were finally starting to "build some momentum." The two committees met for nine hours, discussing everything from free agency to arbitration to playoff money. After the marathon meeting, members from both sides emerged looking peaked and emaciated, but still managed to hold out hope the season could be saved.

"This is a difficult process," Washington Capitals goalie Mike Liut, a member of the negotiating committee, told the Associated Press. "It is laborious. There is a lot to be discussed. We are grinding through it."

Montreal player rep Guy Carbonneau stunned the members of his union by suggesting there would be no strike as long as the two sides were still talking. One of the strengths of the players' union had been its conviction in the cause, its unyielding stance on the issues that kept every player moving in the same direction. But now a major figure seemed to be breaking ranks, exactly what the owners were hoping for.

"We can still play the games," Carbonneau told the *Montreal Gazette*. "If there is progress, there won't be a strike. On Monday, we'll re-evaluate. We'll see where we are and then decide."

Suddenly, players around the league scurried to repair any damage Carbonneau may have caused with his comments. They wanted to make sure the owners still understood the seriousness of the situation and wouldn't get any wild ideas the union was about to break into factions.

"Maybe Guy has trouble understanding English," Garth Butcher said of the French-Canadian player.

Butcher tossed the comments aside as unimportant and irrelevant. The Blues' player rep had other things to worry about, like keeping his teammates informed on the progress of negotiations while also trying to work his broken foot back into playing shape. He, Zombo, Joseph, and Hull were still nursing their injuries when the Blues took on the Whalers just four days before the scheduled strike.

As it turned out, this game was one of the most enjoyable of the year, not just because the Blues walloped the Whalers 7-2, but because so many players achieved personal marks.

"Personal goals are important only if they lead to team success," Brian Sutter once said. Against Hartford, they did.

Late in the first period, with the Blues on a power play, Jeff Brown sneaked down the left side, caught a beautifully placed pass from Craig Janney, and chipped it over Kay Whitmore's right shoulder. Brown's twentieth goal of the year tied Larry Sacharuk's record and made Janney and Nelson Emerson $100 richer for assisting on it.

"We're going to have to go and maybe spend that tonight," said a smiling Brown after the game. "C.J. made a heck of a play. He found the seam and put it right on my tape."

But that was only one of five milestones on the night. In the second period with the Blues once again with the man advantage, Philippe Bozon passed the puck ahead to Emerson, who streaked around a defender and slid it over to Ron Wilson. Wilson beat Whitmore for his eleventh goal of the year, surpassing his previous high with the Blues and his high since scoring 18 with Winnipeg way back in 1980-81. He would add his twelfth later in the game. But few people noticed Wilson's milestone. Instead, everyone looked to Bozon's assist, his first career point in the NHL. He would later assist on two other goals and earn the game's number-three star.

"I feel good," Bozon said. "This was my fifth game, and I didn't have any points. I want to help this be a better team."

And so he was. Bozon had quickly become a fan favorite, surprising everyone in the Arena, most noticeably Brian Sutter, with his physical style of play. With a live television audience looking on, Bozon had leveled Wendel Clark in Toronto the game before with an open-ice check. Few players dare to mix it up with the Leafs' tough-guy captain, but an unimpressed Bozon ran over Clark like a locomotive.

"Do you know who that was?" the *Post's* Tom Wheatley asked Bozon when the Blues returned home. "Do you even know who you hit?"

Bozon shrugged his shoulders and muttered, "Sure, I know him."

Not only was it a pleasure to watch Bozon score his first points in the league, it was even more enjoyable watching Brendan Shanahan score his 30th and 31st goals of the year, surpassing his personal high in New Jersey two seasons before. One of the most likable players on a team full of them, it was great to see Shanahan set career highs after playing the entire year with a huge albatross named Scott Stevens on his back. Not only that, but he scored his 30-plus goals while playing the majority of his time on the second line, with a multitude of different linemates.

"I think I've done as best as I could under the situation," said Brendan. "It's a good feeling. It's kind of like coming in at the start of the year and wondering how things are going to go. It's kind of a nice little side note that coming into my first year here, I was able to get a career high."

And finally, the most surprising and unexpected mark of all, iron-fisted Darin Kimble scored his first goal of the year, a mere 76 games into the season. And it came less than five minutes after he chalked up his third assist of the year. Needless to say, it was his first multiple-point game of the year, as he doubled his season point output in just sixty minutes.

So did Kimble save his stick? Was he going to hang it over the fireplace at home? Or was he going to ship it to the Hockey Hall of Fame? None of the above. Later in the game, Kimble reverted to the player we all know and love. Trying to clear the puck out of his own end, he accidentally fired it into the crowd behind the Blues' bench, striking a woman in the chest. Luckily, it was Kimble who shot it, so the woman was unhurt. But showing his soft, sweet side, Darin skated over to the bench and passed his stick up to the woman as a souvenir. In all seriousness, that was a charitable gesture from a man who probably wanted to have that stick bronzed.

"It feels good to finally get that goal," said Kimble. "I had a lot of chances. Well, not a lot compared to Brett, I guess, but I had a lot of chances, and it finally went into the net for me."

With a crowd of reporters surrounding Kimble for the first time all year, Chase walked nearby and yelled, "They want to talk to you now, eh, Kimby?!"

Indeed, the players were in a lighthearted mood after the 7-2 trashing of Hartford. With the possibility of a strike just a few short days away, it was nice to forget about all that serious crap away from the ice and just concentrate on having fun before more than 17,500 fans.

Unfortunately, the party came to a grinding halt two nights later, when the Blues returned to business against the Maple Leafs, the team that had embarrassed them earlier in the week in Toronto. The game had playoff ramifications for both teams. If the Blues lost, they were out of the hunt for second place. If the Leafs lost, they were closer to being eliminated from the playoffs, period. Obviously, their fight for survival was much stronger than the Blues', and it showed from the drop of the first puck.

The Blues played what had to be their worst first period of the year, and there were certainly plenty to choose from. It was similar to the first period in Toronto, the one Brian Sutter called the worst of their recent road trip. While the Leafs fired 14 shots at Guy Hebert, Brown and Emerson were the only Blues to slap the puck at Grant Fuhr. After that 14-2 barrage, Toronto held a 2-0 advantage.

To their credit, the Blues came out firing in the second period and took control away from the Leafs. It was just like the first twenty minutes, only the roles were reversed. The Blues outshot Toronto 17-4 but could only match goals with the Leafs, with each team scoring once. Curt Giles netted his first goal as a member of the Blues in the third to make things interesting, but Toronto held on for the 3-2 win and stayed alive for postseason play.

As for the Blues, they would definitely open the playoffs in Chicago. The only way they could finish second would be to win their last three games while the Hawks lost their remaining four. Sorry, but there was no way that was going to happen.

Meanwhile, in a Toronto hotel, John Ziegler handed the players' union what he called "the last proposal" from the owners. It was early Sunday morning, March 29, about thirty hours before the Monday noon strike deadline. No question, the two sides were serious about resolving their differences. They had engaged in a 16-hour marathon session Friday and met again for more than 12 hours Saturday night and Sunday morning. Neither side tipped its hand by telling the public what the major sticking points still were. But there's no doubt, the owners and players still couldn't see eye to eye on the issues of free agency and playoff revenue.

It appeared the players' union would have to either accept this latest offer or go on strike as planned. There was little chance the two sides would talk again on Sunday night because of a scheduled meeting in Chicago of the league's Board of Governors. Ziegler said the board members weren't about to break their engagement to do any eleventh-hour negotiating with the players. Take the contract or take a walk, the owners said.

Hoping to give the owners something to think about at their Chicago get-together, Bob Goodenow handed Ziegler a counter-proposal as he left Toronto. The offer was unanimously rejected late Sunday night, and both sides had reached the point of no return. In a matter of hours, the first full-scale strike in NHL history was set to begin. There was no telling how long it would last. Some players feared that if the owners convinced themselves they could weather the financial hit of missing the playoffs, then the beginning of the 1992-93 season would be canceled. The owners would lock out the players and force them into financial starvation, a move that would eventually leave the players with no choice but to accept the offer on the table.

If that really happened, and the remainder of the 1991-92 season was wiped out, how fitting an end it would be for the Blues' 25th anniversary season. It was a year that never got untracked after Scott Stevens was rudely forced out of St. Louis. Ever since then, the Blues had been a rather blasé hockey team that was interesting to watch mainly because of its internal problems.

And now this. A possible end to the season because the owners and players couldn't come to terms on a new collective bargaining agreement. The old one had expired exactly 12 days after Stevens was sold, er, traded to New Jersey. The Blues were one team that could withstand the seriousness of a strike. Hell, they had been through enough already. What was a little work stoppage?

Chapter Seventeen

STRIKE OUT

Ron Caron was fidgeting in his seat. For a man who has trouble sitting still, this was nothing newsworthy. But on this particular morning, Caron felt a sense of urgency to find out the latest information. Were the players on strike today as they had threatened? Or in some unexpected and miraculous turn of events, did they agree to the owners' latest proposal and decide to keep playing hockey?

Unfortunately for Caron, he was in a black hole of information, sitting on the runway of O'Hare Airport in Chicago. The Board of Governors' meeting had ended the night before, and Caron, along with Jack Quinn and Mike Shanahan, were heading back to St. Louis early on the morning of March 30, the day when hockey was scheduled to stand still.

Caron couldn't wait for the aircraft to land at Lambert. He scribbled a message to the pilot and handed it to a flight attendant for delivery. He had to get the latest news. Now.

The message from the pilot wasn't exactly what Caron wanted to hear, but it would have to suffice for now. The pilot hadn't heard what the players' intentions were, but when he got closer to St. Louis he would radio ahead for the very latest. Until then, the Blues' general manager could do nothing but sit and wait.

Meanwhile, in cities throughout North America, player representatives were engaged in a teleconference call with union head Bob Goodenow. He told them it was now time to find out what every union member wanted to do. Goodenow instructed his messengers to go back to their respective teams and ask the players to vote on the owners' "final" proposal. Obviously, this would take time. It couldn't be done in a matter of hours. To make sure each and every player knew exactly what he was voting on, it was imperative the strike deadline be pushed back a couple of days.

"When we got closer to St. Louis the answer came back," said Caron shortly after landing. "John Ziegler said the strike, or the possibility of a strike, has been delayed until Wednesday. Well, if you are aware what Wednesday is, it's April Fool's. I just hope that we don't get an April fool."

So for the time being, the teams would keep playing and practicing as the votes were tallied over the next 48 hours. The delay not only gave union members a chance to digest the issues before voting, it gave the public a chance to hear additional spin from the owners on how the players' demands were completely out of line.

"Costs are really escalating rapidly and that is of concern to ownership, especially when salaries in this particular season have gone up 37 percent," argued Jack Quinn. "Nine out of every ten dollars in ticket revenue is going to the players."

"As you look around (the league), you'll probably see some new (owners') faces in the years to come," added Mike Shanahan. "It'll be very difficult for these franchises to survive with the cost of doing business escalating at the rate of 30 to 40 percent at a clip."

Shanahan went so far as to suggest that many of the players didn't even understand the issues and were being led astray by Goodenow and a group of hard-line veterans. The Blues' chairman admitted to contacting some of his subordinates to make sure they knew what they were doing.

"We've talked with players, and it's obvious with their reaction to us that they really were unsure if they should be striking," Shanahan said. "They had some questions that I think indicated they didn't really have a clear understanding of exactly what that offer consisted of."

Shanahan's method of negotiating through his players was somewhat surprising, to say the least. It was a typical owner's ploy by a very atypical owner. Shanahan is not in fact the team owner, of course. That title belongs to a group of faceless St. Louis business execs known as Civic Progress. But as that group's chairman and governor, Shanahan can at least act as the Blues' owner.

Shanahan was known as a "players' man," a member of the new breed of NHL owners who seemed to have a clear vision of the league's future. This Brat Pack of visionary leaders, Detroit's Mike Ilitch, Pittsburgh's Howard Baldwin, Montreal's Ronald Corey, and L.A.'s Bruce McNall, just to name a few, seemed intent on taking the league out of prehistoric times and into a more modern era of booming popularity. There were even rumblings of a palace coup that would topple the old regime led by Chicago's Bill Wirtz, and replace it with a new contingent of "player-friendly" leaders.

But suddenly Shanahan was toeing the company line. After taking heat from hard-line owners for signing high-priced free agents and jacking up the league's salary structure, Shanahan was now backing away from his renegade image and preaching a conservative philosophy that must have made Wirtz's grinch-like smile grow from ear to ear.

The ultimate proof of Shanahan's metamorphosis, and that of the entire Blues management staff, came on the issue of free agency, specifically the ill-fated Scott Stevens deal. Remember how team officials could barely control their anger when Judge Houston's decision came down? Now, seven months later, Shanahan wanted no part of second-guessing the system in place.

"I think that free agency, as it now exists, works," he said.

Come again?

"If there are ways to improve, they ought to improve it. But we have no complaint about it."

That last line left me speechless. The chairman of the team that had been devastated by the free-agency process had no complaint about it? What would it take for Shanahan to actually find a problem with it? Lose Brett Hull? Curtis Joseph?

In reality, however, Mike Shanahan had no choice but to espouse the league's commitment to fiscal sanity. Just as the players were showing solidarity, the owners had to be equally united. When the television lights were turned up and the tape recorders turned on, the 22 NHL owners had to hide their differing points of view and act as a coalition of responsible businessmen working for the same cause. If there was going to be an overthrow, then it would come behind closed doors away from public view and, more importantly, Bob Goodenow's view. Just like at the Vatican when a new pope is selected, perhaps NHL officials would release puffs of smoke from their headquarters when a new leader was officially chosen. Until then, new-line owners like Shanahan were going to preach old-line sermons.

Meanwhile, the Blues emerged from the locker room and headed straight to the ice for practice. They didn't know what to expect when they arrived at the Arena that morning. But after hearing from co-player reps Butcher and Janney, they put on their skates, grabbed their sticks, and silently walked past a large number of reporters who had lined up outside the locker room door. The season was still in progress. At least for another 48 hours or so.

The delay, of course, was to give each player a chance to vote on the owners' final offer. But some critics, including some of the players themselves, questioned whether the union was backing down a bit. It was an assumption that made Janney bristle.

"If people are thinking that, they're dead wrong," he snapped. "It has nothing to do with weakening. We want everyone to be informed. Information is a very important tool to decision making. Hopefully, we can make a calm, intelligent, rational decision."

Janney was among many players around the league who felt the union wasn't being forceful enough in its demands. In its rejected counterproposal to the owners, the union had dropped its demand that a free agent could be signed without any type of compensation once he reached the age of 27. The players instead agreed to the owner's proposed age of 30. In the old contract, the age was 31.

Also, the players gave a thumbs-up to expanding the regular season from 80 games to 84. The four extra contests would give the owners additional revenue, estimated at $17 million dollars, to help pay for the increased salaries. It was a decision many players found unappealing because of the increased workload. The season was long and strenuous enough, they argued, without adding another week and a half to the schedule.

So with both sides finally agreeing to terms on some of the major issues, what was the holdup? Well, the players and owners had found two additional items about which to argue. They were issues no one even thought important back in September. And when they were made public just before the strike deadline, fans and media alike scratched their heads wondering what the hell the two sides were talking about.

First was the length of the contract. It was always assumed the new collective bargaining agreement would run through at least the 1993-94 season, if not beyond. But the owners insisted that the two sides had so many major disagreements that it would be foolish to lock either side into a long-term deal. Therefore, the owners wanted to sign a contract only through the next season and use the time to hammer out a more workable contract that would please both sides.

"I think a one-year proposition is good, so we can all step back and take some heat out of the situation and really work toward resolving all the issues on both the owners' and the players' sides," said Mike Shanahan.

But paranoid players saw the one-year offer as nothing more than a thinly veiled effort to give the owners an additional year to figure out how to really screw the union, perhaps even destroy it.

Secondly, and this was the biggie, the players wanted the rights to their faces. Sounds a bit funny, doesn't it? However, this was no laughing matter to Bob Goodenow and the gang. The hockey trading card business was booming. And the union was raking in a pretty good haul from it, estimated at $11 million during the 1991-92 season, nearly nine percent of total trading card revenue. That money was the major source of income for the union and had been for 21 years. Without it, the union would die a quick death.

Well, in came the owners, who politely told their employees to read the fine print in their standard player contracts. It contained language, somewhat vague according to Goodenow, that gave owners control of the players' "image." In other words, the owners had every right to take every cent from the trading card business. As it stood now, the owners were raking in about $8 million from hockey cards, or some three million less than the players' union. But being the good guys they were, the owners had over the years allowed the players to fund their union through the hockey card industry.

But now that it was becoming a multimillion dollar business, far surpassing anyone's expectations, the owners wanted a bigger chunk of it. They told the players it was time to form a new partnership in which both sides could prosper. Not only were hockey cards becoming increasingly popular, but the sales of such NHL merchandise as jerseys, hats, pucks, and posters were also becoming big business. Let's take advantage of this boom together, the owners told the players. Let's merge like two corporations and watch the dough just start rolling in.

The players looked at the owners with all the skepticism of a parole board hearing a criminal's profession of new-found religious faith. The union was convinced the owners were up to no good, some even suggesting that the good-faith offer was actually an attempt to bust the union.

"(All of a sudden) they want to address their claim to something that has been ours for 21 years," Goodenow said. "What is the real purpose for their proposal?"

Blues officials had a tough time understanding such mistrust. With both sides sure to make a financial killing, why were the players so reluctant to join hands with their employers?

"I just can't see why anyone would walk away from this package," Shanahan said. "I just can't answer that question. I'm sorry."

"Let's hope these 48 hours that are left now will give us a window to try and finish these other items off," said Quinn.

However, the next 48 hours proved only one thing. The players' union was much stronger and more united than perhaps even Goodenow thought possible when he first took the job. When the votes were tallied on the morning of April Fool's, you could hear the gasps of disbelief from inside executive offices around the league. The players voted 560-4 to tell the owners to take a hike. None of the four dissenting votes came from the Blues, who voted unanimously to reject the owners' offer the day before.

At precisely 2 p.m. St. Louis time, Garth Butcher and Craig Janney officially declared a strike at a news conference in a meeting room at the Brentwood ice rink. With reporters waiting patiently to hear the news, Butcher looked at his watch and stepped forward to the podium.

"Well, I guess we can start," Butcher said. "The players are now on strike as of 2 o'clock our time."

The Blues had been scheduled to jump on a plane about an hour later and fly to Minneapolis for a game against the North Stars that night. But as the votes were being tallied at union headquarters, it became clear that the Blues weren't going anywhere.

"It's very disappointing it came to this point," said Janney. "But it's something we put a lot of thought into as an organization. Obviously, the membership thinks it's the right thing to do by the vote we had."

"I think the players have very strong resolve right now," said Butcher. "The players are very unified. We didn't go into the discussions saying to our members that this is something that's going to be over in a year. Our association laid it on the table that this could go well into next season. Obviously, we hope that's not the case, but I believe we have the resolve to withstand it."

As soon as the co-player reps were finished briefing the media, reporters dashed to the Arena to hear the other side of the story from Quinn and Shanahan.

"We're very concerned about this," admitted the Blues' chairman. "I guess this is the worst possible thing that could have happened. It did happen, and we don't feel good about it."

"Hopefully it can be resolved to save the playoffs because the fans deserve the playoffs," added Quinn. "That's what this sport is all about. It's the fun time of year."

And, of course, the profitable time of year for the owners. According to Ziegler, 13 percent of the clubs' revenue comes from the playoffs, nearly $40 million league-wide. And yet, the owners dish out next to nothing to their players during the postseason. Depending on how far they go, players can earn as little as a few hundred bucks a game. That's a drop in the bucket, considering a team can take in as much as $600,000 per contest.

No doubt about it. This strike was meant to tighten the screws on management. With the arenas quiet and empty, the owners were set to lose millions of dollars. Some clubs could survive a major financial hit. But most, including the Blues, desperately needed playoff revenue to survive on a competitive level.

"The St. Louis Blues, by program and by design, has been what I'll call a 'marginal' operation for lack of a better word," Shanahan explained. "We don't operate to make windfall profits. We make a profit, and we put it back into the team and the operation."

It was that kind of worried rhetoric the players were counting on. As soon as the owners realized the severity of their losses, the union was convinced that management would be more than willing to settle the strike. And fast.

*   *   *

Garth Butcher was moving in slow motion. He absolutely did not want to get his equipment on for the morning skate, because he had a funny feeling he'd be taking it right back off in a matter of minutes. So Butcher just sat there and watched his Vancouver teammates slip into their practice jerseys while slowly following suit. He moved so cautiously it looked as though he had a sunburn over his entire body.

It was the morning of March 5, 1991, the trading deadline. The Canucks were in Pittsburgh for a game that night, and Butcher was convinced he wouldn't be around to see it. The trade rumors were just too strong and persistent. Not only was he hearing them in Vancouver, but some of his ex-mates now skating for the Blues told him to stand by. Not taking any chances, Butcher packed extra clothes for the trip just in case he was dealt elsewhere. It was the first time in his nine-year NHL career that he had brought additional supplies on the road.

Of course, Butcher had survived similar rumors the year before. He heard through the grapevine that he was on his way to St. Louis halfway through the 1989-90 season. Instead, the Blues asked for Rich Sutter and Harold Snepsts, while Butcher stayed behind on the only team for which he had played.

But this year was different. Too many people in the know were telling him about a deal with the Blues. The information appeared solid and accurate. That's why he was taking so long to change into his hockey getup. Ron Caron would have to make the deal within minutes to beat the deadline, and Butcher preferred to stay in street clothes as long as he could.

Sure enough, right in the middle of dressing, the word came down. Butcher and Dan Quinn were going to St. Louis in exchange for Geoff Courtnall, Cliff Ronning, Sergio Momesso and Robert Dirk.

"I got the call from (president/general manager/head coach) Pat Quinn," recalled Butcher. "I just went out and talked to him on the phone and it was done. I was on a plane in about an hour and a half on my way to Hartford (where the Blues were playing that night.)"

The Trade became a study in fan behavior, proving just how fickle some fans can be. Many in St. Louis criticized the deal immediately, saying the Blues had given up too much offense, three forwards who had combined for 51 goals and 117 points. In fact, right after the Blues beat Hartford in Butcher's first appearance, they failed to win a game in their next six, matching their longest futility streak of the year. Many people jumped off the Blues' bandwagon and onto Butcher's back.

But just when The Trade seemed to be a disaster, the Blues tied their longest winning streak in team history, winning their last seven games of the year. Just like that, the criticism stopped. The bandwagon was full again, with many more clambering to get on. The Blues were suddenly the hottest team in the league heading into the playoffs and were considered one of the favorites for a Stanley Cup.

When the Blues beat the Red Wings in their first-round playoff series after being down three games to one, many credited Butcher for making the difference. He was the big bully on the block, knocking people down as they ventured too close to the net. His agitating, intimidating style all but nullified the aggressive play of Bob Probert and Company.

"We would have never won that series without Butch," Brian Sutter would later say. And many Blues backers and media members agreed with Sutter's observation.

However, when the Blues were unable to get past the "lowly" North Stars—so lowly they came within two games of winning it all—the Butcher-bashers were back again. Only this time, they were more vicious and mean-spirited. They blamed the demise of the Blues on their new defenseman, saying if it wasn't for him the team would still be moving forward in the playoffs. The fans needed a scapegoat, and his name was Garth Butcher.

Little did Butcher know it would only get worse during the Blues' silver anniversary season. When Scott Stevens was kidnapped to Jersey, all eyes turned to Butcher. Show us what you can do now, the critics demanded. Our leader is gone. You're supposed to be so tough. Prove it.

Being named captain to replace Stevens put even more pressure on Butcher. He had to be twice as good as the all-star defenseman to make people happy. In the end, Butcher would fail because he was never given a fair shake. But if the truth be known, though Butcher-bashers don't want to hear it, Garth was on a pace to enjoy the most productive season of his career.

Before breaking his foot in Calgary and prematurely ending his season after 68 games, Butcher had five goals and twenty points. If he had maintained that pace over twelve contests, he would have ended the year with 23 points, equaling the career high he set during the 1987-88 season. He was also on a pace to surpass 200 penalty minutes for the sixth year in a row. The numbers were astonishing when considering all the pressure put on Butcher to become nothing short of a Hall of Fame defenseman. But, just like the previous season, Butcher was an easy scapegoat for fans looking for someone to blame. And when Brian Sutter came to his captain's defense, Sutter's stock declined just as rapidly.

Overall, Butcher played much better than expected. But that was only when he was compared to himself. There was no way in the world he could prevail in comparisons to Scott Stevens. It was unfair to draw such parallels. Remember, Butcher was traded to the Blues when they still had Stevens and planned to keep him for the rest of his career. Butcher was never meant to replace Stevens, only to supplement him. After opponents were pounded into the ice by Scott, Garth would make the tag like a pro wrestler and head to the ice to continue the flogging. It was an effective combination that was unfortunately cut short by Judge Houston's decision, forcing Butcher to fulfill unrealistic expectations set by unrealistic fans and media.

But Butcher feels it unnecessary to explain his side. He's not looking for sympathy. He's not looking for understanding. The only thing he's looking for is success in the future. Only losers peer at the past and whine about what might have been.

"It seems to be brought up over and over again," said Butcher, referring to The Trade. "To me, I don't believe in looking back at anything like that. I don't think successful people look back and regret the things that happen. People who are successful look ahead. They see what they can do about today and not about the other days."

For Butcher, that meant rehabilitating his broken foot and getting back to action as soon as possible. Of course, the strike would have a bearing on his return. Garth had been in danger of missing the first round of the playoffs, but the delay bought him extra time to mend.

It also gave him some time to spend with his wife, Tanys, and two kids, Matthew and Megan. For the first time in his married life, the Butcher family was together for a long stretch during the season. By his own admission, he was "driving everyone crazy" at home while his teammates were playing hockey. But don't let his cabin fever fool you. Only his closest friends know, but tough-guy Garth Butcher is mush when it comes to his family. You won't find anyone more devoted and committed to his wife and kids than this rough-edged man with the perfect hockey name.

"I'm a guy who loves his family more than anything else in the world," he admitted. "I'm very normal from that point of view. That's the way most people feel."

Indeed. But once again, we get back to perceptions. It's probably inconceivable to some that Butcher is capable of leaving his hockey persona at the rink while turning into a loving father figure at home. There must be a telephone booth somewhere on the way to Chesterfield where Butcher is able to change into another personality. The man with the deep-set eyes and deep, gutteral voice doesn't exactly seem the Ward Cleaver type.

But Butcher, like many high-profile athletes, is a very private individual. What you see isn't necessarily what you get. Butcher does not live and breathe hockey. Sure, he gives it his undivided attention at the rink. But away from it, he wants no part of any conversation relating to his profession.

"I like to meet people who don't want to talk about hockey all the time," he says. "It's nice to talk to those people and be a normal person, just to talk about their kids and my kids. When we discuss things like that, I found myself very easy to get along with and get to know. Sometimes when the discussion turns to hockey, I tend to hold back a little bit."

But during the strike, Butcher couldn't hide from the sport. While his teammates were playing golf, he was playing the part of a player-representative. He was in constant contact with Bob Goodenow and other members of the union's negotiating committee. He was also the contact for the St. Louis media demanding to know the very latest. At first, Butcher gave his home phone number only to a few selected reporters. But it took only a day or two for others to discover the number and start calling the mucker-turned-manager. He should have established a 1-900 number and made a little money on the side.

Butcher's co-rep, Craig Janney, had flown back home to Boston during the strike. He stayed in touch with Butcher but left the majority of the work to his partner in St. Louis. And since Garth did such an excellent job relaying information to the press, reporters found it unnecessary to track down Janney for further news. Butcher handled his player rep responsibilities with such expertise that many people undoubtedly gained new respect for the Blues' team captain. Not once did he show signs of irritability, despite constant harassment, mainly from journalists trying to stay informed of the situation.

The first few days of the strike, Butcher had little to offer his inquisitors. The two sides had just about come to terms on the major issues of free agency, pensions, scheduling, and the entry draft. The major sticking points continued to be the length of the new contract and the hockey card controversy. The strike moved into the weekend of April 4 with virtually no progress on those two issues. Ziegler and Goodenow talked off and on, but their conversations were described as "exploratory" and nothing else.

In the only major development, the players' union handed the owners a new proposal to mull over during the weekend. The Board of Governors called an emergency meeting for Monday, April 6, and planned to give an answer to the offer at that time. If the bigwigs gave a thumbs-down, the rest of the season was in definite peril. The Blues' 25th anniversary, along with the league's 75th, would forever be referred to as the season that wasn't. How fitting for a league that many felt was a joke anyway.

The two sides not only disagreed on the issues, they also adopted different public relations philosophies. The players preferred a quiet, unassuming approach. Goodenow and his player representatives were quick to update everyone on the progress of the talks but refused to discuss the nuts and bolts of it.

"We want to keep it at the negotiating table and out of the media so we can have productive negotiations," explained Butcher. "We're still at a point where we feel we can get this thing solved and therefore don't want to get into any issues."

John Ziegler couldn't have disagreed more. Trying to win the fans' approval, Ziegler blitzed the public with a p.r. campaign of tributes, tirades, and tears. This man missed his calling. He didn't belong in hockey. He belonged in sales at a Fortune 500 company. He could've made millions.

His most memorable sales job came on the afternoon of April 4. Speaking live on Canadian television, Ziegler went into a diatribe over the strike while remembering his childhood watching "Hockey Night in Canada" every Saturday night.

"Having hockey withdrawal symptoms is not fun," he said, looking straight into the camera while pausing every few words for added emphasis. "Tonight is 'Hockey Night in Canada.' And we're not going to watch hockey. I would hope our players would think about that. Because they're all good, young men and great athletes. And I've never met a National Hockey League player in my life that didn't have an extraordinary love and passion and feeling for this game."

Before you grab for your barfbag, hold on. There was much more. Ziegler followed up his tribute to the players by putting the blame for the strike squarely on their shoulders.

"I would ask the players, do you really want to deprive our fans of this game for the issues that we're talking about? Especially because, knowing the owners, they'll work it out with you. What answer do you have to the fans who say tonight, 'Why aren't we watching hockey?' And I feel very helpless that I can't give them an answer that I would be satisfied with as a hockey fan."

Ziegler's condescending language was unfortunate because, aside from his emotional pleas to gain favor with fans, his speech at times was very informative. He used charts and diagrams to point out the financial status of the league. If the numbers were even remotely correct, it was suddenly difficult to come down against the owners for being so stingy.

One graph showed the league making a $46 million profit during the 1990-91 season. But from there, the profit line dropped so rapidly that just looking at it you got that queasy feeling in your stomach as if driving over a hill too quickly. Ziegler predicted a $9 million loss during the current season, a dramatic dip of $55 million from one year to the next. The NHL president proceeded to forecast another $55 million loss during the 1992-93 season and a whopping $102 million shortfall the following year. Was it really that bad? If so, the league might as well fold its tents and quit while teams were still making money.

"The owners have said, 'We'll take two years, 1991-92 and '92-93,'" Ziegler said. "'We'll take a hit and take the $64 million in losses. But work with us and help us so we don't have a $102 million loss in 1993-94.' And they (the players) have said, 'No. You take that risk. We want a three-year contract and then we'll start talking whether or not we can put something together.' This business cannot stand a $150 million loss.

"It is not an answer, and it is not a responsible answer to say to us, 'That is your problem.' Because that problem is made up of 90 percent of salaries. And for the association to say to us, 'You solve the salary problem,' I suggest is not a very fair approach."

After making his point about the salary structure, Ziegler turned to the other major controversy, the trading card industry, and worked his charm on that, too. He suggested putting the legal jargon aside and formulating an unprecedented partnership in the booming business. After all, he pointed out, the owners had every right to rake in more money from trading cards than they were currently receiving.

"We make money from trading cards also," Ziegler said, continuing to speak slowly and deliberately. "And the trading card position of the players' association has never been collectively bargained. Never. It is not in their collective bargaining agreement. They just took the money. In their standard player's agreement, it is so clear. All of those rights belong to the member clubs. And what we're saying is, 'You took it. You never came to us. You never negotiated it.'"

Toward the end of Ziegler's thirty-minute speech, he tried to make one last point that should have backfired, even damaged his credibility on the points he was hoping to make earlier. A reporter suggested to Ziegler that it sounded as if the owners were asking the players to babysit them over the next few years to make sure they didn't spend recklessly. One might have expected Ziegler just to laugh off a comment like that. Instead, Ziegler couldn't have agreed more.

"I've said it to them (the players) all summer," said Ziegler. "I said, 'Gentlemen, you have to help these guys (the owners) protect themselves from themselves because they will not do it without your help.' Owners don't have to do that. But that's what owners do unless restrictions are imposed upon all of them."

His point was mind-boggling. Grown men who had built financial empires because of their shrewd financial wizardry and business acumen suddenly had no clue how to keep their sport franchises afloat? These owners weren't just plucked off the streets and told to go run a hockey team. Most were multimillionaires who had built their businesses from scratch. They knew a little something about how to run a company. But according to Ziegler, these men were now grossly inept when dealing with employees who demanded six- and seven-figure salaries. Puh-leeze. Gimme a break. The point should've fallen on deaf ears. But it didn't.

If Ziegler's intentions were to sway public opinion, he was doing a damn good job. Much to the delight of his bosses, Ziegler had played the ultimate salesman to perfection and convinced fans of his logic. That's not saying Ziegler was grossly inaccurate with his facts and figures. For all we know, the league was really on a pace to lose $166 million over the next three years. Even Goodenow had a difficult time shooting down that theory. He asked the owners to explain where the expansion money was going, but that's about all the firepower he used in an unsuccessful attempt to invalidate Ziegler's claims.

According to reports out of Canada, a majority of fans were miffed at the players for walking out, and a large chunk of their displeasure could be directly attributed to Ziegler's impassioned pleas. The fans agreed with Ziegler's contention that the league would be in serious trouble if the players received everything they were after. Stop acting like spoiled brats and just play hockey, they demanded. What's an April in Canada without hockey? No one really knew. Until now. And the longer the strike went on, the more vocal and irate fans became.

Seeing that his performances were drawing rave reviews from viewers, Ziegler let it all hang out during another live news conference on Tuesday, April 7. He informed viewers that the hockey season would be officially canceled on Thursday if the players refused to accept the owners' second "final" proposal. The players' negotiating committee had already rejected it the night before, much to the chagrin of Ziegler.

"The question I have is why they didn't allow their membership to vote on the proposal?" he asked.

Still, the owners left the offer on the table for the players to reconsider. If they continued to push it back at the owners during the next 48 hours, then Ziegler said he had no choice but to lock up the rinks and tell everyone to go home for the summer. And that's when his speech turned to the stuff for which the Oscars are made.

"I hope the games resume," he said quietly, starting to choke up and stumble over his words. "It's now in the hands of some of the greatest athletes in the world. I hope they make the right decision."

Suddenly, Ziegler stopped. He was unable to utter another word. He gulped hard, trying to force back tears that were accumulating in his eyes.

"Excuse me," he whispered. With glossy eyes and a deep frown, Ziegler reached for a glass of water and slowly took a sip, hoping to regain his composure. Watching this unfold, I had the urge to stand up and applaud. Sir Laurence Olivier had nothing on this guy. Ziegler must have forgotten for a moment that his league was associated with a Stanley Cup, not an Academy Award.

Ziegler's tearful breakdown in front of a live television audience sickened players around the league. How could they effectively negotiate with a guy who used that kind of behavior to sway public opinion?

"It made me want to puke," Garth Butcher said bluntly.

Butcher's union chief had grown tired of watching Ziegler play the role of master thespian every couple of days, calling Ziegler's antics "theatrics."

"My reaction to John Ziegler's comments are simply that he seems to have decided to go public to say that the players are greedy, that the players don't understand, that the players aren't informed," Goodenow told the Associated Press. "That's unfortunate because that's not true."

The players stood their ground, refusing to enter into a public debate with Ziegler. They let the NHL president talk directly to hockey fans while they adopted a more private approach. And, of course, that's the proper way to solve complex internal problems. When one side uses the media as its own Broadway stage, it's usually a sign of weakness. But in this particular case it was working. Hockey fans, most notably in Canada, would never forgive the players for walking out right before the playoffs. Couldn't the players see how upset they were making the president of the league? Perception IS reality.

*   *   *

"They're back there," the waitress said, pointing to the back of the restaurant.

"Have they been in there very long?" I asked.

"Nah, just an hour or so. They're eating lunch right now."

I had no idea how long they'd be in that back room, so I took a seat in the lobby, accepted a free Diet Coke, and waited for the players to emerge. It was the afternoon of Thursday, April 9, the day the NHL was supposed to officially close for the year if the players didn't accept the owners' offer on the table.

The Blues were meeting at Brett Hull's restaurant in west St. Louis County to get the latest scoop from Garth Butcher. His co-rep, Craig Janney, was still in Boston, so Butcher was holding court by his lonesome once again. The other notable figure missing was Brett Hull himself. Was he tired of spending time in his own place of business? Not at all. Hull had a date with a golf course and didn't want to spurn her. He'd get all the information he needed after his round. At least SOMEONE had his priorities straight.

The deadline of 2 p.m. Central Time came and went, and no announcement was made. The players were still locked in a back room discussing the latest proposals while the season was teetering on the brink of cancellation. As it turned out, NHL owners were meeting in a conference call at the same time to discuss their options. No public acknowledgement was made of their own self-imposed deadline, effectively letting it pass without one mention of it. And that could mean only one thing. The two sides at least still talking, even though they were far apart on the trading card issue, the only major stumbling block remaining. The dispute over the length of the new contract had pretty much been settled with the players agreeing to a one-year extension.

"I certainly don't see the players moving from their position on the issues, and I don't see the owners doing that right now," explained Butcher after emerging from the three-hour meeting with his teammates. Butcher was Mr. Casual, wearing white shorts and a gray golf shirt with a pair of sunglasses hooked into its V-neck. But he was all business when discussing the strike, now into its ninth day.

"We sent an offer to the owners, which they rejected," he pointed out. "They brought back their own offer, which we rejected. We didn't feel the last offer was as good as the one we had on the table before. At this point in time, it looks very, very bad."

Butcher told his mates to stick around St. Louis for at least a couple of days before venturing off to their various postseason destinations around North America or, in Philippe Bozon's case, France. Even though the picture looked bleak, Butcher said, there was a chance this thing could be settled at any moment, so stay close to your phones.

"We're going to keep in touch, and Butch is going to keep us abreast of what's going to happen," said Curtis Joseph, whose sore foot was back in playing shape. "It's a sad feeling to think this could be the last time we see each other for who knows how long."

"Right now, I think the guys are still going to be around for a little bit," said Dave Christian, holding his son Beau, an uninterested participant in the meeting. "In all of us, there's the little kid who loves the game, and we'd love to be playing. But we've also come to find that there's certainly the business side to the game as well."

Many of the players milled about the parking lot for a few extra minutes, engaging in what could be their last conversations with one another for some time. Nelson Emerson, Kelly Chase and Joseph leaned against a car and talked among themselves. Jeff Brown and Pat Jablonski sat in Brown's red Jeep while conversing with a few of their teammates standing nearby. Brendan Shanahan visited with Darin Kimble and Bret Hedican.

These are the moments that bring players closer together. They were far removed from the sport of hockey. They weren't skating endlessly up and down the ice. They weren't listening to Brian Sutter bark out orders. They were just standing in the parking lot of a restaurant talking with one another without the distractions related to their profession. They were more than teammates here. They were friends. And if the strike was having any positive effect, it was bonding this troubled team. Other organizations around the league were having serious problems dealing with the work stoppage. Owners were berating players and vice versa. Threats were being made. Strong words were being spoken. Teams were being torn apart.

But not the Blues. This was one squad that was solid in its commitment to Bob Goodenow, and equally solid in its respect for management. They saw Mike Shanahan, Jack Quinn, and Ron Caron as members of one of the more progressive management teams in the league. Most players around the league held deep admiration for the Blues' top brass. They were among about a half-dozen organizations whom NHL players saw as striving to make the league more prosperous by creating a more player-friendly environment. The only punishment Blues management had handed out to its striking players was depriving a small number of them, primarily the newest members of the team, of their paid hotels and car rentals. However, that was standard operating procedure during a work stoppage, and the players affected weren't surprised. They just found other places to live and different modes of transportation.

Meanwhile, a break in the stalemate seemed to be occurring Thursday evening. After talking to team owners on the phone for more than three hours, Ziegler and Goodenow conversed with one another and agreed to meet in person in New York the next morning. It would be their first discussion since Tuesday, when Ziegler had issued his threat to terminate the season.

Sure enough, the two negotiating committees got together early Friday morning and started to piece together another "final" offer. Late in the afternoon, after nearly nine hours of discussions, it appeared the two sides had finally hammered out a new agreement. Or had they? A Montreal radio station quoted Canadiens general manager Serge Savard as saying "the strike is over." Electronic media outlets throughout the U.S. and Canada picked up on the report and were soon telling their viewers and listeners that the season had been saved.

However, Savard had jumped the gun. The strike was NOT over. The two sides had NOT signed a new deal. At his Chesterfield home, Butcher was forced to temper everyone's enthusiasm. With the phone permanently attached to his ear, the Blues' player rep advised teammates and media alike not to believe what they were hearing.

"Some of the reports that it's done are wrong," he said, standing in the middle of his front lawn with his cordless phone next to him. "But there is certainly a lot of reason for optimism. As of a half-hour ago (7 p.m. St. Louis time), they were still talking and negotiating."

That didn't stop Blues staff workers from preparing as if the strike was indeed settled. The offices were full of employees stuffing letters into envelopes that were to be mailed out to season ticket holders. The letters explained that a settlement had been reached and the season would continue, with the remaining two home games pushed back ten days.

"Your patience and support are appreciated," was the last line of the letter, followed by Jack Quinn's signature. In all, staff employees stuffed over 7,000 letters that night for immediate delivery.

Meanwhile, back in Chesterfield, Brian Sutter was busy with a different problem. He was tirelessly patching up a front lawn damaged by disease.

"I've always had a good-looking lawn and this is the first time something like this has happened," explained Sutter as he was filling in the bare spots with a turf-growing product. Sutter had lived in the same home for twelve years but took care of it as if he had purchased it yesterday. Would you have expected anything less? A few weeks later, the lawn would be full and plush once again.

His hands stained green, the Blues' head coach used his forearm to wipe the sweat from his forehead as he contemplated returning to work at the rink. The strike had been extremely difficult for Sutter to handle, not knowing what to do or what to say.

"It's something that's been out of my control, and it's frustrating at times from where I stand," he said, also a bit perturbed with the premature news reports about the strike settlement. "It's to the point where you want something straightened out one way or the other. I think everybody feels that. I'm no different than anyone else."

In another section of Chesterfield, Dave and Elaine Lowry, who live down the street from Butcher, arrived at the Christian household to pick up Dave and Lisa and head out for a night on the town. Actually, they were just driving to a nearby theater to see "White Men Can't Jump." Not exactly the party atmosphere at Banff.

"I saw you driving around my neighborhood so I hid," Lowry kidded me. "And now I have to run into you here."

The Blues' left winger explained how he was driving his wife nuts not being able to play hockey. But now that there seemed to be some major progress, he expressed optimism that Elaine could regain her sanity.

"We're hoping we can resume play," Dave said. "The players are excited, and we want to play. But you have to look on it from both sides. We want what's best for the players and best for the fans. They want us on the ice, and that's where we want to be."

Christian told a similar story how his family couldn't wait for the strike to be settled. It's great to have you home, Pops. But when can you return to the Arena?

"It's too dark now, but you would notice the yard is mowed and everything's been picked up," he said pointing to the front yard. "We got some chores done around the house. But I think my wife and my family are ready for me to go back to work. Now, with what's happening today, we're pretty optimistic that we'll be back skating tomorrow and possibly playing on Sunday."

Sure enough, just minutes after the two couples watched Woody Harrelson prove that some white men CAN jump, John Ziegler and Bob Goodenow ended 15 hours of talks with the news everyone had been waiting to hear.

"The players get to play hockey," said Goodenow, "and I get to watch." In case you're wondering, there were no tears at this news conference.

So after ten days, the NHL's first big strike was officially over. Serge Savard was correct. He was just about six hours too early. Just before 11 o'clock Central Time, the two sides signed the dotted line and the season was set to continue. The only thing left was for union members to cast their votes the next day to approve or reject the agreement. It was expected to pass over-whelmingly.

Meanwhile, back at the Arena, staff workers were forced to restamp the 7,000 letters. Expecting the strike to be settled earlier in the evening, the employees had been using a different date for mail service. Since the cutoff point was 10 p.m. and the strike wasn't settled until an hour after that, the workers had to repeat the process. Many of them didn't emerge from the Arena until 4 in the morning. Those are some "character" employees, aren't they?

As is always the case after contract negotiations are completed, there's an instinctive urge to label one side the "winner" and the other the "loser." However, it was virtually impossible to do that in this case, because there were so many issues involved. But in breaking them down, you had to give the decision to the players on the most controversial subject matter, the trading card business. Not only were they allowed to keep the share of revenue they had been taking for 21 years, but the owners put it in writing that was specific and to the point.

A slight edge also went to the players on the issue of free agency. Group I free agents, players under 25 years of age, could now move to a new team without the threat of that team's losing a quality player. The free agent was allowed to choose between giving his old team compensation by draft choices or equaliza-tion decided by an arbitrator. If that sounds a bit confusing, look at it this way: Say the new system had been in effect when Brendan Shanahan signed with the Blues. Shanahan would have a choice what to give the Devils in return. He could use the old system and let an arbitrator decide who the Devils should get, OR, thinking that might be too risky to his new team, Shanahan could send a couple of draft choices to Jersey instead. The number of draft choices is based on the free agent's salary. In Shanahan's case, the Blues would have sent two number-one picks to the Devils and kept Scott Stevens.

Speaking of Stevens, who was a Type II free agent, under the new rules the Blues would have had to give the Capitals only two first-rounders for him instead of five. Just think. If this contract had been implemented in 1990 instead of '92, the Blues not only would have Stevens AND Shanahan, but they would have been less likely to make so many other changes to make up for the loss of Stevens. The old rules really hurt this team, which was desperately trying to upgrade its talent.

And for Group III, a player who reached the age of 30 could now move to a new team without compensation. The only restriction was that the player's current team could match the offer sheet to keep him. The players had wanted the age dropped to 28, but agreed to 30. Overall, the new free-agent system still wasn't as free as baseball, but it was a hell of a lot better than the archaic plan it replaced.

And in the third victory for the union, the players won a larger chunk of playoff revenue. They'll get a total of $9 million during the '93 playoffs, almost triple the amount of two years earlier. The Stanley Cup champs will see their take increase from $25,000 to $40,000 per man. Even the slightest increase in ticket prices during the playoffs—and you know that's going to happen in most venues—will easily make up most, if not all, of the difference.

On the owners' side, you can chalk up several victories there as well. The biggest one, of course, was getting the union to agree to just a one-year contract extension. In other words, the two sides have to do this all over again in less than a year. Can't wait.

The owners also got their wish by expanding the season from 80 games to 84, while reducing the entry draft from 12 rounds to 11. Goodenow initially wanted the draft abolished completely, then tried to cut it in half to six rounds before finally agreeing to reducing it by just one round. You can bet Goodenow will try again when the two sides begin working on a new collective bargaining agreement very soon.

There were a number of less-publicized issues on which both sides made concessions. One of the more interesting gives the owners the right to dress only 17 players for each game instead of the current 18, not counting the two goaltenders. If implemented, expect to see fewer "goons" on the ice, as teams are forced to go with only their most skilled players.

The morning after the strike was settled, the Blues entered the locker room for the first time in the month of April. Like other teams around the league, they first approved the new agreement and then promptly headed to the ice for a long-awaited return to practice. Overall, the union voted 409-61 to resume the season, proving there were quite a few hard-liners who wished to stay on strike until the owners made even more concessions. In fact, one member of the media chided Garth Butcher for the union's reluctance to pander to the media the way John Ziegler did.

"All you had to do was inform the media on what the issues were," the *Post's* Tom Wheatley said.

"You don't understand," Butcher responded. "That's not the way you do business."

The two politely argued for a few minutes and then dropped the subject. Good thing, too. The last thing Butcher wanted to do when he came to the rink was start discussing the recently completed negotiations. He'd lived it, breathed it, and eaten it for the last couple of weeks. The bags under his eyes had "strike" written all over them.

"I'm a little burned out," admitted Butcher, who had been on the phone until 3:30 a.m. "It's definitely been a learning experience. You learn how to try and sleep through all this stuff. It's a very intense thing, and it's a very emotional thing."

Brian Sutter couldn't have agreed more. He walked down the ramp and into the rink, wearing his hockey getup for the first time in what probably seemed like ten years instead of ten days. He smiled broadly, thrust his chest out, and quickly skated around the ice like a horse that had just been released from its stable.

"It's great to get going again. I can't express how I feel about that," he said. "This has been very tough. It's devastating for the people that really care. You feel it [when] talking to people who want to come and watch hockey."

Sutter also expressed trepidation about the possibility of injuries. He was very concerned that some of his players might try to do too much too quickly. With a game tomorrow night in Minnesota, Sutter had to be very careful in running practice.

"You don't want to put them into a position where somebody's going to get hurt," he said. "So you try to organize a practice where there's a lot of flow and puck movement and momentum. But at the same time they are going to be into the physical contact tomorrow, so you have to involve that a little bit, too."

Especially worrisome to Sutter was how his injured players would respond. Butcher's broken foot wasn't completely healed so he still wasn't available for duty. Zombo's broken foot was in much better shape, but Sutter wasn't ready to insert him into the lineup just yet. Hull and Joseph, however, the team's top two stars, were finally cleared for action. The two men would be in the lineup against the North Stars, their first contest since falling to injuries in the same Detroit game a month earlier.

"I feel alien in this equipment, let me tell you," Hull said as he was about to take the ice for morning practice. "I'm used to having one glove on my hand."

Hull laughed at his joking reference to his strike pastime, golf, but some players were unamused. During the strike, Hull had showed little interest in what was happening in New York and Toronto, the main sites of negotiations, and some privately criticized Brett for not taking a more active role in the dispute. Wayne Gretzky and Mark Messier, two of the game's biggest ambassadors, were very visible during the last couple of days of the strike. Members on both sides gave Gretzky credit for doing what he could to settle it, though some hard-line players complained that he was instrumental in forcing the union to back off from some of its demands.

Hull just shrugged off the criticism. What could he have done? he asked. His appearance in New York wouldn't have made a bit of difference in the outcome of the strike. Besides, he had no desire to get involved. The only dilemma he wanted to face was whether he should use his 5-wood or 3-iron to clear that creek.

"I have faith in the people in charge or they wouldn't be there," Hull said. "I just stayed clear of it."

For Hull and the rest of the Blues, it was time to get back to the business of just playing hockey. And judging by the smiles and laughter on the ice, this team was more than happy to return to the ice and make a run at the Stanley Cup.

*　　*　　*

The fans made their feelings very clear. They didn't boo. They didn't yell. They didn't utter one profanity. No, the fans did better than that—or worse. They showed apathy, something even more dangerous and contemptuous than a shower of Bronx cheers when the players returned to action. Judging by all the empty seats, many fans were saying they couldn't care less that the season had resumed. Ouch.

Across the league, teams were experiencing season-low crowds when play continued April 12. Barely 11,000 showed up in Toronto to see the Maple Leafs lose to the Islanders. Less than 13,000 bothered to attend the Bruins/Nordiques game at the Boston Garden, the smallest crowd there in four years. There were some 2,000 empty seats in Chicago for the Hawks' matchup with the Red Wings, the first non-sellout in several years. And just 6,500 die-hard fans showed up in Hartford to see the Whalers host the Flyers, the second-smallest crowd in Hartford history!

At the Met Center, an announced crowd of 13,417 attended the Blues/North Stars game. However, you couldn't make too much of that figure. Minnesota had a recent history of fan apathy, so getting more than 13,000 to watch a hockey game there could be seen as a major accomplishment.

The first few minutes of the game were, as expected, slow and uneventful. Like two boxers in the first round, the Blues and North Stars were feeling each other out, just trying to get their legs back in working order without overexerting themselves. In fact, the most exciting part about the early going was seeing the line combinations Sutter was using. To the average fan, that's rarely something to get thrilled about. You won't hear too many champagne bottles being uncorked over a particular line formation. But at the very least, the new-look Blues had to be a pleasing sight to even the most critical Blues fans.

The top line consisted of Brendan Shanahan, Craig Janney, and Brett Hull. It was a combination—substituting Janney for Oates—that fans and media alike had been calling for since Sutter broke them up during the second game of the season. During Hull's absence, Janney and Shanahan played exceptionally well together on the first line, so when the Golden Brett finally returned, Sutter kept them together.

The second line consisted of Nelson Emerson at right wing, Ron Sutter in the middle, and newcomer Denny Felsner patrolling the left side. Felsner was a freshman at the University of Michigan when the Blues drafted him in 1989. Three years later as a senior, Felsner finally signed a contract and immediately reported to the team the day after the strike was settled. If this 21-year-old college phenom was even half as good as scouts promised, he was set to become the second-biggest goal scorer on the team, behind Hull. Felsner had been the top offensive weapon at the college level during the 1991-92 season, with 42 goals and 94 points in only 44 games. He ended his four-year career at Michigan with 261 points in 162 games. His presence on the second line excited St. Louis hockey fanatics.

And on the third line? They're baaaaaack. Yes, the Green Berets were reunited once again. Dave Lowry, Bob Bassen, and Rich Sutter had played together at various times throughout the season, but never for very long stretches. Perhaps, just perhaps, this old checking line could recapture some of its past success and lead the charge into the playoffs.

Of course, the top three line combinations forced a couple of players temporarily out of the picture. It was no surprise that Kelly Chase's stay on the second line proved brief. He would spend the next two games in street clothes and would see virtually no ice time during the playoffs. Philippe Bozon had quickly become a fan favorite, but he was now seeing limited action on the fourth line.

And Dave Christian, hockey's ultimate gypsy, still couldn't find a home on one line. He played in more games during the year than anyone but Jeff Brown and Brendan Shanahan. And yet, he never knew what his role was supposed to be from game to game. For now, Sutter had him on the fourth line with Bozon and Ron Wilson. The Blues were paying Christian $1.76 million over three years, but they had no idea what to do with him. If all they wanted was a guy who could fill a spot role here and there, they certainly could have found a player much cheaper. Someone hadn't done his homework.

With the Blues and North Stars circling one another in the ring, Minnesota drew first blood on Jim Johnson's fourth goal of the year, six-and-a-half minutes into the game. Shanahan tried to clear the puck out of his own end but weakly gave it up to Johnson along the boards. The Minnesota defenseman skated into the right circle and beat Joseph between the pads to give the home team a 1-0 lead.

For the rest of the period, the Blues resorted to their prestrike ritual of frantically chasing the opposition around the rink. It really didn't matter what the offensive combinations were for the

Blues. Defensively, the team just couldn't move the puck out of its own end. Welcome back, Curtis Joseph.

The Stars, firing one shot after another, were averaging nearly one shot per minute late in the first period. But with the Blues short-handed, Hull took a pass off the boards from Wilson and raced as fast as he could toward the other net. From the right circle, Hull ripped a slapper that was stopped by Jon Casey. But the puck rebounded right back to Hull, now at an impossible angle below the circle. Just as he was being tackled from behind by Marc Tinordi, Brett wristed one more shot that mysteriously found its way past Casey and inside the far post. For Hull, it marked the 300th goal and 500th point of his career. Only Wayne Gretzky and Mario Lemieux had reached 300 goals faster.

At the end of twenty minutes, the Blues had managed to hang on for a 1-1 tie. But they had been outshot 16-8, and even that figure was misleading. The Blues fired half their shots in just the last couple of minutes of the period. Hull and Joseph, the two ex-injured stars, didn't look as if they'd missed a beat. Their teammates, however, played as if they were still on the golf course, casually walking the links and deliberating on club selection.

The second and third periods, fortunately, were a different story. The Blues traded in their golf clubs for hockey sticks and started playing with emotion. The Blues' defense finally plugged a few gaps, limiting the Stars to six shots in the second period and ten in the third. Joseph continued to make one spectacular save after another and proved once again that he was the team's most valuable player, even though his exploits went relatively unnoticed outside of St. Louis.

The problem for the Blues, however, was that the Stars' defense, anchored by Jon Casey, proved just as formidable. The Blues managed only 13 shots the final two periods. They had their chances, especially early in the third, when Bassen missed a wide-open net, but they were never able to put any sustained pressure on Casey, and the teams went into overtime tied at one.

The extra five-minute period wasn't exactly what either team wanted after a ten-day layoff. The Blues got the only shot on goal during the overtime, but a slapper by Emerson failed to connect. Each team gained a point for the tie, which meant nothing to the Blues, of course. They were already cemented in third place and were set to start the playoffs in Chicago. It was a different story, though, for Minnesota. The one point clinched a playoff berth for the Stars and eliminated Toronto. The Norris Division playoff schedule was now complete.

"I think a lot of the guys had pretty good jump," said Jeff Brown, who now had only two games left to score his record-breaking 21st goal. "We played a good, solid 60 minutes. We definitely outplayed them the last two periods."

"As the game went on, I felt the team got stronger," observed Ron Sutter. "The play of Curtis Joseph really stood out, and to see Hullie come back and play the way he did was a positive."

As for the newcomer, Denny Felsner didn't exactly turn any heads and was benched for almost the entire third period. But then again, how many players set the league on fire in their first NHL game? For Felsner, it was a learning experience and nothing else.

"I didn't really do anything spectacular," the rookie admitted. "Coach Sutter told me that I need to stick to my wing more and go up and down it. I kind of get mesmerized by the puck sometimes and wander to the center, which is what I did in college. But that's over with. I just have to stick to the wing."

Two nights after tying the North Stars, the Blues were given a preview of their first-round series. The Blackhawks came to town, and each team was primed to send a message to the other. One sign of weakness, and you could bet it would be exploited during the series. Neither team wanted the other to go into the playoffs with added confidence because of something that happened in this game.

Sure enough, the fists were flying early and often. Referee Rob Shick called no fewer than 13 penalties in the first period. The physical play seemed to handcuff the Blues who, like the first period in Minnesota, were pinned in their own end with no room to operate. In fact, the Hawks' Steve Smith scored just 11 seconds into the game, and you had the sinking feeling that a blowout was on tap. That would sure work wonders for the Blues' confidence heading into the playoffs, wouldn't it?

However, after killing a two-man Hawks advantage, the boys in blue turned up the juice and started motoring to the other end of the rink. Using the same line combinations as the previous game, the Blues dominated the last half of the period by working the puck beautifully in the offensive zone. Even the defense, specifically the pairing of Cavallini and Quintal, worked the points to perfection to help sustain pressure. With a little more than three minutes remaining, their hard work paid off.

Cavallini ripped a shot from the left point that was stopped by Eddie Belfour. The puck bounced into the slot, but Bozon was unable to corral it as he was checked from behind. The puck wound up on Quintal's stick at the right point, where he immediately fired another shot on net. Once again, Belfour made the stop, but the results were different. Standing in the slot now was none other than the league's top goal scorer. Hull banged in the rebound to tie it at 1-1.

In the second period, the rough stuff subsided, but so did the fine play the Blues had exhibited late in the first. Once again, the Hawks forechecked the Blues into submission and buzzed Guy Hebert, who was getting his last start of the season. The Hawks outshot the opposition 9-5 in the first ten minutes of the period and took the lead on Smith's second goal of the game.

But once again, the Blues suddenly woke from their funk and returned fire. Rick Zombo caught a Steve Smith clearing pass, faked a shot on net, then passed down low to Shanahan in the slot. Doing a perfect imitation of Hull, Brendan one-timed a shot past Belfour to even the score at two.

Just a minute and a half later, it was Cavallini's turn to fumble the puck. As Paul motored behind his own net, little Tony Hrkac, who is some 35 pounds lighter than Cavallini, bumped the Blues' defenseman off the puck and tried a wrap-around shot on Hebert. Guy was able to stop it, but tough-guy Stu Grimson poked in the rebound to give the Hawks their one-goal lead back.

For Cavallini, it was yet another example of an increasingly disturbing trend of coughing the puck up in his own end. The former all-star seemed to lack the same kind of toughness he had showed in his earlier days with the Blues. The decline in aggressiveness was especially painful for Blues fans to watch, since he had always been one of the most popular players on the team. But even some of the old faithful began to turn on him.

When Rich Sutter tied the score at 3-3 late in the second period, a smattering of boos could be heard when Cavallini's name was announced with the assist. The reaction was shocking, to say the least. St. Louis fans aren't prone to booing one of their own unless they feel he's betrayed them, as in the case of Adam Oates. Cavallini was still trying as hard as he could. He wasn't dogging it. It's just that his mistakes were happening more frequently, and some fans began to voice their dissatisfaction. It was a problem that would reach its apex during the playoffs.

Early in the third period, the 16,181 fans were treated to one of the most magnificent goals they'll ever get the pleasure to witness. This by itself was worth the price of admission. Nelson Emerson, the Blues' prized rookie, dashed out of his own end down the right side. He continued speeding along the boards until he crossed into the Hawks' zone. With a couple of defenders in his way and no teammates to pass it to, Emerson suddenly put on the brakes and spun in a circle, letting Frantisek Kucera fly past him. Emerson then cut to his left, put on the brakes again, and amazingly cut back to his right as if shot from a cannon. With everyone in the building in awe, including the Hawks, Emerson fired a shot that glanced off Kucera's right skate and into the net. The crowd went absolutely bonkers. That one goal was a highlight film by itself. Emerson's speed and grace had electrified the fans on many occasions during the year, but nothing came close to this one. His goal gave the Blues their first lead, and they went on to beat the Hawks 5-3.

"It's just something that happened," Emerson said modestly. "It's important that we use our speed wide. But a lot of times guys are so good, they can cut you off wide, so you have to do something else. I just put the brakes on that time and was fortunate it worked out."

"He lights it up sometimes, eh?" observed Shanahan. "We're always telling him to do that. You'll probably see him do that more often as he gains confidence in the NHL."

While Emerson and others were getting all the attention, Rick Zombo quietly dressed in front of his stall without one member of the media asking him a question. And that was a crying shame. In his first game in exactly a month, Zombo had one of the strongest outings by a Blues defenseman in some time. He was tenacious. He was physical. And he was downright nasty. In other words, he looked like the Rick Zombo that was such a pain in the ass to the Blues when he was skating in Detroit. It was a wonderful sight to see a guy play with such fire around the Blues' net.

"Somebody has to," he said. "We've had a lot of trouble with Norris Division teams. We knew a month ago we were going to play Chicago, and we had to set the tone. Winning tonight really gives us confidence. To find a positive side to the strike, it gave our team an opportunity to rest and heal."

Forty-eight hours later, the Blues ended the regular season with a 5-3 win over the North Stars at the Arena. It was a game of milestones for many of the players. Brett Hull scored his seventieth of the season, becoming only the second player in history, after Gretzky, to score at least that many goals in three consecutive seasons. Dave Christian scored his twentieth goal of the year to become the fifth Blues player to do that this season. It marked the tenth time in his twelve NHL seasons that Christian had netted at least twenty.

As for the rookies, Denny Felsner got his first big league point by assisting on Christian's goal. And Philippe Bozon scored his first career goal early in the second on a two-on-one break with Richie Sutter. As the two men crossed the blue line, Sutter passed the puck to his left to Bozon. Philippe glided toward the net, waited for Jon Casey to commit, then flipped the puck over the Stars' goalie to give the Blues a 2-0 lead. After Bozon jumped into Sutter's arms in celebration, he skated to the bench and slapped gloves with everyone.

"It was nice because I had some good chances the last couple of games and I didn't score," he said. "I had to score one before the season ended."

However, the team's enthusiasm was tempered somewhat by a pair of milestones not reached, a pair that was oddly related. Late in the game, the contest all but wrapped up, the Blues tried desperately to get the puck to Jeff Brown. He needed just one goal to break the all-time Blues record for goals by a defenseman.

However, in their haste to force feed the puck to Brown, they forgot about their good buddy, Curtis Joseph. With 54 seconds left, the Blues were caught making a line change and allowed the Stars to race toward Joseph uncontested. Ulf Dahlen scored, costing Joseph a rare and treasured feat. If that last puck hadn't hit the back of the net, Joseph would have finished the season with a goals-against average of 2.99, the first Blues starting goaltender to finish under 3.00 since Jacques Caron in 1971-72. However, Dahlen's goal left Joseph's mark at 3.01 and left the Blues' head coach in a sour mood.

"It was an absolute horseshit change, and it ended up costing us a goal," Sutter complained. "Him (Joseph) of all people deserved it. That was the personal milestone that you would've liked to see."

"I can imagine," said Brown when informed Sutter wasn't very happy that he was trying so hard to score his 21st. "It's disappointing because Curtis has been there all year. He's done a heck of a job. Maybe we should have beared down a bit more. I was shooting maybe a little more than I should have."

Curtis was extremely diplomatic about the whole thing when pressed for his thoughts. Not one to make a big deal out of anything, Joseph tossed the milestone aside as just a bunch of meaningless numbers.

"I'm not a mathematician or anything. I didn't calculate it up," he said humbly. "The main thing is we won, and Saturday is the real game."

True enough. The Blues had responded well after the strike, gaining five of a possible six points. They were one of only five teams to go unbeaten in three games after the strike. They were going to need that kind of momentum heading into Chicago, a place that had been extremely unkind to the Blues in postseason play over the last 25 years.

As the Blues geared toward the playoffs, a disturbing and somewhat surprising rumor began to circulate around the Arena. Brian Sutter's job was in jeopardy. Just 12 months after winning the NHL Coach of the Year award, Sutter had to prove he was worth keeping. Can a coach really become so bad in one season? Then again, who was the real Brian Sutter? The one who guided the Blues to 105 points the year before? Or the one who couldn't get his team out of neutral this season?

Those were the questions that would have to be answered as the Blues traveled to Chicago. It didn't seem possible, but the man who took over the label of "Mr. Blue" from Barclay Plager was now in danger of being kicked out of St. Louis.

Chapter Eighteen

PLAYOFF BOUND

Stephane Quintal walked up the steep stairs leading from the visitors' locker room to the ice surface. Holding a cup of steaming coffee in his hand, the Blues defenseman gazed around the empty arena and pictured what it would look like in a few hours.

Quintal must have been very successful with his afternoon snooze. His hair was disheveled and his eyes a bit red, as if he had just been rudely awakened from a deep sleep. Brian Sutter soon joined him and began pointing to various sections of the rink as Quintal sipped his java. The Blues head coach had been routinely criticized for burying his young players and not giving them a chance to grow. But this was a scene that most people never got a chance to witness. The mentor was patiently teaching the student. There was no yelling. No words of anger. No evil stares. Just a one-on-one conversation conducted without an audience.

After visiting for a few minutes, the two men slowly turned away from the ice and made their way back down the stairs and into the locker room. It was 5:45 p.m., just an hour and fifty minutes before the start of Game 1 between the Blues and Blackhawks.

Brian looked remarkably calm, considering all the pressure that was being put on him to win. The word was out. Win or you're gone. Blues management had not released an official statement on the matter, but rumors and speculation strongly suggested that the winningest coach in team history would be looking for employment elsewhere if he couldn't get past Chicago in the first round of the playoffs. Sutter had proven his merit as a regular-season coach. But his postseason record was mediocre; he had never gotten past the second round of the playoffs in his first three years at the helm. And in the game of hockey, where a team is judged only by what it does in April and May, Sutter's résumé wasn't enough to save his job. He HAD to beat the Hawks. Period.

No question, the odds were stacked against Brian. Not only was he going up against the Hawks, a team the Blues had beaten in the playoffs only once in their history, but Sutter had other problems to contend with as April 18 rolled around. Perhaps the most disturbing involved Craig Janney. The Blues center, unlike most of his teammates, had not kept himself in shape during the strike. He huffed and puffed his way through the first two regular-season games when the season resumed. He failed to tally a single point in those contests, the first time that Janney was scoreless in consecutive games as a member of the Blues. Sutter did him a favor in the season finale and sent him to the press box instead of the ice. Janney had a reputation in Boston of choking in the playoffs. Was it deserved? We'd soon find out.

The other problem Sutter had to deal with concerned his injured captain, Garth Butcher. His broken foot was healed, and doctors had cleared Butcher to play, but that didn't necessarily mean he'd jump right into action. Over the last several weeks, Garth had given 100 percent of his time and effort to his player rep duties. Was he fit to return? Would it take him a few games to get back into the swing of things? The Blues had to have a healthy Garth Butcher to have any chance at getting past the Hawks.

As Wayne Messmer sang the national anthem, a truly inspiring performance that motivates every fan in the joint to yell and scream with every note, I began to think back on the Blues' recent history here in old Chicago Stadium. And I cringed. Time after time, it seemed, the Blues would become frazzled in the early going and find themselves a couple of goals down before they even got their bearings. The worst thing a visiting team can do in this building is let the fans get involved in the game from the very first drop of the puck. If the Blues were to have any chance, and I mean ANY chance, they had to take the crowd out of it. They didn't necessarily have to score a goal right away. They just had to play responsible hockey and keep the Hawks off the scoreboard the first few minutes of the game. If not, you could kiss this baby good-bye.

Right away, it became apparent that Brian Sutter was up to a few tricks. Instead of keeping it simple, it seemed as if he would try to out-think and out-coach Mike Keenan. The first line Sutter threw out there had Ron Sutter centering Dave Lowry and Brendan Shanahan. Excuse me, but how many times had we seen this combination? Twice? Once? Never?

But before the fans and media could figure out what was going on, the second line took on an even stranger appearance. Bob Bassen was on the left wing. Okay, that's fine. Ron Wilson in the middle. Sure, we can buy that. And Brett Hull on right wing. WHAT? The league's top goal scorer was playing with two checkers? The collective cry around St. Louis was that Brian Sutter had finally lost his marbles. But the fans hadn't seen nothin' yet.

The third line consisted of Craig Janney in between Philippe Bozon and Rich Sutter. All right. Where was the hidden camera? This was a joke, right? Was Alan Funt going to suddenly appear on the ice? Here we had a finesse player, Janney, in between two physical players who didn't exactly show a penchant for scoring goals. And that's where Janney's talent lay: feeding a guy who could put the puck in the back of the net.

Finally, the fourth line seemed to prove Sutter had gone off the deep end. Dave Christian was on the left side and Darin Kimble on the right. Fair enough. Many fans thought Christian deserved a more prominent role, but they had grown accustomed to seeing him shifted from one position to the next. This was nothing new. But the shocking figure on this line was Nelson Emerson at center. To many observers, Sutter had gone too far. Hiding Emerson on the fourth line was akin to making Ray Lankford the bullpen catcher.

The defensive pairings yielded no surprises. Paul Cavallini was teamed with Rick Zombo, Jeff Brown with Stephane Quintal, and Murray Baron with Curt Giles. In other words, rookie Bret Hedican was sitting, and Garth Butcher still wasn't ready. Not a good sign.

But just as everybody was set to drive down to the Arena and protest the offensive combinations, a groan suddenly filled

Chicago Stadium. The nomadic Christian one-timed a slapshot from the slot that clanked off the crossbar and in. Just three-and a-half minutes into the contest, the Blues had a 1-0 lead. The visitors had played it beautifully, scoring the game's first goal and forcing the more than 17,000 fans to sit on their hands.

The expected Chicago onslaught never came. Instead of forechecking the Blues into coughing up the puck, the Hawks appeared out of rhythm. Missing was the aggressive pursuit that makes them almost unstoppable on their small ice surface. Their lack of intensity allowed the Blues to escape to the locker room at the first intermission with a one-goal lead and a 9-7 advantage in shots on goal. The impossible had happened. Using a variety of unexpected line combinations, the Blues had come here and outplayed the Blackhawks the first twenty minutes. Perhaps no one was giving Brian Sutter the credit he deserved.

"C'mon!" one fan shouted as the two teams skated off the ice. Even a few boos could be heard throughout the stadium. The Blues were in a perfect position to pull the upset now. They had the lead and had effectively taken the crowd out of the game.

The Blues continued to play sound hockey in the second period. The Hawks finally woke from their slumber and started to pressure Curtis Joseph, but for the most part, the Blues were able to move the puck out of their own end with little trouble. In fact, the boys from St. Louis had several opportunities to add to their lead. Bozon hit a post. So did Brown. Shanahan appeared to have a sure goal until Ed Belfour made a spectacular glove save. It's unfortunate one of those shots didn't light the red lamp. The Blues would need it.

Right after Shanahan missed his golden opportunity, the Blues turned the puck over in the neutral zone when Janney's pass to Brown hopped over his stick. Steve Smith grabbed it and poked it ahead to Mike Hudson, who broke into the Blues' zone. Hudson quickly passed it over to Brian Noonan, who headed straight at Joseph. With Christian draped over him like a tight-fitting suit, Noonan managed to flip the puck under Joseph's right armpit to tie the score with under five minutes to play in the second period.

Chicago Stadium's loud and obnoxious horn sounded and the fans broke into bedlam. The crowd was now back in it. And as expected, its deafening roar finally kicked the Hawks into action. They began dumping it into the offensive zone and forechecking the Blues with precision hits in the corners. The Blues, so effective in getting the puck out the entire game, suddenly had no idea how to move that piece of rubber. The Hawks continued to pressure until scoring the go-ahead goal with just 37 seconds remaining in the period. Steve Smith retrieved a loose puck at the left point, skated toward the middle, and fired a shot wide to the left of Joseph. The puck bounced off the endboards right to Chris Chelios near the post. The Hawks' defenseman tried to flip the puck over Joseph but instead poked it right into his chest. However, Jocelyn Lemieux, while being knocked to the ice by Giles, managed to backhand the rebound just inside the far post to put Chicago up 2-1.

There went that obnoxious noise again. It's actually a fog-horn off an old ship built by a now-defunct company in Wisconsin. After every Hawks' goal, a man sitting next to the penalty box presses a button to turn on the foghorn. The sound, which blares through a set of speakers below the scoreboard, is so deep and loud it echoes through the bottom of your gut, rattling every rib and internal organ. To a visitor, it makes you want to vomit. To a local, it's music to the ears. And in this particular case, it symbolized the home team's first lead of the game.

The Blackhawks rode the momentum into the third period. With just thirty seconds gone in the final frame, Noonan scored his second goal of the game, sweeping in a loose puck near the left post. The ear-splitting horn shot through the Stadium and sent the crowd into a frenzy again. It was so darned frustrating to see how this game had turned in just a matter of minutes. The Blues dominated play the first 35 minutes but found themselves down by two goals five-and-a-half minutes later.

The teams traded quality scoring chances the remainder of the period, both Joseph and Belfour kicking out one shot after another. The third period turned out to be a classic, as the Blues and Hawks took turns pressuring the opposite net, but neither side could sneak the puck past the goal line. Chicago held on to beat the Blues 3-1 and take a 1-0 lead in games. St. Louis had played well enough to win. But you just can't give up goals at the beginning and end of periods and expect to come out on top. Especially in Chicago, where the crowd plays such an important role in mood swings.

"The fans got back into it in the second period, and we got caught standing back and watching a little bit too much," said

Ron Sutter. "But we know we can win here. We just have to come back Monday with the same attitude we started tonight with."

The Blues were left to ponder what might have been. What if one of those shots that hit the post in the second period had gone in? The Blues would likely be ahead in the series instead of Chicago.

"There was that five-minute span where we hit the post twice and I kind of put that one into his glove," Shanahan said. "Eddie made a big save. You never know what it'd be like if one or two of those go in. We've just got to remain positive. We're still confident."

"Bozon hits a post, Brown hits a post, and Eddie makes a big save on Shanahan," observed Coach Sutter. "Right after that, we turn the puck over in the neutral zone and the score is 1-1. They got the jump back, the flow going back their own way again."

Now the Blues had to get that flow going back THEIR way again. Two nights later, Sutter still juggling the lines to keep the Hawks off-balance, the Blues visited Chicago Stadium again in hopes of evening the series. The only major change for the Blues came on defense, the pairing of Giles and Baron replaced by Hedican and Butcher. Yep, Garth reclaimed the "C" from Hull and took to the ice to bang heads for the first time in 44 days.

As for Hedican, he was getting his first taste of a playoff atmosphere. Sutter was looking for a little extra speed to move the puck up-ice, and Hedican had the capability of doing that. The only question was, did the rookie have the mental toughness to succeed in his first NHL playoff game? If he could play a strong game tonight, then this kid just might be for real.

The Blues were in a confident mood before the game. Even though they had lost two nights earlier, they had been able to dictate the flow of the game—except for a small stretch at the end of the second period and the beginning of the third. The team was brash and bold as it skated onto the ice to begin Game 2.

"The guys are really loose," observed trainer Mike Folga. "They're confident they're going to win this thing."

They gained even more confidence 93 seconds into the contest. With the Blues on the power play, the Hawks were caught too deep on a short-handed rush. Janney quickly controlled the puck and moved it the other way. Just as he crossed the blue line and was hit by Bryan Marchment, he slid the puck to his right where Quintal grabbed it and quickly shot it on net. Eddie Belfour must have been trapped in his cocoon because his butterfly move was a split-second too late to stop Quintal's shot from going between his legs. Just like 48 hours before, the Blues had taken the crowd out of the game by scoring the first goal early.

However, just a minute later, Nelson Emerson was ejected from the game for cutting Chris Chelios with a high-stick. (Chelios probably deserved it, but I guess it's still against the rules). Chelios, one of the league's ultimate competitors and a guy opposing fans hate with a passion, made the Blues pay for the bloody lip he was now sporting. Given a five-minute power play on Emerson's penalty, Chelios scored twice in less than a minute and a half to give Chicago a 2-1 lead.

That damn horn blared away and an arena full of black and red-clad fans erupted in celebration. Even George Wendt, the actor who plays Norm on "Cheers," was clapping away between sips of his beer and bites on his bratwurst. The raucous crowd was back in it. But not for long.

With Marchment in the penalty box for tripping Hull, Janney, who was playing his best game since before the strike, went behind the net to fetch the puck and quickly backhanded it to Ron Sutter at the left faceoff dot. Sutter immediately slapped it over Belfour's left shoulder to even the score at 2-2. It wasn't a difficult shot to handle by any means. Belfour seemed to be struggling in the early going, which was great news for the Blues.

What wasn't such great news was the Blackhawks' goal late in the period. Keith Brown dumped the puck in from the neutral zone, sending it flying to the right of Joseph. The puck came out hard off the endboards directly to Tony Horacek, who ripped a one-timer past a startled Joseph. It was the first even-strength goal in a period that saw 37 minutes in penalties. It was difficult for either team to implement any kind of a game plan with so many power-plays.

The second period started off much the same. Just four-and-a-half minutes had ticked away when Butcher was caught for holding. It was one of three penalties called on the Blues captain on the night. He was obviously trying to play the role of the intimidator, hoping he still had it after missing so much time. Perhaps he just pretended every Blackhawk looked like John Ziegler.

With the Hawks pressuring on the power play, Cavallini managed to gain control of the puck and tip it out of his own end. Steve Smith, hanging out in the neutral zone, appeared to have a bead on it. But as he casually skated toward the puck, he was beaten to it by Hull, who tipped it past Smith and off the boards. Hull then danced around the Hawks' defenseman and scooted alone down the right side. As he entered the circle, Hull snapped a shot that whizzed past Belfour to tie the score at 3-3. Once again, a "normal" Belfour probably would have made the save. But not on this night.

Later in the period, the Hawks did everything but put the puck across the line. With Shanahan off for roughing, Chicago blitzed the Blues' net with a continuous barrage of shots. Joseph the stick save. Joseph the pad save. Joseph the glove save. Curtis proved he was up to the challenge. Were his teammates?

You bet. Just a minute after Shanahan's penalty expired, Jeff Brown sneaked into the right circle, took a pass from Bassen, and slapped a shot over Belfour's left shoulder to give the Blues a 4-3 lead with a little more than three minutes left in the period. Belfour, like Joseph, had a reputation for falling to his knees with each shot, and the Blues were exploiting that. Three of the four Blues goals were directed at the upper half of the net.

Barely a minute later, Belfour was knocked to the ice during a scramble around his net. He didn't seem to be seriously hurt, but he just lay there with his legs and arms spread out. As he stood up, he was face-to-face with his replacement, Dominik Hasek. Did Mike Keenan assume Belfour was hurt and promptly push Hasek to the ice? No, but it didn't matter. It was a perfect excuse to yank Belfour. Eddie "the Eagle" had looked awful, and it was time for him to take a seat on the bench.

The third period turned into a battle of the goaltenders. Hasek was so sharp, it looked as though he had been playing every game. He stopped Hull three times in the first six minutes. At the other end of the rink, Joseph was matching Hasek save for save. There were 27 shots on goal during the final period, and only one turned the red lamp on. Fortunately, it didn't also turn the horn on. Dave Christian scored an empty-net goal to seal the Blues' victory, a 5-3 win that evened the series at one game apiece.

The fans groaned and started to file out slowly, heads down, probably because their frowns were so heavy. One of the few groups of people still left in the stands was the Blues' contingent of scratched players that included Pat Jablonski, Murray Baron, Curt Giles, and Kelly Chase. Nelson Emerson had joined them after being tossed from the game in the first period.

Chase somehow drew the ire of one fan who couldn't deal with the fact that his team had been beaten. The kind of fan who would contemplate suicide because there seemed to be no reason to continue breathing after watching his heroes lose. The guy didn't appear to be drunk. He just looked like a real fruit loop.

"You're a zero, Chase!" the fan yelled from a couple of rows away. "You have zero talent! You're outta here next year! You got me?! You're a big, fat zero!"

Chase just looked at the guy and smiled. But as the fan continued heckling the Blues' boxer, Chase couldn't let it go any longer. He climbed down a few rows and started to walk right toward the fan.

Oh, no. Please don't let it happen. I thought Kelly Chase had more intelligence than this. He was going to start something with this guy and probably punch his lights out. As some of his teammates looked on, Chase walked within a foot of the fan, stepped down another row and continued walking down toward the ice, where he eventually disappeared to the locker room.

Whew! That sigh of relief wasn't from me. It came from the suddenly quiet loudmouth. As Chase approached him, the fan obviously forgot what to say. He just watched Kelly walk toward him, probably praying that he hadn't gotten himself in too deep. With that, the rest of the Blues filed out, as did the heckler. Just another night at the old ice rink.

As expected, the Blues were in a jovial mood after the game. Not only had they beaten the Hawks in their own building when nobody gave them a chance, but they were now heading home for the first time during the playoffs. The Blues had effectively taken the home-ice advantage away from Chicago. They had three of the final five games scheduled at the Arena.

"We feel very good," admitted Hull. "We played very well, especially after losing a key player like Nelson Emerson in the first few minutes of the game."

Hull was showing another sign of his continued growth as a leader. For the second game in a row, he was teamed with a couple of checkers, this time Bassen and Ron Sutter. Hull wasn't getting a lot of great scoring chances as he might expect with

Janney. But he wasn't sulking. He wasn't complaining. He wasn't questioning Sutter's decision making. At least not publicly.

"That's what Sudsie's been teaching me over the last few years," Hull said. "You can't get upset. You can't get frustrated. You can't get uptight. You've got to go out and play. There are certain times when you don't score, but as long as I'm not getting scored against and I'm working hard and I'm doing the things I'm supposed to be doing, the puck's going to get into the open, and I'm going to put it in."

Now the Blues were in command. But don't tell Brian Sutter that. The last thing he wanted to hear was how the Blues were now in the driver's seat. What if his team was able to win Game 3 at home and take a lead in the series? Don't even think it.

"Somebody might run over me after the third game when I'm walking out of the parking lot," said Sutter, displaying rare postgame jocularity. "If you look ahead of yourself, something tends to jump up and kick you where the sun don't shine. We're going back to win the third game at home. We'll look at the fourth game when it comes."

Sutter's opposing head coach was in a completely opposite mood. No surprises there.

"Here comes your highness," quipped one reporter as Mike Keenan approached the podium to answer questions.

How would you assess your performance tonight?

"You don't even have to ask that question, do you?" snapped Keenan.

I know what I think. I want to know what you think.

"I think the same as you."

Oooh, boy, this was fun. Sutter could sometimes be argumentative following a tough loss. But so could Keenan, as I was learning. The banter with reporters continued.

You've lost home-ice advantage now. How tough...

"I can't hear your questions," responded Keenan, peering into the bright lights.

Mike, do you feel you dominated...

"I can't hear you!"

I couldn't help but snicker while this was going on. Keenan very well may have had trouble picking up questions from the back of the room, but there was no doubt he was irritated as hell that he even had to be there in the first place. He was very frustrated with his team's performance. His two biggest offensive stars, Jeremy Roenick and Steve Larmer, had only one point between them in the series, an assist by Roenick in Game 2. Why were they a non-factor?

"You'll have to ask them that," Keenan answered. "We mixed the lines tonight to get somebody to put the puck in the net."

Many of the Blues remarked how the Hawks just didn't seem as aggressive as they had during the regular season. They lacked the fire and intensity that had been their trademark under Keenan the last four seasons. But after the first two games of this playoff series, it was obvious that something was bothering the Blackhawks.

"They're dogging it," said one Blues' player. The innuendo was clear. Some of the Hawks didn't seem to give a hoot about advancing past the first round. Like Sutter, there was speculation that Keenan would be ousted from his head coaching position if his team didn't have some success in the playoffs. And because Keenan was despised by a number of his players, rumor was that an internal coup was being hatched to make sure Keenan wouldn't be around next season.

That line of thinking was probably off-base. According to some Blues players, most professional athletes will tell you it's next to impossible to intentionally stop playing because of some ulterior motive. There's too much pride at stake. A player may not like his coach, but that's no excuse to roll over and quit performing.

But on the other hand, athletes can be beaten up so often that there's nothing left to give anymore. And that's what some of Keenan's ex-players in Philadelphia and Chicago had complained about in the past. They didn't purposely dog it. It was just difficult to get motivated anymore when a guy was screaming at their every move and not showing SOME sign of respect for his players.

Was that starting to happen with this Blackhawks team? Were they beginning to wear down under the weight of their head coach? If so, it couldn't have come at a better time for the Blues. They were heading back home with the series tied at 1-1, a wonderful opportunity to take the lead against a team that seemed uninspired.

*   *   *

Paul Cavallini was in a rage. He had just been informed of some very troubling news and he couldn't believe it. Cavallini dashed into Brian Sutter's office and, according to insiders, heated words were exchanged. Few players would dare to confront Sutter in this manner, but Cavallini obviously felt he had nothing to lose. Someone inside the locker room, and not one of the coaches, had just told the Blues defenseman that he was being scratched for Game 3 tonight at the Arena. And he had to hear it from the top man himself.

Sure enough, the former all-star defenseman was told his services were not needed tonight. For the first time in his career, Paul Cavallini would sit out during a playoff game. And it wasn't because he was injured, as Sutter tried to tell the *Post's* Dave Luecking. The reason was simple and everyone knew it. Sutter, like many people, had been unhappy with Cavallini's play, and it was time to give someone else a chance to strut his stuff. Cavallini was out. Giles was back in.

The move wasn't entirely displeasing to Blues fans, either. When the scratches were announced just minutes before the game, a small cheer erupted at Cavallini's name. It was unbelievable that he had fallen this far in the eyes of his ex-supporters. One could only imagine the pain Cavallini, an extremely sensitive individual, was going through watching his teammates skate around the ice. This had to be the low point of his NHL career.

With a few minor adjustments here and there, the line combinations were much the same for Game 3. And just like the previous contest, the Blues didn't get much of a chance to use them early on because of a multitude of penalties. The first one came after only 63 seconds, and it started with a beauty of a hit on Chelios. The Hawks' agitator skated into the corner to retrieve a loose puck. But trailing his every step were Brendan Shanahan and Philippe Bozon. As soon as Chelios touched the puck, the two Blues simultaneously leveled him against the boards. Chelios had been double-teamed, an extra bang for the buck. The hits were clean, but they were so devastating, you knew the Hawks weren't going to take them without a fight.

Sure enough, Brent Sutter went after Shanahan, and several other players paired off as the Hawks objected to the check on Chelios. When order was restored, three Blackhawks were tossed into the penalty box for roughing, as were two Blues,

Shanahan and Ron Sutter. That gave the Blues a power play, and they didn't waste it, pumping a goal past Dominik Hasek, who had started the game in place of Belfour.

Ron Wilson won a faceoff in the Chicago zone and kicked it back to Giles at the left point. His shot missed to the right of the net and caromed off the endboards to Jeff Brown at the right point. Brown fired a shot straight at the net, but before the puck got to its destination, Hull, who had positioned himself between Brown and Hasek, deflected the shot with his skate to Nelson Emerson, standing atop the left post. The Blues rookie scored his first NHL playoff goal by slapping the puck into the open left side of the net. Once again, the Blues had taken the early lead.

Still looking for revenge on the earlier hit, Chelios rammed Emerson against the sideboards just seconds after the puck was dropped at center ice. Just as the Hawks did for Chelios, the Blues came to Emerson's aid, and here we went again. Lowry and Noonan were given four minutes each for spearing, while Rich Sutter was sent to the box for unsportsmanlike conduct. Chicago now had the power play but was unable to connect.

Perhaps their ineffectiveness with the extra man made the Hawks especially ornery. At 7:31 of the first period, Mike Peluso was called for charging, and just thirty seconds later, Roenick was whistled for hooking. The Blues now had two extra men, which made Hawks coach Mike Keenan decide to switch goaltenders. Inexplicably, he yanked Hasek and sent in Belfour, perhaps thinking his star goaltender had a better chance of stopping the Blues' extra attackers.

Sorry, it didn't work. Nelson Emerson made Keenan pay with one of the prettiest goals of the series. Emerson controlled the puck at the left point, sizing up the situation. He passed it over to Brown on the right side, who immediately sent it down to Hull in the left circle. The Golden One skated toward the net, drawing everyone and his brother toward him. Instead of shooting, Brett passed across to Janny in the right circle, where he quickly sent it back to Emerson, now stationed above the left circle. With Shanahan and Steve Smith fighting one another for position inside, Emerson ripped a shot that flew into the upper right corner to give the Blues a 2-0 lead. The entire play lasted only a few seconds. It was bang, bang, bang, bang. Crisp, on-target passes. It was the kind of power-play goal that coaches diagram on chalkboards. Out came Belfour and in went Hasek. Mike's strategy obviously hadn't worked.

Forgive the fans—and yes, some members of the media, cough-cough— for starting to picture a Stanley Cup banner hanging from the rafters. Let's see, where would it go? Down by the jerseys that had been retired? Nah, leave those alone. Up with the divisional champ banners? No, too cluttered. This one had to stand out alone. How about right in the middle, hanging just above the scoreboard? Yeah, that'd be great. I mean, wasn't it in the bag now? The Blues were well on their way to taking the lead in the series. And everyone figured if the homeboys could get past the Hawks, then the rest was downhill. Just beat those guys, and Lord Stanley, here we come.

Meanwhile, with such giddiness enveloping our souls, we watched Keenan go bonkers right before our very eyes. The man had finally lost it. They needed to fit him with a straightjacket and take him away. Just because he had changed goalies twice didn't mean he was finished. No, no, no. Not by a long shot. Just 37 seconds after his second switcharoo, Keenan tried it again. With a faceoff in the Hawks' zone and the Blues once again with a two-man advantage, Belfour changed scenery with Hasek one more time. Twenty-two seconds later, and the Blues now down to a one-man advantage, Keenan played musical goaltenders for the fourth time. Belfour to the bench. Hasek to the net. This was getting a bit ridiculous. The Blues were starting to complain that Mike Keenan was causing delays in the game and should be called for a bench minor.

"The referee is in control there," said Coach Sutter. "He let them go a little bit. There's supposed to be a time limit on changes."

"I thought we were getting the bad end of things, the tough end of the things," explained Keenan, hinting at HIS frustration with the officiating. "I mean, the whole thing was initiated with the two guys running Chelios with the high-stick, and there was no call. From that point on, it just deteriorated. It was unfair, to tell you the truth."

But you know what? Keenan's plan worked to perfection. It didn't matter so much who was in the net. He just wanted to take the momentum away from the Blues. They were up 2-0 and had a two-man advantage before the first half of the period was even finished. Facing the possibility of a blowout, Keenan had to find some way to slow the game down and turn attention away from the scoreboard. By making a mockery of his goaltenders, he would take the wind out of the Blues' sails. His diabolical scheme worked.

With the snap of a finger, the Blackhawks scored three unanswered goals in a seven-minute span to take a 3-2 lead after the first period. All three came on the power play as the Blues— and the Hawks, for that matter— continued to take stupid penalties. There was no flow in the game's first 20 minutes. Each team took turns on the power play, pelting the opposing goalie with shots. Joseph faced 18, and the tag-team duo of Hasek and Belfour 15, and all five goals came on the power play. After just one period, the Blackhawks were just one away from tying the most power-play goals scored against the Blues in a playoff game. Mike Keenan had gone from joke to genius.

Since the Hawks seemed to have so much trouble moving the puck with the teams at even strength, it seemed the worst thing the Blues could do was take penalties. Stay out of the bad boy's box, and you have it made. Roenick had scored on the power play, but he, Larmer, and the rest of their mates were still finding it difficult to operate when the penalty box was empty.

Ooops. Spoke too soon. Just 42 seconds into the second period, Shanahan made a bad pass to Bozon as the Blues were starting to rush up-ice. Mike Hudson picked off the puck and backhanded it to Dirk Graham, who skated in between the circles and shot it past Joseph. The even-strength goal gave Chicago a 4-2 lead. The Hawks had scored four goals in exactly eight minutes of play.

The Blues got back-to-back power-play opportunities after Graham's goal, but they couldn't cash in. As the second period started to wind to a close, it looked as though the Blues would have a tough time coming back to win this thing. Both sides had started to play defensive, playoff-style hockey, cutting down the number of scoring chances. After 33 shots in the first period, the two teams combined for only 15 in the second. If the third period was even remotely similar, it didn't seem likely the Blues could sneak two goals past Hasek.

As it turned out, they didn't have to. With under a minute left to play in the period, Rick Zombo raced behind his own net to retrieve the puck that Noonan had dumped back there. With Jocelyn Lemieux breathing down his neck, Zombo put on a beautiful spin move and evaded the Hawks forward. As he started out of his own end, Zombo lost the puck for a split-second as it hit the back of Christian's skate. Fortunately, Giles was playing prevent defense. He scooped up the puck and gave it right back to Zombo, who continued his journey to the other end of the ice. He maneuvered his way through the neutral zone and across the blue line down the right side. This guy looked like Emerson all of a sudden. As a couple of Hawks converged on Zombo, he flipped it over Igor Kravchuk's stick and ahead to Christian, who had quietly sneaked behind the defense. Christian raced across the front of the net and backhanded the puck between Hasek's legs to cut the lead to one.

What an enormously important goal that was. Instead of starting the third period down by two goals, the Blues were now faced with only a one-goal deficit. It didn't matter how tight and cramped the quarters were out there. Anything could happen now that the Blues were down by just a single tally.

As expected, the third period was similar to the second, each team trying to bottle up the other. It was terrific strategy for the Hawks, but not necessarily for the Blues. They still had to score a goal. So in an effort to create a little offense, Sutter put his number-one line back together halfway through the period. It was the first time in the series Shanahan, Janney, and Hull had skated on the ice at the same time. Right after that, the checking line of Lowry, Wilson, and Rich Sutter banged a few bodies before giving way to the second scoring line of Christian, Ron Sutter and Emerson. Finally, the Blues were looking more like themselves. And you know what? It paid immediate dividends.

Hull did an imitation of Zombo and motored from end to end with the puck. As Hull entered into the Chicago zone, Kravchuk poked the puck away, but Emerson, who had just replaced Janney, scooped it up and quickly fed Butcher, who had pinched in on the right side. The Blues captain slapped a shot under Hasek, and the game was knotted at 4-4.

The rest of the contest was a classic. One for the ages. One that everyone will brag that they were there that night. Sometime in the future, somebody will conduct a poll and find out that the Arena amazingly had 120,000 people there that night. But that's all right. Millions of people also claim they were at Woodstock.

The last seven minutes was fingernail-biting time. With the fans on the edge of their seats, teams took turns racing up and down the ice to try to win this game in regulation. To their credit, the Blues and Blackhawks played exceptional defense to limit the scoring opportunities. No one on the ice wanted to be blamed for making a last-minute blunder that cost the game. Remember, whoever won this contest took a 2-1 lead and control of the series. The stakes were much too high to take an unnecessary chance offensively.

With just seven seconds left in the game, the Blues had one last chance at putting the puck in the net. Many of the fans stood on their feet as Ron Sutter and his older brother Brent crouched around the faceoff dot in the Hawks' zone. Ronnie had been having quite a bit of success against his sibling, so it seemed likely the Blues could gain control of the puck for one last shot on net.

Everyone's heart must have been beating a mile a minute. The linesman stood over the pair and dropped the puck. The Sutters' sticks chopped down on the ice and frantically searched for control. Brent was able to fight off Ronnie for the puck, but the Blues got it right back. As the clock ticked down, five...four...three...the Blues desperately worked the puck around but were unable to get a quality shot away...two...one. The horn sounded, the fans fell back into the seats, and the players skated off the ice for intermission. Unlike the regular season, teams get a full 15-minute break between the third period and overtime, since they play a full 20 minutes in OT instead of just five.

During intermission, I ran into Paul Cavallini and Pat Jablonski standing outside their box near press row.

"Well, who's it going to be?" I asked the pair.

"Hullie," answered Jablonski. "It's got to be Hullie."

"I'm going with Zombo," said Paul. "He's going to do it."

Jablonski didn't go out on much of a limb predicting Brett would score the winning goal, but Cavallini sure did. I actually hoped he'd be right. A guy like Zombo certainly deserved to be a hero in a situation like this. I'm always rooting for the hard-working players who never get much recognition in their careers. That's why it had been such a treat to watch a guy like Lee Norwood score the game-winning goal in overtime in his first game with the Blues back in November.

Near the end of the break, KMOX's Randy Karraker walked down press row asking everyone if they wanted in on the overtime pool. Throw in a buck and pull a name out of a hat. If your guy scores the winning goal, the money's yours.

Not about to turn down the chance to earn a few extra greenbacks, I tossed in a dollar and stuck my hand in the hat. I circled my fingers around as if that would magically help me pull out Hull's name. I grabbed a slip of paper, opened it up, and it read "Larmer."

Oh, man. Talk about mixed emotions. Obviously, I wanted the Blues to win this thing. But suddenly $35 was on the line. I guess if the Hawks had to win it, Larmer might as well pump in the winning goal. I had a deep sense of guilt even thinking like that. That is, until I realized I had given my last buck away. C'mon, Larmer. You can do it!

During the overtime, it didn't look like anyone would score. Once again, the teams opted for a defensive approach. Neither side was going to take stupid chances venturing too far into the offensive zone while leaving their backsides exposed. There was always at least one defenseman back to cause interference. Someone would eventually win this game, but it wouldn't be on a breakaway.

After the first five minutes, only one puck had been directed at the net, and it belonged to Chicago. Amazing. Whoever had the puck was immediately smothered. There was more breathing room in a sardine can. The two sides were bottling up quicker than an assembly line at an Anheuser-Busch plant. The Blues' first shot finally came at 5:30 of the extra period, when Hasek made a glove save on Hull. The Hawks came right back, and Joseph stuck out his mitt to rob Dirk Graham. Where was Larmer, for heaven's sake?

Halfway through the OT, the game started to open up a bit. We would have been there all night at the current pace, so the teams started to take a few extra chances. Quintal skated in, rifled a shot, and CLANK—hit the post. Awwwww, the fans groaned. The loudest yell came from a guy in the press box. He obviously had drawn Quintal.

Then, with four-and-a-half minutes left, Brett Hull skated around a defenseman and headed toward the net. This was it. Jablonski would be right. Whoever had picked Hull was about to count his money. With a Hawk perched on his back, Hull managed to poke a shot at the net, but Hasek kicked it out. Bassen was right there for the rebound, but he was unable to put the puck at the net.   The ole' heart couldn't take too much more of this.

The first overtime ended without a winner being declared. It was back to the dressing room for yet another 15-minute intermission. Reporters hurriedly scanned the record book for the last time the Blues had gone into double-overtime. There it was in fine print, and who could forget it? Back on April 7, 1984, the Blues beat Detroit with under three minutes remaining in double-OT, the longest game in franchise history. Interestingly, the Blues would clinch that series two nights later by winning another overtime game. However, they were ousted in the second round by the North Stars. How did it happen? Yep, Minnesota eliminated the Blues in the seventh and deciding game by winning 4-3. In overtime.

As the extra-extra period started, most of the fans were still in attendance. It was exactly 12 minutes before midnight, but who wanted to tell their co-workers the next day they walked out of the game before it was over? No matter if this became the first triple- or even quadruple-overtime in Blues' history, these fans wanted a chance to brag about it the next day. Who knows? If the game went long enough, the fans could leave the Arena, drop the kids off at school and head straight to work.

The first couple of minutes looked good for the Blues. Shanahan whacked a shot from the right circle right into Hasek's chest. In the first 150 seconds of play, the Blues fired three shots at the Hawks' net and were dominating early play. That made it even more exciting for the fans. The Blues appeared to be on the brink of a dramatic, double-overtime playoff victory. You could just feel it. The Blues were aggressive. The Hawks seemed tentative. If the world was a just place, the Bluenotes would leave the building victorious.

With a little more than three minutes gone in the period, Chicago's Stephane Matteau lazily skated out of his own end with the puck and into the neutral zone. Dave Lowry caught him from behind and wrapped his stick around Matteau's midsection, taking him off the puck and into the boards. Butcher picked up the piece of rubber and skated back to his zone so his teammates could get in position to work a play. The Blues captain passed it ahead to the rookie, Bret Hedican, who tried to dump it in. However, the puck hit Chelios and ricocheted to Ron Sutter, who was stationed along the far boards, right on top of the blue line. Sutter passed it all the way across the ice to Bob Bassen, who only had one defenseman in front of him.

As the fans started to jump to their feet again, Bassen felt the presence of a big stick over his left shoulder. Fortunately, it was a friendly stick, resting comfortably in the hands of a guy named Brett Hull, who had just jumped to the ice on a line change. Bassen knew what he had to do with the puck. Without even acknowledging his teammate, Bassen dropped the puck back for No. 16 to work his magic.

Every sports fan in the world remembers those special games he witnessed in person. He was actually in the stands that day, watching the classic consequences unfold. I'll never forget, as a 15-year-old, watching Bob Forsch throw the first of his two no-hitters on a rainy spring day in 1978. Or how in 1982, Mizzou upset Oklahoma 10-0, at Faurot Field, prompting thousands of wild-eyed college students to tear down the goal-posts. Little did I know when I came to the Arena on this particular night, I would add another great sports moment to my memory banks.

Hull put the puck on the end of his stick and made a beeline for Dominik Hasek. The poor guy never had a chance. The only man left to interrupt the play was Hawks defenseman Steve Smith. He glided across the front of the net, waiting to take Hull's shot in the gut. However, Hull had all the patience in the world. It didn't matter that the game was on the line. It didn't matter that more than 16,000 screaming fans were already jumping up and down in celebration. Brett Hull was calm, cool, and collected. He waited for Smith to glide on by, so he had nothing but Hasek between him and the net, which, to Hull, suddenly looked as big as an empty warehouse. Smith was out of the picture when Hull arched his weapon high over his head and uncoiled it with the ferocity of a cannon. The puck took off like a rocket and whizzed under Hasek's pads, snapping the back of the net. The clock stopped just a few minutes before midnight. Cinderella could now stay out and party.

With his stick raised high in the air like King Arthur's sword, Hull slowly skated toward his bench while his teammates hurried over to greet their superstar. Brian Sutter jumped into the arms of his assistant, Bob Berry. Even trainer Mike Folga took a few seconds out of his busy schedule to raise his arms in triumph next to the two coaches. It was a sight to behold, that sea of blue and white crowded into a circle, smothering the man with the golden locks. Sure, it would've been nice to see a guy like Zombo win it. But it was only fitting that Mr. Hull ended the game with one of his patented slapshots from the slot. No one was happier than a certain Blues intern who was jumping a little higher than everyone around him. He had drawn Hull's name. I guess he had circled his fingers around the hat a little better than I had.

As the Hawks slowly skated off the ice, Steve Smith bashed his stick across the net. No question, he was probably kicking himself for not staying in the goal crease a little longer. But showing SOME signs of intelligence, he opted to get the hell out of the way. As Smith continued his journey to the dressing room, he flew into a rage and turned over a table of cups filled with Gatorade. The liquid splashed on a couple of bystanders, including a KTVI cameraman who got an unexpected bath.

The Blues took their sweet time getting off the ice. They, like everyone else in the building, wanted to savor the moment. As they finally made their way to the locker room, the fans showered them with ear-splitting cheers. They could now head home, though they'd probably get little sleep as pictures of Hull winning the game played over and over again in their minds.

"I think everyone got their money's worth here," Coach Sutter said. "If you went into the dressing room right now, you'll see a lot of very tired athletes."

No question, the Blues were exhausted. But you didn't hear anyone complaining about it. They were now up two games to one, with Game 4 right back here in St. Louis 48 hours later.

"That was the first time I've done that since my first year in college," Hull said. "That was a long, hard game. A lot of ice time. I've got to give all the guys in the room a lot of credit."

"I knew Hullie was there, so I just dropped it a little bit," explained Bassen, replaying the game winner. "He made no mistake. We're all excited about that."

You can say that again. The 5-4 win could prove to be the final nail in the Hawks' coffin. Keenan was still unhappy with his top players and, no question, they still weren't playing up to their capabilities. There were times during the regular season when the Hawks looked enormously better than the Blues. But not during these playoffs. The Blues still weren't playing up to their potential, either. But they were now in control of the series. And with another win in two nights, you could pretty well secure a trip to the second round, which could very well secure Brian Sutter's job.

Chapter Nineteen

OVER AND OUT

Fear.

That emotion, perhaps more than any other, is the biggest motivator for a professional athlete. Fear of failure, fear of being only second-best, can single-handedly drive an athlete to success.

"You have to have a little bit of fear everytime you hit the ice," Brian Sutter said earlier in the year. "That's what pushes you to succeed."

And that's exactly what the Blackhawks were up against as they skated onto the Arena ice the night of April 22 for Game 4. The Blues had backed them into a corner. If they lost tonight, they'd be on the brink of elimination. There was fear in their hearts. They were staring smack dab at an early playoff departure.

The Blues weren't exactly coming to the rink feeling over-confident. They knew they'd have to earn a win tonight just like the two previous games. But their sense of urgency couldn't compare to the Hawks'. While Chicago was fighting for survival, the Blues were coming off a highly emotional win. Would they still be feeling the effects of it?

"I think yesterday was a day, whether guys will admit it or not, where guys were still drained not only physically, but emotionally, too," said Janney of the off-day between games. "I think that whole day was taken and needed to get back together emotionally and physically."

The Blues had to guard against being too soft in Game 4. With Chicago coming out of the chute like a bunch of wild animals, the Blues would have to match the Hawks blow for blow. There could be no letdown. They had to pretend Game 3 never occurred. They had to forget Brett Hull scoring the game winner. They had to get that dramatic victory completely out of their system. This was the pivotal game of the series. The consensus was that whichever team won this contest would eventually advance to the second round.

It was clear from the start that this was going to be a brutally physical game. As expected, the Blackhawks played as if they had just lost a bitter divorce battle. They were the ultimate Nasty Boys, banging bodies and crunching skulls. Mike Keenan even dressed both of his fighting goons, Mike Peluso AND Stu Grimson, a surprising move with the Hawks so desperate for a win.

The Blues, however, weren't about to be intimidated. When the sides engaged in their first scrum, just 42 seconds into the game, Mike Hudson and Stephane Quintal were given two minutes each for roughing, while Stephane Matteau and Dave Lowry were slapped with fighting misconducts. (Remember, it was Lowry who had aggressively stolen the puck from Matteau in Game 3, starting the winning play.)

A mere 17 seconds later, Chicago forward Brad Lauer was whistled for elbowing, and just like that, the Blues had their first power play of the game. The home team couldn't connect—in fact, couldn't even get a shot on goal—but there'd be plenty more chances the next 59 minutes.

A little more than six minutes into the first period, the Blues had their second chance with a man advantage, as Brian Noonan was forced to the penalty box for high-sticking. It wasn't until a few seconds into the power play that the Blues finally fired their first shot on goal. No question, they had been totally outplayed in the early going. But the scoreboard is what counts most, and, for the fourth game in a row, the Blues lit it up first.

Bret Hedican, who continued to look more confident with each shift, dumped the puck behind the Hawks' net, where Janney picked it up. The Blues' center tossed it out front to Shanahan, who quickly slid a pass to Hull above the left post. The Golden Brett wristed a slapper that hit Belfour's pad and trickled in for a 1-0 Blues lead on only their second shot of the game.

By the time Chicago was given its second power play at 10:43, the Hawks were enjoying a 9-2 advantage in shots. Their tenth proved the charm as Jeremy Roenick scored his second of the series to even the score at one. And that's when things started to get REAL nasty.

Kelly Chase, playing his first game of the series in place of Kimble, tussled with Bryan Marchment in the most spirited fight of the first four games. The two went toe to toe and landed some major blows on each other's noggins. But it was Chase, who has one of the best fighting techniques in the game, who eventually got the better of his opponent, dropping some hellacious haymakers on Marchment's face. Chase was given seven minutes in penalties for fighting and high-sticking. But Marchment was slapped with nine minutes for fighting, roughing, and holding. This guy was a little ticked off.

The Blues were given their third power play of the game but managed only two shots for a total of four after 14 minutes of play. Meanwhile, the Hawks had slapped twelve shots at Curtis Joseph, despite being short-handed for much of the game. The worst-case scenario was developing. The Hawks were playing with much more intensity because they had much more to lose. Chicago was playing with fear.

With less than three minutes to play in the opening period, the visitors took a much-deserved lead when Brent Sutter scored his first of the series. The Hawks continued shelling Joseph until, mercifully, the horn sounded to end the first twenty minutes of play. When all the numbers were tallied, the Blackhawks enjoyed a 2-1 lead, a 15-4 advantage in shots, and the comfort of knowing the home team was as lifeless as a beached whale. The Blues were still living off the fat of the last game and were in no shape to match the Hawks' aggressiveness tonight.

Fortunately, the Blues were given a chance to break out of their doldrums at the start of the second. With 36 seconds remaining in the first period, Brian Noonan was whistled for high-sticking and roughing, and the Blues were given a four-minute power play. They still had most of it left to start the second, but if the first twenty minutes were an indication, would it really matter? After all, the Blues had managed only four shots on three power plays. Why would it be any different now?

It wouldn't. Janney, in control of the puck in the Hawks' zone, nonchalantly passed it back to Emerson. Trouble is, it never got there. The puck hit Dirk Graham's skate and bounced to Matteau, who had just jumped off the Hawks' bench on a line change. He raced unmolested to the Blues' net and scored past Joseph's right skate on the breakaway. It was now 3-1 Chicago, and the game would only deteriorate from there. No matter what line combinations Sutter threw out there, the Blues seemed to have no clue what they were doing. If the Hawks were the Nasty Boys, the Blues were the Lost Boys.

When St. Louis was given its sixth power play halfway through the period, the Blackhawks were enjoying a 24-5 edge in shots on goal. Did I say edge? I meant gap. Did I say gap? I meant black hole. Which is what the Blues seemed to have fallen into. They had disappeared from sight. The only reason the score was still so close was that the Blackhawks were confused by how easy the game had become.

To no one's surprise, the Blues once again failed to shoot even one puck at the general vicinity of Eddie Belfour. Six power plays. Two shots. As the song says, how low can you go? This wasn't just the worst game of the series, this was turning into the most hideous contest of the entire season.

Shortly after embarrassing themselves on their sixth power play, the Blues were given their seventh when Keith Brown was caught for cross-checking. The Blues should have done the only humane thing possible. Decline the penalty. Why look foolish again? Not only had 18,089 people crammed into the building, but a large audience was watching this horror movie on television. There was no need to look silly in front of so many people time and time again.

But suddenly, and without warning, Murphy's Law was turned upside down. Everything that could go right, did. Despite being blown out in every facet of the game so far, Curt Giles and Brendan Shanahan scored on back-to-back power plays to tie the score at 3-3. I repeat—the Blues knotted up the game on consecutive power plays. And it wasn't as if the Blues had worked for them, either. Both goals were of the junk variety. Belfour should have easily made the saves. The Chicago netminder had obviously grown bored of the game and was caught napping.

The contest had gotten a little ridiculous, to tell you the truth. Not only were the Blues back in a game they had no business being in, but referee Bill McCreary had gotten a little carried away with the whistle when it came to the Blackhawks. In one of the most amazing statistics you'll ever see, the Blues had the man advantage for more than eleven minutes of the second period, and yet they were outshot 10-8. Go figure. The Hawks must have thought the scoreboard was malfunctioning when they left the ice after two periods. How could it possibly be 3-3 when they were living in the Blues' zone?

After the Hawks killed yet another power play to start the third period, they finally got the play they were looking for to bury the half-dead Blues. Five minutes had expired when Roenick made the kind of dazzling move that Blues fans thought had been reserved for Emerson. Roenick motored down the left side and across the blue line. Just as he approached Zombo, the Hawks' top scorer spun around in a pirouette worthy of a ballet dancer. Roenick breezed by Zombo and headed toward the left post. Joseph had the angle cut off nicely and stopped Roenick's shot. But Noonan had followed up the play and got a couple of whacks at the rebound before smacking it into the net for the go-ahead goal. That's all the Blackhawks needed to put the game away.

They continued to batter Joseph with a flurry of pucks, outshooting the Blues 9-3 through the first 15 minutes. In case you're keeping score, that's 34-15 with just five minutes left in the game. Just to make sure the score didn't look so close, Mike Hudson added his second of the series, and Chicago held on for the 5-3 win to even it up at two games apiece. The Blues' performance was so pathetic, it was enough to make blood relatives take a few swings at each other. And that's exactly what happened when the final horn sounded.

Ron and Brent Sutter had been going at it all game. A slash here. A cross-check there. Not exactly brotherly love. The second the game was over, Ronnie smashed his older brother into the boards for an earlier slash. Feeling a bit left out of the family get-together, Richie raced behind Brent and started tugging him down with a sleeper hold. Others crashed the party, and it was soon one big pileup to the left of the penalty box. Order was eventually restored, and the two sides skated off to their respective dressing rooms.

The twins were obviously jealous of something Brent had and they didn't. Something called a driver's seat. Brent and his teammates were firmly entrenched in it now with just three games left, two of them in Chicago. After that draining, double-overtime victory two nights earlier in which the Blues took command of the series, the Hawks had staged a coup and recaptured control 48 hours later. The Blues looked completely defenseless against the Hawks' attack. Instead of the Stars and Stripes, the Blues should have hoisted the surrender flag during the national anthem.

"It appeared from the start of the game they wanted it a little bit more than we did," a very subdued Brendan Shanahan remarked. "I'm sure from the moment Brett scored his overtime goal two nights ago to the moment the puck was dropped tonight, they knew it was do-or-die for them."

"Maybe the legs weren't working. I don't know what it was," said Joseph, the only Blues representative who played exceptionally well. "Give them credit. They were flying pretty hard. They forced us into some bad plays."

"They came out jumping and certainly set the tempo of the game in the first period," said Brian Sutter. The Blues' head coach complimented his team for coming back in the second period to tie the score but conceded that his players just weren't very sharp for most of the game. Now he was faced with the daunting task of going to Chicago, where they had to steal yet another game.

"I can't wait," Sutter said.

Oh, yes you can, Brian. Yes you can.

*   *   *

The kid pointed the gun directly at my head. I mean, right between the eyes. I just stood there, frozen in my tracks. With a wry smile, the youngster pulled the trigger. Click.

"Pow!" the kid yelled. "You're dead." And with that, he ran down the sidewalk to catch up with his two friends.

I was still standing in place. My whole body felt numb. I had to look down at my feet to make sure they were still there because I couldn't feel them.

I had been waiting for a co-worker outside Chicago Stadium when several kids, probably about 10 to 12 years old, walked past me. The Stadium isn't in a very safe section of Chicago, but who was going to bother me in broad daylight? The game was still a few hours away, and there were no police in the vicinity. But I felt absolutely no sense of danger standing outside the Stadium's front doors.

But when that kid stopped, yanked a black pistol out of his jacket and pulled the trigger, I thought I was a goner. It turned out to be only a toy gun, and the smart-aleck kid was just having fun at my expense.

As I walked back into the Stadium, I just laughed it off. So what if my heart was still beating like a jackhammer? It's good to get frightened every once in a while. It clears out the system. As I'm prone to do, I started to look for a little symbolism in what had just happened. Would the Blues be like that kid or like me? Would they come out firing and freeze the Hawks in their tracks? Or would they look for the quickest escape route to avoid being shot down and humiliated? If they showed even the slightest bit of timidness, this series was all but over.

As Bernie Federko and I took our seats under the press box, we heard a loud crash above us. What the hell was that? Was this old building finally starting to crumble? One of the ushers hurried upstairs to find out what was going on. He arrived to find Blues assistant coach Wayne Thomas sitting on the floor. It seems that a metal folding chair collapsed as he was sitting down in it. A second ominous omen.

"There's electricity in the air," Ron Caron told Dave Luecking after Thomas went flying. Let's just hope the Blues wouldn't get shocked.

For this all-important Game 5, Brian Sutter put Paul Cavallini back in after a two-game hiatus, and Murray Baron after a three-game absence. Sitting on the sidelines were Curt Giles and Stephane Quintal, who had suffered a wrist injury in Game 4. Dave Christian also was forced out due to a hurt wrist and was replaced by rookie Denny Felsner, seeing his first action of the series. In the final change, Sutter switched tough-guys Kimble and Chase.

The Blues had played extremely well in Chicago in Games 1 and 2. They had scored the first goal early and taken the crowd out of each game. To have any chance on this night, they'd have to repeat the script. They had to forget about their woeful performance a couple of nights ago and play sound, positional hockey. And that's exactly what they did from the start.

Less than two minutes into the game, Brendan Shanahan carried the puck around the Hawks' net and moved out toward the blue line. Using his patented stiff-arm to keep a defender at bay, Shanahan slid the puck with one hand across to Butcher at the right point. The Blues' captain passed it down low to Ron Wilson, who quickly whirled and shot. Belfour made the save, but Bozon was in the right place at the right time, slapping in the rebound to give the Blues a 1-0 lead on his first and only point of the series.

The Blackhawks tied it halfway through the period when Matteau scooted past Zombo down the right side and blistered a shot at Joseph. The Blues' goalie made the save, but Matteau poked in the rebound to make it 1-1. Matteau had suddenly become an offensive threat. He had five points in the series, all in the last three games. Heck, Larmer and Roenick only had six points COMBINED coming into this game. Players are often judged on how they respond during the playoffs, and Matteau was responding just fine, thank you.

The Blues then started to make a multitude of mistakes, as if it were the first day of training camp. Twice they were called for penalties while they were on the power play, thereby negating the man advantage. Their defense was also an embarrassment. In fact, it was a defensive breakdown that allowed the Hawks to score late in the period to take the lead. Baron unsuccessfully tried to clear the puck out as the Hawks were breathing down Joseph's neck. Keith Brown kept it in and fired a shot that Steve Larmer tipped in for his first goal of the series. That was not a good sign. The Blues had kept Larmer off the scoreboard the first four games. If he was going to start getting hot now, the Blues were in a heap of trouble.

The first period ended with the Hawks leading 2-1. The visitors had played very well in the early going, then slacked off the last ten minutes. There was still plenty of time for the Blues to right themselves. If they could just pretend the game was starting over again, perhaps they could score an early goal as they had in each of the five games.

Sure enough, Brett Hull needed only 36 seconds of the second period to score his fourth of the series. He was the overall points leader and top goal scorer so far, and the game was tied at 2-2.

Just 89 seconds later, the Bluenotes took the lead on a typical Shanahan goal. The Blues' forward was mucking it up in front of the net when he poked in a loose puck as he was being knocked to the ice. The Blues not only were leading 3-2, but they were now completely dominating the home team. After three-and-a-half minutes of play, the Blues had pelted Belfour with seven shots. Can you imagine keeping a pace like that throughout an entire game? That's 120 shots!

As I made a note of the Blues' seventh shot, and wondered how many they were going to get this period, little did I know I wouldn't need my pen to write down any more Blues shots for quite some time. The dry spell they were about to embark on was unparalleled. It was so dry it made the Sahara look like a swampland. Suddenly, the Blues couldn't buy a shot if their very lives depended on it.

Meanwhile, the Blackhawks had no trouble finding Curtis Joseph. In fact, they occasionally went one better and found the back of the net. With nine minutes left in the period, Steve Larmer showed he was indeed back in the series, pounding in his second of the game to tie it at 3-3. Blues-killer Matteau assisted on the goal, his sixth point of the series. Only Hull and Keith Brown had more.

Four minutes after that, the Blackhawks rushed across the blue line and waltzed through the Blues' defense like it was standing still. Brad Lauer cruised behind the net, with Craig Janney nearby. Did Janney run interference? Did he try to gain control of the puck? Nope. The Blues' center must have remembered he left the iron on back home. He skated out of there like a bolt of lightning. His sudden departure allowed Lauer to simply move around to the front of the net and score past a beleaguered and defenseless Joseph. The second period ended with Chicago up 4-3.

Blues fans had to be befuddled and bewildered watching this series. Where was the killer instinct on this squad? How could a Sutter-coached team not stay motivated after taking a lead? How could a group of players decide to take the night off after coming from behind to take a 3-2 lead early in the second period? There wasn't a quitter on this team. If there was, he wouldn't be playing. And yet the Blues had shown a season-long inability to kick the opposition when it was down. There was no rage. There was no fire. Hell, there wasn't even smoke. The burning smell was the Blues self-destructing.

Unfortunately, the third period began like the second had ended, with the Blues forgetting that sometimes you have to shoot the puck at the opposing net to have a shot at winning. With the boys in blue unable to clear the puck once again, Chris Chelios scored on a slapshot from the right point to give the Hawks a 5-3 lead. It seemed impossible that the Blues could come back now. Not the way they had been playing since the start of the second period.

The Blues finally gathered up enough strength to muscle a shot on net at 8:00 of the third period. Incredibly, they had gone over 24 minutes without recording one shot on goal. That was more than a full period's vacation for the goalie. And this was the playoffs, for crying out loud. A time when guys were supposed to come to the fore and play bigger and better than during the regular season. Instead, the Blues had meekly retreated to their own end without any desire to engage the enemy. Pitiful.

With less than five minutes left, Jocelyn Lemieux slapped in his second goal of the series to give the Blackhawks an insurmountable 6-3 lead. Jeff Brown scored a cosmetic goal 45 seconds later in hopes of making the game appear a little prettier than it really was. It didn't work. Everyone watching knew the Blues had quit playing after the start of the second period, handing control of the series to the Hawks, who now held a 3-2 lead in games. One more loss, and the Blues were heading to the golf course for the summer. And you had to wonder if that was their intention. Ever since Hull's double-overtime goal in Game 3, the Blues were as limp as a wet noodle. Except for brief stretches here and there, Brian Sutter's team looked as bad the last two games as at any time during the regular season.

"There are no excuses when you play teams at this time of year," Sutter said after the game. "We're going to see how strong some people are. I'm looking forward to going home (for Game 6). We're going to see how some individuals respond."

For now, his individuals were despondent. They were in a haze so deep that even a Brett Hull slapshot couldn't penetrate it. They now had to return to St. Louis and try to regain some of that magic that had been lost the moment Hull netted the winner in Game 3. If not, the season of turmoil would officially come to a close.

"I don't know what it is," an exasperated Hull said. "We just quit working. We go up 3-2, and we just seem to think that was it, and they're going to quit and it was going to be easy. We should know better than that."

"We gave up a lead and it's very frustrating, especially in a game like this," said Cavallini, who admitted to being a little rusty at the start of the game. "Now it's a do-or-die situation. Sometimes a team has to get in that situation to play its best."

And that's what it would take. The Blues had to play their best. The Blackhawks, led by the resurgence of Larmer and Roenick, had finally come out of their funk and were starting to play up to their capabilities. There was more than a season-saving victory at stake here. A man's job depended on the Blues winning the next two games.

*   *   *

"I think it's a bunch of garbage," an irritated Garth Butcher said. "The thought of that is just stupidity."

Yikes. I decided to drop the subject immediately. But I just had to ask the team captain what he thought about all the rumors concerning Brian Sutter's job security. They were now stronger than ever, and they were coming from people in the know. We had to report them as rumors, because we weren't allowed to quote anybody. But they were definitely more than that. It was being spelled out in plain English. If the Blues failed to win the last two games of the series, the team would begin an immediate search for a new head coach. The news was being leaked from the very top.

"I find it hard to believe his job is on the line," said Hull. "He's done such a great job with the young people and with all the changes we've had around here. He's a tremendous person. He's a tremendous coach. I'm not sure if there'd be one or two guys very happy if he had to leave."

Do you get what he was saying? Reread that last line. Hull was admitting, in his own way, what many already assumed. There were at least a couple of players who weren't exactly going to mourn the loss of Coach Sutter. In fact, Hull looked over at one particular locker when he said that. Coincidence? Maybe. But the locker belonged to a guy who had had occasional run-ins with Sutter during the course of the year. Brett was talking Hull-speak again, making reporters think for themselves.

Meanwhile, Brian was handling the rumors extremely well. Here's a guy who had been loyal to the same organization for 16 years. He had literally given his blood, sweat, and tears to the Blues since he was 19 years old. But he was now in danger of being tossed out the door like an uninvited guest. It hardly seemed fair. But then again, hockey is no different from any other business. We all see things in our respective professions that are unfair, but we're generally powerless to do anything about it.

"There are a lot of people in town that patted me on the back last year," Brian said. "And those same people are the ones that are doing the yelling this year. But that's part of the profession. I remember talking to Whitey Herzog. He said, 'Some guys are going to be friends one day and wish you good luck and pat you on the back. The next day they're going to be throwing things at you.' I've given my heart and soul to everyone on the hockey club, and I'm proud of it."

And now Sutter would have to give his heart and soul one more time in an effort to stay employed. In hopes of shaking up his team defensively, Brian took Baron out of the lineup and inserted Lee Norwood for the first time during the series. Norwood had played in only nine of the last 31 games, and no one was quite sure why. The 32-year-old defenseman led the team in plus/minus and was generally one of the strongest players on the ice. That is, when he was on the ice. Fans and media alike clamored for his reappearance. And now, with the season on the line, he was finally being given a chance.

During the morning skate when it was announced that Norwood would be playing, his teammates couldn't help but needle him. As Norwood walked into the dressing room after practice, a number of players began clapping, saluting, and cheering. Some bowed in a reverent tribute to his "greatness."

"I'd hate to be the first guy to feel his number!" shouted Shanahan from across the room.

That first guy was Brent Sutter, who was nailed by Norwood just seconds into the game. He then piled on a couple of Hawks near the Blues' net when play was stopped. His aggressive play inspired the team to take control of the game from the very start. The Green Berets followed Norwood's physical lead with a few crunching checks of their own. Butcher then sent Larmer flying with an open-ice check to which Matteau took exception, crunching Butcher even though the puck was nowhere in sight. That should've been a roughing penalty, but referee Mark Faucette plugged his whistle and let play continue. Norwood had set the stage. This was going to be war.

Seven minutes into the period, however, Faucette made a questionable call on Philippe Bozon. The Blues' forward, who had continued to impress observers with his aggressive play, bashed Chelios into the boards with a clean check. However, Faucette blew the whistle and sent Bozon off for high-sticking. Replays clearly showed Bozon's stick was below his waist but, of course, replays can't be used to reverse penalties. Off went Philippe and on came the Hawks' power-play unit.

With forty seconds left in the penalty, Keith Brown slapped a shot from the right point that hit the post and trickled to the front of the net. With a group of players fighting for control, Cavallini accidentally nudged the puck with his skate and kicked it to Roenick, who easily tapped it in for the 1-0 lead. It was the first time in the series that Chicago had scored first.

Any fears that the Blues would roll over and die were quickly forgotten as the homeboys went on an offensive rampage the last half of the period. The Blues outshot the Hawks 12-7 during the first period and generally outplayed the opposition.

Unfortunately, they came out as flat as stale beer for the second period. They were given a power-play opportunity at the start but failed to get one shot away. Playing at even strength was no better as Sutter tried to mix lines to get something going. That's fine. Every coach does it. But one combination had Hull teamed with Ron Sutter and Dave Mackey, making Sutter-bashers smile with delight. We've got him now, they were saying.

With play stopped six minutes into the period, a wayward pigeon swooped down from the rafters and landed on the ice, presumably to look for water. The fans dusted the cobwebs off their hands and cheered for the first time of the period. What a way to end the season, with the crowd more excited about a pigeon than the game itself.

Less than two minutes later, Jeremy Roenick effectively ended the Blues' season. Or so it seemed. Chelios one-handed a pass to Roenick, who was high above the circles. The Hawks' center made a nice move side-stepping Hull, who rushed in from behind. Roenick then rifled the puck over Joseph's left shoulder to give Chicago a 2-0 lead. It was as if Roenick had skated over to the Blues' bench and knocked Brian Sutter down with one final blow.

But the Blues' head coach was partially resurrected at 12:35 of the second period on a controversial call. With the Hawks caught up-ice, Janney and Emerson dashed toward Eddie Belfour, with only Igor Kravchuk in the way. Controlling the puck, Janney crossed down the left side and glided toward the net. Just when it looked like he was in too deep to do anything, he guided the puck over to Emerson, who was crashing the far post. The puck hit Kravchuk's stick, bounced high into the air, and was slapped into the net by Emerson with an apparent high-stick. The red lamp went on, the Blues huddled in an embrace, and the fans jumped in celebration as the Blues had cut the lead to 2-1.

Or had they? The referee and his two linesmen gathered near the penalty box and put in a call to the replay official upstairs. If he ruled Emerson had used a high stick to whack it in, the officials had no choice but to wave off the goal and send the crowd into riotous behavior. No question, the fans would shower the ice with debris if the goal was disallowed.

However, after consulting over the phone for a minute or two, Faucette turned toward center ice and pointed to the faceoff dot. The goal stood, and the Blues had cut the lead in half. It was a popular call, if not the right call. Replays clearly showed Emerson had his stick over his head when he slapped the puck into the net. That's right. It wasn't just above his shoulders. It was clearly above his head as he scored the Blues' first goal.

The crowd was into the game for the first time as Brian Sutter paced up and down behind the bench, pounding his fist into his hand and glaring toward the ice with a look that could kill.

"C'mon, boys!!" he shouted over the roar of the crowd.

But just a minute later, the emotional tide turned when Bozon was sent to the penalty box for four minutes after cutting

Roenick's mouth with his stick. Once again, it was a tough call. Bozon tried to slap at the puck, but his stick hit the top of Roenick's blade and bounced all the way up to Roenick's face. The Blues would have to play nearly the rest of the period short-handed, minimizing any offensive threat to tie the game.

The Blues killed off Bozon's double-minor and headed to the dressing room still down by a goal. The entire season now came down to twenty minutes of play. A season that saw the banishment of Scott Stevens, the controversial trade for another Sutter, the contractual demands of Oates, the injuries to key players, the ten-day strike, and every other event that made this a season to forget, suddenly was reduced to one period of hockey. Just twenty more minutes of ice time, and the Blues could be packing their belongings and heading home for the summer.

At the start of the period, the Blues didn't exactly play with the desperation of a team about to be eliminated from the playoffs. They had trouble creating much pressure in the Hawks' zone even though Chicago was letting them in. The Blackhawks were adopting the dangerous game plan of sitting on the lead. Belfour still wasn't on top of his game and was fighting almost every puck shot his way. Nonetheless, the Blues were unable to create any quality scoring chances.

The clock slowly ticked down. Ten minutes left. Then nine. Then eight. Then seven. Finally, the Blues started opening things up. They forechecked the Blackhawks into the corners, fought for control of the puck, and worked it around for the right scoring opportunities. Emerson missed on a wrap-around. Shanahan blasted a shot from the right point that Belfour stopped. Butcher clanked one off the left post. The clock continued counting down the numbers, while the Blues continued missing the back of the net.

Now down to six minutes. Five minutes. Four minutes. The Blues were finally skating in desperation. They flung their bodies at the Hawks, dove for loose pucks, and skated ferociously from one end to the other. The Hawks were being completely shut down. They were just hoping to survive the final few minutes against a team willing to risk it all to stave off elimination.

Three minutes. Two minutes. The tension was thicker than Grimson's head. The nerves were more frazzled than Don King's hair. A puck flies across the crease, and Bassen is unable to connect. Damn! C'mon! There's another loose puck near the crease, but Lowry is held up from getting to it.

One minute. Fifty seconds. There goes Joseph to the bench. The Blues' net is now empty, as an extra attacker is sent to the ice. No one is resting comfortably any longer. Every person in the building is either standing or sitting on the very edge of his seat. Fingernails are littering the aisles. The entire arena is about to suffer one collective coronary.

Forty seconds. The Hawks finally clear the puck to the other end of the ice, wasting precious time. The Blues quickly work it back but can't get anything going. The puck is held along the boards, creating the most important faceoff of the season, Ron Sutter against Jeremy Roenick. Sutter has to win it to have any chance at salvaging the season. If Roenick controls the puck, it's all over.

Exactly 27 seconds left as the linesman drops the puck. With the two sticks chopping the ice for possession, Sutter is able to swat it away, but the puck never reaches a man in blue.

Twenty seconds. Fifteen. Ten. The puck has been cleared to the other end. The Blues race frantically back to retrieve it. Five. Four. They can't get across. C'mon! Just one last shot! Three. Two. The puck is still floating around the neutral zone. One. That's it. Bzzzzzzz.

The 1991-92 season had just come to an end for the St. Louis Blues. There was no celebration. There was no pileup at center ice. There would be no drinking from the Stanley Cup. A troubled silver anniversary season unceremoniously ended on home ice on April 28, 1992. A season that held such promise in September ended with utter disappointment seven months later. For the 25th year in a row, the Blues had lost their last game of the season.

Keeping with tradition, the two teams lined up in single file and shook hands with one another. One team still had dreams of winning it all. The other only had dreams of what might have been. As the players would say, the Blues left it on the ice. They gave it everything they had until the final tick of the clock. Unfortunately, they couldn't say the same for Games 4 and 5, in which they looked pathetically inadequate. As it turned out, Hull's game-winning goal in Game 3, was the last highlight, and one of the few, of the season.

"I'm sure 27 of us would like to have those games over again," said Jeff Brown. "We should've won this series. That's the bottom line. They're not a better hockey club. We should've won."

That was the consensus among Blues players in a deathly quiet locker room after the game. Neither team played exceptionally well. It's just that the Blues played worse. They had their spurts when they looked like a championship-caliber team. But they also had their moments when they looked like a group of rejects trying out for an expansion team.

"I'm very disappointed in myself," a dejected Janney said, his eyes staring at the floor. "To put it bluntly, I thought I sucked the whole series. Right now, I'm pretty bitter and disgusted with myself."

Janney had been unable to dispel his reputation as a playoff choker. In his defense, however, he rarely saw No. 16 to his right. Janney's primary skill is getting the puck to a proven goal scorer, and he was teamed with Hull on only a few occasions.

Janney would retreat to Boston with only sour memories of his playoff performance. Meanwhile, the man he was traded for, Adam Oates, was leading the upstart Boston Bruins all the way to the third round of the playoffs, where they ran into the eventual Stanley Cup champs, the Pittsburgh Penguins. The trade suddenly didn't look as one-sided as when it was made.

You couldn't help but quickly replay the entire season as reporters gathered in the dressing room. And you had to start with the Scott Stevens controversy. People were upset at the time, no doubt about it. But few realized the devastating impact it would have on the team. Many expected the Blues to overcome his loss and compete as they had the year before. But as it turned out, those expectations were foolish. With so many changes following Stevens' departure, there was little chance the Blues would fight for the ultimate piece of silver during their silver anniversary.

"I don't think the expectations were as high from our point as they were from you guys' point of view," Hull told reporters. "We knew of all the changes that had been made, and we knew there was going to be an adjustment period. I thought we played above what we should have."

Of course, that didn't matter. The fact that the Blues had lost in the first round of the playoffs would likely spell the end for

Brian Sutter in St. Louis. He was as crushed as anyone. For the 16th year in a row, he failed to reach the Stanley Cup finals.

"There's nobody, unless you actually played and actually care the way certain individuals do, who understands how much it hurts," said Sutter, tears gathering in his eyes. Damn the objectiveness. I felt for the guy. I, like almost everybody else in St. Louis, questioned some of his decisions. That's the beauty of sports. We're all experts after the fact. Some fans and media members publicly crucified Sutter for almost every move he made. Such negative criticism had finally taken its toll.

"I do the best job I possibly can, and I try to be oblivious to everything that goes on," Brian said at the postgame news conference. "But obviously some people think they're experts. That's not something I've ever declared myself to be. If you guys want to coach the team and decide what's going to happen, you guys go right ahead."

Well, somebody had to play head coach. In just three days, the Blues would lose theirs.

Chapter Twenty

END OF AN ERA

Brian Sutter sat alone. He stared intently at the television, watching the Canucks take a 1-0 lead over the Jets in the seventh and deciding game of their first-round series. It was shortly after 10 p.m. on the night of April 30, just 48 hours after the Blues were eliminated from the playoffs.

Brian's 12-year-old son, Shaun, walked into the room to tell his dad some urgent and distressing news. Shaun had been watching the nightly news on another television set when a sudden announcement was made.

"Dad, they said you're getting fired tomorrow," Shaun told his father. "They said they're going to announce it at a news conference."

Shaun's younger sister, Abigail, walked into the room to give her dad the same information. Brian listened to his kids in disbelief before turning his eyes back to the hockey game. However, he couldn't see the players. He couldn't hear the announcers. The television could have been showing color bars, and it wouldn't have mattered. His mind was in another world. His gut started churning. His heart sank to the pit of his stomach. Brian Sutter was starting to feel a mix of emotions. First shock. Then depression. Then anger. Unmitigated, unbridled, passionate anger. How in the hell could they tell the media without telling me first? His blood started boiling. Like Julius Caesar, he suddenly felt betrayed by the very people he had trusted.

Within seconds, the phone started ringing off the hook. Journalists, friends, neighbors, you name it. Everyone wanted to hear it from Brian himself. Was he indeed fired? And was Bob Plager really his replacement, as one station had reported? Brian had no idea. No one from the Blues' front office had talked to him about any of these unsubstantiated stories.

When Sutter finally got a chance, he placed a call to Ron Caron. Surely his general manager would tell him the truth. Instead, Caron refused to divulge anything.

"Let's talk about this tomorrow morning," Caron told him. "We'll all meet at the Arena and go over everything."

Needless to say, Sutter didn't sleep a wink. He replayed his 16 years with the organization over and over in his mind. Instead of sheep, he counted goals. 303 of them. And assists. 333 of those. Both those marks are second in team history to Bernie Federko. He tallied his wins as a coach. 153 of them. First in team history, far above legendary coaches Scotty Bowman and Al Arbour.

He saw his jersey hanging from the rafters, one of only four numbers retired in Blues history.

But what have you done for me lately? That's what team officials were asking and Brian Sutter didn't have a suitable answer. His last team had fallen 22 points from the year before, when he was named the NHL's top coach. For the first time, he was unable to survive the first round of the playoffs. It seemed few people cared about his previous accomplishments. That wasn't good enough anymore. He had shown an inability to motivate his players during the postseason, and that was intolerable. So without telling him, Blues management fired its head coach, named team scout Bob Plager to replace him, and then secretly leaked it to selected people, none of whom was named Brian Sutter.

Sutter finally got the word firsthand the following morning at 7:00. Mike Shanahan, Jack Quinn, and Ron Caron tried to explain why the move was being made. He was stubborn. He wouldn't hear the advice of his assistants. He mismanaged and misused his players. His defense was ridiculously inept, giving up 35 shots a game. He was impatient with the youngsters on the team.

But none of the reasons made any sense to Sutter, who was still in a state of denial. He couldn't believe he was being let go from the only organization he had called home. The man voted the best left winger in Blues history by the fans had just been voted an ex-coach by his superiors.

When I arrived at his house later in the day, I expected to see a man who had devastation written all over him. I expected to find him slumped in a chair with glassy eyes and a dazed look. How else was he supposed to appear? Hell, he had just been fired. He didn't resign. He wasn't transferred to another department. He didn't have his pay docked. He had been canned. Terminated. Kicked out. Dumped on his ass. Good-bye. You're gone.

But Sutter didn't have the look of a beaten man. And I should have guessed that. He was the strongest individual I've ever known. A bit too strong, actually. I always figured an occasional dose of relaxation could do the man a world of good. But that wasn't his style. Sutter attacked whatever he was doing—I don't care if it was reading a book—with conviction and dedication.

I can just picture him on a beautiful Caribbean beach, surrounded by people who had traveled thousands of miles to get away from it all. While everyone else is tanning and floating in the waves, Sutter stares at the sun and dares it to burn him. He ventures into the ocean intent on pushing the waves back where they came from. He snorkels, not to take in the wondrous sights, but to catch a few eels with his bare hands.

Okay, okay. So he wasn't THAT intense. In fact, Brian always got a kick out of people's perceptions that he was such a hard-ass 100 percent of the time. He insists that he can relax and enjoy himself as much as anyone.

"I'm dead serious, but I like to have fun," Sutter said in paradoxical fashion, then followed up with another paradox. "I'm very private, but I love being with people."

That kind of mixed makeup helped him deal with being fired. He was devastated, but relieved. He was hurt, but determined to move on. I found him on the phone—what else—talking to supporters who wished him good luck in his job search. Ironically, the man Sutter was talking to when I knocked on his door was Kings coach Tom Webster. He would be canned in a few days, and Sutter's name would pop up as a possible replacement.

"I'm just glad it's over with, to tell you the truth," Sutter said after hanging up with Webster. "The focus wasn't on the hockey club and winning. It was getting Brian Sutter the heck out of town."

Brian wasn't referring just to outspoken fans. He had grown tired of reading derogatory things about himself in the paper. He was absolutely steamed hearing loud-mouth Kevin Slaten, a controversial radio personality, tell his listeners that Brian Sutter was a joke of a coach. In fact, following the Blues' loss to the Hawks in Game 6, Sutter accused Slaten's station, KASP, of giving out his home phone number so angry fans could call and harass his family. The accusation was never proven, and some speculated Brian made it up in an underhanded attempt to make Slaten and his station look bad.

No question, Sutter desperately wanted the media on his side. The day after the season ended, Brian invited 13 reporters to the Arena for an informal meeting to clear the air. He wanted to set the record straight and explain why he operated the way he did. He wanted the opportunity to defend his actions. He talked for nearly two-and-a-half hours, carefully outlining his every move. Some explanations made sense. Others didn't. In fact, a couple of his answers were out and out wrong. I asked him about Lee Norwood, wondering why we hadn't seen him in the play-offs until the last game.

"Where was Lee Norwood during the winning goal last night?" Sutter asked back. The room was quiet. No one had the answer. "I'll tell you where he was. He was back near his own blue line watching the play. Lee can't catch up to the play like he once could."

Mmmmm. Sounded good to me. Until I got back to the station and looked at the tape. Brian couldn't have been more incorrect. Norwood was very much involved in the play. In fact, he was back near his own net when Roenick scored, ready to take on any Blackhawk who ventured by. It wasn't Joseph who fished the puck out of the net. It was Norwood. That's how close he was.

In the end, of course, Sutter's media briefing had absolutely no effect on his status with the team. Two days later he was fired, making the get-together virtually meaningless. Everything he had said became moot. Perhaps he should have held the meeting elsewhere. It just so happened he gathered the group of reporters in the dreaded conference room, where traded players go to say their last words. Another one bites the dust.

I visited with Brian for only a few minutes the day he was fired. He had so many other things to accomplish we agreed to meet at a later date. Meanwhile, the Blues' new head coach was holding a news conference that afternoon to meet the press. Not that he had to introduce himself to reporters. Everyone knew who Bob Plager was. The 49-year-old former defenseman played in the Blues' very first game on October 11, 1967 and didn't take off the Bluenote until eleven seasons later. But just like his older brother, the late Barclay Plager, Bobby would stay in the organization after his playing days were over. He served in virtually every capacity, going wherever management asked him to, like a loyal foot soldier.

In 1990-91, Plager earned national recognition when he was sent to Peoria to coach the Rivermen. All he did there was lead the minor league team to the Turner Cup championship, while setting a professional hockey record with 18 consecutive wins. In all, the Rivermen broke over forty records in the International Hockey League and established Plager as a possible contender for an NHL coaching job in the future. Just one year later, Plager was named the Blues' 16th head coach. (By the way, how can an organization have 16 head coaches in 26 years and expect to be successful? Just wondering.)

"Right now, I'm a little scared about what's going to happen next year," admitted Plager. "But I think you should be scared. It's a challenge. I was scared to go to Peoria last year. I didn't know what to expect."

It's difficult to imagine Plager being scared about anything. He's a well-known jokester and prankster, a hockey Henny Youngman. The day before he was named head coach, he was seen walking around the Blues' dressing room, cracking jokes as he went.

"Did you hear Mike Tyson has already been challenged in prison?"

Is that right?

"Yeah, Jeffrey Dahmer wants a piece of him."

Oh, geez. Plager followed with another joke that's not fit to print. But I have to admit, it had me rolling. Plager's humorous nature, by his own admission, is a facade for the nervous juices that constantly flow in his stomach. Fear is what motivates him. Jokes are what cover it up.

"I've always said I didn't want to coach," said Plager. "But I think that was a little fear that I had that I might not succeed."

And now he was back to being fearful again. He was suddenly with the big boys, hoping to accomplish what no other man in the history of hockey had before: take the Blues to a Stanley Cup title. His predecessor, the most successful Blues coach in regular-season history, had failed on four occasions. His brother, Barc, had also failed in the late '70s.

"I thought about my brother a lot throughout this whole thing," confided Plager. "I had all the respect for him. In fact, I'm just wondering what he'd do in my position. This is a challenge. It was a challenge for him. I'm going to take the challenge."

Plager admitted the hardest part about taking the job was replacing one of the Blues' all-time greats, a man he deeply respected and cared for. The last thing he wanted was to force Sutter out the door.

"I talked to Bob (Berry) this morning," recalled Plager. "I told him, 'I don't want to take Brian Sutter's job.' I was told that Brian Sutter had been relieved. He no longer had a job. It's something that I didn't campaign for."

In fact, some insiders suggest that Plager was strongly advised to take the job by his superiors. Management had made up its mind who would take over without consulting Plager first. The plan had been formulated well in advance of Sutter's firing. Brian was out. Plager was in. Assistant coach Bob Berry moved into the front office to become Caron's assistant. Peoria coach Harold Snepsts was called up to take Berry's place while the other assistant coach, Wayne Thomas, stayed put.

All were at the news conference to announce the changes. Every one of them remarked what a bittersweet day it was. They were excited about taking a new direction under the new managerial alignment. But they also had to part company with a man who lived and died by the Blues.

"This is not a happy day for Ron Caron," the Blues general manager said. "I faced these same circumstances in 1983 (when he was fired in Montreal). I had the Montreal Canadiens tattoos all over my body, my mind, and feeling good about what I had done for the team. And all of a sudden it happens.

"(But) this team will be more solid. We will have a very precise approach. We will share the wealth of knowledge. And basically this is the reason why we made the move."

Exactly. Caron hit the nail right on its proverbial head. According to countless people in the organization, Sutter had become a one-man management team. He suggested who to draft, even though he had never personally seen the players, according to one co-worker. He wanted to be a part of every decision made by the people in the front office. He wanted to be more than just the coach. He demanded to be an assistant-everything. And he very rarely asked for input from those around him, specifically his assistant coaches.

"Brian Sutter was the most focused man I've ever known," Wayne Thomas said. "And we, as assistant coaches, didn't want to interrupt that focus. Many times we stayed clear."

Sutter had two of the finest assistant coaches in the game and he didn't take advantage of their knowledge and expertise? Something was terribly wrong there. As it turned out, that was one of the principal reasons for Sutter's ouster. He had become a bit too powerful for management's liking.

"It is time for a change, in our opinion, here in St. Louis," remarked Mike Shanahan, who lauded Sutter's accomplishments as a player and coach. "That doesn't make us right or anyone else wrong. It's just the direction we're heading."

And so it was done. Brian Sutter was unemployed for the first time in his life as the St. Louis Blues headed into their next quarter-century with a new coach and a new direction. Team trainer Mike Folga and equipment manager Jim Pickard were fired shortly after Sutter. Ron Caron promised an influx of foreign players (he used his first three draft picks a few months later to take Russians), improved puck control, fewer shots on goal allowed, and "better entertainment for our fans," as he put it. If that's not pressure, I don't know what is. Bob Plager better get the jokes ready. He may need them.

*   *   *

He busily poured solution into his pool, mixing it in to clean the water and make it ready to dive into. Viewed from the deck above, the pool looked inviting. I felt like shedding my tie and plunging right in.

"Dad, can I jump in yet?" asked Shaun Sutter.

"No, not yet," Brian answered, dragging hoses in and out of the water. "Not for another thirty minutes."

Every time I visited the Sutters', the father of the household was busy doing something. Just once, I'd like to see Brian sitting in a rocking chair with a bag of Doritos in his lap, a mess of empty beer cans thrown about the living room, and the television tuned to an afternoon soap opera.

"Hey, Dave, c'mon down," Brian demanded. "Do you want to talk down here?"

It was an absolutely gorgeous morning. The sun was shining brightly, but the temperatures were still rather mild. It was Tuesday, June 9, nearly six weeks after Sutter had been fired. The anger had subsided only slightly, and the pain was as sharp as the moment he first heard the news.

"The hurt and the scars from what went on and how they did it will never go away," Sutter said in a hushed voice. "I trusted them, and I respected them. And I expected them to call me."

Brian said he could handle the rejection. He had started to prepare himself long before it happened. But when he had to hear about it from his kids, he felt as if his heart had been carved out. After 16 years, he deserved better.

Sutter and I talked for a couple of hours that day, reliving what went wrong during the silver anniversary season and what he could have done differently to save his job. At first, Brian shied away from ripping his ex-employers. He didn't want to get involved in name-calling. But the longer we talked, the more his outrage began to surface. The bitterness was still there. And it was difficult for him to contain it.

"I have to be careful to say the right things, because you can't burn your bridges," he said. "But they're saying things, and I'm not supposed to? That's not right."

The criticism that burned Sutter the most was that he was too stubborn and wouldn't listen to anyone. He said it was a case of the pot calling the kettle black.

"They were 100 percent wrong when they said I wouldn't listen," Brian said of Jack Quinn and Ron Caron. "They're the ones who are stubborn. Ronald has a history of when he talks, he's right. And the whole world knows that. You can talk to him, and he can't even hear you. He's more interested in getting HIS point across. You can't close your eyes and have the blinders on and say this is the way we're going to do it.

"I took time to understand Ron. I'm probably the only guy to get along with him in that way. Those aren't opinions. Those are facts."

No question, Sutter and Caron could no longer share the relationship they once had. They were never best friends, but they shared a common goal: take the Blues all the way to the top. They disagreed many times on how to do that, but their commitment to excellence was shared. That never wavered. Now Sutter is left to remember how his old general manager treated him during D-day.

"That man never looked me in the eyes when he was firing me," Brian said, his voice rising in tone. "He just sat there and stared at the table. He kept talking about his days in Montreal and how hurt he was when he was fired. You know what? He still hasn't called me. What are we, five or six weeks later? Not one call. Not one."

When Caron started talking about his Montreal days, which he often did, Sutter would shudder. According to Brian, Caron was unable to forget his past with the Canadiens and move on. Everything the Blues did was compared to the glory days of an era gone by.

"You can't be the Canadiens of the 1950s," Brian said. "The game has changed. It's so much different. But certain people don't understand that."

Brian reflected on the day he took over as coach, June 20, 1988. He knew there was a lot of work ahead of him, not just on the ice, but in the front office. As the coach, he had to become more involved in the day-to-day operation of the club. It was never that way before. But it would be now with Sutter at the helm.

"There wasn't a lot of communication when I took over," he said. "There was minimal input from the coaches. Everybody in hockey knew that. That's not a kick in the ass. That's just the way it was. When I took over, this organization had an awful conception of the people within it. There was no communication. We worked hard in four years to get the coach's input."

Perhaps a little too hard? It was easy to make Sutter the fall guy now. If he had concentrated just on his coaching duties, he would've been responsible only for what happened on the ice. But since he became so intertwined with management, he could also be blamed now for so many of the decisions that backfired. The much-maligned Garth Butcher trade was attributed to Sutter. So was the Ron Sutter deal that sent Brind'Amour to Philadelphia, where he promptly scored 33 goals and 77 points, the second-highest on the team. And the biggest disaster of all, the loss of Scott Stevens as compensation for Brendan Shanahan, was linked directly to Brian Sutter.

Hogwash, says the ex-coach. He accused team officials of distancing themselves from the Stevens controversy so he was left to take the heat. It took the cooperation of everyone in the front office to make the deal work, he said.

"I was so disgusted when we lost Scott Stevens," remarked Sutter. "I never once heard from management how much we were going to miss him. Everyone was involved in that decision. A sign of strength for any management group is spreading the praise around and not pointing fingers when things go wrong."

You'd think Sutter would love nothing more than to see the Blues collapse over the next couple of years. Quite the contrary, he says. He claims he cares for everyone on the team, especially the youngsters he got to see grow from the day they were signed. He wishes the Blues the best of luck in the future. But that future will consist of decisions being made by only Quinn and Caron. Plager and his staff will have virtually no input into what happens off the ice, according to Sutter.

"It's getting back to how it used to be when two people had all the say in the organization," Brian observed. "The decision they made on me was typical of how it used to be. Everything is based on public relations. When p.r. interferes with the decisions of the hockey team, you're not going to have success. To run a successful business you have to hire good people, give them responsibilities, and don't interfere."

As the clock approached noon, the sun started beating down on our heads, making it difficult for us to see one another through squinted eyelids. We found shade on the deck overlooking the pool but weren't able to continue the interview right away. Sutter's real estate agent arrived with an offer on his house. His cherished home had been on the market since the day he was fired, and seeing that "For Sale" sign in his front yard was a constant reminder of what had happened May 1.

"It pisses me off everytime I look at it," Sutter said.

He visited with his agent for only a minute before returning to the sundeck. The offer was way too low, and he rejected it immediately.

"I'm just trying to get back what I put into this place," he said. "I'm not going to make any money, but I'm certainly not going to lose any, either."

Brian and I talked for about another 30 minutes, mainly discussing the media's role in his ouster. I happen to think the media didn't have much bearing on the decision. That's giving too much credit to the media's influence and power. I know certain people in this town would like to THINK they had that kind of power, but I'm not buying it.

However, Sutter bought into it big-time. Constant second-guessing by uninformed reporters helped sway public opinion against him, Sutter said. And as the outrage became stronger and louder, team officials had no choice but to eliminate the problem to keep the fans' support.

"There are some people (reporters) in this town who sound like they know what's going on," Brian said. "These guys who criticized line changes didn't watch other games on television. They didn't switch the channel. They didn't see that every team changes lines during the playoffs. But in the end, management listened to those people."

Later that afternoon, Sutter signed a contract to coach one of the most storied franchises in the NHL, the Boston Bruins, one of the Original Six. The Bruins have been the most successful franchise in the NHL over the last quarter-century. Ironically, their streak started in 1967-68, the Blues' inaugural season. That year, Boston made the playoffs for the first time in nine seasons. They haven't missed postseason play since, qualifying for the playoffs 25 consecutive years. Now Sutter has the daunting task of continuing that unequaled streak of success.

Just making the playoffs wasn't good enough in Boston. You had to win it all. The Bruins made it all the way to the Wales Conference finals in 1991-92 where they were eliminated by the Penguins. Making it to the third round would have been a rare feat for the Blues. They had gone that far only once in the last 22 years. But in Boston, it wasn't enough to save Rick Bowness' job. That's the kind of environment Brian Sutter was about to enter.

"I'm certainly delighted and excited," a beaming Sutter said. "Over the last 25 years, their tradition of winning is absolutely incredible. I'm going to do my darnedest to uphold them."

One of Sutter's players would be Adam Oates, the all-star center the Blues traded in February because of his contractual demands. Sutter never publicly complained about Oates' off-ice problems, but other members of the team remarked how livid the head coach was over Oates' "selfish interests."

"There's no question he's one of the most skilled people in the game," he said when I asked him about those reports. That was it. End of discussion. Sutter's refusal to talk anymore about Oates made it clear he still harbored resentment about Adam's financial feud. That had been one of several incidents during the season that blurred the team's focus, and there wasn't a damn thing Sutter could do about it.

I shook hands with Sutter and wished him good luck. I probably wouldn't see him again until the Bruins came to town next season. It was hard to believe, but "Mr. Blue" was severing his ties completely with the city of St. Louis. Unlike so many other athletes, Sutter and his family were leaving the Gateway City for good, never to return except on business or to visit friends.

"I wish it didn't have to be that way," Brian said solemnly. "But they left me no choice. If the situation was handled differently, I might have stayed."

Once again, the ex-coach was referring not to the actual firing, but to the method in which it was done. He'll never forget how his kids had to tell him of his dismissal. For that reason alone, Sutter couldn't stand to stay in a place that suddenly had a bitter taste to it. He said he'll always love the city and its people. But his bosses showed him the door, and he decided never to come back and knock on it again.

*   *   *

The Blues' 25th anniversary season certainly was a memorable one, but it had very little to do with the standings. Few people realized that when Scott Stevens left for New Jersey, it would be the beginning of perhaps the most tumultuous season in team history. I don't care what anyone says. No one understood exactly what the loss of Stevens would mean to the club. It's easy to look back now, point a finger, and say, "I knew it, I just knew it." But remember, after the Blues lost their first two games of the year, they lost only once in their next 12 games, vaulting to first place after one month. No one talked about Stevens then. It was only after the team was blitzed a couple of times by Detroit in November that people started longing for their former captain again. And as the season continued to sputter along, Stevens' talents looked more impressive all the time.

Of course, the man most affected by the constant focus on Stevens was the person responsible for his departure, Brendan Shanahan. Shanahan was treated terrifically by Blues fans, a testament to their appreciative nature. But the newcomer could never escape the shadow of Stevens because the conversations about the infamous deal continued throughout the year. No one blamed Shanahan. They blamed Brian Sutter, Ron Caron, Judge Houston, and the league itself.

Despite a season shadowed by the man he'd replaced, Shanahan set a career high with 33 goals. Still, team officials weren't wholly satisfied with his performance. After the season ended, Sutter met with Brendan and told him he could do much, much better. He didn't use his size and physical strength enough. If he didn't improve, he'd be nothing more than a mediocre player at the prime of his playing career.

Those are some harsh words for a guy who'd just scored 33 goals. But Sutter always pushed his players to the limit, sometimes beyond. He never let a guy rest on his laurels, no matter the accomplishments. After Hull's first year in St. Louis, when he scored 41 goals, the Blues' head coach had a meeting with his fledgling superstar to discuss the 1988-89 season. Hull figured Sutter would pat him on the back for a job well done. Wrong. The Blues coach preached to Hull about giving it even more, not being satisfied with scoring "only" 41 goals. Brett was a little stunned by his coach's failure to recognize his stellar season, but the session paid dividends. All Hull did the next year was net 72 goals to set an NHL record for goals by a right winger. He followed with 86 the next year, and suddenly Brett Hull was the top goal scorer in the game.

Blues officials are counting on Shanahan's continuing improvement. With the Stevens controversy and Brian Sutter long gone, Shanahan signed a three-year deal for about $3 million on June 13, less than two days before he would have become a free agent. Shanahan might see more ice time on the top line, a spot he was promised when he came to the Blues in the first place.

(One thing here. Why on earth would a tight-budgeted organization pay a guy a million bucks a year after he scored just 69 points? The figures gave more credence to suspicions that Shanahan indeed signed a multimillion-dollar deal as a free agent in the summer of 1991, while the Blues submitted only a one-year contract at $650,000 to the league office. Shanahan certainly had potential to develop into a star. But did he deserve an extra $400,000? Perhaps Devils general manager Lou Lamoriello was right all along when he accused the Blues of pulling a fast one.)

While the Blues struggled during their silver anniversary, the league itself fell flat on its face during its 75th anniversary season. And its troubles actually started with the Scott Stevens situation. His forced move to Jersey did more to unite union members than any other event in recent memory. It culminated in the ten-day players' strike in early April, and it eventually cost President John Ziegler his job. That's right. The man who was willing to shed a tear on live television would now have to take his act to the unemployment line. Publicly, at least, Ziegler resigned. But there was so much pressure from the so-called "moderate" or "progressive" owners, that Ziegler had little choice but to step down after 15 years.

In another startling move, NHL czar William Wirtz, the owner of the Blackhawks and the most influential man in the game of hockey, also stepped down from his post as chairman of the Board of Governors and was replaced by Kings owner Bruce McNall. During strike talks, Wirtz was kindly told to get the hell out of the way, because his condescending attitude toward the players was impeding progress. Such strong language directed at Wirtz would have been intolerable in the past. But in a new age of player-power and progressive ownership, Wirtz was told to keep a lid on it.

Perhaps the National Hockey League is finally ready to make that big leap into the national spotlight. Perhaps the league will finally shed its unfortunate image of being a basement league that promotes fights, not its stars. And just perhaps the

NHL will join the big boys of baseball, basketball, and football in terms of respect and popularity toward its profession. It's a sport waiting to explode across the national scene. It just needs the proper leadership to get it there.

And as the league finds more success, let's hope the St. Louis Blues do, too. Here's wishing the boys in blue start their second quarter-century on a winning note and eventually bring their deserving fans their first Stanley Cup.

Appendix A
Team Statistics

Key:GP=games played, G=goals, A=assists, PTS=total points, +/- is the plus/minus rating, PIM=penalty minutes, PP=power-play goals, SH=short-handed goals, S=shots on goal, PCTG=scoring percentage.

Player	Team	GP	G	A	PTS	+/-	PIM	PP	SH	S	PCTG
B. Hull	STL	73	70	39	109	2-	48	20	5	408	17.2
C. Janney	BOS	53	12	39	51	1	20	3	0	90	13.3
	STL	25	6	30	36	5	2	3	0	37	16.2
Total		78	18	69	87	6	22	6	0	127	14.2
A. Oates	STL	54	10	59	69		12	3	0	118	8.5
B. Shanahan	STL	80	33	36	69	3-	171	13	0	215	15.3
N. Emerson	STL	79	23	36	59	5-	66	3	0	143	16.1
J. Brown	STL	80	20	39	59	8	38	10	0	214	9.3
Ron Sutter	STL	68	19	27	46	9	91	5	4	106	17.9
D. Christian	STL	78	20	24	44	2	41	1	3	142	14.1
P. Cavallini	STL	66	10	25	35	7	95	3	1	164	6.1
B. Bassen	STL	79	7	25	32	12	167	0	0	101	6.9
R. Wilson	STL	64	12	17	29	10	46	5	2	100	12.0
Rich Sutter	STL	77	9	16	25	7	107	0	1	113	8.0
D. Lowry	STL	75	7	13	20	11-	77	0	0	85	8.2
G. Butcher	STL	68	5	15	20	5	189	0	0	50	10.0
S. Quintal	BOS	49	4	10	14	8-	77	0	0	52	7.7
	STL	26	0	6	6	3-	32	0	0	19	0.0
Total		75	4	16	20	11-	109	0	0	71	5.6
R. Zombo	DET	3	0	0	0	3-	15	0	0	1	0.0
	STL	64	3	15	18	4	46	0	0	47	6.4
Total		67	3	15	18	1	61	0	0	48	6.3
G. Cavallini	STL	48	9	7	16		40	0	0	72	12.5
M. Mongeau	STL	36	3	12	15	2-	6	2	0	23	13.0
L. Norwood	HFD	6	0	0	0	0	16	0	0	1	0.0
	STL	44	3	11	14	14	94	1	0	51	5.9
Total		50	3	11	14	14	110	1	0	52	5.8
M. Baron	STL	67	3	8	11	3-	94	0	0	55	5.5
C. Joseph	STL	60	0	9	9	0	12	0	0	0	0.0
P. Bozon	STL	9	1	3	4	5	4	0	0	19	5.3
D. Kimble	STL	46	1	3	4	3-	166	0	0	12	8.3
K. Chase	STL	46	1	2	3	6-	264	0	0	29	3.4
C. Giles	STL	31	1	1	2	3-	8	0	0	4	25.0
J. Marshall	STL	2	1	0	1	0	4	0	0	2	50.0
B. Hedican	STL	4	1	0	1	1	0	0	0	1	100.0
D. Mackey	STL	19	1	0	1	4-	49	0	0	12	8.3
D. Felsner	STL	3	0	1	1	0	0	0	0	2	0.0
D. Lovoie	STL	6	0	1	1	3-	10	0	0	11	0.0
G. Hebert	STL	13	0	1	1	0	0	0	0	0	0.0

Player	Team	GP	G	A	PTS	+/-	PIM	PP	SH	S	PCTG
M. Marois	STL	17	0	1	1		38	0	0	11	0.0
R. Robinson	STL	22	0	1	1	4-	8	0	0	9	0.0
R. Hoover	STL	1	0	0	0	0	0	0	0	1	0.0
R. Skarda	STL	1	0	0	0	0	0	0	0	0	0.0
V. Riendeau	STL	3	0	0	0	0	0	0	0	0	0.0
P. Jablonski	STL	10	0	0	0	0	4	0	0	0	0.0

Keys: GP=games played, AVE=goals-against average, MINS=minutes played, GA=total goals against, SHOTS=shots against, PCTG=percentage of shots saved, Record=overall won/loss/tie record.

Goaltenders	GP	AVE	MINS	GA	SHOT	PCTG	Record
G. Hebert	13	2.93	738	36	393	.908	5-5-1
C. Joseph	60	3.01	3494	175	1953	.910	37-20-10
V. Riendeau	3	4.20	157	11	96	.885	1-2-0
P. Jablonski	10	4.87	468	38	259	.853	3-6-0

Shutouts —Joseph (2)

1991-1992 NHL Scoring Leaders

Player	GP	G	A	PTS	PIM
Mario Lemieux, PITT	64	44	87	131	94
Kevin Stevens, PIT	80	54	69	123	252
Wayne Gretzky, LA	74	31	90	121	34
Brett Hull, STL	73	70	39	109	48
Luc Robitaille, LA	80	44	63	107	95
Mark Messier, NYR	79	35	72	107	76
Jeremy Roenick, CHI	80	53	50	103	98
Steve Yzerman, DET	79	45	58	103	64
Brian Leetch, NYR	80	22	80	102	26
Adam Oates, STL/BOS	80	20	79	99	22

Top Goal Scorers

Player	GP	G
Brett Hull, STL	73	70
Kevin Stevens, PITT	80	54
Gary Roberts, CAL	76	53
Jeremy Roenick, CHI	80	53
Pat LaFontaine, BUF	57	46
Steve Yzerman, DET	79	45
Luc Robitaille, LA	80	44
Mario Lemieux, PITT	64	44
Mark Recchi, PHI	80	43
Owan Nolan, QUE	80	42

Top Assist Leaders

Player	GP	A
Wayne Gretzky, LA	74	90
Mario Lemieux, PITT	64	87
Brian Leetch, NYR	80	80
Adam Oates, STL/BOS	80	79
Dale Hawerchuck, BUF	77	75
Mark Messier, NYR	79	72
Craig Janney, BOS/STL	78	69
Kevin Stevens, PITT	80	69
Joe Sakic, QUE	69	65
Phil Housley, WIN	74	63
Luc Robitaille, LA	80	63

Top Goaltenders
(Minimum 1500 minutes)

Player	AVE	RECORD	PCTG
Patrick Roy, MON	2.36	36-22-8	.914
Ed Belfour, CHI	2.70	21-18-10	.894
Kirk McLean, VAN	2.74	38-17-9	.901
John Vanbiesbrouck, NYR	2.85	27-13-3	.910
Bob Essensa, WIN	2.88	21-17-6	.910
Curtis Joseph, STL	3.01	27-20-10	.910

Appendix B
Final Standings

Clarence Campbell Conference

Norris	W	L	T	PTS	GF	GA	Home	Away	DIV
Detroit	43	25	12	98	320	256	24-12-4	19-13-8	19-10-3
Chicago	36	29	15	87	257	236	23-9-8	13-20-7	15-12-5
BLUES	36	33	11	83	279	266	25-12-3	11-21-8	11-17-4
Minnesota	32	42	6	70	246	278	20-16-4	12-26-2	12-16-4
Toronto	30	43	7	67	234	294	21-16-3	9-27-4	14-16-2

Smythe	W	L	T	PTS	GF	GA	Home	Away	DIV
Vancouver	42	26	12	96	285	250	23-10-7	19-16-5	20-10-5
L. Angeles	35	31	14	84	287	296	20-11-9	15-20-5	16-13-6
Edmonton	36	34	10	82	295	297	22-13-5	14-21-5	15-14-6
Winnipeg	33	32	15	81	251	244	20-14-6	13-18-9	15-14-6
Calgary	31	37	12	74	296	305	19-14-7	12-23-5	16-15-4
San Jose	17	58	5	39	219	359	14-23-3	3-35-2	8-24-3

Prince of Wales Conference

Patrick	W	L	T	PTS	GF	GA	Home	Away	DIV
NY Rangers	50	25	5	105	321	246	28-8-4	22-17-1	19-15-1
Washington	45	27	8	98	330	275	25-12-3	20-15-5	22-12-1
Pittsburgh	39	32	9	87	343	308	21-13-6	18-19-3	16-16-3
New Jersey	38	31	11	87	289	259	24-12-4	14-19-7	14-16-5
NY Isles	34	35	11	79	291	299	20-15-5	14-20-6	13-15-7
Philadelphia	32	37	11	75	252	273	22-11-7	10-26-4	10-20-5

Adams	W	L	T	PTS	GF	GA	Home	Away	DIV
Montreal	41	28	11	93	267	207	27-8-5	14-20-6	16-10-6
Boston	36	32	12	84	270	275	23-11-6	13-21-6	16-10-6
Buffalo	31	37	12	74	289	299	22-13-5	9-24-7	12-14-6
Hartford	26	41	13	65	247	283	13-17-10	13-24-3	10-16-6
Quebec	20	48	12	52	255	318	18-19-3	2-29-9	11-15-6

Playoffs (in games)

1st Round—Chicago def. St. Louis 4-2, Detroit def. Minnesota 4-3, Vancouver def. Winnipeg 4-3, Edmonton def. L.A. 4-2, NY Rangers def. N. Jersey 4-3, Pittsburgh Def. Wash. 4-3, Montreal def. Hartford 4-3, Boston def. Buffalo 4-3.

2nd Round—Chicago def. Detroit 4-0, Edmonton def. Vancouver 4-2, Pittsburgh def. NY Rangers 4-2, Boston def. Montreal 4-0.

3rd Round— Chicago def. Edmonton 4-0, Pittsburgh def. Boston 4-0
Stanley Cup—Pittsburgh defeated Chicago 4-0.

Appendix C
Blues' Game-by-Game Results,
1991-1992

Game	Date	Opponent	Score	W/L	Record	PTS	Goalie
1	10/5	@New Jersey	2-7	L	0-1-0	0	Rien/Jos
2	10/7	@Toronto	0-3	L	0-2-0	0	Joseph
3	10/10	Edmonton	3-2	OT W	1-2-0	2	Joseph
4	10/12	San Jose	6-3	W	2-2-0	4	Joseph
5	10/15	Toronto	5-1	W	3-2-0	6	Riendeau
6	10/17	@Detroit	3-6	L	3-3-0	6	Riendeau
7	10/19	Chicago	4-4	OT T	3-3-1	7	Joseph
8	10/20	@Chicago	4-1	W	4-3-1	9	Jablonski
9	10/24	Boston	6-5	W	5-3-1	11	Jablonski
10	10/26	Calgary	2-2	OT T	5-3-2	12	Joseph
11	10/28	@Toronto	1-1	OT T	5-3-3	13	Joseph
12	10/30	@Edmonton	2-2	OT T	5-3-4	14	Joseph
13	11/1	@Vancouver	3-2	W	6-3-4	16	Joseph
14	11/3	@Winnipeg	3-3	OT T	6-3-5	17	Joseph
15	11/5	Philadelphia	3-4	L	6-4-5	17	Jos/Jab
16	11/7	@Detroit	3-10	L	6-5-5	17	Jab/Jos
17	11/9	Hartford	3-4	L	6-6-5	17	Joseph
18	11/10	@Detroit	4-6	L	6-7-5	17	Joseph
19	11/14	Winnipeg	2-1	OT W	7-7-5	19	Joseph
20	11/16	Minnesota	5-3	W	8-7-5	21	Joseph
21	11/17	@Chicago	1-5	L	8-8-5	21	Jablonski
22	11/20	Toronto	5-2	W	9-8-5	23	Joseph
23	11/23	NY Rangers	0-3	L	9-9-5	23	Joseph
24	11/28	Quebec	5-2	W	10-9-5	25	Joseph
25	11/30	Detroit	7-3	W	11-9-5	27	Joseph
26	12/3	@Minnesota	3-3	OT T	11-9-6	28	Joseph
27	12/4	@Minnesota	2-5	L	11-10-6	28	Joseph
28	12/7	Pittsburgh	6-1	W	12-10-6	30	Joseph
29	12/10	@NY Isles	7-7	OT T	12-10-7	31	Joseph
30	12/11	@Buffalo	6-3	W	13-10-7	33	Hebert
31	12/14	@Quebec	4-2	W	14-10-7	35	Joseph
32	12/16	@Montreal	2-4	L	14-11-7	35	Joseph
33	12/19	San Jose	4-0	W	15-11-7	37	Joseph
34	12/21	NY Islanders	6-2	W	16-11-7	39	Hebert
35	12/22	@Chicago	2-5	L	16-12-7	39	Joseph
36	12/26	Chicago	3-1	W	17-12-7	41	Joseph
37	12/28	@Minnesota	2-5	L	17-13-7	41	Joseph
38	12/31	@Buffalo	3-4	L	17-14-7	41	Hebert
39	1/2	Minnesota	6-2	W	18-14-7	43	Joseph
40	1/4	Detroit	2-6	L	18-15-7	43	Joseph
41	1/6	@Toronto	2-3	OT L	18-16-7	43	Joseph